The Complete Book of

SAILING

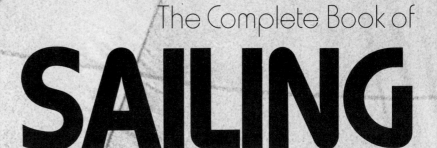

The Complete Book of

SAILING

Edited by Peter Cook and Barbara Webb

Consultant editor Theodore A. Jones

Doubleday & Company, Inc.
Garden City, New York 1977

Library of Congress Catalog
Card No. 76-19620

© Ward Lock Limited 1977

ISBN 0-385-11531-8

First published in Great Britain in 1977
by Ward Lock Limited, 116 Baker Street,
London, W1M 2BB, a member of the
Pentos Group.

Layout by Jill Leman

Text filmset in Times
by Servis Filmsetting Ltd, Manchester

Printed and bound in Hong Kong by
Toppan Printing Co.

CONTENTS

Introduction

Sailing has probably been the fastest growing recreational activity in the world over the last twenty years or so, and the rate of increase shows little sign of abatement. Although, earlier, yachting was a rich man's sport, today sailing is a sport available to all as the result of increased affluence and more leisure time.

Arguably, sailing has a wider range of appeal than any other pastime. It can be followed from childhood to old age at every level of mental and physical involvement. It is relaxing, it is a challenge, it allows man to control his own destiny and to benefit or suffer directly from the result of his own decisions and actions. It provides adventure and, although it develops self-confidence and fitness, it seldom calls for the ultimate in physical prowess.

Competitive yearnings can be satisfied at every level – from a friendly, private race between two boats that find themselves on the same piece of water heading in the same direction, right up to the cut-and-thrust of international championships and Olympic regattas. Offshore racing calls for pitting one's skill against the elements, accurate navigation and driving a boat at her optimum speed day and night, at times in conditions of considerable discomfort. Social and gregarious requirements are met in the club bar after the race where every move made on the water, and many more that might have been made, are talked over until the small hours.

The cruising man seeks a totally different type of relaxation. His ingredients are identical to those used by the racing man – a sailing boat, the water and the weather – but his ultimate enjoyment is achieved by 'doing his own thing', away from the rush and pressures of daily life. He may not even wish to see his fellow men but prefers to find some deserted creek in which to anchor his boat with nature as his only companion.

The reason for the wide appeal of sailing is the vast range of conditions that can be experienced. Nothing could be more different than sailing on a quiet river or sheltered lake on a summer's evening on the one hand, and battling around Cape Horn in the teeth of a gale in sub-zero temperatures on the other; or sailing a beach boat under a hot tropical Caribbean sky, and sailing the North Atlantic single-handed in a race lasting forty days or more. Even if you sail one boat on the same stretch of water year in, year out, the conditions will seldom be the same – the wind will vary in strength and direction, the tidal conditions will be different, the weather will change. And all the time it is a matter of weighing up the elements and harnessing them to your advantage.

Sailing can cost as much or as little as one cares to spend. The smallest sailing boats can be bought for less than the cost of a ten-year-old car, and maintenance costs can be limited to a couple of pots of paint a year. The most expensive yachts cost a fortune to buy and maintain. In between there are sailing boats to suit every pocket. It is not even necessary to own a boat, for the owner of even the smallest dinghy usually requires one person to sail with him, small cruisers may carry a crew of four to six, while the largest yachts can need as many as fifteen or twenty. Because owners of larger boats are usually more interested in finding keen, knowledgeable people to form a reliable team than in looking for wealthy friends to help pay for their boat, sailing in even the most expensive yachts is possible for nearly everyone.

The choice of the correct type of boat to buy is vital and depends on the sailor's temperament, fitness and financial position. If a man is gregarious and competitively minded, the choice of boat will often be decided not so much by the virtues or shortcomings of a design but, more often, by the character of the people who sail in the boats. On the other hand, if cruising is the main objective, the choice of boat will depend more on the waters where he wishes to sail, and a degree of comfort will be more important than optimum performance. The prospective purchaser should, therefore, consider carefully what type of sailing suits his requirements and whether he can afford to buy and maintain the boat of his choice. He should also employ an expert to check whether she is sound.

Years ago the only way to start sailing was either to know someone who would take you sailing or buy a boat and go it alone. The system worked satisfactorily because there were far more experienced people sailing ready to give advice than there were trying to learn. Today a higher percentage of people are novices, but in most countries there are club training programmes and establishments specializing in all forms of sailing instruction, so no one need forego a thorough grounding in the subject before he is let loose on his own.

One great thing about sailing is that the novice is usually frightened of the strength of the wind and roughness of the sea long before his boat is in any danger or the limit of his own capability is reached. But there is always a risk of being caught out by unexpected, rapidly deteriorating conditions. There is no substitute for first-hand practical experience, but there are many excellent books on every aspect of the sport from which the reader can benefit from the knowledge of others.

This book is called *The Complete Book of Sailing* and includes contributions from a number of authors, all experts in their own particular field. The editors would hasten to add that in no way does this book tell everything there is to know about sailing – that would be impossible in even a hundred books. What it sets out to do, however, is to give the reader an overall picture of the sailing scene in the English-speaking world and sufficient information on sailing boats, their construction and use, to enable him to obtain the maximum enjoyment from what many believe to be the most satisfying of all pastimes.

Part I
Sailing worldwide

1
Centreboard dinghies

Wendy Fitzpatrick

1.1 The parts of a sailing dinghy:
1 Burgee. 2 Main halyard.
3 Headboard. 4 Mast. 5 Mainsail.
6 Sail batten. 7 Boom black band.
8 Boom. 9 Mainsheet. 10 Headsail
sheet. 11 Tiller extension (hiking
stick). 12 Tiller. 13 Rudder stock.
14 Rudder blade. 15 Headsail sheet
fairlead. 16 Centreboard. 17 Shroud
plate. 18 Gunwale rubbing strip.
19 Foredeck. 20 Bow (starboard).
21 Stem. 22 Spinnaker pole
downhaul. 23 Kicking strap (vang).
24 Gooseneck. 25 Spinnaker.
26 Spinnaker pole. 27 Spinnaker pole
lift. 28 Shroud. 29 Spreader.
30 Headsail. 31 Headsail hanks.
32 Headsail halyard. 33 Forestay.
34 Spinnaker halyard crane.

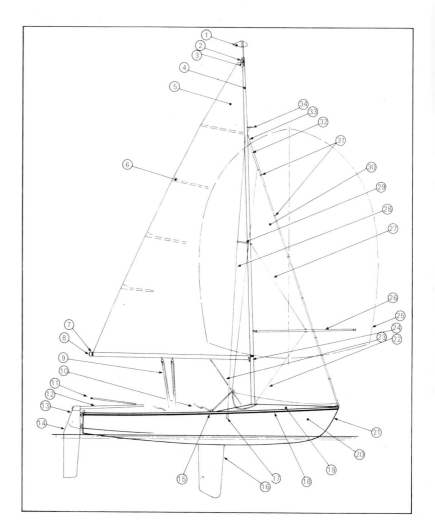

Dinghy sailing can mean anything from spending a leisurely afternoon enjoying the wind, the sun and the sea, to racing a highly-tuned dinghy against skilled opposition, squeezing out the last ounce of speed and using wits and muscles at full stretch for the duration of the race.

A boat is as personal as a pair of shoes: it must fit or its owner will never feel comfortable in it. It is easy to recommend some very good designs in almost any size or category, but they may not be right for the individual who, pronouncing them either dull and boring or hair-raising, immediately applies for membership of the local tennis club and leaves the sea to the gulls.

Centreboard dinghies can be sub-classified into general-purpose day boats and racing boats. Day boats are dinghies for relaxed sailing and are designed more for comfort than for speed, having a relatively small sail area. They are a comparatively slow and stable type, make less physical demands on the crew than the racing dinghy, and are suitable for novices because they call for slower reactions than do more high-powered designs. They are also ideal for those who want to sail purely for the pleasure of sailing, for whom speed is not the ultimate objective.

It is easy to allow the term 'racing dinghy' to conjure up a picture of a boat flying along in a welter of spray, crew out on the trapeze and fighting an enormous spinnaker with all his might. But a racing dinghy is for the most part a dinghy which is raced, and therefore some day boats are included in this category. The breed starts at the bottom end of the size scale with the little Optimist, all 7ft 6in of it, and finishes somewhere around the Olympic Flying Dutchman at nearly 20ft. In between there is seemingly a class for everyone, but that is no deterrent to a new design taking the world by storm every now and then. Many of the simpler racing dinghies are also used for day sailing and are therefore suitable for beginners, whereas the out-and-out racing dinghy which carries a large sail area, and probably a trapeze, is suitable only for skilled sailors who want the stimulus of competition and physical exertion, and who are prepared to sacrifice comfort and stability for speed.

The most important factor influencing the choice of boat is your temperament and physical condition. If you want to relax, avoid the sensitive, high-performance racing dinghies and go for a slower day boat or racing boat. But if you want excitement and exercise, the faster

Optimist dinghies racing in the 1969 World Championship. Designed by American Clark Mills as a training boat for youngsters, 106,000 of these simple hard-chine prams are spread throughout the world, and this figure increases annually by over 9,000 boats. Optimists can be built from plans or wood kits and are also available in glassfibre. The photograph on p. 65 shows the new sail insignia. Loa 7ft 6½in; beam 3ft 7½in; sail area 35sq ft; hull weight 77lb.

The crew of this Olympic 470 dinghy drive her to windward in a fresh breeze, using their weight to balance the force of the wind on the sails. The helmsman sits or hikes out while the crew is suspended from a trapeze. Loa 15ft 6in; beam 5ft 6in; sail area 137sq ft; spinnaker 140sq ft; weight 259lb. Over 30,000 boats increasing by 2,600 boats each year. Designer, Frenchman André Cornu.

Two people can lift a boat weighing up to 130lb on and off a car roof. With a special combined roof rack and trolley one man can manage the same weight. This is a 10ft Mirror dinghy.

Below A traditional clinker-built, wooden day-sailing boat with a gaff rig and loose-footed mainsail. Note the reef points used for reducing the sail area in strong winds.

racing dinghies are the answer, once you have acquired the skill needed to sail them. The size and weight of the boat, the strength of your crew, and the question of transport all affect your choice. The maximum weight of a dinghy which a husband and wife or father and son can man-handle easily on and off a car roof is about 130lb. This will increase to an all-up sailing weight of about 160lb with spars, sails and rudder – still a reasonable load for two people to carry to the water's edge. Heavier dinghies need to be carried on a trailer.

Then there is the question of the waters in which you will be sailing. A good sea boat, for instance, may feel as dead as a dodo on a small inland pond. A lightweight flier may be totally uncontrollable at sea. If you are new to an area or new to the sailing game, play safe and seek expert advice locally. Better still, put your name on a club's crew list and go afloat in a variety of classes to see for yourself.

Maintenance also influences the choice and depends partly on the material of which a boat is built. Many people are prepared to accept the maintenance which a wooden boat requires, but if yours is a busy life, opt for glassfibre. The maintenance of a competitive racing dinghy is obviously more time-consuming than that of a simple day boat.

Finally cost, which is not a question of size alone: the more complex the boat, the more expensive will it be both in purchase price and in the maintenance of fittings and gear. Trailer and launching trolley will need to be budgeted for, the cost of a mooring or, more usually, a site where the boat is to be parked, and if you plan to travel on the open meeting circuit, there is also the cost of fuel, meals and hotel bills.

General-purpose dinghies

We shall consider first some of the many types of general-purpose dinghy, for this is the category of boat which so often gives the novice his first taste of the sea – and a wrong choice of dinghy can so easily lead to disillusionment with the sport of sailing as a whole. To be satisfactory the boat chosen must be able to perform the duties required of it. The minimum practical length for a knockabout sailing dinghy is about 8ft, but it would be foolhardy to expect such a boat to take a family of three estuary cruising for extended periods. Similarly, it is obvious that two small children could not cope happily with a heavy 16-footer, either ashore or afloat.

A small dinghy makes a good children's boat. Very often an 8-footer will be little more than a revamped yacht tender, reasonably stable, and with good carrying capacity for its size – but do not forget those three words 'for its size'. A dinghy of less than 10ft should be used with care and only in sheltered waters. Make sure that, even in light winds, its performance is sufficient to make way against an adverse tidal stream or current. It is unlikely to be suitable for more than one adult or two children.

A dinghy of 11ft or so is more versatile. It is still light enough to be carried on a car roof rack, large enough to carry two or even three adults, has more stowage space and the potential to carry a larger, more powerful rig which gives better performance under sail.

Over about 12ft the choice is seemingly boundless. Some very good traditional clinker-built dinghies still exist; some of the family orientated racing classes are suitable for day sailing; or you could choose a purpose-designed modern family day boat which takes advantage of glassfibre construction to incorporate a clever accommodation layout with plenty of stowage space and built-in buoyancy.

A general-purpose day sailing boat needs stability, both inherent stability in the hull and directional stability under way. That heart in the mouth, unsteady feeling encountered on stepping gingerly aboard a racing dinghy has no place here. Lateral stability comes with full sections and a firm turn to the bilge, but look to see that the generous water-line beam is not carried all the way through to the transom. The after end of the hull should tuck up and narrow a little to prevent the transom digging into the water. The weight of the helmsman aggravates this tendency which, at best, creates drag and slows the boat, but at worst could drastically alter the handling characteristics and, in heavy weather, result in a capsize.

A sailing dinghy should have about 8–10° rise of floor. In simple terms, the more steeply veed the hull and the narrower the water-

A small, modern, general-purpose family dinghy built of glassfibre which requires less maintenance than wood. The simple rig has no shrouds or stays to support the mast, and the mainsail is sleeved over the mast and boom.

15

1.2 Dinghy hull sections. *(top)* A
stable hull shape suitable for general-
purpose dinghies. A relatively wide
waterline beam and firm turn of bilge
contribute to stability; the flare above
the waterline helps to deflect spray and
provides reserve buoyancy. *(centre)*
A much less stable section which
might be found in some racing
dinghies. The slack turn of bilge means
that the boat will heel easily and
could be difficult to control when
heeled. *(bottom)* Bow sections. The
outer shape is too full and will buffet
into the waves and create much
spray. The inner section, shown by the
chain line, is rather fine and is typical
of some racing dinghies. The middle,
dotted, section is about right for
general-purpose boats. It is not too
full on the waterline and so will slice
through the waves fairly easily but
there is plenty of reserve buoyancy.

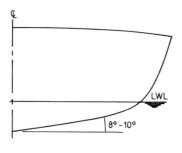

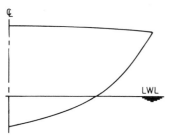

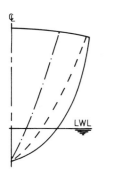

line beam, the more unstable the boat will tend to be. A moderately beamy dinghy will carry a generous payload without sinking unacceptably below her marks.

Sailing is necessarily fraught with the possibility of getting wet, but the shape of the boat can do much towards keeping the crew dry. The bow is no place for over-full sections: neither should it be needle-sharp for its entire depth. The former will punch at the waves and make a lot of fuss for little forward progress; the latter will knife happily through the sea but, lacking reserve buoyancy, will carry on knifing, maybe burying the bow under the next wave, maybe just building up a hobby-horse motion.

The ideal boat for comfortable sailing should have a slight overhang forward – not too much, for speed is related to overall length *at* the waterline and not above it, centreboard dinghies being sailed level, not heeled – a generous but not exaggerated flare in the topsides and a fine entry below the waterline. This boat will drive into the sea with the minimum of fuss, and most of the spray will be deflected away from the crew by the flare of the hull itself. In dusty going some water is bound to find its way on to the foredeck, but washboards will stop most of the unwanted water infiltrating the cockpit.

A pram bow is often employed in very small dinghies as it provides more buoyancy, and thus load-carrying ability, than would be found in a stem dinghy of similar length. It must be swept up so that the bow transom is well clear of the water when the boat is carrying her normal payload, and the weight of the crew and their gear should not be loaded too far forward or the bow will be depressed, the flat bow transom will slam into the waves and the boat will be stopped just as surely as a car which is driven into a bale of straw.

Gunwale rubbing strakes perform several useful functions besides acting as a buffer between a dinghy's topsides and anything she may hit or lie alongside. A generous rubbing strake will help to deflect spray and will provide a handhold to lift the boat ashore.

Buoyancy and stowage are often considered in the same breath, for often a buoyancy compartment will double as a stowage compartment when space is at a premium. Buoyancy here means reserve buoyancy, called upon to float a dinghy in the event of a capsize or immersion, so all compartments must be capable of being sealed effectively and easily. A block of foam or an inflated air bag should be carried in any buoyancy (flotation) compartment which is not permanently sealed.

Distribution of flotation tanks is important. Reserve buoyancy in the floor is unsatisfactory, for when capsized the boat will tend to roll over completely, and recovery will be difficult because the buoyant area must be pulled below the water before the boat can be righted.

Too much reserve buoyancy is as bad as too little. Forward, aft and side tanks together can provide so much buoyancy that a capsized dinghy will float too high in the water to be manageable. Not only will it be impossible for the swimming crew to reach and climb on to the centreboard, but the boat presents so much area to the wind that it blows away from the crew very fast indeed – possibly too fast for even a good swimmer to catch.

Ideally, there must be sufficient buoyancy to float the boat and her crew in safety while they bail. Dinghies which come upright with a lot of water aboard may suffer from water slopping up through the centreboard case slot as fast as the crew can bail. If the centreboard pivots (a daggerboard case must necessarily have an open top), a capping piece can be fitted to close the top of the centreboard case. The buoyancy must be distributed evenly fore and aft so that the boat lies calmly on her side when capsized and has no tendency to bury either her bow or stern. Too much buoyancy in side tanks can be a disadvantage: if the sidedecks are submerged, the centreboard is easy to reach from the water. If the water which is in the boat when she is righted can be kept to one side by a baffle or spine along the centreline of the cockpit, the weight of the crew will be balanced as they clamber aboard on the other side.

A small amount of buoyancy at the masthead of a dinghy helps to discourage complete inversion. It can be a block of foam lashed to the masthead or a panel of unicellular foam contained in a double panel at the head of the mainsail. Alternatively, a hollow mast can be filled with a chemical foam which expands and sets *in situ*.

Fittings should be robust and simple. The rudder hangings should be bolted through the transom and attached securely to the rudder itself. Pintle lengths should be staggered so that one can be located while the second is lined up. Aligning both fittings simultaneously while the boat is bobbing to the waves can range from difficult to impossible. A retaining clip is needed to prevent the rudder floating off. Are the rudder blade and tiller strong enough?

The area of hull or deck where the mast is stepped should be adequately strong. If the mast is supported by shrouds and a forestay, their anchor points should be through-bolted to a strong area of the hull. A transom-mounted mainsheet system is probably best for a family dinghy as it keeps most of the sheet away from the passengers. A centre mainsheet, or one which is led from the transom forward along the boom and down to a central take-off block, encroaches on the cockpit area and so reduces the crew's working space.

Jib fairleads need be no more than simple plastics mouldings, but it is a good idea to have jib sheet cleats which make for easier single-handed sailing, save the helmsman having to remind the crew constantly to trim

Left This Flying Dutchman has too much built-in buoyancy and is consequently floating high on her side. The crew must not become separated from the boat because the wind would blow her to leeward faster than they could swim. One crew member is in the water pulling the mainsail down the mast, the other stands on the lowered centreboard holding the jib sheet to prevent the boat turning completely upside down. When the mainsail has been lowered they will be able to pull her upright.

Right Although this Flying Dutchman has too little buoyancy, she can be sailed in this swamped condition. Inflatable bags beneath the decks keep her afloat. The bag here was not held securely in place and broke away under pressure, presenting the helmsman with a problem as he cannot steer with the tiller.

17

Right A Windsurfer. The mast is attached by a universal joint. The sailor lifts the rig and sails by controlling the angle and attitude of the sail and moving his weight. There is no rudder.

Below right The cheap and simple Sunfish is a very popular off-the-beach sailing surfboat and provides keen racing. Loa 13ft 10in; beam 4ft 8½in; sail area 75sq ft; weight 139lb.

Below The helmsman of this una-rigged Laser leans out as a puff strikes the boat.

the jib and ease the load on the crew's hands. Cam cleats are probably the best type; they are not too uncomfortable to sit on, can be cleated from many different angles and released quickly.

A 'boaty' boat is not necessarily everybody's requirement; many will derive tremendous enjoyment from a pure fun machine. The Windsurfer type is a surfboard powered by a single sail set on a mast which pivots on a universal joint on the board itself. There are no controls: no rudder, no sheets, no shrouds. The sailor stands on his board in the manner of the best surf riders, holding the rig in his two hands, and steering by inclining it forward or aft and by moving his weight. If the wind becomes excessive or the boat starts to go out of control, he just drops the whole rig into the water and the boat stops dead. Windsurfing is not an easy art to acquire and needs plenty of sea-room in the early stages. It is a sport suitable only for adult swimmers and requires a good sense of balance and a strong back and arms.

One step removed from the Windsurfer, and nearer to a conventional boat, is the sailing surfboat type often known as a sailing surfboard or off-the-beach boat. This incorporates a flat skimming hull with vestigial cockpit and, usually, a simple single sail sleeved over an unstayed two-part aluminium alloy mast. Capable of exhilarating bursts of speed, these designs provide tremendous excitement because the helmsman is so close to, and often in, the boat's own bow wave.

Racing dinghies

The performance of racing dinghies varies as much as the personalities of the people who race them. They can be relatively heavy and slow with just a mainsail and jib; they can be extremely fast planing boats with mainsail, genoa and vast spinnaker for off-the-wind work; or they can be single-handers, mostly una-rigged, of all shapes and sizes.

Unlike keelboats, dinghies are designed to be sailed on an even keel, and the weight of the crew is used to counter the pressure of the wind on the sail. In most classes the sail area is kept small enough to be controlled by the crew sitting on the sidedecks who, as the wind increases, hook their feet under straps mounted in the cockpit and lean outboard so that their weight is as far removed as possible from the centreline. To exert the maximum righting moment some of the more serious racing classes, which carry greater sail area to improve performance, have an exaggerated flare in the topsides where the crew sit so that crew weight can be sited further outboard in strong winds. Some classes allow one or both crew members to use a trapeze; others still use a sliding seat (hiking board), usually a hollow wooden box which slides across the

With their crews trapezing the helmsmen of these International 505s racing in the 1976 British championship are balancing their boats on a broad reach by spilling the wind from their mainsails. Loa 16ft 6in; beam 6ft 2in; sail area 200sq ft; spinnaker 215sq ft; minimum weight 280lb. 6,000 boats. Designed by Englishman John Westell.

The single-handed International 10sq Metre Canoe is possibly the most difficult racing class to sail and only about 340 boats are registered. Their 17ft overall hulls have only 3ft 4in beam, sailing weight is 200lb and sail area 107sq ft. The helmsman sits out on a sliding seat or hiking board to balance the boat, and when he tacks this has to be pushed across the boat so that he can sit out on the new windward side.

Opposite (top) Some classes are ideally suited to a husband-and-wife or boy-and-girl team. Here the 1971 Irish Enterprise champions show the fine form that won them their title. Around 20,000 boats worldwide increasing at about 850 per year. Designer Englishman Jack Holt. Loa 13ft 3in; beam 5ft 3in; sail area 113sq ft; weight 250lb.

(bottom) The Finn, the Olympic single-hander designed by the Finn, Rickard Sarby, has no trapeze or sliding seat. Only a strong, heavy crew with considerable stamina can drive it effectively in strong winds. Because the low-sweeping boom prevents him seeing to leeward, a window of transparent material is sewn into the foot of the mainsail. Loa 14ft 9in; beam 4ft 10in; sail area 110sq ft; weight 319lb.

crew's part of the boat and supports him as far outboard as does the trapeze – only this time he is not suspended from the mast but merely sitting on his seat.

The racing dinghy tends to be leaner beneath the water than her general-purpose sister, while the knife-like bow and flat planing sections aft are typical of the more extreme racing classes. With very few exceptions, dinghies cannot sail sufficiently fast on a close-hauled course to lift and plane.

Some of the older racing classes grew from flourishing general-purpose dinghy designs. A few owners would go to a regatta, form a class at the home club and, inevitably, seek improved performance. In some cases the racing modifications eventually precluded the lighter crews from competing in the class – the husband and wife teams for example – and they would turn elsewhere.

One-design racing classes are boats built to the same design of hull and sail plan, and they are controlled by a rigid set of rules to ensure that they are all as alike as possible. Measurements are taken at many points over the hull and deck to check that each boat has been built within the permitted tolerances – usually only 5mm – and the area of the sails and shapes of the centreboard and rudder are strictly controlled, together with materials and construction methods. A few classes follow very strict hull tolerances but allow the deck and cockpit layout to be to individual specification.

Other classes, known as restricted or development classes, are controlled by much freer rules, and variation in design of hull shape and sail plan is encouraged. Some – the International Moth is an example – allow considerable freedom, restricting only the overall length, sail area, mast height and hull configuration (no multihulls); others, like the International Fourteen, have some fairly basic outline hull parameters and control the total sail area, sometimes relating it to mast height.

The most successful racing classes are not necessarily the fastest, most attractive or most spectacular. They tend to be the designs which

The type of people who sail in a class is just as important as the characteristics of the boat. If you do not like the people who sail the boats, you will not enjoy your sailing. Here a group of Fireballs prepares for a race at Hayling Island in Chichester Harbour, England.

best fit a variety of conditions and which have active class associations.

The fact that a racing dinghy does not carry a spinnaker does not necessarily make it uninteresting but places a premium on team-work between helmsman and crew. Those who make constant small adjustments will pull away from those in the fleet who are content to cleat the sheets and wait for the wind to do the work. A boat with a spinnaker can even be an embarrassment – for example, on small inland waters where conditions are fluky.

Choosing the right class is easier than the first glance at a list of perhaps 100 designs might suggest. First there is the type. An out-and-out racing machine requires a regular and enthusiastic crew, prepared to work hard and possessing a drip-dry outlook on life. If you are forced to rely on a succession of enthusiastic but unskilled volunteers, you should look for a simple layout and a relatively stable boat. If the crew problem is acute, consider a single-hander and look for the one best suited to your weight and sailing ability. An agile person will do well with a fast single-hander with trapeze or sliding seat, but a larger, heavier person will find a heavier boat, such as a Finn, which needs body power to drive it hard, more suited to his needs.

Where will you sail? If you and your regular enthusiastic crew have decided to travel on the open meeting circuit, you have only to choose the right size and type of boat for your combined weight and ability, and – most important – make sure that you like the type of people that the class has attracted already: they are the people with whom you will be spending most of your weekends.

If all you seek is local competition and the occasional open meeting, it is unwise to buy a boat which will be the only one of its kind at your home club. You can never enjoy the satisfaction of beating the opposition boat for boat and knowing that it was your skill that triumphed. Handicap racing can be good fun, but anyone seriously interested in racing finds it a poor substitute for class racing – the very best way to sharpen sailing skills.

The class that is raced locally will have proved suitable for the conditions in the area, and you will be more likely to find a second-hand market should you later decide to change to a more testing class. Some very keen racing takes place in most unlikely classes between crews that one would expect to find in the more thoroughbred international classes. It may be worth sailing in a class which you regard as less than ideal if the competition offered is excellent.

Competition is keenest between boats of one class, but in many waters there are too few boats of one class to make a good race. Some clubs organize regular racing for handicap or menagerie boats to enable boats of different classes to race against each other. Rivalry between classes can be as great as that between individuals. Here co-editor Peter Cook in a Fireball leads a 505 and a Hornet round a mark in the annual classic Burnham Icicle race sailed on England's East Coast.

Buying a centreboard dinghy

Your mind is made up. You have answered an advertisement in a yachting magazine for the boat of your dreams. It seems to be a bargain, but how can you be sure?

The boat must be sound, and if you are new to the sport, it is as well to take a really experienced friend with you to make sure that there is no rot, no sign of damage or second-rate repair to the hull, to check the state of the gear and fittings, and to advise on the condition of the sails and rigging.

23

A simple, uncluttered cockpit layout in a dinghy. The centre mainsheet traveller runs on a length of stainless-steel tube, and the final mainsheet take-off point is a swivel jam block mounted on the aft end of the centreboard case. The toe straps can easily be adjusted to suit different wind conditions and sizes of crew simply by sliding them along the stiffening tubes.

In general the older the boat the less you can expect to pay for it. Those old boats which seem to be expensive will probably turn out to be in excellent condition and may boast a brand new rig. If a boat is basically sound but neglected, it can be brought back to life with determination and hard work. Do not be put off by blackened wooden decks, but by all means use them as a bargaining point when discussing the price. Stripped and dried out there is no reason why those decks should not regain most of their former glory. They are a sign of negligence on the part of the previous owner, for the boat has probably been damp for months or even years and will need to be dried out to bring her down to her designed weight. Water may have entered the wood in very few places, but it will usually spread so that the timber is damp, if not completely soaked. If the boat has been subjected to the heat of the sun, the water will have expanded and tried to evaporate through the surface coating of paint or varnish. Some surface coatings such as polyurethane paints are almost impervious, and if sufficient moisture has been trapped in the wood and enough heat applied, the whole coating will have lifted. All this points to a major refit, completely stripping off paint and varnish by using either expensive paint stripper or a blow lamp – so take this into account when agreeing a price.

Even if sound and maintenance-free, an old glassfibre racing dinghy is not necessarily a good investment – and may depress you beyond measure. In the early days of glassfibre construction less was understood about stiffening, and, whereas top dinghy builders now are producing very stiff boats right down to minimum weight, you may find that an old boat feels soft. The whole hull will flex and twist in a sea, transmitting shock waves to the rig that the sailmaker never bargained for, causing the mast to perform extraordinary contortions, the sail to lose power, and the boat to feel dead.

An old boat with an original rig will need to be re-rigged if she is to race competitively. Ask a sailmaker who is currently successful in the class to quote the cost of new sails, and then consider whether it might be better to look for a slightly newer boat.

Do not worry about a sparsity of fittings. Provided they work efficiently, learn to use the ones already fitted before adding the latest go-fast gadgets. The top half of the fleet may be using them to advantage, but in the early days your hands will be full just learning about the new boat. There will be time for improvements later.

Maintenance

Glassfibre boats require little maintenance – usually just a scrub with washing-up liquid and warm water. If the boat is to be dragged frequently up a stony beach or hard, white is probably the most practical hull colour, because invisible cosmetic repairs are effected easily, whereas bold colours require great care in matching and filling. While the penalties for allowing a glassfibre boat to remain wet are not immediately as great as with a wooden boat, the aim should, nevertheless, be to dry the boat after every sail. Eventually water will permeate glassfibre, and it is particularly important that water is not allowed to lie in the boat during the winter months when there is risk of freezing. Water expands as it freezes and if it has found its way into the glassfibre through an unnoticed damaged area it can crack the hull.

If a wooden boat is to be kept in good condition, it should be washed down with fresh water after use, sponged dry and covered to prevent dew and rain forming puddles in the bilges. Lightweight plastic covers are not recommended if the boat is to be stored in the open for long periods, because the boat will tend to sweat and remain permanently damp. A good quality waterproofed canvas cover is a worthwhile investment. The boom should be attached firmly to the gooseneck, track or groove downwards in the case of a wooden boom, to ensure that it remains dry, and the cover should fit over the boom in the manner of a ridge tent. There should be a generous overlap at the gunwale and down the topsides to prevent rain being blown into the boat. Free circulation of air is important.

Glassfibre hulls can easily be repaired by the amateur handyman, and even quite large holes in modern plywood dinghies can be patched very successfully by the use of a glassfibre repair kit.

Trailers and trolleys

Dinghies over 130lb should be transported on a trailer, and care must be taken that the regulations of the country or state in which you are towing are fully complied with. These laws vary considerably.

It is often better to buy a trailer which will carry a larger and heavier dinghy than the one you are intending to purchase, especially if you have children in the family, because you may well decide to move to a bigger boat later on, and you are sure to use the boat to carry luggage which will not fit in the car.

Remember that a road trailer should never be immersed in water. Wheel bearings, although packed with grease before every journey, will be hot on arrival, the grease will have thinned, and any air trapped inside will have expanded. Plunge the whole outfit into cold water, and your elementary physics will tell you what to expect. Everything contracts, there is no air available to fill the gaps, water rushes in, and sooner or later the bearing rusts and collapses.

A launching trolley is needed for larger dinghies. There are some excellent combination trailer/launchers on the market and a variety of good trolleys. Plastics trolleys are very light, can be taken apart easily, but not all are sufficiently robust. Some types use large balloon/fender-type wheels, some of which are excellent and some suitable only for a given launching site. The best all-round type is one with large diameter pneumatic wheels which will take sand, slopes, rocks and hollows in their stride.

It is most important to have a buffer at the front of the trolley to protect the forefoot of the dinghy, which can easily be chipped if the boat is dropped on to rough ground. Always use the dinghy's painter to lash the bow on to the trolley when launching and recovering.

The transom of an Enterprise showing a lifting rudder. On the transom the lower rudder fitting is the pintle and the upper the gudgeon; on the rudder the reverse applies. The transom flap, made of clear acrylic sheet, can be opened to allow large quantities of water to drain out when the boat is swamped. The mainsheet block is attached to a slide running in a length of track the full width of the transom.

2
Keelboats

Malcolm McKeag

Just what is a keelboat? Odd though it may seem to the non-sailing reader or the newcomer to sailing, there are several definitions, each offered at some time or other by various authors, from which we may choose. In the most narrow sense a keelboat is a fully decked yacht used solely for racing. In the broadest sense it is any boat that has a keel – which would just about include any boat ever built. For our purposes we shall consider a keelboat to be any sailing yacht that does not rely on the weight of the crew as the primary means of counteracting the heeling moment caused by the wind in the sails, but relies instead upon ballast (which is simply weight put to a specific purpose) attached to or built into the hull. In other words, any ballasted monohull sailing craft.

In this chapter we shall look briefly at the various types of keelboat that exist and see how they are used for many different ways of sailing, and how specialized types of keelboat have developed for each aspect of the sport – open and fully decked day sailers; racing keelboats; keelboats with cabins for living aboard and cruising; their half-sisters, the motor sailers, with their relatively larger engines; and that special breed of keelboat, with a cabin and possibly little else in the way of creature comforts, developed for that hardy branch of the sport, offshore racing.

When yachting first became a pastime it was carried on in a grand manner, but the first small racing sailboats were the workboats of the inshore sailors and longshoremen: the oyster smacks and crabbers of England, and the fishing catboats of Narragansett Bay, Rhode Island, USA. In these the working sailors would race on high days and holidays, and when amateurs first began to think of racing small yachts, they naturally thought in terms of the craft available.

By the end of the nineteenth century many small craft had been built for pleasure use on both sides of the Atlantic, but it was in England that interest began to centre on keelboats as opposed to centreboard craft. In fact the first recorded class of small boats for amateur racing – the Water Wags of Dublin Bay, Ireland, designed in 1887 – were centreboarders. Boats developed from unballasted fishing skiffs had been in amateur use for many years before then on both sides of the Atlantic, but in England a series of small ballasted classes, built in the same manner as the large racing yachts of the day, began to evolve.

From carrying ballast inside the craft to steady the boat there grew the idea of bolting it on to the keel on the outside, and as more was learned of the science of naval architecture, the underwater shape of yachts became more streamlined until, well before the turn of the century, the fin keel which we know today was a feature of these small yachts.

Early keelboats were not built, as most are today, to a small number of designs but, as was the vogue with the larger yachts they imitated, to a great number of individual designs, each differing from the other to a greater or lesser degree in an attempt to find improved performance. They therefore raced each other on a handicap system and were rated, or measured for their handicap, in the same way as the biggest yachts. Because the same measurement rule was used for all sizes of racing keelboat, there was a general trend towards a common shape, this shape, of course, being greatly influenced by the rules of measurement.

26

At this stage the small keelboat proper was used almost exclusively for racing and day sailing. The pastime of cruising in small boats did not enjoy anything like the popularity of yacht racing, and such small cruisers as did exist were based much more on the sturdier working craft of the time.

Keelboat racing, as opposed to the racing of unballasted craft, probably enjoyed more early popularity in Britain than in America, but in 1895 an English yachtsman, J. A. Brand of the Minima Yacht Club in London, challenged the Seawanhaka Corinthian Yacht Club of Oyster Bay, Long Island, New York to a series of races in $\frac{1}{2}$ Raters, a small British keelboat class of the time. The Seawanhaka accepted, which was pretty generous of them since they not only had to provide the silver trophy but had to build a fleet of $\frac{1}{2}$ Raters as well, none being raced in America at the time. Not only did they build the boats in time but they won the series (albeit in a centreboarder), and the trophy became the Seawanhaka International Challenge Trophy for Small Yachts. It is still raced for today but in different boats, and is regarded as one of the premier international matches for small racing keelboats.

Meteor and *Germania*, two of a group of Grand Yachts that led to yachting being labelled the sport of kings and millionaires. *Meteor* on the left was owned by the Kaiser. They required large professional crews and competed in a series of regattas round the coasts of Britain at the end of the nineteenth and early twentieth centuries.

27

A modern Twelve Metre, *Dame Pattie,* the Warwick Hood-designed Australian challenger for the America's Cup in 1967. Twelve Metres used to race as a class in America and Britain before World War II but are only built now for America's Cup racing. The crew are to windward to provide righting power and are lying flat to reduce windage. Note the clutter of winches on deck and, just forward of the helmsman, the strong mainsheet track which has holes in it to make it lighter. The windward running backstay is set up, and the leeward one is slack.

From these racers, now established on both sides of the Atlantic, there developed a breed of small, fast keelboats with accommodation. These cruiser racers developed from the desire of some yachtsmen to race their small keelboats not only in different centres, sailing along the coast for a new series at a different club, but also to race from one centre to another.

While interest in the many developing small keelboat classes increased at the end of the last century and in the first decade of this one, the lime-light was always stolen by the Grand Yachts. It was in this size of yacht – boats like the 15, 19 and 23 Metres – that the great match races of the day took place.

In the larger yachts and at international level keelboat racing continued on the handicap basis, but even at the turn of the century amateur yachtsmen, racing in their own locality, were baulking at the expense of building individually designed yachts and appreciating that it was cheaper to build several yachts to just one set of plans, using the same building jigs and moulds. This was the one-design concept.

The pinnacle of the development of keelboats for handicap racing was reached with the introduction of an international rule of measurement giving rise to the various Metre-boat classes. Of these we might take special note of just three: the Twelve Metres, the Eights and the Sixes. Very few Twelve Metres (once considered small yachts, but now at the top of the keelboat size range) are built nowadays, and these few all in connection with the challenges for and defences of the America's Cup. Eight Metres are still raced, although few are now built, but Six Metres are built and raced in America, Scandinavia and Australia.

In the impoverished years after World War II few yachtsmen could afford to build new Six Metres, and so a new rule was drawn up to

30 Square Metres racing in light airs in Table Bay. The class rules restrict sail area to 30sq m (323sq ft) and encourage a long, slim hull. Introduced in 1908 the class prospered in the Baltic and gained International status in 1928. A fleet raced at Marblehead in the 1930s and eighteen boats were racing in the Solent in 1938. A 30 Square Metre, Colonel 'Blondie' Hasler's *Tre-Sang*, was raced successfully offshore and won the 1946 Class II RORC championship. The photograph on p. 108 shows a 30 Square Metre under construction.

Below The International Soling has been the Olympic three-man keelboat since 1972. Designed by the Swede Jan Herman Linge, about 2,300 of these boats are raced worldwide. Loa 26ft 9in; Lwl 22ft 2in; beam 6ft 3in; draft 3ft 3in; sail area 233sq ft; spinnaker 355sq ft; weight 2,233lb.

produce a cheaper, lighter boat, the International Five-Point-Five which replaced the Six Metre as an Olympic racing class in 1952.

Metre boats represent the ultimate in pure racing keelboat development; during their racing life they are used for nothing else, and yet are alarmingly expensive to build, especially as each one is not only designed individually but tank-tested in model form before being built. Building to a stock design is much more economical, and modern production methods, using glassfibre moulding techniques and mass production processes for fittings and sails, render the one-design concept more attractive.

Another change is taking place in racing keelboat design. Since speed is the ultimate goal in any racing yacht, and weight is the antithesis of speed in small yachts, modern keelboats are becoming lighter and lighter. Consequently crew weight becomes a greater proportion of the all-up racing weight. Because the crew can exercise greater righting moment, designers have demoted the keel in importance, and instead make use of the human ballast carried on board. So far has the trend advanced that, like dinghies, some modern keelboats can even be capsized in quite moderate weather.

Two keelboats were used in the '76 Olympics; in one, the two-man Tempest, one crew member on a trapeze assists in keeping the boat upright, while in the other, the three-man Soling, the helmsman and his two crewmen hang so far over the side when racing that only the soles of their feet remain inside the boat!

Let us take a closer look at the various keelboat types which exist today, and try to catch a glimpse of the special attractions that each aspect of the sport has for its followers.

A Herreshoff 12½ one-design sailing on Buzzards Bay. These wood, day-sailer keelboats were designed by the American Nathaniel Greene Herreshoff in 1914 and are still actively raced in several New England yachting centres. A jib-headed rigged glassfibre version called the Bullseye is popular as a day-sailer, but few are raced.

Day-sailing boats

Used, as their name suggests, for short sailing trips, day sailers are usually half- or three-quarter-decked keelboats, with seats in the cockpit but, by definition, with no accommodation. Varying between 15ft and 30ft overall, the most usual length for such craft is between 18ft and 23ft. They spend most of their time lying to a mooring or sitting in a marina berth, waiting for their owner to come and use them for only a short trip – perhaps a picnic with the family to a nearby cove, but usually just for a short sail. In some respects day sailing is pleasure sailing at its purest, and certainly its simplest form: the owner and his friends (or maybe the owner alone, for sailing singlehanded can be a wonderful way to relax) take the boat out for the afternoon with no particular destination in mind. They just go out, enjoy a sail, and come back – sailing for sheer pleasure. Other sides of the sport usually have a definite end in view: the racing man wants to test himself against his rivals; the cruising man has somewhere to go; but the day sailor enjoys sailing purely for its own sake.

Keelboat racing – which we shall examine more closely when considering one-design craft – is a specialized form of day sailing, and many small keelboats are designed to fulfil the dual function of day sailer and racer. Either way the day sailer is probably the most under-utilized keelboat of all and, because of its short range, tends to spend most of its time in one locality. Thus, each area, each estuary and stretch of coast, has tended to breed its own variation on the general theme, variations which can be so slight as to be unnoticeable to the outsider to the sport. Not so to the insider, however: a little more sail area here, a different form of construction there – all serve to make the local class distinguishable from another class a few miles down the coast.

The advent of the glassfibre day sailer, produced in large numbers and sold across a nation, has tended to undermine the individuality of the local breeds, but older, wooden boats survive due to the loving care of their owners often in the hands of one owner for many years, sometimes passing from father to son. Many long-established yacht clubs have members who have owned, sailed and raced the same boat for twenty or thirty years, and sometimes the boats were raced by their fathers before them.

One-design classes

One-designs are racing keelboats, each of which is built to the same set of plans. The idea behind one-design racing is to remove any artificial advantage which the possession of a different type of yacht might produce, and to limit what is sometimes known as 'cheque-book racing' when the owner with the deepest pocket can win by out-equipping his rivals. Human nature being what it is, there are literally hundreds of different one-design classes, each designed to fulfil a different need: only a small number of racing yachtsmen, it seems, can agree on the sort of boat they should all race.

Each class interprets the one-design philosophy in a different way: in some everything that can be standardized is standardized – even to the point that all the boats' sails must be bought from the same maker at the same time. Others are less restrictive, allowing individual variation in matters not deemed fundamentally important, such as the placing of fittings, deck layout and so on.

One-design keelboat racing can be a close, cut-and-thrust business, often much more so than dinghy racing where the wider variation in speed can cause the boats to become more widely separated, especially in marginal planing conditions. There tends to be less variation in the speed of keelboats with the result that the contest involves more split-second timing and, at the same time, more cerebral activity. Sometimes it can be more like chess than racing!

Handicap racing

Boats of different classes, or of no special class, which want to race against each other, need some means of giving all boats an equal chance. Yacht racing is somewhat peculiar in that the object of the race is not, in fact, to find the fastest yacht, but the best skipper and crew – and yet, in

International One-Designs, designed by Norwegian Bjarne Aas in 1935, racing in Bermuda. Most of these elegant wooden boats were built in the 30s or 50s, but they are still raced on Long Island Sound, at Marblehead, San Francisco, and in Bermuda and Scotland. Loa 33ft 5in; beam 6ft 9in; draft 5ft 4in; displacement 7,120lb. About 150 boats worldwide.

Battlecry, a modern offshore racing yacht designed by the New York firm of Sparkman and Stephens, is a development of the very successful German-owned *Saudade. Battlecry*, owned by John Prentice and built of cold-moulded wood by Souter of Cowes, was a member of the successful 1975 British Admiral's Cup team. Loa 47ft; Lwl 37.2ft; beam 13.5ft; draft 7.8ft; IOR rating 36.1ft. Note the clear decks and separate cockpits. The helmsman, navigator and tactician occupy the aft cockpit which has an instrument consol ahead of the hatch. The crew work in the forward cockpit out of the way of those in the aft cockpit. Sails can be handed below easily and quickly through the main hatch.

keelboat racing especially, it is the name of the winning yacht and not that of the crew which is engraved on the trophy after the race is over. However, particularly in dinghy sailing, more and more races are being won by people rather than boats. Yachts are rendered equal by being given a handicap, expressed in units of time. And, indeed, the word 'handicap' here is a misnomer!

The handicapper, knowing one yacht to be faster than another due to some physical feature (more sail area or a differently shaped hull for example) expects her to complete the course in, say, one hour, and might expect a slower yacht, yacht B, to take an extra two minutes to do the same course. Yacht A then has a handicap of 'two minutes in the hour' against yacht B. If there are more than two boats in the race, yacht A's handicap might be 'two minutes against B, three minutes against C and a minute and a half against D' – quite a mouthful. So common usage takes a sometimes mythical yacht as the 'scratch' boat which gives time to all the others. They then express their 'handicap' – which should properly be called their time allowance – simply as 'so many minutes in the hour'. In our example yacht B's 'handicap', or time allowance bonus, would be two minutes if A were a scratch boat.

Such arbitrary handicapping is all very well for local racing where the handicapper knows each boat's capability, but a more scientific, more objective approach is required at national and international levels. The currently accepted method is to take an agreed series of measurements of each yacht which, when put into a mathematical formula, gives an indication of her potential performance. From this is derived the yacht's rating which is expressed as a theoretical length. This rating is then used, again via a mathematical formula, to find the theoretical or corrected time which the yacht has taken to complete the course. The corrected times of all the yachts in the race are compared, and the yacht with the shortest corrected time is declared the winner.

Offshore racing

Most of the racing in keelboats to which we have referred so far takes place around specially laid courses in sheltered water, not far from the yacht's base, and is of only a few hours' duration. Offshore racing takes place in open water, over much longer courses, and the race can last several days. The sport began with cruising yachts racing from one place to another, but competition is now between specially designed and built craft. Furthermore, these yachts normally start and finish in the same place, having completed a course of, maybe, 200 miles.

To some yachtsmen such sport is great fun; to others it is the height of pointlessness. For the latter the offshore race should be the means to an end, a diverting way of adding zest to going somewhere different. To the dedicated, however, the race has become an end in itself.

Offshore racing, in which a wide variety of different designs of yacht compete, is carried out almost exclusively under handicap racing rules, the yachts being measured to the International Offshore Rule (IOR) or a local offshore racing rule. One highly specialized branch of the sport – level-rating racing – has taken the handicap principle full circle.

Level-rating racing

The original intention of the IOR was to assess the potential speed of existing yachts, but once the rule was published, designers could, as it were, put the cart before the horse, deciding first what rating their yacht should carry, and then designing the boat to that rating. The whole idea of this 'designing to the rule', as it is known, is to finish up with a yacht which will sail faster than the rule thinks it will – to 'beat the rule'.

In level-rating racing a specific rating – say 27.5ft – is chosen as the common base, and yachts of that class are designed to that rating. They can then race as one-designs do on a first-home-is-the-winner basis, without handicap. But because each yacht can be different in spite of having the same rating as the others, level-rating racing is as much a battle between the designers as between the skippers, each designer trying to outsmart the rule to give his owner an advantage. However, it is very difficult to outwit the rule, for as soon as someone finds an advantage that the rule-makers had not foreseen – why, the rule is changed and the advantage taken away!

If our example level-rating figure of 27.5ft IOR is puzzling (it can hardly be said to be a round figure, after all), we should explain that the origins of the current level-rating groups or classes is something of an historical accident, and that the actual rating figures themselves have no other special significance. The principal level-rating classes for which world championship meetings are held, are the Quarter Ton (18ft IOR), the Half Ton (21.7ft IOR), the Three-Quarter Ton (24.5ft IOR), the One Ton (27.5ft IOR) and the Two Ton (32ft IOR). These were followed by the Eighth Ton (16.4ft IOR) and Mini Ton (16ft IOR) levels, supported and promoted by the British and the French respectively, but so close together that both countries soon announced their intention of finding an acceptable single level, and the Offshore Racing Council approved the Mini Ton (16ft IOR) as a new level-rating class for 1978.

Cruising keelboats

Cruisers are simply keelboats with beds in them. Unlike racing yachts the cruiser is used by its owner to go places for the sake of going. It can be across a wide ocean to a foreign land or just a mile or two up the coast. The joy of cruising is the joy of living aboard and working one's own small ship, being one's own master and dependent upon one's own efforts. Most of us take a delight in visiting new places or renewing old friendships, but there is a special magic in arriving somewhere by boat that can never be found when arriving by car. The thrill can be just as great when entering a familiar port five miles from home as when making a landfall after crossing 5,000 miles of ocean. For many cruising folk, especially those who live in densely populated areas, the joy lies in being able to find a quiet, peaceful anchorage far from towns, roads, noise and – people.

Many types of cruising keelboat exist: one-off wooden boats, stock glassfibre boats, boats with engines and boats without. In both America and Europe there has recently been a swing away from modern yachts back to older-style craft. In Britain the trend is to restore old working craft which are past their working days: old smacks, bawleys and pilot cutters are restored by dedicated owners who spend as much time maintaining these old boats as they do sailing them. In America, where there are perhaps more people chasing fewer old boats, and where the consumer may himself be more used to buying than building, the trend is towards reproduction period sailing craft – modern boats built on traditional lines.

Motor sailers

Sailing and especially cruising mean different things to different people. Some sailors will curse the internal combustion engine with their dying breath, along with every other mechanical contrivance man ever devised to render his life on board a small ship more comfortable; others, while still delighting in the quaint challenge of progress under sail (there are, after all, so many easier and quicker methods of travel), are prepared to accept some of the less obtrusive modern conveniences. While the traditionalist scorns not just engines but electric light, winches, and

modern materials which require less maintenance than good old tree-wood, most modern sailors welcome creature comforts.

The motor sailer carries creature comfort in the sailing yacht to its logical conclusion, while remaining a sailing boat and not a powered craft. Many writers describe the motor sailer as a fifty-fifty: 50% sailing boat, 50% motor yacht. Unfortunately, the problem is rarely so simple for the requirements of the two power sources, sail and engine, are often opposed. What is a good shape for the hull of one might be quite the wrong shape for the other. This is especially so in the smaller sizes of craft, and, unfortunately, some so-called fifty-fifties are only 50% as good as a proper sailing boat and 50% as good as a fully-fledged power craft.

Properly executed, however, the motor sailer concept can work well, with the yacht having much of the comforts of a motor yacht, such as an enclosed wheel-house or raised central steering position, and yet be able to provide the joy of progress under sail when conditions are favourable. An advantage of motor sailers is an abundance of power so that small crews, lacking in great physical strength, can cruise safely in a much

Many yacht designs were based on traditional working boats of this type. This Colchester Oyster Smack from England's East Coast has been restored and sails in her original form in Old Gaffers races. She is a gaff-rigged cutter with a long bowsprit and loose-footed mainsail. The number CK 431 on her bulwark just forward of the shrouds indicates that she is still registered as a fishing craft.

35

The 52ft *Delfina* was built in England for American owners and is kept in the Virgin Islands. This distinctive cruising boat is from the board of the American designer Frank MacLear of MacLear and Harrison, New York, who specialize in the development of easily handled rigs. The mainsail luff has a wire which is stretched between the head and the tack but is not attached to the mast in between. Electrically driven furling gear is fitted to both headsail and mainsail so that sail can be reduced by rolling them round their luff wires. Reducing sail area and stowing sails is an easy matter, even when short-handed.

larger vessel than would be possible under sail alone. For example, many retired couples, and indeed many younger couples with small children, find their motor sailer allows them to enjoy cruising which otherwise might be denied them by lack of muscle power.

The keelboat, then, with its versatility and the many specialized types that have been developed through the years, is a thoroughly comprehensive vessel. It is the basic unit of the very broad spectrum of yachting as a whole and gives enjoyment to countless thousands. The humble working craft of the fishermen, the crab catchers, the shrimpmen and the longshoremen of the last century have indeed come a long way.

3
Multihulls

Pat Boyd

Multihull is the generic term used to describe boats with more than one hull. The most common types are catamarans, which have two similar hulls, and trimarans, which have a main, central hull and a smaller hull either side to provide stability. Single-hull boats are sometimes referred to as monohulls to differentiate them from multihulls.

Hull stability

A sailing monohull relies on its hull shape to provide the initial stability to enable it to float level on the water. As the boat heels to the wind, initially there is an increase in the righting moment produced by the hull shape. In a dinghy this inherent righting moment is complemented by the weight of the crew as they move further to windward as the wind increases. In a deep-keel boat the more the boat heels, the greater the righting moment provided by the ballast keel, until the mast is horizontal. As the wind increases, more drive is obtained, and the boat travels faster up to a point. The main limiting factor is the righting moment available to counteract the heeling moment produced by the pressure of the wind in the sails. In a dinghy there comes a stage when it is necessary to ease the sheets to spill the wind from the sails in order to avoid capsizing, and in a ballasted keelboat the sheets must be eased and the sail reduced, or the boat merely lies on her beam ends, and forward progress is impeded.

The more beam a monohull has, the greater the inherent stability of the hull, but beamy hulls are usually less easily driven through the water than slim hulls. In a keelboat a high ballast ratio will produce optimum stability, but more ballast means more weight, and weight slows a boat. So there are practical limits to the beam and amount of ballast that can be provided to counteract heeling, and achieving the happy medium is amongst the many compromises that have to be made by the designer. The designer of a multihull relies entirely on the hulls to provide stability, and ballast is not normally required. By having two or more relatively slim hulls joined above the water and easily driven through the water, he can effectively increase beam without increasing resistance. Given the right conditions, multihulls are capable, therefore, of much higher speeds than monohulls of comparable size.

Types of multihull

Catamarans usually have identical hulls. The smaller catamarans, which are sailed like dinghies, have beams to tie the hulls together, and the area between the hulls and the beams, on which the crew sit, is usually filled with cloth or netting called the trampoline. Larger catamarans have a continuous, rigid bridge deck between the hulls, and in cruising catamarans this will usually be covered to provide part of the accommodation.

Trimarans have a central hull in which the crew work and, in a cruising boat, live, and wing hulls, called outriggers or floats. The leeward hull provides stability while the windward hull usually rides just clear of the water.

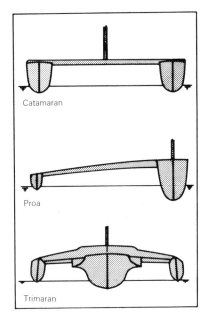

Catamaran

Proa

Trimaran

3.1 Multihull cross-sections. *(top)* A racing or day-sailing catamaran. The mast is stepped on the centreline on one of the beams that join the two hulls. *(centre)* A proa has one main hull and a single outrigger which is usually to leeward when the boat is sailing. To change tacks the rig is reversed and the boat steered from the other end. Some proas carry their outrigger to windward, and the boat is balanced by the weight of the crew on the outrigger. *(bottom)* A cruising trimaran has accommodation in the main hull and stowage in the outriggers. In large trimarans the outriggers may also be used for accommodation.

The third type of multihull, and less common than the other two, is the proa which has a main hull and just one outrigger to provide stability. In most proas the outrigger is to windward, and the weight of the crew in the outrigger helps to keep the boat upright, while in others the outrigger is to leeward and its buoyancy provides the righting force. In either case the outrigger is always carried on the same side – windward or leeward. A proa, therefore, cannot tack in the normal way but has to sail in the opposite direction, the rig being reversed and the bow becoming the stern and vice versa, there being a rudder provided at each end.

Development history

Catamarans have their origin in Polynesia where the natives have used them for hundreds of years as a means of transport between the far-flung Pacific islands. Built of local materials, the larger, cargo-carrying catamarans looked like floating villages, complete with palm-thatched huts, while the flying proas were notable for their speed.

In Europe the eccentric Irish baronet Sir William Petty is thought to have been the first person to build catamarans. He built three in the years 1662 to 1664. A catamaran built in 1664, and appropriately named *Experiment*, was sailed successfully to Portugal but sank on its return voyage in the Bay of Biscay in a storm.

The original Polynesian catamarans were virtually two boats lashed alongside one another and separated by cross-beams. Sir William's looked much more like one boat sawn in half with the resultant vertical sides planked and separated by the bridge deck.

The classic American designer Nathaniel Herreshoff re-kindled the multihull flame in the latter half of the nineteenth century. His catamaran *John Gilpin*, for instance, looked like a trimaran in which the designer had forgotten the main hull. The hulls were slim with shield-shape sections and resembled racing rowing skiffs. The rest of the boat was slung between these hulls, an oval cockpit, like a giant doughnut, and a main beam, projecting forward from the foot of the mast to form a bowsprit. The hulls were allowed to pitch independently on flexible ash cross-beams – an arrangement adopted almost 100 years later by the British designer John Westell for his *Trixia*. Herreshoff built six catamarans between 1876 and 1879, and in 1898 the Canadians built a 37ft-long racing catamaran called *Dominion* which was designed by G. Herrick Duggan. She represented the Royal St Lawrence Yacht Club in a series of races for the Seawanhaka International Challenge Trophy for Small Yachts and won four out of four races. *Dominion* was very shallow draft, the hulls being almost semicircular in section, and the junctions of the bridge deck were so curved that the cross-section had the appearance of an unbroken, wavy line, like a figure 3 on its back.

Both Herreshoff and Duggan had their catamarans banned from competing with monohulls. As a consequence the multihull movement went underground from a sailing point of view until 1937 when Eric de Bisschop and Joseph Tatibouet built a 45ft catamaran called *Kamiloa* in Hawaii, and took fourteen months to sail her to Cannes in the south of France.

One of the requirements for a successful multihull is a strong, light structure, and with the introduction of marine plywood and glued construction for boatbuilding after World War II, the way was clear to build multihulls relatively cheaply.

The first development of racing catamarans took place in England in the early 50s deep in the Essex marshes on Canvey Island. A couple of Olympic canoeists experimented with a pair of racing canoe hulls connected by a bridge deck with a dinghy rig on top. The result was crude by today's standards but it was nevertheless efficient enough to encourage the Prout brothers, Roland and Francis, to go further. They were assisted in their efforts by Ken Pearce who commissioned them to design and build an 18ft catamaran, *Endeavour*.

The early racing catamarans were unsophisticated by today's standards. Centreboards were housed in a short trunk in the middle of the bridge deck. As they were surface piercing, they were not very efficient, and to compensate for this they had to be exceptionally large. Heavy strains were imposed on the bridge deck calling for strong and heavy structures, and it was several years before centreboards were fitted into the hulls, thus saving weight. Weight saving has been a high priority for designers ever since.

During the mid-50s in the Pacific Woody Brown designed and built the 40ft *Waikiki Surf*, a derivative of the 1947-built *Manu Kai*, a 38ft 6in day boat used to take trippers for runs off the Hawaii beaches. Back in England Bill O'Brien designed the hard-chine Jumpahead of which around 200 were built, and James Wharram, with £200, a pile of plywood, a hay loft, and a burning desire to build a Polynesian-type catamaran and sail it across the Atlantic, succeeded in his aim and eventually returned in another, larger catamaran which he built on the beach in the West Indies during the trip.

Trimaran development has always seemed to lag a few years behind that of the catamaran. In 1868 the trimaran *Non Pareil* sailed from New York to Southampton in forty-three days. After World War II the work of Arthur Piver, an ebullient American fired by energy, optimism and enthusiasm, did much to popularize cruising trimarans round the world. He hit the multihull headlines in 1960 when he crossed the Atlantic in his 30ft prototype *Nimble*, and in the following years a world-wide cruising multihull explosion took place.

In England Bill O'Brien moved up from his Jumpahead in size and introduced the first of his Bobcats – a chunky 8m cruiser offering considerable accommodation for the size of boat. Rod MacAlpine-Downie designed racing cats, including some to the C-Class rule, before graduating to performance cruising catamarans, and Derek Kelsall designed and built one-off boats. In the United States Robert B. Harris, Robert E. Harris, Jim Brown and Norman Cross were trying out various multihull ideas while in Australia Lock Crowther and Hedley Nicol were very active. In the West Indies Dick Newick was designing fast trimarans and even from behind the Iron Curtain came news of multihull development.

When multihulls first gained popularity in the 50s, a strong multihull camp developed, some of whose supporters made wild claims for their

C-Class catamarans. These large, expensive racing catamarans are built almost exclusively for Little America's Cup racing, the correct name being the International C-Class Catamaran Challenge Trophy. Here final adjustments are made to the rig of *Red Roo* before leaving with *Quest III* for Denmark in 1970 to challenge for the trophy. This was finally won by the 25ft long, 14ft beam *Quest III*, designed by Australian father and son Charles and Lindsay Cunningham. The 300sq ft maximum permitted sail area includes both the wing mast and the sails, and *Quest III*'s 40ft 7in mast measured 3ft 7in fore-and-aft low down.

performance. There formed an equally hard anti-multihull camp of conservative-minded, traditional yachtsmen who understood little of multihulls but devoted their time to damning the whole concept. Both sides supported their arguments with unfounded claims and sweeping statements, but the vast majority of keen multihull sailors appreciated the virtues and limitations of their craft and contributed towards steady progress and development.

A fact that surprises many people who have not studied the multihull scene is that there is considerably more design variation to be found in multihulls than there is in monohulls. There are small catamarans designed primarily for use as day boats for pottering, and there are out-and-out racing catamarans, as highly tuned as the most extreme racing dinghy. There are cruising catamarans designed to provide as much comfortable accommodation as possible, and there are ocean-racing greyhounds designed to put up the fastest time in trans-ocean races.

Catamaran racing classes

While the growth in popularity of racing multihulls and cruising and offshore multihulls has been parallel, each type has followed its own course. In 1959 in Miami, Florida the American magazine *Yachting*'s one-of-a-kind regatta was dominated by catamarans. The American, Robert Harris-designed *Tigercat* won four of the five races whilst the Prouts' latest cat, *Cougar*, won the other. During this regatta international rivalry, albeit friendly, began to run high, and out of this was born the International Catamaran Challenge Trophy – now popularly known as the Little America's Cup. A Royal Yachting Association sub-committee dealing with multihulls had fixed the parameters for a restricted class to stimulate design development. They were: 25ft over-all length; 14ft beam; a sail area of not more than 300sq ft to include the area of the spars; and the boat was to be sailed by a crew of two. This resulted in the C-class catamaran.

The Little America's Cup was first held in September 1961 in America on Long Island Sound with the British *Hellcat II* beating the American

An International Tornado being put through its paces by world champion and Olympic Gold medal winner Reg White. Loa 20ft; beam 10ft; sail area 235sq ft; weight 279lb. 2,500 boats worldwide, growing by 200 annually.

Below The Hobie 14s shown here are single-handers designed by Hobie Alter. They have no jib, and the helmsman hikes to keep the boat upright in strong wind. The Hobie 16 has mainsail and jib and a crew who use a trapeze.

Wildcat. Britain successfully defended the cup against American and Australian challenges each year until 1969 when the Danes were successful. They lost it the following year to the Australians who retained it until 1976 when the American *Aquarius V* beat the Australian defender *Miss Nylex.*

In 1967 the IYRU instigated selection trials for catamarans to be chosen for international racing in the A and B classes. An Australian boat, Australis, narrowly secured selection as the A class and was granted international recognition but gained little ground, and recognition was rescinded in 1975. However, the two-man, B-class boat selected, Tornado, went from strength to strength. Designed by Englishman Rodney March, she completely dominated the 1967 trials and in 1972 was chosen as an Olympic class for Canada in 1976.

New racing classes spring up all over the world. Some wither and perish while others gain a substantial hold. The largest class numerically, the Hobie Cat, designed by American Hobie Alter, has spread all over the world, thanks to an enlightened marketing policy. The Hobie design is such that centreboards are not required, making it ideal for sailing off a beach, and the racing is a light-hearted affair except at championship time. In 1975 Rodney March designed an 18ft catamaran without centreboards called Dart and it was recommended as a new international class after trials in California early in 1976.

During the early 70s there was a resurgence of interest in the Little America's Cup. The Australians led the world in the development of solid wing masts but these proved somewhat difficult to control as well as being heavy. There was also a move towards the use of conventional sails and less complicated rigs, as underlined by the simple rig of *Aquarius V* when she won the Cup in 1976.

Larger multihulls

Because a cruising multihull achieves its stability without having to carry a large lump of lead as ballast, scantlings can be lighter and internal volume greater for a given length of boat. Light weight means smaller

41

A Dart catamaran flying her weather hull as she slices to windward. The simple but high-performance Dart, designed by Englishman Rodney March in 1975, can be sailed either with a crew of two using mainsail and jib, or single-handed with the mainsail alone. In the first year 200 boats were built, and she was selected as a new International class at trials held in California in 1976. Neither centreboards nor dagger boards are required, and the fully-battened mainsail has no boom. The hulls and main beams can be dismantled quickly for transport and storage. Loa 18ft; beam 7ft 6in; draft 11in; sail area, mainsail 139sq ft; jib 34sq ft; weight 280lb.

A typical cruising catamaran. The 8 metre Catalac provides spacious accommodation for her length and has a 10ft × 6ft 6in self-draining cockpit. She can sleep five and has a saloon, separate toilet compartment and galley. Catamarans make ideal family cruising boats as they tend to remain on an even keel, but sail area should be modest to reduce the risk of capsizing. Loa 26ft 3in; beam 13ft 1½in; draft 2ft 2in; sail area 377sq ft. Built by Tom Lack Catamarans Ltd of Christchurch, England.

winches and a lighter-weight crew can cope, while a strong one can carry on longer without fatigue. But mast sections and rigging often have to be greater, especially on the heavier cruising cats, because it is possible to drive multihulls much harder than monohulls. There is no built-in safety valve like that when a monohull heels, spilling the wind from her sails and reducing the effective lateral area.

It is really in the accommodation area that the larger multihulls score. In a cruising trimaran over 40ft in length there is room for four double cabins of considerable luxury. Over 45ft size really starts to pay dividends – in catamarans it is possible to achieve full standing headroom over the bridge deck. A big trimaran is like three monohulls lashed together – the main hull can contain a superb saloon, a navigator's cabin, bath, shower and a full-size galley while up to six double cabins can be provided in the outriggers.

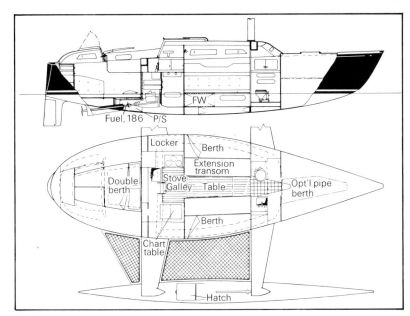

3.2 *Left* The accommodation plan of a 33ft cruising trimaran designed by Robert B. Harris of Vancouver. There are two cabins separated by a centre cockpit. The saloon provides a galley to port, two berths set up high in the flared topsides and seating that can be converted to two more berths. The aft cabin has a double berth, and a single pipe cot can be fitted in the fo'c's'le forward of the toilet compartment. A cross-section of this hull is shown at the bottom of figure **3.3** below.

A catamaran provides considerable internal volume but its usefulness is dependent on the cross-section of the hulls. A V-shape hull gives plenty of deck space and width at shoulder level but lower down is more restricted. A U-shape hull section is better and allows for locker stowage at floor level in the cabins. If the hulls are very slim, the ends will be virtually useless for stowage, so a slim hull 50-footer might only have the accommodation of a fuller section 30-footer.

In the smaller catamaran designs below 35ft overall it is difficult to obtain an elegant profile as well as providing standing headroom over the bridge deck. Only by incorporating a chunky-looking doghouse can standing headroom be achieved. The Prout-designed Snowgoose overcomes the problem by having a nacelle beneath the bridge deck which provides standing headroom along the centreline. Some designers have provided a sunshine roof at the aft end of the saloon, while others accept the lack of standing headroom over the bridge deck in the interests of appearance and reduced windage. Of course most cruising catamarans have full standing headroom in each hull.

As trimarans come down in size their accommodation plans become more like those of monohulls. Most cruising trimarans around the 30ft mark have a flared main hull to allow room for bunks in the flares. Even some considerably larger trimarans, if built with an eye to speed for racing, have only scanty stowage space in their slim outriggers.

There is a very sharp division in accommodation levels between racing and cruising multihulls. Above 30ft overall a trimaran will probably provide better accommodation for cruising while a catamaran is better below this length. In cruising multihulls, especially, centreboards are losing popularity since their cases take up valuable accommodation space and are a possible source of leaks. Also, there is a school of thought that maintains that by not having centreboards the hulls have less lateral grip in the water and slide sideways more easily

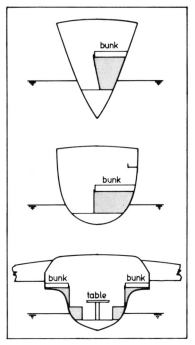

3.3 Comparison of stowage space available in different hulls. *(top)* A vee-shape catamaran hull has ample width at shoulder level. *(centre)* A U-shape hull has more space at floor level, and the bunk does not have to be positioned so high to obtain sufficient width. *(bottom)* The cruising trimaran illustrated in figure **3.2** above. The main hull is flared above the waterline to take the bunks, but there is little useful stowage space beneath them.

should the boat be struck by a sudden heeling gust of wind or by a large sea which might tend to turn it over.

Performance

A 30ft cruising catamaran will hold her own against most monohulls of similar size to windward in most wind strengths, but as soon as she gets off the wind in anything other than the lightest airs she will be at an advantage and can accelerate to 12 or 15 knots when surfing on waves in quite modest wind strengths. Many cruising multihulls over 35ft have put up passage speeds of over 10 knots average.

When it comes to ocean racing there is a strong argument between the trimaran and catamaran factions, with trimarans possibly winning the day. The most famous ocean-crossing multihull is arguably the French *Manureva* sailed by Alain Colas and built as *Pen Duick IV* for Eric Tabarly. This 70ft trimaran is an out-and-out ocean racer built of welded aluminium, and with masses of tubular struts and two vast semi-circular sheet tracks she looks like a plumber's nightmare. In December 1968 she crossed the Atlantic from the Canary Islands to Martinique in the West Indies, a distance of 2,640 miles, at an average speed of 10.47 knots and the following year in the Pacific covered 2,225 miles in 8 days 13 hours – an average of 10.85 knots. In the 1974 Round Britain Race the 70ft catamaran *British Oxygen*, sailed by Robin Knox-Johnston and Gerry Boxall, finished a day ahead of *Manureva*, but in the same race the honour of the trimarans was upheld by Mike McMullen in his 46ft *Three Cheers* which was snapping at the heels of *British Oxygen* all the way to the finish.

Proas are potentially the fastest multihulls but offer little in the way of accommodation. Tom Follet, the American, sailed the 40ft proa *Cheers* in the 1968 Singlehanded Transatlantic Race and finished third in a fleet of thirty-five, while the world sailing speed record of 31.09 knots was set up in 1975 by *Crossbow*, a 60-footer designed by Rod MacAlpine-Downie just for the record attempt. She is completely useless for anything other than speed attempts in one direction as the rig cannot be reversed and she can sail only on one tack, having a single outrigger far out to starboard of the main hull in which her crew of four operate the rig and rudder by remote control.

Handicap racing

There has always been opposition to allowing multihulls to take part in organized races with monohulls because each type behaves in a different manner in varying conditions of wind strength and direction. This has been interpreted by many multihull enthusiasts as stubborn and obstructive behaviour on the part of the establishment, but what it really represents is an intelligent appreciation of the difference in performance potential between multihulls and monohulls, for there is no way that the two can be rated and handicapped fairly in relation to each other.

In 1974 the International Offshore Multihull Rule (IOMR) was introduced and adopted but was not welcome universally. It was drawn

Left Manureva, a ketch-rigged trimaran, was built of aluminium for Eric Tabarly as *Pen Duick IV*. Alain Colas, won the 1972 OSTAR with her in a record time of 20 days, 13 hours and 15 minutes. Loa 70ft; Lwl 67ft; beam 35ft; draft 2ft.

Below left The 60ft, purpose-designed proa *Crossbow* held the world sailing speed record at 31.09 knots. She can be sailed only on starboard tack and is controlled from the outrigger. Loa 60ft; Lwl 50ft; beam 1ft 10in; beam overall 31ft 6in; pod 15ft overall.

Below Cheers, Tom Follet's slim 40ft proa finished third in the 1968 OSTAR. Because the outrigger is always to leeward, she cannot tack normally and, instead, the rig and steering arrangements have to be reversed.

Left FT, David Palmer's 35ft loa, 26ft beam trimaran, was designed by Derek Kelsall for the 1976 OSTAR and finished seventh. She is an out-and-out racing machine with accommodation for her crew in the main hull and only minimal storage space in the outriggers. Note the self-steering gear hung over the transom, the circular mainsheet track, the life-raft attached beneath the track and the radar reflector hanging from the backstay.

Righting a capsized catamaran. The Dart can be righted easily after a capsize without outside assistance. The crew are pulling on the jib sheet which has been led over the upper hull. When the mast and sails lift clear of the water, the boat will come upright quickly and the crew must immediately roll themselves on board and trim the sails.

Below These Victress trimarans can easily be moored alongside a wall in a spacious harbour, but in many marinas where space is at a premium multihulls are often charged one and a half times or twice the rate for a monohull craft.

up to a great extent by Dr Vic Stern, Commodore of the American Ocean Racing Catamaran Association, and was based on experience gained on the west coast of the United States and in the Pacific. There is a strong feeling that more account should have been taken of conditions and experience in other parts of the world, but for the time being it is the only international rating rule for offshore racing multihulls.

Trailing and mooring

One factor that has to be considered when contemplating the purchase of a multihull is the width of the boat. Since most countries have restrictions on the maximum width of a load that may be trailed behind a car, many small catamarans have to be dismantled or trailed on their sides – a design feature of many class-racing catamarans is the ease with which they can be taken apart and put together again. Many marina operators charge extra for multihulls, but charging for a catamaran twice the rate levied for a monohull, on the basis that it has two hulls and not one, does seem somewhat excessive. However, multihull owners will often be called upon to pay half as much again as the rate for a monohull. Some trimarans have overcome this problem by having outriggers which fold alongside the main hull when the boat is in harbour.

Stability and safety

A multihull is very stable both when floating in the water upright and when inverted. If a multihull is driven too hard with too much sail for the strength of wind and the crew is not alert, there is a risk of flipping over, and righting the boat can be a difficult operation. Small class-racing catamarans often need the assistance of a rescue boat to help the crew right them after a capsize, while the recovery of an offshore or cruising multihull is a salvage operation. With a modicum of care and

46

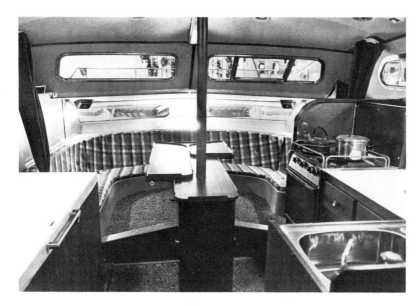

This picture gives a good indication of the spacious accommodation available in a cruising catamaran. This is the saloon of a 35ft Cherokee, a Macalpine-Downie design with eight berths built by Sail Craft Ltd of Brightlingsea.

good seamanship the risk is slight indeed. The anti-multihull brigade will point to a handful of documented disasters and unexplained disappearances to try to prove the unsuitability of multihulls for off-shore and ocean sailing, but similar fates befall monohulls and there are many successful recorded voyages by multihulls to prove their reliability. Even if a multihull should be turned over in the open ocean, all is not lost as was proved by the experienced American, Philip Weld, who was sailing his 60ft trimaran *Gulf Streamer* from Florida to Britain for the 1976 Observer Singlehanded Transatlantic Race when a 40ft high, double-crested wave overturned the boat 350 miles off the east coast of the USA. Weld and his crew were prepared for such an emergency and, having cut an access hole in the bottom of the main hull, were able to live on board for nearly five days until they were rescued by a passing ship which responded to their distress flares.

Multihull advantages

Multihulls have much to offer in terms of performance and accommodation for money. The racing multihulls are exhilarating to sail and even cruising catamarans can put up exceptionally fast passage times given the right conditions. A cruising catamaran of only 25ft or 30ft overall has a spacious living area, a huge cockpit – ideal for a social party or a vast playpen for toddlers – and the great advantage that the boat tends to remain on an even keel at sea, which means that items stay where they are placed, and the crew do not become fatigued through having to brace themselves continually against the angle of heel.

4
Sailing in Britain

Peter Cook

Boating is reliably held to be the most popular participant sport in Britain. It is claimed that there are more people afloat on a Saturday afternoon in July than are watching football on a Saturday afternoon in February – and football is Britain's greatest spectator sport.

In Britain no one lives further than 100 miles from part of the coast where sailing is available, and there are numerous sailing clubs on reservoirs, flooded gravel pits and rivers where dinghy sailing takes place.

As there is no legislation in Britain calling for registration of craft, it is impossible to quote an exact figure for the number of boats in the country, but a good indication of the spread and level of activity was given in a report produced in 1973 by a firm of management consultants, commissioned by the national administrative authority, the Royal Yachting Association (RYA). This report concluded that there were 750,000 yachtsmen in Britain who were committed to the sport, '. . . either by owning a boat or making substantial financial or time commitments as crew, part owner or working partner'. It was, however, estimated that well over two million people had some interest in boating. The 750,000 'committed yachtsmen' were divided into: 200,000 racing restricted and one-design sailing boats; 20,000 offshore cruising; 2,000 powerboat racing; 15,000 offshore racing; and 500,000 partaking in 'inland, estuarial and local sea cruising, non-competitive dinghy sailing, and day cruising in trailed or locally parked open runabouts'. No breakdown was given for the last, and by far the largest, category, but it would be fair to assume that the interest of at least half these 500,000 was in sailing boats, which would mean that in spring 1973 nearly half a million people in Britain were 'committed' sailing yachtsmen.

Class racing is very popular in Britain. In 1975 there were seventy-two active classes of which sixteen were International classes and twelve National classes. Some classes were only a dozen or two strong, but the total number of boats was an estimated 120,000. There are also a number of purely local one-design classes not included in this total, seven active keelboat racing classes and four catamaran classes.

Background

Yachting developed in Britain during the nineteenth century, until in the 1890s and early 1900s there were a number of well-established racing classes of cruising yachts led by 'the Big Class' – magnificent cutters, over 100ft in length and manned by large professional crews. During the sailing season the Big Class moved from one coastal resort to the next, racing in different regattas. This was the heyday of grand yachting and certainly a time when yachting was predominantly the sport of millionaires and kings. World War I put a stop to yachting activity for five years, and although the Big Class was revived in the 20s with the J class and similar size vessels, 1935 was the last year that saw them racing round the coast.

There is a long tradition of competition between Britain and the United States stemming from 22 August 1851, when the schooner *America* defeated a fleet of seventeen British yachts in a race round the

Opposite Standfast II, a member of the 1975 Dutch Admiral's Cup team, beating under a well-reefed mainsail in dusty conditions.

Isle of Wight. The trophy she won, the Hundred Guinea Cup put up by the Royal Yacht Squadron, went back to New York and became the America's Cup. It has rested in the New York Yacht Club ever since, despite many challenges from Britain, and others from Canada, Australia and France. Early challenges took place in the large schooners and cutters of the day; after 1930 the smaller J-class boats were used, and when the competition was revived in 1958, Twelve Metres were adopted. Although the America's Cup competition has faded in importance with the growth of major offshore competition) it still remains a pinnacle of international sport yet to be surmounted by any challenger.

Dinghy sailing

From the turn of the century until World War II numerous local one-design dinghy classes developed in Britain. Some were raced by just one club, others might be concentrated on a particular area, but all were designed to suit local conditions. Sometimes no more than a dozen or so boats were built to a class and few reached three figures, but the majority were raced keenly and kept in immaculate condition. Many of these boats still enjoy regular class racing, although, in some cases, all the boats were built over fifty years ago.

Three of these early classes, all 14ft long, joined forces to produce the rules for a 14ft restricted class, the National (later International) Fourteen. This was by far the largest dinghy class raced on a national basis, but small by modern standards. By the mid-30s sail numbers had reached only around 300 with about thirty new boats being built each year.

In 1936 the National Twelve was introduced – a restricted class, with similar rules to the International Fourteen but with a price limit. It was an immediate success with 170 boats built in the first six months, and over 400 when the war put a stop to further growth in 1939. After the war, the National Twelve class grew at an average of 100 boats a year, and in 1946 the magazine *Yachting World* launched a 14ft, clinker-built restricted class which became the Merlin Rocket. In 1947 the moulded plywood 12ft Firefly one-design was introduced. Used as a single-hander in the 1948 Olympics, it afterwards became established as a two-man class especially popular with universities and the armed forces.

In the 50s dinghy classes proliferated, all designed for quantity production and home building, using plywood and waterproof glues. Leading the field as a designer was Jack Holt, who had designed the original Merlin in 1946. In 1947 he designed the 10ft 6in Cadet as a training racing dinghy for young people – the rules restrict the age of the crew to under eighteen for racing – and this class later attained International status. In 1950 came the GP14, a general-purpose, half-decked dinghy suitable for family sailing, and in 1951 came the GP's small brother, the 11ft 3in Heron. Also in 1951 he designed the 16ft Hornet, a high-performance racing dinghy with a sliding seat for the crew. All these boats were hard chine, but in 1956 the first of the double-chine boats appeared – the Holt-designed 13ft 3in Enterprise and, from Ian Proctor, the 11ft Gull, which was followed in 1958 by the 15ft 10in

Inland sailing on the river Thames at Teddington. The almost windless conditions call for considerable patience and concentration from the crews of International Fourteens competing in this Tamesis Sailing Club race. Loa 14ft; beam 5ft 6in; sail area 190sq ft; spinnaker 260sq ft; weight 300lb approx. About 1,100 boats.

Opposite Flying Dutchman dinghies racing in Weymouth Olympic Week in England in the 1976 British Olympic selection trials.

51

J-Class racing in the 30s with *Yankee* leading the British boats *Shamrock V* and *Endeavour. Yankee,* designed by Frank C. Paine, was one of four J-Class boats built in America when Sir Thomas Lipton challenged for the America's Cup with *Shamrock V*, but *Enterprise* won the trials and successfully defended the Cup. *Yankee* raced across the Atlantic in 1935 beating the three-masted schooner *America* by about thirty miles. *Atlantic*'s 1905 time of 12 days 4 hours and 1 minute still stands as a record for an Atlantic crossing under sail. *Yankee*'s dimensions: Loa 125.5ft; Lwl 84ft; beam 22.4ft; draft 15ft; displacement 148 tons; sail area 7,550sq ft.

Wayfarer. Although these dinghies were all designed for production in plywood, they are now built in glassfibre.

Many other dinghy classes made their appearance during this period but there is not room to mention them all here. There are two classes, however, the Mirror and the Fireball, that cannot go unrecorded.

The 10ft 10in Mirror, designed by Jack Holt and do-it-yourself expert Barry Bucknell in 1963, was the first boat to use the stitch-and-glue construction method (see Chapter 10). The boat takes its name from the *Daily Mirror*, the newspaper that sponsors and markets it. It has been responsible for introducing to sailing many people who would otherwise never have gone near the water and by 1975 over 50,000 boats had been sold throughout the world.

The 16ft 2in Fireball was a completely new approach to dinghy design by Peter Milne in 1962. Intended for home building, she has a scow-like hull with a flat bottom panel, two bilge panels, and two topside panels. The cheeky, unconventional shape, moderate price and high performance caught the imagination of a spirited group of young sailors and spread quickly to other countries. The Fireball is now an International class and sail numbers world-wide had reached 10,000 by 1975.

Although some round-bilge dinghy designs were introduced in the late 60s for construction in glassfibre, few have enjoyed the popularity of the well-established classes despite their being twenty or thirty years old.

Cruising

Britain is ideally suited for cruising. There are many harbours where a cruiser may be kept, and interesting home and foreign cruising waters are within easy sailing distance.

The largest concentration of cruisers and ocean-racing yachts has always been in the Solent and Southampton Water area in the middle of the South Coast, seventy or eighty miles from London. The Solent is a strip of water between the Isle of Wight and the mainland; it stretches over twenty miles from Spithead in the east to Hurst Narrows in the west and is two to three miles in width. Southampton Water runs north-west from the centre of the Solent for ten miles to the port of Southampton. Along the shores are a number of creeks and harbours providing yacht anchorages and they include some of the best-known yachting centres in the country – Cowes, Hamble, Bursledon, Beaulieu, Lymington and Yarmouth – all with marinas and yacht repair facilities. Portsmouth Harbour lies at the eastern end of the Solent, and a few miles further east are the entrances to Langstone and Chichester Harbours; twenty miles to the west of the Solent lies Poole Harbour, while the Cherbourg Peninsula in France is only sixty miles to the south. The whole area is an ideal cruising ground. There are some shallow patches and mud banks but usually they are all well marked, and there are few off-lying dangers. The novice can potter gently from one yacht haven to the next. When he becomes more adventurous, Chichester and Poole Harbours involve only a few hours' passage in open water, and France is an easy day's sail away. The complex tidal streams add spice to what might seem rather unchallenging sailing, and the double high water extends the cruising opportunities for shallow draft boats. No wonder that many yachtsmen spend their whole lives sailing in the area.

The deep-water estuaries of Devon and Cornwall lie 100–150 miles west of the Solent and are an attractive cruising ground. To the south is the rocky coast of Brittany in France with its many small harbours, superb shellfish and soft wines.

East of Chichester Harbour along the south coast of England and through the Dover Straits there are few sheltered havens for yachts, and such harbours as Newhaven, Folkestone, and Dover are far too busy acting as ferry terminals for millions of passengers, cars, and lorries travelling to and from the continent of Europe each year to concern themselves very much with yachting. There is a small yacht marina at Newhaven, and a huge marina complex and harbour has been built at Brighton where previously there was just an open beach, but this part of the English Channel is not good for cruising. There are few places for

A small, gaff-rigged family cruiser motoring into Cowes Harbour from the Solent. This Westerly is towing an inflatable dinghy which is used as a tender for getting ashore from a mooring and which can be deflated and stowed on board for offshore passages. In the background is the premier British yacht club, the Royal Yacht Squadron.

Dartmouth is typical of the West of England harbours. A deep water inlet with steeply wooded banks passes between the small towns of Dartmouth and Kingswear. The tidal river Dart meanders nearly ten miles inland and can be explored by smaller yachts and dinghies. On the hill in the background is the Brittania Royal Naval College where future naval officers receive their initial training.

Dragons racing at Burnham-on-Crouch. The East Coast is very flat and wind blasts down the fairly narrow river uninterrupted by hills or high banks. Designed by Johan Anker in 1926 the Dragon was an Olympic class until 1968. Six or seven fleets of these International keelboats race in the British Isles. Loa 29ft 3in; beam 6ft 3in; weight 3,740 lb; sail area 237sq ft.

the cruising yacht to anchor, and there is considerable congestion of shipping in the Dover Strait and its approaches, so the area is best avoided by the cruising man.

North of the mouth of the Thames estuary on the East Coast a series of rivers and creeks, running into the counties of Essex and Suffolk, provides another popular cruising ground. It includes such yachting centres as Burnham-on-Crouch, Maldon and West Mersea on the river Blackwater, Brightlingsea on the river Colne, Pin Mill on the Orwell and Waldringfield on the Deben. The area has a totally different character from that found on the South Coast. Here the shore is flat, and sand-banks stretch a few miles to seaward, so local knowledge is an advantage. But it is a relatively safe coast, and the worst fate that befalls the unwary is often the inconvenience and ignominy of having to spend a few hours sitting on a sand-bank waiting for the tide to return. East Coast cruising yachtsmen have the equally flat coasts of Belgium and the Netherlands the other side of the North Sea available for foreign visits, and the more adventurous with the time to spare can head for Denmark and the other Scandinavian countries.

Another cruising area in Britain is centred on the river Clyde on the

A cruiser motoring out of Mallaig Harbour on the west coast of Scotland, a ruggedly attractive area with numerous outlying islands. Yachts can spend years exploring this spectacular coastline, but these are cruising grounds for experienced sailors.

west coast of Scotland. Here the water is deep, and the west coast of Scotland, possibly one of the most spectacular cruising grounds anywhere with its sea lochs and outlying islands, offers rugged cruising to the experienced sailor. This is no place for the novice, for the coast is exposed, and outside the islands one is open to the full force of the Atlantic swell. The shore is steep-to with many off-lying rocks both above and below the water, and winds can increase suddenly and funnel down in gusts between the mountains and high cliffs. Although there are plenty of islands to shelter behind, the water is often unsuitable for anchoring, being too deep with a rocky bottom. The Western Isles of Scotland provide the most satisfying cruising to be found in Britain and are the ultimate for many cruising men.

The main yachting centres around the coast of Britain have been mentioned, but yachts will be found nearly everywhere there is somewhere for them to moor. In the popular centres moorings are hard to come by, and even where marinas have been built, berths are usually at a premium. Today it is essential, therefore, to secure the promise of a mooring or marina berth before being committed to buying a boat.

The dinghy explosion in the 50s was followed by a similar increase in interest in small cruisers as dinghy sailors graduated to larger boats. Until this time the traditional small cruiser had been relatively narrow in the beam and was built individually by an established boatyard – a fairly expensive and time-consuming exercise. The new demand was met first by plywood boats with hard-chine hulls, the best known probably being the two-berth 17ft 3in Silhouette. Later came the first production glassfibre cruisers.

Today there is a wide selection of good quality cruisers available up to 40ft overall. Above this size the choice is more limited, but there are at least two British-built production cruising yachts over 70ft in length.

There are a number of clubs devoted to cruising which have accumulated a considerable wealth of information on cruising grounds and this is available to members. In England are the Royal Cruising Club and the Cruising Association, in Scotland there is the Clyde Cruising Club, and in Ireland the Irish Cruising Club. Membership of one or more of these is most useful if extended cruising is planned.

Racing

Ever since the Ocean Racing Club was formed in 1925 (it became the Royal Ocean Racing Club in 1930), offshore racing has developed steadily in Britain, with a pause during the years of World War II. In 1950 the Junior Offshore Group (JOG) was formed to organize racing for yachts down to 16–20ft on the waterline, smaller than were allowed to compete in the RORC events. The detailed development of offshore racing is covered in Chapter 16.

The RORC is the major organizer of offshore events in Britain and is responsible for about twenty races each year. The main programme takes place from the Solent round courses set in the English Channel, usually just over 200 miles in length. RORC races also take place to ports in France and across the Irish and North Seas. Other organizations run their own offshore events. On the East Coast the East Anglian Offshore Racing Association (EAORA) has a full programme of races, shorter in length than those of the RORC. The Irish Sea Offshore Racing Association (ISORA) runs races in the Irish Sea which take place in Scotland and North Wales as well as Ireland, and there are other offshore events off the north-east coast, from the Firth of Forth on the east coast of Scotland, and in the West Country from Plymouth and Falmouth. The major events for offshore boats in Britain are the 605 mile Fastnet Race and the Admiral's Cup international team-racing series that take place every other year.

Many of the older clubs run races two or three times a week for keelboat one-designs, dinghy classes, and cruising boats, which are owned by local residents rather than weekend visitors. If sufficient boats of a particular class turn out regularly for handicap racing, they will qualify for their own class racing while, conversely, lack of regular support can mean relegation to the handicap fleet. Many of the centres running this type of sailing have a regatta week each year, the most famous being Cowes Week which takes place at the beginning of August. Every other year Cowes plays host to the Admiral's Cup competition where the

Opposite A varied selection of British cruisers, including an ocean racer, an old gaff cutter, a Folkboat and a family cruiser, sail out of the Medina river at Cowes for the start of the annual Round the Island Race. This classic race round the Isle of Wight brings together about 400 boats, ranging from pure cruising boats to out-and-out Admiral's Cup contestants.

three inshore races of the event are held. The Fastnet Race starts from Cowes on the Saturday at the end of the week. Even in non-Admiral's Cup years Cowes teems with visiting yachts from other parts of the country and from abroad. With something like five IOR classes, two cruising keelboat classes, and ten one-design keelboat classes, it is the biggest and most spectacular regatta in the country. On the East Coast Burnham Week takes place at the end of August, and in July there is a regatta week on the Clyde. Other centres hold their own sailing weeks for cruisers and dinghies.

Another major event from Cowes is the annual Round the Island Race. Up to 400 boats take part in a mass start for a course which circumnavigates the Isle of Wight, a distance of about sixty miles. In the Solent there is a points series running throughout the season from May to September. There is also regular, round-the-buoy racing for the level-rating classes which also have their own annual championship week.

Learning to sail

The RYA administers a National Proficiency Scheme and a National Coaching Scheme which cover every aspect of sailing. There are numerous sailing schools, many of which are RYA approved, teaching from the very elementary day-boat level right up to full ocean navigation standard. Evening classes in theoretical subjects are available at colleges and adult education centres, but full qualification in any form of sailing calls for practical experience and a practical test. The armed forces, the Scout and Guide organizations, and many schools also adopt the RYA teaching method, and so a uniform standard of teaching and qualification is available throughout the country.

An association of sail training organizations lists a selection of large boats that take young people sailing, and two purpose-built schooners, *Sir Winston Churchill* and *Malcolm Miller*, are run by the Sail Training Association (STA) and provide sail training cruises for boys and girls.

Administration and organization

The racing classes are administered by their own class associations, but for national classes changes to class rules must be endorsed by the RYA. International classes are similarly controlled by the IYRU.

The RYA is the national administrative authority for most forms of boating – there are other organizations for canoeing, water skiing, and inland waterways. It administers the national sailing classes in conjunction with their own associations, the National Proficiency Scheme and RYA/DTI Yachtmaster's Certificates, the racing rules, and competitive powerboat racing; it is involved with the training and appointment of class and tonnage measurers, the issuing of sail numbers for non-IOR rated cruisers and is engaged in continual consultation with national and international maritime organizations; it publishes a host of booklets on many subjects allied to boating varying from *Regional Lists of Sailing Clubs and the Classes they Race* to *Notes on Planning for Going Foreign*, and from *Lists of Films* to *Notes on*

Reservoir sailing in the Midlands miles from the sea. All over Britain reservoirs and flooded gravel pits are used for dinghy sailing and racing. This promises to be a rather slow race at Hollowell Sailing Club. The dimensions of the Mirror dinghies are: Loa 10ft 10in; beam 4ft 7½in; weight 135lb; sail area 69sq ft; spinnaker 65½sq ft. Around 55,500 worldwide, annual growth about 4,000 boats.

Insurance. Possibly the RYA's most important function is that which receives least publicity – dealing with government, local and harbour authorities, and keeping a watch-dog eye on boating interests.

Entry to most sailing and yacht clubs is relatively easy – merely a matter of finding a proposer and seconder. Some clubs are more exclusive than others and, therefore, more selective, but the greatest difficulty in joining a club is likely to be encountered when membership lists are full and there is a waiting list. This happens frequently at inland clubs sailing on reservoirs where the number of boats and club members is restricted owing to lack of space. Club subscriptions in Britain are low by world standards and so, sometimes, are the facilities. Subscriptions can vary from a few pounds a year to £100 ($200) or more – the latter more often being levied not by the old established royal yacht clubs but by recently formed clubs on new reservoirs with high mortgage charges to meet for their modern clubhouse. Sailing clubs have their own character – in some the emphasis is on keen racing while others provide a more relaxed atmosphere catering more for the family man. Most clubs organize racing for a selected number of classes and may also have a handicap class.

During the summer months, especially, open meetings are popular, and most clubs run one open meeting each year for each of the dinghy classes they race. Some dinghy sailors spend every weekend during the summer on the open meeting circuit, preferring the challenge of different competition and different conditions each weekend to the more predictable conditions at their own club. All classes have one national championship each year, and some of the larger ones have area championships at which boats may qualify for the main national event if numbers have to be limited. The major dinghy regatta, Weymouth Olympic Week (WOW), which is usually held in June each year for the Olympic classes, attracts top overseas competition.

Each year there is a National Team Championship in which sixteen clubs compete for the title, over a weekend in October, after a knock-out competition lasting the whole year and involving 200 or 300 clubs.

There is also a National Youth Championship and a Ladies' Championship.

Each club has its own burgee, and the red ensign is the national flag to fly afloat. The union flag, flown ashore, may only be flown afloat as a jack by the Royal Navy who, together with the Royal Yacht Squadron, are the only people allowed to fly the white ensign. Members of some clubs are allowed to fly the blue ensign or a defaced red or blue ensign but must first obtain a warrant, and their yachts must be registered as a 'British ship'. A red ensign should be flown by visiting yachts as a courtesy flag, not the union flag which renders the owner liable to a fine.

Regulations, registration and licences

The only statutory regulations affecting someone in charge of a boat in tidal waters are those of the *International Regulations for Preventing Collisons at Sea* and any local regulations enforced by harbour authorities. Most inland waterways are covered by regulations affecting navigation, speed, pollution, and other matters laid down by the administrative authority.

Any vessel over 15 tons net must be registered with the Registrar of Shipping, and vessels under 15 tons net must be registered if they are to leave British territorial waters. Details of registration and safety-equipment regulations are set out in booklets obtainable from the RYA. Registration is normally necessary if the boat is to be subject to a mortgage agreement, and is extremely useful abroad as proof of ownership. For unregistered yachts an International Certificate for Pleasure Navigation obtainable from the RYA is a useful proof of ownership.

There is no statutory requirement for insurance, but many clubs make insurance, with a minimum amount of third-party cover, a condition of entry for races, and it is advisable to have third-party cover up to at least £100,000. Class-racing boats are required to have up-to-date class-racing certificates, and offshore-racing yachts have to be measured to receive a rating.

Britain has very strict laws concerning the import of certain animals from abroad. Any animals brought into the country must be reported to the health authorities immediately and confined in an approved anchorage or berth before being placed in quarantine in an approved establishment for a number of months. The restrictions apply equally to animals imported from abroad and those that have visited another country. The spread of rabies across Europe has meant that heavy penalties have been awarded to offenders – large fines or even imprisonment – and there is pressure to increase the penalties to include destruction of the animal and confiscation of any yacht involved. So the best advice is to leave your pet at home.

Rescue services round the coasts are co-ordinated by the Coastguard who can call upon lifeboats, helicopters, or surface ships to carry out rescue operations. The Royal National Lifeboat Institute (RNLI) have over 250 sea-going lifeboats stationed round the coasts of Great Britain and Northern Ireland, and nearly sixty inshore lifeboats which are outboard-powered inflatables. The Coastguard operates a safety service for yachtsmen known as the 'CG66 Scheme'. Yachtsmen are asked to complete a card, (CG66A), giving details of their boat and its normal area of operation. When making passages outside this area yachtsmen can complete form CG66B, giving details of their intended passage and the name and telephone number of someone ashore who can be contacted if the yacht is overdue.

Weather

For many years Britain was subject to prevailing winds from the west and south-west which were associated with depressions moving in from the Atlantic. June was usually a fine, settled month with light winds, while the beginning of August usually produced variable conditions and a gale or two. In the early 70s the pattern changed, and the depressions passed clear of the British Isles to the north, resulting in dryer weather and lighter winds, more frequently from an easterly direction. The meteorologists are unable to predict whether the old predominance of westerlies will soon return or whether a more permanent change in the weather pattern has become established.

Publications and charts

Britain is served well with boating publications. There are a number of publishers who specialize in yachting books, and each of the five leading magazines covers a well-defined field of interest, while a number of fringe magazines cover minority interests.

Charts issued by the Hydrographic Office of the Admiralty used to be most detailed, but with the change to metric charts and a reduction in the funds available for survey work, many of the smaller channels and harbours and the inshore waters which are seldom used by commercial craft are not being resurveyed. On the metric charts soundings are not shown for some inshore areas. Charts and other Admiralty hydrographic publications, including sailing directions and tidal atlases, are available from Admiralty Chart Agents who can also supply the weekly *Notices to Mariners* which list the latest alterations and additions. Two publishers produce yachtsmen's charts which often give more detailed information on inshore waters.

Reed's Nautical Almanac, published annually, contains a mine of information for the cruising man – everything from tide tables to how to cope with childbirth on board! As well as books written by yachtsmen as guides to certain waters the Cruising Association produces a valuable handbook with information on many ports and harbours, and the Clyde Cruising Club and Irish Cruising Club also produce pilot guides covering their own waters. In addition, there are Admiralty sailing directions for all areas.

5
Sailing in the United States of America

Theodore A. Jones

Sailing was a way of life for Americans from the earliest settlement days of the Colonies. Not only had all the early settlers endured the rigours of a long ocean passage, but they depended on sailing vessels for their livelihood. Commerce was carried on in small sailing vessels up and down the many protected waterways of the east coast where harbours abound in infinite numbers – sometimes several to the mile. America's sailing warships and privateers, though small, possessed legendary speed. The New England and Nova Scotia fishermen developed outstandingly seaworthy and fast schooners capable of staying at sea in the worst winter storms and racing home with their catch to be first to market. Slavers, pilot schooners, and clipper ships developed speed as a necessity for survival. Those with speed reached their destination first, leaving the rest behind and forgotten. It is natural, then, that sailing is rooted in the very fibre of many Americans and is a heritage of great importance.

The United States of America has thousands and thousands of miles of coastline and a deep-rooted heritage as a maritime nation, but there are also many millions of its people who live inland, who have never seen the sea, who are afraid of the water, and cannot even swim. It would be

The 1970 United States national junior champions sail their Snipe into Miami Yacht Club harbour. Although somewhat heavy by modern standards, the International Snipe, designed by American William Crosby in 1933, is still popular especially in North and South America. Loa 15ft 6in; beam 5ft; sail area 128sq ft; weight 440lb. About 23,000 worldwide and 1,000 built annually.

a mistake to characterize all Americans as seafarers – only a relatively few would claim to be – but while the bulk of the US population may care little for sailing or the sea, the country is so vast and its population so large that there are still many millions of people who sail. Numbered among them are some of the finest seamen, yacht racers, and accomplished cruising men in the world. Surveys indicate a fleet of small sailing yachts (centreboarders and small, keel day boats) that numbers around 600,000. Add to this a fleet of offshore racers of 5,000 – about a third of the world's total; cruisers numbering somewhere between 10,000 and 20,000; an armada of literally millions of large and small powerboats; and the result is a sizeable number of participants. There is no way to know for sure, but there are probably more people sailing in the USA than in any other country in the world. The newspapers carry very little coverage of sailing events, and even the America's Cup has a hard time of it on the sports pages, vying with baseball, golf and tennis. But, nevertheless, there are many people out sailing and having fun.

While sailing now spreads to every sound, bay, estuary, river and lake in the country, it has its origins in the New England coastal states, not only because the early settlers in this area were sailors, but undoubtedly also because the area is unsurpassed for summer sailing. One of the most popular sailing and cruising grounds in the country is the area from Maine to New York City which, with its legendary islands, harbours, and unspoiled natural beauty, is not unlike the Stockholm Archipelago in the Baltic.

It would be possible to spend years in Maine and not see all there is to see, nor visit every harbour, nor smell the smells and taste the joys of cruising this largely unpopulated coastline. Maine is not, primarily, a small sailboat area, as the water is cold, the tide range is great, and the currents are swift. The cruising man must come prepared to spend some anxious moments groping through the fog, sometimes for days at a time, but the charts and aids to navigation are accurate and plentiful. While the water is too cold for swimming by most people's standards, it does help to produce a moderate climate and wonderful sailing breezes. Days will be spent sailing in Force 4–5 breezes with the sun tanning bare backs, while nights will be spent swinging gently at anchor snuggled in bunks under two blankets. Harbours are so ridiculously close together that it becomes a chore to decide which one to choose for the night's anchorage.

Heading west from the Maine Coast one soon comes to more populated areas, the first probably being the great fishing town of Gloucester, Massachusetts, located on Cape Ann. Gloucester is still a fishing town without much yachting activity, but visiting yachtsmen are welcome and find it a fascinating port to visit. At the height of the season one can almost walk across the harbour at Marblehead by stepping from one moored yacht to the next. Cohasset, Duxbury and many other places similarly offer shelter, interesting sights and complete services for visiting yachtsmen.

West of Cape Cod to New York are some of the finest sailing waters to be found anywhere. This area is more populated than the Maine

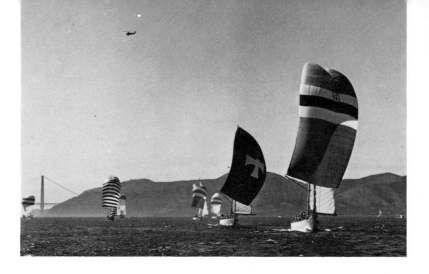

Large offshore racers sailing in the annual St Francis Yacht Club Trophy series held in San Francisco Bay. The Golden Gate bridge is in the background.

Coast, but it offers every variety of sailing, racing, cruising and related activities imaginable. The summer climate is ideal with warm to hot weather from June through to September. The normal yachting season seems to lengthen each year and extends from April until October (whereas east of Cape Cod the season runs from late May until early September). Natural harbours exist everywhere, usually only a few miles apart, and almost every one of them has a marina, yacht club or some sailing facility.

Virtually every class of one-design racing boat is raced somewhere in this area of the USA, the most popular keelboat classes being Solings, Etchells 22s, International One-Designs and Tempests, while centre-board classes include 470s, Fireballs, Lightnings and many local classes such as the Blue Jay (a small Lightning), Thistle, and Rhodes 18s.

There is a wide choice of offshore sailing events every weekend. Fixtures such as the 220 mile Stamford to Vineyard Race and the Block Island Race regularly draw over 200 entrants, as does the biennial Block Island Week, a week of day racing patterned on the British Cowes Week. The famous Newport to Bermuda Race starts from this area, and the Annapolis to Newport Race finishes here. These biennial events are held on alternate years.

There is excellent, though shallow, protected water sailing in New Jersey from about thirty miles south of New York City to Delaware Bay where the abundance of commercial traffic and the open, shallow water are not conducive to sailing either large or small boats. However, Delaware Bay is an important link when cruising between the South Jersey Coast and Chesapeake Bay via the Delaware-Chesapeake Canal.

Chesapeake Bay is approximately 250 miles long with a maximum width of about thirty miles in its centre at the mouth of the Potomac river. Sailing is most popular in the spring and fall months as the summers are generally hot and there is little wind. Chesapeake Bay has thousands of miles of delightful shoreline for cruising, and is also a popular place for one-design racing. Many large northern yachts winter in this area since the harbours and river estuaries do not generally freeze during the winter months as they do east and north of New York.

The Inland Waterway is a series of canals, rivers and bays which are interconnected, allowing moderate size cruising sailboats to travel over

64

Optimist dinghies racing on Biscayne Bay in Florida. This 7ft 6½in trainer has become an extremely popular International class since it was first introduced to provide sailing for deprived youngsters in Boston.

Class B ocean racers crossing the starting line at Biscayne Bay, Florida at the start of the seventh biennial Miami to Montego Bay (Jamaica) race. Boats are required to carry their sail numbers on large overlapping headsails because, as is apparent here, the whole of the mainsail can be obscured by the genoa.

The Lightning is a day-sailer and three-man racing class popular in North America. This rather heavy centreboard boat was designed by Sparkman and Stephens in 1938 and over 12,000 have been built. Loa 19ft; beam 6ft 6in; sail area 177sq ft; weight 700lb.

1,000 miles from Norfolk, Virginia, at the southern end of Chesapeake Bay, all the way to Miami, Florida. Hundreds of yachts, both power and sail, traverse this waterway in the autumn and spring, travelling to and from the winter cruising grounds in the south. Along the way are many unspoiled areas, small towns with friendly citizens, and large cities with comprehensive facilities. One finds more and more local sailing activity every year in places like Pamlico Sound, Charleston and Hilton Head, South Carolina, and the Indian River, Florida.

As one moves south, the climate becomes increasingly moderate. Miami enjoys almost continuous summer weather with summer temperatures hovering between 30° and 32°C (mid to upper 80°sF), and winter temperatures usually between 20°C (high 60°sF) and 23°C (low 70°sF). Here sailing is a year-round pastime, but there is more activity in the winter months when many northern yachtsmen either take their own boats south or charter sailboats for cruising. St Petersburg on the west coast, and Miami on the east coast both host several one-design midwinter series for several popular classes.

A well-known ocean racing fixture is the Southern Ocean Racing Conference series of races which takes place in February and March each year. As many as 200 yachts participate in races from St Petersburg and Miami, and to the Bahama Islands in what is traditionally one of the toughest and most demanding series of ocean races held anywhere in the world. The Gulf Coast from Key West, Florida to Corpus Christi, Texas also enjoys year-round sailing weather. Yachting centres in this area are New Orleans in Louisiana, and Houston and Corpus Christi in Texas.

The west coast of the USA does not enjoy the natural harbours that abound in the east and Gulf States but, nevertheless, it has many vast armadas of sailboats. Seemingly everything in California is larger than life, and sailing is no exception. While natural harbours are scarce, many man-made harbours and marinas have been built. There would surely be even more sailing in Southern California were there more places to keep sailboats. Mooring off is uncommon in this area, and dock space is at a premium. Boat salesmen have first to assure a customer that they can have a slip before a sale can be made.

A few very small dinghies (8ft Sabots, Lehman 10s and 12s, and Hobie Cats) race actively inside harbours in the San Diego and Los Angeles areas, while Stars, Five-Point-Five Metres and similar keelboats race in the open ocean. This is the area where large cruising yachts are used as racing day sailers, and many of the older Eight, Ten, and Twelve Metre yachts race actively here against the more modern ocean racers. Sailing in Southern California is a year-round activity for both large cruisers and small dinghies.

San Francisco Bay is the third major sailing area in California. It is an entity unto itself with hundreds of miles of shoreline lying within the bay area, which is known for its strong prevailing winds. Very few yachts find it necessary or desirable to venture outside the Bay although there are a number of cruising races with courses to or around outlying islands. Many sailing cruisers venture up the Sacramento river delta country, but the sailing possibilities among these narrow channels are

Opposite Close racing between two American Three-quarter Tonners during the first Three-quarter Ton World Championship held off Key Biscayne in Florida in 1973.

limited. Nevertheless, cruising is excellent, with many miles of protected waters in unpopulated areas.

Puget Sound in the State of Washington in the Pacific Northwest, and Vancouver just over the border in Canada, have excellent sailing facilities similar in many ways to the Maine Coast in the east. The season is longer here as the winters are moderate compared to the north-east. For the very hardy there is much unspoiled cruising water to the north of Vancouver or into Alaska, but the further north, the shorter the season. This is not an area for small boat sailing, but cruising under sail is extremely popular.

If in our thumbnail cruise we had turned eastward from Miami instead of westward, our course would have taken us 1,000 miles to and through some of the finest cruising grounds in the world – the West Indies. Unless starting from Miami one would not normally deliberately sail there first in order to reach the islands of the Lesser Antilles, because the prevailing trade winds make the voyage nearly dead to windward. Most northern yachtsmen wishing to take their yachts to the West Indies depart instead from Moorhead City, North Carolina, avoiding the treacherous shoals of Cape Hatteras and ignoring the supposed dangers of the 'Bermuda Triangle'. Scores of 35–70ft yachts make this passage every year unnoticed and unscathed by the mysterious evils supposed to lurk in this part of the ocean.

Once the islands separating the Caribbean from the Atlantic are reached, sailors find themselves in an unparalleled cruising area. Winter temperatures range from 20°C (70°F) to 32°C (90°F) and the trade winds blow at a nearly constant 15–25 knots in daytime. During a comfortable day's run, reaching along under a bright sun with dry decks, it is possible to cruise leisurely from island to island as they are never more than forty miles apart. The islands themselves are very different, largely primitive, and virtually all possess excellent anchorages either in secluded areas or bustling harbours. Services are not universally available, but with proper planning yachtsmen should encounter no difficulties in providing for their vessels. This is mostly a cruising area with little activity in day sailers or racing dinghies except in Puerto Rico where there are active fleets of Olympic classes in the protected waters around San Juan.

Antigua Week, a cruiser-racer regatta held annually in late winter, started as a racing series for charter yachts but has become a well-organized and serious racing series for privately owned yachts. This is the only organized racing of note which takes place in the area.

The Bahamas, which lie just off the Florida Coast, provide exceptional cruising for those with limited time and less ambitious plans than those heading for the Lesser Antilles. Bimini and Gun Cay are just sixty nautical miles east of Miami, and another 100 miles across the Great Bahama Bank takes one to the capital of the Bahamas, Nassau, on New Providence Island. From Nassau it is possible to range for hundreds of miles in any direction to beautiful, low coral islands with excellent, though shallow, harbours and sunny, summery weather 18°–27°C (65°–80°F).

There is one-design keelboat racing at Nassau – Stars, Solings and

Opposite Congested conditions as a fleet of Solings round the gybe mark during a light weather race at the CORK (Canadian Olympic Regatta, Kingston) week in 1974.

The Bahama Islands are a favourite cruising ground for American yachtsmen. The nearest is only about 60 miles from Florida and acts as a stepping stone for cruises which can stretch for 1,800 miles, hopping from island to island in the West Indies. Here the fourteen-man crew of the eventual winner of the annual three race Family Island Regatta is off to a fast start. These workboats start traditionally at anchor.

Five-Point-Five Metres being the active local classes. Over the years other US and Canadian centreboard and keelboat classes have held midwinter regattas in Nassau, although increasing difficulty in transporting boats to the Bahamas has hindered these events in recent years. There is, nevertheless, much small sailboat activity in the Bahamas which have ideal harbours, bays and beaches for enjoying day sailing and off-the-beach boating.

Number of people who participate in sailing

It is only possible to estimate the number of people who sail in the United States of America. The area is large and widespread. Fleets of one-design classes and, increasingly, cruisers up to about 35ft overall sail and race in the many thousands of lakes in the interior states. The Great Lakes of the USA and Canada have fleets of many thousands of offshore racers and large cruisers. These range a shoreline from Lake Ontario in the east to Lake Superior in the west which is conservatively estimated at 4,000 miles, not counting harbours and estuaries.

Part of the difficulty in estimating the size of the sailing population stems from the many different governments and regulating agencies, each with their own set of laws and methods of reporting, which influences the count. While the US Federal Government has a uniform

The 1976 world Star champion Jim Alsop and his crew Mike Duhin hiking out at Nassau in the Bahamas. This flat-bottomed keelboat was designed with a gaff rig in 1911 by William Gardner, and the rig has been modified three times. It is very popular in North and South America and in some European countries but has never become established in Britain or Australia. An Olympic class for many years until 1968, it was dropped in 1972 but reinstated for the 1980 Olympics in Russia.

model boating law, it is open to different interpretations by different states. The Federal Government requires that every motorboat over 10hp be registered with either a state or federal agency. Many states have chosen to register the minimum and only account for powerboats with 10hp or more, which includes sailboats with engines. Some states, however, require registration by all powered craft regardless of horsepower, again including all sailboats with engines. A few states require registration of everything that floats, including all sailboats. Registration figures, therefore, include some sailboats, but since regulations vary so greatly, no trends or assumptions should be derived from government registrations.

The magazine *Boating Industry*, which conducts extensive surveys, estimated that there were 780,000 sailboats without inboard power in use in the USA in 1974, and an untold number of inboard powered auxiliaries included among 770,000 inboard motorboats registered by all states during the same year. Their estimate of 2,440,000 'miscellaneous craft' also includes some sailing dinghies, prams and canoes not accounted for in other statistics.

Racing classes provide more reliable numbers. Classes such as the Lightning which numbers over 14,000, the Sunfish with 50,000, the Laser with 10,000 in North America, and the Optimist Pram which is sailed by 10,000 to 15,000 youngsters, provide a more definitive idea of the numbers of people involved. In addition, there are new people coming into sailing every day, as shown by the experience of a small 'board boat' company which sold 50,000 sailboats for under $50 each as a premium offered by a cigarette company. Virtually none of these people had ever owned sailboats before.

There are 5,000 active ocean racers throughout North America which are rated to the International Offshore Rule. There are easily twice that many racing under local and regional handicapping systems, and probably five or six times as many larger cruising sailboats which do not register as racers anywhere. *Yacht Racing* magazine claims that its surveys show a sailboat-racing population of approximately 90,000, which represents offshore racing in every form, and includes all International one-design and open classes except the French-designed International Vaurien which is not sailed in North America.

THE COMPLETE BOOK OF SAILING

According to the magazine *Boating Industry*, this vast, widely dispersed armada is serviced by almost 6,000 marinas and yacht clubs. There are about 2,000 yacht clubs of all types in the USA and Canada, with 560 clubs participating as individual members of their respective national authorities.

Approximately 31,000 people earn their livelihood through sailing, and while no one has an accurate count of the dollars spent on sailing and related items, extrapolating from the overall marine sales estimate of 1974 yields a figure of $300,000,000 spent on sailing.

Sailboats, an annual catalogue of all types of sailing craft, lists over 1,000 classes, including all sailing yachts which are available for sale on a production or limited production basis, from the smallest 7ft dinghy to the largest 80ft motor sailer. Not included are the myriad custom-built boats which are available or have been built in ones, twos or threes over the last two or three decades and are still in active service. *Sailboats* lists over 700,000 sailing craft in all categories in existence in the USA.

Living aboard

Whether or not one lives aboard one's sailboat depends on the climate of the area and, to some extent, on local regulations. Many municipalities have ordinances which prohibit people from living aboard boats in permanent anchorage areas or marinas. Where it is permitted and the climate is warm, living aboard is popular. Most, however, do not live on competition sailing craft in these areas. In many places like Sausalito, California or Miami, Florida whole floating colonies have developed which do not pertain especially to sailing yachtsmen. A small percentage of cruising sailors and families live aboard their yachts while they cruise. A particularly popular 'live aboard' scheme is to cruise the east coast's Inland Waterway to Florida and the Caribbean in the autumn and winter months. As everywhere sailors tend to be rather a hardy lot and are not usually burdened with elaborate refrigeration, air-conditioning, or heating systems as are so many power-driven yachts. An ice-box, plenty of ventilators, and a small, charcoal-heating stove serve the needs of most cruising live-aboard sailors.

Development

The United States is not the scene of as much dinghy development as is found in other parts of the world. Apart from a very small number of International Fourteens there is little in the way of design innovation in monohulls. A few enthusiasts pursue the fine art of multihull design and building, but these number but a handful when compared to the many tens of thousands of people who sail.

A type of dinghy indigenous to the inland lakes regions of the Mid-West is the scow. The scow classes are mostly open or restricted designs. Hulls must fit within the dimensions of a box, and this has led towards the scow shape, blunt at both ends. Scows have developed in relative isolation over a period exceeding 100 years, and the classes, which range in size from 13ft to over 40ft overall length, are very fast in the smooth

lake waters. The type has not proved suitable for open water sailing and, therefore, has not spread far beyond the inland lakes regions. Scows have bilgeboards and twin rudders. Most popular are the E-boats which are built to an open design formula with a maximum overall length of 28ft. The most popular one-design scow is the M-20 which numbers about 500.

Offshore racing is another matter, with a large and enthusiastic number of offshore racers actively developing their craft to the ultimate in speed potential. There is much interest in all the level-rating classes, and it is probably here that innovation is greatest. In 1975 US designs won four of the five World Level Rating Championships. Except in California, where all sorts of weird and wonderful things are attempted, US designs tend to be more conservative than many of the strange experimental craft seen in other countries. Many of the popular offshore races off the California coast are predominantly downwind affairs – the Transpac Race from California, a regularly scheduled event of 2,225 miles mostly downwind, being the ultimate. These spawned what are not so affectionately called ULDBs, or ultra light displacement boats, by their more conservative detractors. ULDBs have won Transpac Races in spite of severe penalties added to the IOR ratings of these types.

Another interesting development from Southern California is the cruising/racing bilgeboarder. Centreboard cruising yachts have always been a national type in the USA because of the shallowness of many cruising waters. The logical development of the centreboarder is the bilgeboard design which was tried by Bruce King with the One Ton class yacht *Terrorist*. This yacht raced with great success in England in 1974, and many observers felt that she could have won the One Ton World Championship had she not lost her mast during the series. Other bilge-board designs have appeared racing in the Transpac, the Southern Ocean Racing Conference, the Two Ton Class, the Canada's Cup, and the Half Ton Class. While they have proved very fast in some conditions, the design trend cannot yet be described as a breakthrough.

In the larger custom offshore racers US designs are world renowned for their abilities. Designs by Dick Carter, Gary Mull, Doug Peterson and Olin Stephens are likely to show in the winner's column wherever important offshore racing events are held.

The Class E scow, a popular racing boat on the lakes of the Midwest, is an open-design class. The boats are 28ft long with the hull shape limited only by what would fit into a theoretical rectilinear box. Rigs are one-design. The E scows are fitted with bilge boards which are useful when righting them after a capsize – a common occurrence. Like most scow classes they also have twin rudders.

Shark catamarans racing in Florida in the Midwinter Multihull Championships. The Shark's 20ft hulls can be folded after one bolt is removed, reducing the 10ft beam to 5ft for trailing. Sail area 272sq ft; weight 350lb.

Sailing schools

Most people in the USA learn sailing by the self-teaching method. They become interested, perhaps when sailing with a friend, and then, often with that friend's help, they strike out on their own, learning as they go. While this may be the usual way to begin, many do eventually take some sort of formal course to improve their overall skill or to learn some specialized aspect of sailing such as racing or navigation.

Many commercial schools teach sailing and are to be found in virtually all sailing centres. Commerical schools are relatively new, having appeared within the past five or six years. Their course content and effectiveness vary widely. Costs depend on the facilities, equipment, number of students and experience of the instructors, and effectiveness varies accordingly.

Most yacht and sailing clubs also provide instruction for their members, but these courses usually concentrate on children's programmes. Many provide special classes for women, while some make instruction available to all members. Children's programmes in the northern parts of the country are usually held during the summer months for the ten- to seventeen-year-old age group. In the south-east and south-west children often begin sailing as young as six, seven or eight, and tend to sail throughout the year, although formal instruction is usually held during the summer months when schools are on holiday.

The United States Yacht Racing Union started a junior racing seminar in 1974. Prior to that time it had not been involved in education in any way. This type of activity will undoubtedly be extended to encompass other types of instruction such as race committee seminars and adult courses in boat handling. Organizations such as the Boy Scouts of America, the Girl Scouts, and their related Sea Scouts and Mariners also offer instruction in practical boat handling and sailing to young people.

The United States Power Squadron (USPS), despite its name, has many active sailing flotillas which teach sailing. The USPS itself conducts one of the finest series of courses available anywhere leading to a thorough, practical understanding of celestial navigation. These formal, nationally uniform courses consist of evening classes which meet weekly throughout the academic year. It takes four years of study to achieve the highest level, grade 'N'. Schools and colleges do not generally offer formal instruction in sailing.

Administration of sailing in North America

The national authority for sailing in the USA is the United States Yacht Racing Union. This organization existed for fifty years until 1975 as the North American Yacht Racing Union, embracing Canada and, occasionally, Mexico. As such it was probably unique as a multi-national administrative body. Changes in national laws and US Olympic Committee policies made it essentially mandatory for the USA to have its own national authority which was accomplished by changing the name from North America YRU to United States YRU.

This change did not affect Canada adversely, as the Canadians have had their own organization, the Canadian Yachting Association, since 1931. The CYA and the USYRU administrations have made plans to continue working closely together, particularly in those areas in which sailors from both countries race together on common bodies of water. Thus, little actual change has taken place as far as the individual sailor is concerned, although the thrust of the administration has altered considerably.

Mexico, Jamaica, Puerto Rico and the Bahamas all have their own sailing federations or national authorities, but the USYRU handles the administration of the International Offshore Rule (IOR) for all of these countries as well as Bermuda, Canada and Venezuela.

Individuals can join the USYRU, which is governed by representatives from thirty-six member area associations representing 1,175 clubs, fleets and local associations. This organization structure was subject to radical change in 1976. 560 individual yacht clubs also belong as separate members of the USYRU. A *Boating Industry* survey taken in 1974 listed 1,320 yacht clubs which serve both sailing and other boating interest.

The USYRU conducts North American single, double and triple-handed championships in men's, women's and junior sailing championships each year. There is also a match race championship and single-handed championships for men, women and juniors. A person is considered a junior if he will not have reached his eighteenth birthday during the calendar year in which a championship takes place. USYRU also conducts North American championships in each of the five level-rating classes recognized by the International Offshore Racing Council. One-design classes conduct their own national and North American championships.

Major events such as the Bermuda Race, the Transpac Race, the Southern Ocean Racing Conference, the America's Cup match and the Canada's Cup match are conducted by individual clubs without specific USYRU or CYA sanction.

6
Sailing in Australia

Bob Ross

Sailing in Australia has become a recreation touching every level of the social strata. A kind, warm climate has always encouraged outdoor activity, and the fact that the largest centres of population sit on the edge of the island continent's 12,446 mile coastline makes it possible for many people to take their leisure in boats.

Although there are no accurate national statistics available, an estimated 200,000 of Australia's thirteen million people sail regularly. The Australian Yachting Federation says that each summer weekend at least 60,000 Australians compete in organized races. Industry statistics show that the sales of stock-production sailing boats are increasing at a steady yearly rate of 10%.

The climate and generations of separate development owing to isolation from the ideas and materials of the world's great yachting centres, have shaped a distinctive character for Australian yachtsmen. In summer sea breezes – from the south-west in the west and south of the continent and from the north-east on the east coast – are generated firmly by the warming of the land mass into a very steady 10–12 knots, sometimes rising everywhere, and almost always in the west, into the full-blooded 15–20 knot wind range. The Australians' boats, boat and sail handling, and psychological attitudes, therefore, have been tuned strongly to the medium to fresh wind range. In international company the Australian is at his best in fresh winds. He lacks the practice, and perhaps the patience, to do as well in light, variable breezes as the European or North American.

The idyllic sea-breeze pattern is interrupted violently now and then, sometimes without warning, by southerly or south-westerly fronts and storms spinning off from the Roaring Forties to the south or, in the north of the continent, by malevolent tropical cyclones. Seas around the coastline are seldom quiet for long. Even when the winds are light, they pound the cliffs of the east coast relentlessly, setting up a backwash wave train counter to and across the top of the Tasman Sea rollers, producing an utterly confused result.

The Australian offshore sailor has, therefore, become skilled through familiarity at handling bad seas and driving boats hard in strong winds. The most important Australian ocean race, from Sydney over 630 nautical miles to Hobart, is almost always punctuated by a gale. The winning crew is often the one that is able to pound its way hardest and longest to windward, or is prepared to blow out spinnakers and hang on grimly through broach after broach downwind. A mild winter has made sailing an accepted year-round pastime in northern centres, while racing fanatics don wet suits and heavy waterproofs for winter racing in the colder winds and colder waters of the southern coastline.

The earlier isolation that led to such interesting separate development as the monster sail area carriers, the Sydney Harbour 18ft skiffs, has ended. In the late 60s and early 70s the eagerness of Australia to compete internationally and to assert itself aggressively as the new boy in the hard school of international competition forced it to import more overseas classes of yachts and ideas on sails, rigs, and fittings. With the communication lines to the rest of the sailing world firmly established through regular international competition and direct affiliation with

An old 18ft Skiff sailing in Sydney Harbour in 1910. The class was introduced around the turn of the century. At least nine crew can be seen in this photograph, and crews were reputed to jump overboard and swim ashore in order to lighten the boats on the last run to the finishing line.

A modern 18ft Skiff screams across Sydney Harbour in a flurry of spray balanced by three men on trapezes. Racing is spectacular as weight and sail area are unrestricted, and the boats carry as much sail as the crew can manage. Races in Sydney Harbour are watched by spectators on shore and following in specially chartered ferries. Boats advertise the names of their commercial sponsors in large letters across the mainsail. A few 18ft Skiffs race in Britain where two or three are built each year. Loa 18ft; beam 6ft. About 150 boats in the world.

policy-making bodies like the International Yacht Racing Union and Offshore Racing Council, Australia is a full member of the international yachting community. Just as clothing fashions, pop music, and hair-styles are transmitted almost instantly to Australia from Europe and North America, so are trends in yachting.

While some of the old individuality has gone, submerged in the much freer flow of information and off-the-shelf equipment, Australia contributes innovation in yacht and dinghy design and in the making of spars, sails, winches, and fittings to the mainstream progress of inter-national yachting. It has contributed some fine individual racing per-formances as well. It won the Admiral's Cup in 1967 and, through its devotion to preparation and training as a team, did much to lift the competition for the trophy to its present status as ocean racing's major international encounter. Olympic gold medals and the International

Catamaran Challenge Trophy have been won, and although they were unsuccessful, the America's Cup challenges between 1962 and 1974 showed the world that the new boy had become a skilled, fierce competitor in international yachting.

Class structure

Many Australians begin their sailing as children. Then follows a natural progression through boats from more than seventy different recognized racing classes, plus many types of non-competitive boat, to suit every age and taste in sailing.

Children, nine years old and sometimes much younger, are most likely to learn to sail in an 8ft Sabot – a class with more than 1,200 boats registered – or the 8ft 7in Manly Junior with more than 1,500 boats. The 10ft 6in International Cadet class is popular in the southern States where the ancient, indigenous 12ft Cadet dinghy is also to be found as a training class in some clubs. There are some purely local trainer classes like the Pelican in Western Australia, and the Wright Intermediate in Queensland.

Teenagers may begin in, or move on to the well-established local classes like the 12ft skiff, Vee Jay, Flying Ant, Thorpe 12, Cherub, Rainbow, Moth, Flying 11, or perhaps into international classes like the Flying Junior, 420, 470, or Laser. After these, out-and-out high-performance boats with strong followings are the 18ft and 16ft skiffs, Flying Dutchman, Lightweight Sharpie, Javelin, OK, Finn, Fireball, and Contender.

The quite separate movement to family dinghy classes – crewed by husband-and-wife and parent-and-child teams – is strongly represented by the Mirror, which claims class numbers exceeding 3,000 boats, the Heron, and to a lesser extent by the Enterprise, Lazy E, GP14, and Puffin Pacer.

A fairly advanced locally developed family dinghy, the Northbridge Senior, adapted from the 14ft Javelin hull by John Spencer, with a modest 100sq ft sail area, designed by Frank Bethwaite, has evolved through the Nova class, which has slightly more sail area, to a new two-man dinghy, the Tasar.

The trailer-sailer is one of the many sailing concepts that has spread to Australia from New Zealand 1,200 miles across the Tasman Sea to the east. It has a strong following among family sailors in Australia. Basically this is a miniature cruiser-racer hybrid of dinghy and small keel yacht, with metal centreplate, sometimes lead-weighted, pivoting upwards into a trunk for trailing or beaching. It has a half-cabin, usually sheltering two bunks and perhaps a spirit stove and WC, a big self-draining cockpit suited to Australia's sunny skies, moderate sail area, and built-in buoyancy to support hull and occupants in the event of a capsize or swamping. The concept was introduced by Richard Hartley of New Zealand with his plywood TS16, a 16-footer designed especially for amateur builders. Seventeen different classes of trailer-sailer between 14ft and 24ft overall are to be found in Australia, most of them marketed as stock glassfibre production models. Some of them race, but most are just trailed about to cruise coastal estuaries and inland waterways.

Catamarans, their speed potential fully realized by Australia's brisk summer breezes, have captured a big following with an estimated 2,400 of many types forming a complete hierarchy that includes trainer cats for children, designs suited to teenagers, high-performance models like the Cobra, Stingray, Australis, A class, Quest B, the Olympic Tornado class, up to those aerodynamic miracles, the International C class, that race for the International Catamaran Challenge Trophy. There are, however, few big offshore cruising or racing multihulls. This sector of sailing in Australia never fully recovered from a series of tragedies in the 60s when seventeen were drowned in trimaran mishaps within three years.

Among the one-design racing keel yachts, the Soling remains the most popular with racing enthusiasts, with the Etchells 22 a growing class. The once extremely popular Dragons and *Yachting World* Diamonds are fading from the scene. The Five-Point-Five Metre class has retained an élitist following, the Tempest has a hard core of supporters but is not generally popular, while the Star class has retreated to a pocket of enthusiasm on the sheltered waters of Lake Macquarie, 100 miles north of Sydney.

Mass production in glassfibre led to a boom in the cruiser-racer classes in the 60s. These are little yachts with ballast keels, most of them ranging from 22ft to 28ft overall, fast enough for a man to race with his friends on a Saturday, and big enough for family day cruising on Sunday with perhaps a short coastal cruise on long weekends or annual holidays. More than twenty cruiser-racer classes are to be found in Australia. Some of them are equipped as Junior Offshore Group ocean racers and compete offshore; others race in mixed inshore handicap fleets or as separate classes.

Ocean racing has become the glamorous, big money showcase of the sport – America's Cup challenges excepted. The level-rating classes, especially Half and Quarter Ton, have become firmly established, and some owners are still prepared to find the money for custom-built thoroughbred ocean racers to fight for places in an Admiral's Cup team.

Where they sail

Yachting in Australia is most strongly based on the main centres of population: Sydney, Melbourne, Brisbane, Adelaide, Perth, and Hobart, although there are many clubs in the country on inland waterways and coastal estuaries.

Sailing's growth in popularity has exceeded the facilities available, and almost everywhere there are long waiting lists for marina berths. Public launching ramps in cities and suburban areas are invariably overcrowded on summer weekends. Some dinghy clubs offer undercover storage or space in open-air compounds, but most dinghy sailors trail their craft home. Moorings are usually controlled by the maritime authority of the appropriate state Government department. They have to be rented from the authority for a small annual fee, or may be laid privately with the permission of the authority, still with a fee required in most places. Typical dinghy club or class association subscription fees are low, but fees are much higher for the more elaborate yacht clubs with marina berths, moorings, and clubhouses with bar and dining facilities.

All racing boats have to be registered with class associations and/or with clubs, but cruising boats do not. No documentation is needed for racing boats apart from class certificates, and in the case of offshore boats and some one-design classes, safety inspection certificates. Insurance is not compulsory. Yacht racing in Australia is administered by the Australian Yachting Federation through its affiliated separate state authorities in New South Wales, Victoria, South Australia, Northern Territory, Queensland, Western Australia, Tasmania, and Papua and New Guinea. Up-to-date addresses of these associations may be obtained from the Australian Yachting Federation.

Clubs and class associations are affiliated to the state authorities whose sub-committees formulate policies on such matters as safety, rules, offshore safety and racing, Olympic classes, and even cruising. The Australian Yachting Federation itself has policy-making sub-committees for ocean racing, rules, multihulls and Olympic planning. The Olympic planning committee, formed after the 1972 Games, has successfully organized sponsorship assistance for Olympic class yachts-men travelling overseas to gain experience in international regattas and has instituted a series of successful annual Easter regattas bringing together all the Olympic classes. The Australian Yachting Federation was formed in 1950. It gained direct affiliation with the IYRU in 1967, and each year a representative is sent to the annual meeting in London. Before 1967 it was represented through Britain's Royal Yachting Association.

Racing in Australia follows IYRU rules, with the exception of the skiff classes which sail to a mixture of IYRU rules, the *International Regulations for Preventing Collisions at Sea* and a few traditional club rules, including a system of using umpires on the water to report breaches of the rules.

Cruising visitors are sometimes surprised by Australia's tough entry formalities. Visiting yachts are permitted to stay only one year in Australia, with one year extension free of import duty. If a visiting yacht is sold in Australia, or overstays its visiting time, the owner is liable to pay import duty, to which is added sales tax – and the charges can total more than 50 %. The rates of duty vary according to the country of the yacht's origin, and according to changes of Government import policy. Intending visitors should check the current Customs and Quarantine formalities with their nearest Australian Government representative before setting sail.

Australia's cruising waters include the exotic, tropical Great Barrier Reef off the north-east coast. The waters surrounding hundreds of is-lands and coral reefs within the one great reef system are ripped by strong tidal currents and are subject to cyclones, especially between December and March. Cruising yachtsmen should study carefully the relevant sections of the *Australian Pilot* and seek out sources of local knowledge before visiting the reef.

History

The earliest recorded regattas were organized by naval officers between ships' boats on the Derwent River, Tasmania and on Sydney Harbour in 1827. Australia's first sailing club, the Tamar Yacht Club, was formed in 1837 at Launceston on the north coast of Tasmania and is still active today. The Victoria Yacht Club, later the Royal Yacht Club of Victoria, was founded in Melbourne in 1856. The Sydney Yacht Club, formed in 1856, collapsed and was replaced by the Royal Australian Yacht Club which became the Royal Sydney Yacht Squadron.

Among early clubs formed to cater especially for smaller yachts was the Sydney Flying Squadron, established in 1890, which initially adopted 22ft open boats manned by up to seventeen men sitting in each other's laps on the windward gunwale, under spreads of more than 3,000sq ft of sail. The 18-footers followed around the turn of the century. They were more modestly rigged than the 22s they superseded but still carried main booms up to 32ft long, bowsprits extending 30ft over the stem, and 45ft-long spinnaker poles. The skiffs, open boats without decking or buoyancy, derived from the watermen's rowing skiffs that used to ply Sydney harbour on business. The 16ft skiff class, founded in 1901, and the 12ft skiffs came from the same source.

Towards the end of the nineteenth century New Zealand, home of that supreme boatbuilding timber kauri pine, sent the first of a steady stream of yachts across the Tasman Sea to Australian owners. Two Auckland families, the Baileys and the Logans, added design flair to their building skills to create a strong demand among Australians for their yachts. This trade led in turn to racing competition between Australia and New Zealand which exists strongly to the present day in all classes and types of yacht.

Within Australia rivalry between colonies (which were federated as states into a single nation in 1901) began in January 1887 with a match between *Janet*, a 60ft cutter owned by Sir William Clarke, Commodore of the Royal Yacht Club of Victoria, and the Royal Sydney Yacht Squadron's champions *Magic* and *Waitangi*. The latter, owned by Vice-Commodore Alfred Milson Jr, won the two-race match on time allowance.

Inter-state competition firmed into an earnest exchange of matches, reminiscent of the America's Cup in format and intensity, for the Sayonara Cup, named after its first winner, a 58ft cutter built in South Australia for Alfred Gollin of the Royal Yacht Club of Victoria. *Sayonara* was a superb yacht designed by William Fife of Scotland, carrying hollow spars imported from New York and sails from Cowes. She can still be seen today sailing Sydney Harbour as a charter boat with parties of day trippers. The Sayonara Cup stayed in Melbourne until 1910 when Walter Marks of the Royal Sydney Yacht Squadron defeated *Sayonara* with his Ten Metre *Culwalla III* after sailing to Melbourne from Sydney via Hobart, a distance of 1,073 nautical miles, to give his crew some practice!

Inter-state competition was also fostered by the Northcote Cup, a perpetual challenge trophy for Six Metre class yachts, and the Forster

Right Rani, designed by A. C. Barber in 1935, was bought by Captain John Illingworth RN who won the first Sydney to Hobart Race with her in 1945. This three-quarter rigged wooden yacht has a canoe stern. The mast has two pairs of spreaders and jumper struts to prevent the top bending. The cotton sails have narrow panels and one line of reef points. Although she has guardrails and stanchions, there are no pulpits. Compare her with *Apollo* on p. 84. *Rani:* Loa 34ft 9in; Lwl 29ft 9in; beam 9ft; draft 5ft 8in; displacement 14,340lb; ballast ratio 41%, RORC rating 22ft.

Even the helmsman of an 18ft Skiff has a trapeze. Sailing a boat with a huge sail area and three or four men on trapezes requires skill and teamwork.

Cup, sailed in ballasted 21ft half-decked boats, depending heavily on the swinging power of six hefty crewmen to keep them upright. Competition for all three trophies continued until World War II and revived briefly after the war before finally being snuffed by the rise of ocean racing and more modern classes of inshore boat.

The interruption of World War II set Australian yachting off on a completely new tack. In the first ten post-war years lightweight, strong, waterproof plywood, then freely available and cheap, was quickly accepted for hard-chine dinghy hulls. Charles Cunningham, later to become best known for his catamarans, designed the hard-chine Gwen 12 dinghy in 1943 and it quickly became popular. From New Zealand came the Cherub in the 50s, a slimmer, fast 12-footer by John Spencer, making full use of plywood's properties, followed by his 14ft Javelin and the smaller Flying Ant trainer.

The techniques of cold-moulding thin timber veneers into lightweight round-bilge dinghy hulls were passed on from those who had used them to build Mosquito bombers in Australia during the war, and this method of construction was universally adopted for the skiffs and scow-design Moths. The first Australian Moth had been designed in box-like hard-chine shape by Len Morris back in 1928. This humble 11-footer that

The Gwen 12, the first Australian lightweight plywood dinghy class, has a lively performance and carries a trapeze. The tack of the jib is attached to a bowsprit, and a long spinnaker boom extends the spinnaker clear of the headsail. In this photograph both helmsman and crew are sitting to leeward to help the sails fall into shape in the light wind, and their weight is well forward to reduce wetted surface by lifting the flat aft sections clear of the water. Loa 12ft; beam 5ft 1¼in; sail area 110sq ft; weight 140lb. Designer Charles Cunningham.

could be knocked together by schoolboys became Australia's most popular class for the young, matched in numbers by the hard-chine, two-man Vee Jay, a fully bulkheaded 12-footer designed in 1931. In 1968, as the Australian Moth fleet numbers neared 1,000, the Australian restrictions became the basis for the new International Moth class rules.

Through this post-war decade and into the early 60s glassfibre was not freely available to Australian dinghy builders so, while the northern hemisphere tended to duplicate its proven timber dinghy hull shapes in glassfibre for similar hull weights, Australians tended to dinghy hulls that became lighter and lighter. The trapeze, first tried in England before the war, filtered into Australia from New Zealand towards the end of the 50s, helping to spread the concept of finer, lighter hulls, carrying a compact sail area suited to the prevalent medium to strong breezes. With plywood a thoroughly accepted medium, the series of easy-to-build family dinghies by Jack Holt of England found ready popularity in Australia through the 60s.

Ocean racing in its modern concept of pressing on through gales and unrelenting twenty-four-hour effort was introduced to Australians by one of the sport's founding fathers and authorities, Captain John Illingworth. Towards the end of the war he was stationed in Sydney as Engineer Commander of the Royal Australian Navy's Garden Island dockyard. In 1945 he persuaded a group of Sydney yachtsmen from the newly formed Cruising Yacht Club to make a race of their proposed Christmas cruise to Hobart. Illingworth bought himself a yacht for the race, a 34ft 9in light displacement cutter, *Rani*, designed by A. C. Barber of Sydney. When the fleet ran into a southwesterly gale off the coast of New South Wales, the cruising men, as was considered prudent in those days, hove-to or ran for shelter. The crew of one yacht sheltered behind Gabo Island even went ashore and shot rabbits. Meantime *Rani* raced on, beating the best of her bigger rivals into Hobart by seventeen hours and easily winning the race on corrected time. Illingworth returned to England, leaving behind the tradition of pushing boats and crews beyond normally accepted limits in bad weather that has become a trait of Australian offshore crews.

Right An Australian Flying Dutchman with a floral-painted hull reflects the holiday mood off this Adelaide beach. The Flying Dutchman is the largest International dinghy and has been an Olympic class since 1960. Designed by Dutchman Uwe van Essen, it requires a strong, heavy crew to sail it at its best, and only careful and knowledgeable tuning will produce the boat speed needed to be competitive. It is expensive to campaign due to its size and the high standard of competition. Loa 19ft 10in; beam 5ft 10in; sail area 180sq ft; spinnaker 190sq ft; weight 370lb. 7,000 boats.

Soon after the war Australians began to venture north in search of international competition – the movement that was finally to involve it completely in the international yachting community. Olympic yachting became firmly established in Australia with the 1956 Olympic Games in Melbourne, where Australia was represented in every class. Soon after the Melbourne Games the Flying Dutchman class became the two-man Olympic dinghy and won an immediate following in Australia. The class it replaced, the Twelve Square Metre Sharpie, was given an immediate breath of new life with the design by Les and Bob Addison of the Lightweight Sharpie, repeating the European Sharpie hull shape in lightweight sheet plywood, and replacing the gunter rig with a modern bermudan sail plan. The three-man Lightweight Sharpie became one of Australia's most popular high-performance dinghies. The 505 class, main rival to the Flying Dutchman for two-man Olympic selection, came to Australia about the same time, and both classes have since been well supported by relatively small but high quality fleets that have done well in international competition.

Ocean racing through the 60s developed into an expert compartment of the sport as the cruising yachts and converted metre harbour racers gave way to yachts which were specially designed for the task. The Sydney to Hobart race became an internationally recognized event and began to attract overseas entries. In 1965 Australia entered the Admiral's Cup for the first time, won it in 1967, and has been a strong competitor ever since. Its own version of the Cup, the Southern Cross Cup for teams from overseas countries and the Australian states, was founded by the Cruising Yacht Club of Australia in 1967. The first Australian level rating championships for Two, One, Half and Quarter Ton classes were held by the CYCA from Sydney in 1974.

Australia challenged four times for the America's Cup. The US defender *Intrepid* beat *Dame Pattie* 4-0 in 1967, and *Courageous* similarly made a clean sweep against *Southern Cross* in 1974, but the Alan Payne-designed *Gretel* took one race from *Weatherly* in 1962, and his *Gretel II* was finally beaten 4-1 by *Intrepid* in 1970. Disqualification after a collision on the starting line cost her a second win.

After three unsuccessful attempts, *Quest III*, designed by Charles and Lindsay Cunningham, won the International Catamaran Challenge Trophy from Denmark in 1970 and successfully defended it in 1972 4-0 against the US challenger *Weathercock*. The full aerofoil-rigged *Miss Nylex* defeated a New Zealand challenge in 1974 but lost the Trophy in 1976 to the US *Aquarius V*.

In general, more and more yachtsmen ride the jets to international venues to participate in world championships, and more and more world championships are staged in Australia.

Opposite Alan Bond's *Apollo* (No. R100) and Sidney Fisher's *Ragamuffin* in close quarters on a shy spinnaker reach on Sydney Harbour. The Sparkman and Stephens-designed *Ragamuffin*, built in 1968, was in the 1973 Australian Admiral's Cup team: Loa 48.6ft; Lwl 36ft; beam 12.3ft; draft 7.75ft; sail area 952sq ft; IOR rating 31.8ft. *Apollo* was built in 1969 to designs by Miller and Whitworth. Loa 57.9ft; Lwl 50ft; beam 13.4ft; draft 8.5ft; sail area 1,500sq ft.

7
Sailing in Canada

Sandy McPherson

Sails in history

Boys who lived on the Atlantic coast of infant Canada's maritime provinces in the time of square-rigged ships had little choice but to turn seaward and sign their articles. In 1875, the golden age of sail in Canada, there were over 4,000 ships of Canadian registry sailing the oceans, but Canadian shipbuilders did not convert to building steel square riggers in the latter part of the nineteenth century and therefore did not take part in the last era of commercial sail. The only commercial sailing ships built in the first forty years of the twentieth century were fishermen, the fine schooners of the Grand Banks. The age of wooden ships and iron men was rapidly coming to an end, but Canada had three kicks left that would attract world-wide attention to her sailors and wooden sailing ships.

In 1895 Captain Joshua Slocum set out to be the first man to sail around the world alone. In his 36ft sloop *Spray* he completed the voyage in 1898, and for the next ten years man and boat sailed thousands of solo miles until one day in 1909 *Spray* and Slocum set sail and were never seen again.

Tilikum, owned by John W. Voss, was originally a west coast dug-out canoe, shaped from a single red cedar log. She sailed from Victoria, British Columbia in 1901 and, after logging 40,000 miles, Voss and his crew reached Margate, England. *Tilikum* is preserved in Thunderbird Park in Victoria.

The schooner *Bluenose* is Canada's best-known sailing ship, although not the biggest. She was perhaps the fastest sailer close on the wind of all the commercial vessels built of wood. Designed by W. J. Roue and built at Lunenburg, Nova Scotia in 1921, she was always skippered by her owner Captain Angus Walters and was never defeated in international fishermen's races. Sadly she was converted to a diesel freighter in 1939 and foundered off Haiti in 1946, but her ghost survives in Halifax in the form of an exact sea-going replica, and every Canadian carries a picture of *Bluenose* in his pocket to this day, for she appears in all her glory on the tail side of the dime.

While the brigs and barques, ships and schooners were disappearing, a new form of sail had arrived – the yacht. The first recorded use of the word yacht in Canada appears to have been in 1795, describing an 80-tonner attached to the naval base in Kingston. The first freshwater sailing Olympics were held 181 years later in 1976 at this Lake Ontario port.

Canadian pleasure-sailing yachts date back to about 1820, and the first Canadian yacht club was formed in Nova Scotia in 1837. In 1861 it became 'Royal' but unfortunately was plagued with dissension. Reorganized in 1875 it became one of only five 'Royal' squadrons in the world, and is known to this day as the Royal Nova Scotia Yacht Squadron.

In 1852 a group of men gathered on a leaky scow in Toronto harbour and founded the Royal Canadian Yacht Club, the oldest and largest of the Canadian clubs to have operated without interruption. Before yachting spread west to Vancouver and Victoria, other clubs were

formed, notably the Yacht Club de Québec, established in 1861 and inactive from 1872 until 1884. It was the first French-speaking club in the country and boasted 300 members in 1888.

During the first half of the twentieth century there were perhaps no more than fifty yacht clubs in Canada, but as the country developed, yachting fever spread gradually westward. By the time World War II burst upon us Canadian yachtsmen had competed in the Olympic Games and the America's Cup, they had sailed around the world in company and alone, and they had built some of the finest yacht clubs in the world.

The real explosion in pleasure sailing in Canada came in the years 1950 to 1965, not only in the east and on the west coast, but in the most unlikely area of all, Canada's famous wheat belt – the prairies. Boats sailed on small lakes, ponds, irrigation ditches and any depression that held water, and it was not long before a flatlander became National Junior Champion. On being asked by a distinguished gentleman what water he sailed on, the proud reply flashed back 'one of those western ditches'. With an estimated 100,000 active sailors and a total investment in sailing of probably over $100,000,000 sailing has truly reached its second golden age in Canada.

Bluenose, the splendid 143ft schooner built at Lunenburg, Nova Scotia, in 1921 was designed by W. J. Roue on the lines of a commercial fishing boat and had holds to carry 210 tons of fish. Owned and always skippered by Captain Angus Walters, she was built for schooner racing against the USA and was never beaten. She appears on the tail side of the Canadian dime. Converted to a diesel freighter in 1939, she foundered off Haiti in 1946, but an exact replica was launched in Lunenburg in 1963. Loa 143ft; Lwl 112ft; beam 27ft; draft 15ft 10in; displacement 285 tons; sail area 10,000sq ft. Some construction details: keel 12in sided, frames doubled 9in × 10in spaced 27in apart; planking 4in thick; ceiling 4in; deck beams 9in × 9in; deck 4in; rudder stock 12in diameter; mainmast 20in diameter; foremast 19in diameter.

Weather and general conditions

There is no way to describe Canada's general weather conditions in a line or two. It can be extremely cold or very hot, with piles of snow or torrential rains, and gale-force winds at the same time as day-long calms. All are part of Canada's weather pattern. It is 4,000 miles from east to west, the most northerly yacht club is 750 miles closer to the Arctic Circle than the most southerly, and the country rises in places to 16,000ft. With 30,000 statute miles of ocean coastline, and 291,000 square miles of fresh water spread over these great distances, the weather can vary greatly from place to place at any given time.

The Pacific west coast is Canada's most temperate area, making British Columbia the only province where year-round sailing is possible. In winter the temperature seldom falls below 5°C (40°F), while in summer over 22°C (72°F) is thought to be hot. Rainfall is considerable. The Prairie Provinces have the shortest season, normally June to September. Temperatures dip as low as $-46°C$ ($-50°F$) in winter and often reach 32°C (90°F) in summer. Whistling winds are common during drought conditions in July and August.

Quebec has a slightly shorter season than Ontario's early May to late October, but the weather is very similar: inhabitants can shiver at $-29°C$ ($-20°F$) and boil at nearly 38°C (100°F). The best winds occur in spring and fall, while July and August can be relatively calm except in thunderstorms. The eastern maritime provinces can be wet and cold, even during the summer season, but the Atlantic coast does not suffer the extremes of Ontario and Quebec. Fog and ice-bergs off the coast in spring and early summer contribute to tough cold-weather sailing.

Safety and policing in Canada is carried out by numerous authorities, and rescue work is effected by Air Force and Coast Guard air-sea rescue and various police forces. Outsiders are often very surprised to find that the 'Mounties' have had a marine division for many years, and it was the Royal Canadian Mounted Police's auxiliary schooner *St Roch*, commanded by Superintendent Larsen, that first navigated the elusive North-West Passage, making the return voyage across the top of Canada between 1940 and 1944.

Clubs and facilities

Nearly all Canada's major yacht clubs are situated in the cities of Halifax, Quebec, Ottawa, Kingston, Toronto, Hamilton, Sarnia, Vancouver and Victoria. Some metropolitan areas have as many as fifteen yacht clubs within their boundaries, but smaller towns and cities are usually close to water as well, and their sailing clubs are not far distant. Canada is lucky in that most of her major clubs support and encourage the smaller ones in many ways invisible to the average sailor. There are 370 clubs affiliated to the Canadian Yachting Association. The large yacht clubs usually have substantial clubhouses, yards with marine railways, and ample winter storage space. Nearly all have reached their membership limits and have waiting lists for mooring space. Many middle-sized clubs have comparable facilities but are a little less grand or extensive. Fees and rentals are somewhat lower, but quality and enthusiasm is just as high. The grass roots of Canadian sailing lie in the dinghy clubs that abound everywhere: they may not have clubhouses but they have boats, jetties or ramps, available water – and spirit.

Public marinas are scattered throughout the nation, particularly in British Columbia where boats can stay in the water all the year round. Here marinas have often become substitutes for private clubs. Chandlers exist in all major cities, as do builders, designers, sailmakers and yards, but yachtsmen in provinces such as Saskatchewan must do most of their purchasing by catalogue and mail order.

Canadian navigable waters are well marked and charted. Radio beacons, weather forecasting and marine radio-telephone systems operate along all ocean coasts and in the Great Lakes, and the Department of Transport (Marine) provides an abundance of printed material to aid the yachtsman as he cruises the oceans, lakes, rivers and canals.

The safety equipment to be carried is laid down in regulations by the Department of Transport and is subject to inspection by various policing authorities, as are the holding tanks for galley and head waste which some provinces and states stipulate must be carried by yachts with sleeping accommodation.

All boats require a licence in order to operate, although personal licences to sail are not generally required in Canadian waters. Certain harbours and approaches require permits for which written and practical tests must be passed. There are speed limits in areas such as approaches, harbours, canals and rivers. These are well marked on charts, and fines are levied for violations.

A C & C 25 cruiser/racer, typical of the work of Canadian designers Cuthbertson and Cassian. Note the extruded aluminium slotted toe rail introduced by the designers to provide a strength member running the full length of the boat. The bolts joining the deck and hull mouldings can be fixed through this, and holes provide a wide choice of secure anchor points for blocks, vangs and fenders.

Building and design

Until the end of World War II the market for substantial yachts was minimal. Several sailmaking firms were specializing in yacht sails by the 30s and a few yards built yachts, but these were quality builders who produced only one or two boats per year.

The post-war growth in sailing offered encouragement and opportunity to potential builders, designers, sailmakers and retailers. From 1950 thousands of yachts have been built in Canada, many of them from the boards of Canadian designers Roue, Brandlemeyer, Hatfield, Cuthbertson & Cassian and Hinterhoeller. Whitby Yachts have produced over 600 of one class of 30ft cruiser-racer, and a smaller, four-berth keel yacht called the Shark numbers over 1,000 throughout the world. Canadian-designed and -built yachts have won the Canada's Cup, the Seawanhaka Cup, the SORC twice and the Victoria to Maui race, while others have been victorious, or simply done well, in major offshore events.

While the yacht-building industry was struggling, many fine dinghies were designed and built in Canada during the first half of the twentieth century, and, of these, examples of the International Fourteen were, and perhaps still are, the leaders. This class produced fine designers such as George Corneil, Charlie Bourke, Fred Buller and Bruce Kirby who, between them, designed nearly twenty Canadian-built versions, nearly every one of which has been successful in international racing.

Although many fine wooden yachts have been produced in Canada, it was the appearance of glassfibre that caused the building industry to boom. Canada has been a leader and innovator in this field. Advanced glassfibre designs enabled Canadians to enter the dinghy export market in recent years, and to lead the way in the glassfibre dinghy construction of classes such as the Albacore, Cadet and Enterprise which were designed outside Canada.

The Laser, designed by Bruce Kirby along with Ian Bruce and Hans Fogh, burst upon the scene in 1970 as no previous boat has ever done and now sails in the four corners of the world. In the sailmaking field there are some twenty Canadian firms as well as five or six of the major world-wide lofts.

Boat types

Apart from the Olympic classes there are nine national classes that are members of the Canadian Yachting Association (CYA): the Dragon, Enterprise, Fireball, International Fourteen, 505, Laser, Lightning, OK and Snipe. Other classes which are members of the CYA are the Albacore, Arrow, Cadet, Caprice, CL 14-16, Cygnus, Dingo, Flipper, 420, GP14, Invitation, Lazy E, Mirror, Optimist, Petrel, Sabot, Sea Spray, Star, Tanzer, Y-Flyer and Wayfarer. Other racing classes are not members, two of which are the Eight Metre and Six Metre, and both still race actively.

General racing

The bulk of yacht racing in Canada is organized by clubs every weekend during the summer when tens of thousands of sailors take part. These are not the highly competitive sailors who race at national and international level. Every type of racing is held in Canada, around-the-buoys, long-distance, point-to-point, junior, ladies, team, class, handicap and, more unusually, races for schooners, brigantines and even ice boats. The forty-eight class associations have organized races involving 15,000 dinghies, and there are between 3,000 and 4,000 offshore racing boats.

Small-boat regattas abound and vary from little local fleets to enormous events hosting over 500 dinghies. Many world championships have been held in Canada since 1966 and the 1976 Olympics were sailed off Kingston at the north-east corner of Lake Ontario.

The largest and most active offshore fleets are located in Toronto on Lake Ontario and the Pacific coast city of Vancouver where starts of over 200 yachts are not uncommon for round-the-buoys racing, or up to 250 boats for offshore events. Europeans may not realize that a very high percentage of Canada's offshore racing takes place on the Great Lakes where races of 200–300 miles are usual.

The best-known offshore events are Lake Ontario's Freeman Cup, 150 miles, and International Race, 225 miles; the Pacific coast's Swiftsure, 125 miles, and Victoria to Maui, over 2,300 miles; and the Eastern

With a backdrop of snow-capped peaks this Canadian Tempest is working up for the 1976 Olympic Games. The boat, *Seeker II*, was donated by Rothmans to help promote Olympic sailing in Canada. The Ian Proctor-designed Tempest, an international two-man keelboat with trapeze, was an Olympic class in 1972 and 1976 but was then dropped in favour of the ageing Star. The fin keel with lead bulb can be raised for beaching and transport ashore. Loa 21ft 11½in; beam 6ft 5½in; draft 3ft 6in; sail area 247sq ft; spinnaker 225sq ft; weight 1,010lb. About 850 in the world, with fifty or so new boats annually.

Seaboard's Marblehead to Halifax, 365 miles. Canadian offshore yachts have competed in many American classics and have also taken part in such races as the Fastnet, Bermuda, Capetown to Rio and Sydney to Hobart.

The Canada's Cup match race series between Canadian and US yachts on the Great Lakes was first held in 1896. Canada has fared better in this series than others have in the America's Cup. The score stands at USA 8, Canada 4, although it is often the same builders and designers such as Herreshoff, Stephens and Hood that Canada must face.

Canada has had two cracks at the America's Cup: in 1876 with the *Countess of Dufferin* and in 1881 with *Atlanta*, but in both cases the challengers were soundly beaten. A third challenge was issued for 1974 by the Royal Vancouver YC but was abandoned. Canada is also active in the various world Ton events, and level racing in offshore yachts is gradually becoming popular.

A fleet of forty-five boats starting in a race in the 1970 North American 505 Championship in Vancouver, British Columbia, on the Pacific West Coast. The climate in this area allows boating all the year round.

Cruising

When one considers the enormous size of Canada with its long coastlines and vast expanse of fresh water, it is obvious that every type of cruising imaginable is possible. The Pacific coast offers the longest season in some of the world's most spectacular scenery with vast fjords. Cruising is even possible in the mountains in areas such as the Okanagan. The prairies are really dinghy country and not suitable for cruising in the normal sense, but although the Lake of the Woods near the Ontario–Manitoba border has a very short season, it boasts thousands of miles of beautiful cruising waters.

The five Great Lakes are really small oceans and, with the exception of Lake Heron's magnificent Georgian Bay, do not offer the scenery and quiet waters available elsewhere. There is, however, ideal cruising in the eastern end of Lake Ontario from the Bay of Quinte down the St Lawrence river to Montreal. The lower St Lawrence to the Atlantic is difficult water with tides, strong currents, and ever-shifting sand bars. The Atlantic coast offers challenging and spirited sailing for the cruising yachtsman, although the rugged but beautiful coast has a habit of hiding behind fog banks. There are magnificent bays and sheltered areas such as the Bras d'Or lakes open to yachts of all sizes.

Beautiful and protected cruising waters are accessible from the Great Lakes by means of canals and rivers, and lead to thousands of miles of additional inland cruising. It is also possible to cruise to Florida and the Bahamas from a thousand miles inland on the Great Lakes, with only a very few miles of open ocean, and many Canadians travel this route each year.

The Canadian Yachting Association

The CYA was formed in 1931 with a total of only twenty-one individual members and eighteen clubs with the prime and, really, sole objective of raising a team for the 1932 Olympics. After the 1936 Olympics the CYA hibernated until 1948 when it was revived by the combined efforts of the Royal St Lawrence and Royal Canadian Yacht Clubs. It then concentrated on youth sailing and the raising of funds to support and establish Canada's Olympic and Pan American Games teams. From 1930 Canada was represented on the International Yacht Racing Union by NAYRU, supported by an unofficial Canadian observer. In the 60s one of the three NAYRU seats on the Permanent Committee was allocated to Canada, and in the past few years this country has taken an ever-increasing interest and part in the affairs of the IYRU, with representatives on the Permanent, Youth, Class Policy and Rules Committees.

Training

There are now nearly 300 locations in Canada where some sort of sail training is available to youth and adults. Member clubs of the CYA have organized 214 sailing schools with CYA qualified instructors who run courses prescribed by the national authority. About 20,000 youths and 5,000 adults attend these courses annually. There are also mobile schools that travel to the far-flung areas of this vast country and sometimes bring sailing to people who have never seen a dinghy. In addition, there are sailing courses offered by public concerns, summer camps, Sea Cadets, Scouts, colleges and prep schools, while three brigantines on Lake Ontario offer training to an additional 300 youngsters each year. Seminars are held throughout Canada offering lectures on racing and navigation, as well as special courses for the grading of CYA qualified instructors, and the CYA publishes various booklets in both English and French.

8
Sailing in New Zealand

David Pardon

The growth of yachting in New Zealand has been a compact and fast-moving process. In contrast to most of the other major yachting nations it spans little more than 100 years from the days when the Auckland race tradition was begun by the flat-bottomed timber scows, ugly gaff-rigged coastal traders built to haul kauri timber from the Northland forests through the Hauraki Gulf to the port of Auckland, to the present day when the annual regatta attracts 1,000 yachts for what is claimed to be the largest one-day event of its kind in the world. The 1975 Auckland Regatta included, for instance, racers in nine keelboat divisions, twenty-eight centreboard classes and assorted other groups such as trailer-sailers, multihulls, navy whalers and 14ft Bosun dinghies.

In a country which prides itself on being remarkably free from the grip of bureaucrats and statisticians, exact figures are hard to come by. Nevertheless, estimates are that one quarter of the 1975 population of 3,026,900 owned a boat, crewed on a boat, or at least sailed in some sort of pleasure craft several times a year.

It is virtually impossible to trace the number of craft afloat or parked on trailers or back lawns up and down the country. There is no compulsory registration of pleasure craft, and club or class association lists are the only means of assessing interest. And these, of course, make no account for the countless thousands of New Zealanders who own a boat but are not club members, and use their craft purely for weekend family outings.

The only general source of statistics is the *Auckland Yachting Association Handbook* which covers all craft registered with the Association. As over 600,000 New Zealanders live in Auckland itself, and a little over 80% of all yachting takes place on Auckland Harbour and the Hauraki Gulf, it offers a fair indication of the strength of yachting in New Zealand as a whole. The 1975 *Handbook* listed 9,984 sailing craft in forty-nine classes from the 7ft P-class dinghy to ocean racers, such as the 73ft Sydney to Hobart line winning *Buccaneer*.

Yachting is controlled at the top by the New Zealand Yachting Federation working through eleven regional associations, seventy-eight class associations and 114 clubs catering for cruising and racing (but excluding clubs which cater only for power craft). The Federation itself comprises four executive officers – president, vice-president, secretary, treasurer – two registrars and eight committees, each with its own permanent chairman. The committees are: Olympic, national contests, appeals panel and racing rules, keeler and powerboat, offshore, multihull, finance and youth.

In co-operation with the country's two major offshore clubs, the Royal New Zealand Yacht Squadron and the Royal Akarana Yacht Club, the Federation was responsible for New Zealand's 1975 challenge for the Admiral's Cup. But day-to-day administration is very much in the hands of the clubs, and it is the smaller clubs with mainly centreboard membership which host Olympic trials and national championships in co-operation with the various class associations.

Although remote from the main yachting centres, New Zealand offers some of the finest sailing waters in the world. Although some sailing takes place on New Zealand's many lakes, difficulty of access, particularly in the South Island, means that by far the majority of skippers keep to the superb, island-speckled waters of the Hauraki Gulf and Bay of Islands, and the deep, extraordinarily peaceful sounds at the northern end of the South Island.

Sitting between 34°S and 47°S the two main islands of New Zealand are within a belt of strong westerly winds which encircle the hemisphere south of latitude 35°S. Slightly to the north is a sub-tropical high-pressure ridge from which pressures decrease southwards to a deep, low-pressure trough located near latitude 70°S.

The weather pattern is dominated by a succession of anticyclones separated by low-pressure troughs passing regularly west to east across the Tasman Sea from Australia to New Zealand. A typical weather sequence might begin with a trough from the west bringing fresh north-westerly winds followed by rain and, possibly, gale-force blows. The passage of the trough with its associated cold front is usually accompanied by a change to cold south-westerly or southerly winds, often with hail or thunder. Winds then moderate, and fine, warm weather prevails for several days as the anticyclone moves across the country.

Occasionally in summer depressions form rapidly, developing into fierce storms, and the capital Wellington is famous as 'The Windy City' where gusts up to 80mph are not uncommon. This weather pattern strongly dictates the design and development of yachting, and it is a fact that Wellington yachtsmen, reared on heavy-weather sailing, rarely score highly in events held on Auckland Harbour a mere 400 miles north.

Winds from a westerly quarter prevail throughout the year, generally tending to increase in strength from north to south. The mountain range extending almost the length of both islands does, however, produce local modifications to the pattern, particularly in the southern provinces of Canterbury and Otago where strong gales are frequent in late spring and summer.

Figures produced by the New Zealand Meteorological Service show that Auckland averages 2.5 days a year with gusts reaching 60mph or more and 49 days a year with gusts up to 40mph or more. Comparative figures in Wellington are 13 and 146, and in Christchurch, the other main sailing area, the figures are 24 and 56.

The same source shows Auckland averaging 2,102 bright sunshine hours a year, Wellington 2,020 and Christchurch 1,974. Auckland's mean annual maximum temperature is 27°C (81°F) and minimum 3°C (37°F), comparative figures for Wellington being 26°C (79°F) and 1°C (34°F), and for Christchurch 32°C (90°F) and −4°C (25°F).

The comparatively light winds of Auckland and the Hauraki Gulf, as against the infamous 'Southerly Busters' which can make Wellington and the Cook Strait area one of the most rugged in the world, account for the fact that while Auckland's top designers – men such as Bruce Farr, John Spencer, Jim Young, John Lidgard, Paul Whiting and so on – build their reputations on light displacement, often high-rating boats (*Tohe Candu, 45 Degrees South, Gerontius, Buccaneer*), Wellington's big names are noted more for traditional designs. Men such as Hal Wagstaff and Bruce Askew still produce carvel, and even clinker boats that have long gone from the Auckland scene. In recent years both have designed

A typical New Zealand trailer-sailer. As their name implies, trailer-sailers are small enough to be trailed behind a family car but have minimal accommodation for restricted cruising and overnight use.

a lot for steel. Plywood, still very popular with Spencer in particular, Farr, Young, and that mass-producer of build-it-yourself plans, Richard Hartley, is seldom advocated in Wellington, and it is significant that in the past two or three seasons no Wellington yacht has been successful in Auckland competition.

The type of yacht cruising and racing in New Zealand waters varies enormously, though there is a strong leaning towards simple hull shapes, chine design and timber or sandwich construction which allows full rein to the national fetish for do-it-yourself building! Nevertheless, New Zealand supports a highly efficient and productive boating industry. The 1974 figures produced by the Department of Statistics show 116 boatbuilding and marine engineering companies operating throughout the country and employing 1,875 people. The industry's wages and salary bill is put at $NZ7,727,000 a year and material costs at $NZ8,528,000. Net value of production is $NZ20,944,000, increasing at something a little more than 4.2% per year.

Popular centreboard yachts include all the Olympic classes, international classes such as the Finn, Fireball, Flying Fifteen, Flying Dutchman, Laser and a whole host of national designs ranging from the most popular of all, the 7ft P-class junior (age limit sixteen), designed in 1924 by Harry Highet and still the backbone of New Zealand yachting, to the 12ft Cherubs and 14ft Javelins which have pushed the name of Auckland designer John Spencer almost as far around the world as have his major keelboat projects, the ocean racer *Buccaneer* and, of course, the shock 1973 Transpac winner *Ragtime*, the lightweight 62-footer that first earned Spencer the title of 'The Plywood King'.

More than forty stock keelboat designs are currently available on the New Zealand market, but the biggest boom in recent years has been in trailer-sailers, ranging from the old but still popular Richard Hartley TS16 to a giant 32-footer just off the board of Wellington designer Hal Wagstaff. Thirteen trailer-sailer designs are currently available either in kit-form for timber construction or as glassfibre mouldings, complete

45° South II, a light displacement, Bruce Farr One Tonner, finished fourth in the 1976 One Ton World Championship. Note the wide, open-backed cockpit with alloy tie beam, and the horseshoe life-belts with automatic flashing, floating lights attached, one of which is hanging at the windward end of the beam. Stowed in a tube through the transom – see the hole just to the left and slightly below the letter R – is a dan buoy which can be released to mark the position of a man overboard. Instruments can easily be seen by the helmsman and crew when trimming the sails.

95

craft or hulls only. The national trailer-sailer championships are fast becoming one of the most popular events on the calendar.

The cost of sailing to a New Zealander can be as small as a week's wages or as big as the ocean, which no matter where in the land he lives is never more than eighty miles away. The plywood 7ft P-class trainer can be built at home (many have even been built on the living room floor) from a $NZ3 set of plans and put on the water, complete with sail and all gear, for less than $NZ200. The 50ft aluminium Sparkman and Stephens-designed Admiral's Cup racer *Corinthian*, built in aluminium for Auckland industrialist Russ Hooper, cost $NZ130,000, and in between lies the whole field of timber, glassfibre, aluminium, steel and, of course, ferro-cement, which method of construction was developed in New Zealand and is still vigorously promoted throughout the world by the New Zealand Ferro-Cement Marine Association (PO Box 26–073, Epsom, Auckland).

To look at a few popular averages: a timber kit for a Richard Hartley 18ft trailer-sailer, complete with plans but without mast, sails and rigging, costs $NZ924. A glassfibre Lawrie Davidson-designed M-20 trailer-sailer, 20ft by 7ft 11in beam, with accommodation for five adults, 210sq ft of working sail, and complete with toilet, squabs, carpet, all sailing and deck gear, galley etc. but no auxiliary, sells for $NZ3,290.

Moving up the scale is a 727 Quarter Tonner which gives a glassfibre hull 23ft 10in overall, 8ft 3½in beam in racing/cruising trim but without auxiliary for $NZ9,600. (This model, which won the 1975 Quarter Ton World Championship, was designed by Bruce Farr, one of New Zealand's youngest and most promising designers who previously dominated the world 18-footer championships, and designed the New Zealand Half Ton Cup challenger *Tohe Candu*.) As a basic Quarter Ton racing craft the cost is down to $NZ8,300.

Further up the scale is one of the most popular cruiser-racers, about seventy of which were produced and sold in the two years after Aucklander Bob Salthouse completed the design. The Cavalier 32 is one of a

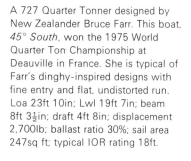

A 727 Quarter Tonner designed by New Zealander Bruce Farr. This boat, *45° South*, won the 1975 World Quarter Ton Championship at Deauville in France. She is typical of Farr's dinghy-inspired designs with fine entry and flat, undistorted run. Loa 23ft 10in; Lwl 19ft 7in; beam 8ft 3½in; draft 4ft 8in; displacement 2,700lb; ballast ratio 30%; sail area 247sq ft; typical IOR rating 18ft.

range of glassfibre hulls by the same designer and produced by the same company. With a 32ft overall length, 9ft 9in beam and drawing 5ft 3in it carries 500sq ft of working sail, can be made to rate and race successfully as a Half Tonner, or to take the family for a comfortable offshore cruise. For the do-it-yourself man who wants to do all he can himself, a basic hull, with bulkheads, frames etc. moulded in, sells for $NZ3,850 while a complete yacht, ready to sail and fitted with a 10hp diesel auxiliary, can be bought for $NZ27,000. Complementing these are many other interesting designs, including racing and cruising multihulls and a number of popular and excellent twin-keel craft by yet another Auckland designer, Alan Wright. A list of stock craft available in New Zealand, with basic details, yacht clubs and organizations, is published each year in *Sea Spray Annual*.

Once owning a boat the New Zealand yachtsman faces few other major expenses, though marina and mooring facilities are scarce in the Auckland area and a long waiting list can run into several years. This helps account for the popularity of sailing craft in the trailerable range and of twin keelers, which sit happily on the many beaches and estuaries around the coastline.

New Zealand's most exclusive yacht club, the Royal New Zealand Yacht Squadron, charges an entry fee of $NZ35 and an annual subscription of $NZ44. At the other end of the scale many clubs with fewer facilities have no joining fee and an annual subscription as low as $NZ25. Somewhere in between is the average. Squadron membership is open, and though active sailing members are preferred to social members, there is no waiting list.

Sailing in any part of New Zealand is pleasantly free from rules and restrictions. There is no compulsion to register or insure any pleasure craft, and only when a boat cruises or races outside territorial waters do normal customs and health regulations apply. However, the Federation and individual clubs have their own regulations covering the safety and operation of boats taking part in events for which they are responsible.

Like most things New Zealand training and tuition is very much a do-it-yourself affair. Most popular of all training craft is the 7ft P class of which more than 2,000 are currently sailing around New Zealand. The New Zealand Yachting Federation has no training programme as such, but a large number of clubs do run their own sailing schools, all in dinghies such as the P class or the Rothmans Father and Son. Only one professional school for keelboat sailing exists and almost without exception New Zealand racing and cruising keelboat sailors graduate from dinghies. In a recent move the New Zealand Department of Education has given its approval to the introduction of sailing as a physical education option in schools, and a pilot scheme, run by clubs in conjunction with individual schools and the department, has been introduced in Wellington.

New Zealand has a purely volunteer coastguard service which is, nevertheless, highly efficient. The Post Office and Radio New Zealand operate an efficient and frequent weather forecast service for yachtsmen. The Post Office, Harbour Board and private radio stations maintain an open watch on 2,182 kHz or Channel 16 (156.8 mHz), and international

Corinthian, an impressive Sparkman and Stephens-designed 50-footer built in aluminium alloy for Auckland industrialist Russ Hooper and favourite for selection for the 1975 New Zealand Admiral's Cup team. The radical Farr-designed *Gerontius* beat her into fourth place and was selected in her place because of her outstanding all-round performance. *Corinthian:* Loa 50ft; Lwl 38ft 2in; beam 13ft 8in; draft 8ft; sail area 1,080sq ft; displacement 35,000lb; ballast ratio 51%; IOR rating 38.6ft.

Sabots racing off Auckland's North Shore. This locally designed lightweight training class is 7ft 11in overall and built in plywood for youngsters up to sixteen years old.

distress frequencies can be used where a ship or station is known to be nearby. A complete list of all radio stations, with call signs, frequencies and listening times, together with weather forecast information and general radio procedure is available in *Sea Spray Annual*.

New Zealand's system of charts is in accordance with the International Hydrographic Organization and the uniform system of buoyage is used. British Admiralty charts and Royal New Zealand Navy Hydrographic Office charts cover North and South Island coastal and lake waters, and adjacent ocean areas such as the South Pacific, Tasman and Coral Seas, Antarctica, etc. Port Information Manuals, including complete aerial views, berthage plans etc. are available for all major ports, and the *New Zealand Pilot* gives full sailing directions for the coast of New Zealand and its offshore islands.

New Zealand Navy charts are progressively being metricated, but at the moment the majority are still in Imperial measurements. A chart catalogue, the *New Zealand Pilot* and Port Information Manuals are available through the Royal New Zealand Navy Hydrographic Office, PO Box 33341, Takapuna, Auckland.

9
Sailing in
South Africa

Brian Lello

The South African coast is long and hard with few harbours and fewer havens suitable for small craft, hardly any estuaries and bays of sheltered waters, and no really navigable rivers. In the south is the Cape of Good Hope, once called the Cape of Storms, and to the north, east and west the robust winds persist. Down the east coast flows the mighty Moçambique or Agulhas current, 1,000ft deep, 100 miles wide, and up to 4 knots over the ground. Up the west coast sweeps the cold Benguela current, creating the arid hinterland. Only 200 miles from Cape Agulhas the remote southern ocean lives alone with its great westerly winds system, and the long south-west swells from the turmoil down there roll up unceasingly against the coastline.

It all adds up to a rather forbidding picture – but at least there are few off-lying dangers. Coastal sailing is often a straightforward slogging match against wind and current. If the yacht is able and weatherly, South African offshore men come to terms with their sailing. Some, finally, even revel in it.

Among world circumnavigators this stretch from Durban round the Cape of Storms to Table Bay with its wonderful backdrop of Table Mountain is justly respected. But the main rule is keep away from the edge of the continental shelf at all costs. Here – and more often in summer than winter – if out-of-season depression winds contest the Agulhas current with a long enough fetch, rare rogue waves appear, big enough to maim the largest ships afloat. Before people fully appreciated this phenomenon there was the long-remembered classic disappearance of the fine new liner *Waratah*, but a dozen or more well-found new freighters and super tankers have also been damaged or sunk.

The characteristics are a long sloping trough, perhaps 2,000ft in length, with a huge out-of-step, vertical-faced swell or comber at the end of it, too steep for any ship to surmount. Yachtsmen will escape them only if they obey this single precept – keep away from the edge of the continental shelf, or the 100 fathom line. Inshore the weather may be horrible, but never too much for a modern cruising yacht.

The interior of South Africa is mostly plateau, the Karroo and the Highveld, and here more great dams arise year by year. Since 1945 these waters have attracted those who hunger for a life afloat. The result is that inland dinghy sailing is stronger than at the coast, and keelboat sailing has also flourished. On Vaaldam in the Transvaal province at the beginning of 1975 one handicap race for cruisers attracted a fleet of 254 yachts. This great stretch of yellow-brown water has an intricate coastline of about 400 miles. In 1974 the South African Navy published a proper Vaaldam chart.

On the coast the people who often put in the most sea-time are not the sailing men, but the game fishermen. There are two main groups: the members of the Marlin and Tuna Club, whose favoured craft are usually about 42ft overall and capable of anything up to 30 knots, and the owners of ski-boats, the small 18–22ft trailer boats, who launch them wherever they can, often through the surf. There are 15,000 of them – a fact that many sailing men hate to admit.

Sailing as an organized sport in South Africa began in the 1850s in Durban and Table Bay. The pioneer and Grand Old Man of Cape

Above The magnificent 88ft ketch *Ondine*, owned by American Huey Long, leading the fleet out of Table Bay at the start of the 1973 Cape to Rio Race. Run every three years, this takes yachts 3,600 miles across the South Atlantic and has become established as one of the classic ocean races. *Ondine* put up a first day's run of 267 miles — an average of over 11 knots.

Right South African-designed keelboats racing on the Vaaldam. Boating is very popular on this stretch of inland water, with one of the handicap races attracting over 250 entries, and in 1974 the South African Navy published a special Vaaldam chart. The spinnaker on the boat in the foreground is stowed in its bag attached to the pulpit ready for hoisting on rounding the weather mark.

yachting was J. G. Steytler, and the first recorded regatta was in 1857 with a local sea-rescue hero, Captain Robert Granger, and one James Ansdell playing leading parts.

The history of Durban's Royal Natal Yacht Club goes back to May 1858 when the Durban Regatta Club, out of which the RNYC grew, was formed. Old diaries of the 1840s mention sailing on Durban Bay; in the Cape the Dutch East India Company had yachts in the earliest days. But these were the small, nimble, commercial craft which eventually gave their name to today's world-wide sport.

The first meeting of the Table Bay Yacht Club – a progenitor of the Royal Cape Yacht Club, which received its royal charter in 1914 and is South Africa's premier ocean-going club – was held on 7 April 1905. Its contemporaries were the Beira Yacht Club, the Royal Natal (charter 1891), the Point, the Congella, the Buffalo Sailing and Aquatic Associations, the Beaconsfield Sailing Club (now Zwartkops Yacht Club) and the Redhouse Sailing Club. A Lakeside Boating Association had been formed at the Sandvlei, Muizenberg, in the Cape Peninsula where a marina is being built.

Today there are at least 30,000 sailing yachtsmen in South Africa and a rapidly increasing community of powerboat folk scattered throughout the length and breadth of Southern Africa, most of them members of the 130-odd water-sport clubs. This whole community is represented nationally by the South African Yacht Racing Association for sail, and the South African Power Boat Association, both with headquarters in Johannesburg. The deep-sea men have their headquarters in Cape Town, where the Cruising Association of South Africa is based. The body is backed by the South African Ocean Racing Trust, which is dedicated to getting people to sea and sponsoring South African participation in the world's offshore and trans-oceanic classics. The Navy is a strong protagonist for sail training, especially for midshipmen. The South African Naval Sailing Association had four entries in the 1976 Rio Race.

Regatta sailing flows from three Olympic classes, the Flying Dutchman two-man dinghy, the International Finn single-hander, and the small group of Soling two-man keelboats, which can be sailed in deep water, but are small enough to be trailed to inland sailing venues. There are many Fireballs, Enterprises, Lasers, Phantoms, Mirrors, OKs, GP14s and other class dinghies. As in most countries dinghy sailing has thrown up many local designs. Before the current addiction to the international Optimist for children, local sailmaker Jack Köper produced a version of the sailing surfboard or simple scow-type hull for children, but with mainsail, jib and centreboard, that had real sailing capacity with the ability to plane in breezy coastal weather. This class is still strong with nearly 3,000 sail numbers, and feeds youngsters who are already well-used to aggressive fast sailing into the bigger classes. Köper also produced a rather shapely scow-type called the Tempo before the Fireball appeared on the world scene. But the Tempos have, understandably, waned a bit because of the chances of international sailing provided as a reward for trying hard in Fireballs. South Africa has the world's fifth largest fleet of these International dinghies.

101

Sprogs racing in the South African
National Championship on False Bay.
This easy-to-build hard-chine dinghy
was designed by Herbert McWilliams
of Port Elizabeth just after World
War II and over 700 have been built.

Frank Spears produced the Spearhead in the late 50s, a lean, mettle-some 16-footer, very demanding to sail in gusty winds but, with its flat-reaching spinnaker, able to hold the Flying Dutchman when conditions are right. After the war the Port Elizabeth architect Herbert McWilliams launched a range of hard-chine plywood dinghies for easy home construction and high performance. The earliest and most successful was the Sprog (700 or more), and many people have enjoyed sailing the Extra and the Winger.

For sheer excitement latter-day sailing seldom matches the old Durban Bay 25ft scows – lovely sailing machines that achieved 20 knots when the afternoon busters scorched along the sheltered channels between the sand-banks.

In 1975 the national regatta of mixed classes, held in open water on False Bay from Simonstown, saw no less than 400 dinghies out at the same time on three Olympic courses. There is a great stimulus among these eager-beavers to compete overseas, and in 1974, a typical season, thirty-eight crews campaigned overseas, travelling to California, Tahiti, Switzerland, Italy, Spain and England.

The strength of dinghy sailing was again well demonstrated at the end of 1975 when the provincial championships for the inland Transvaal or Highveld province saw a turnout of 450 boats in the various classes. At Plettenberg Bay on the coast the Hobie catamaran championship fielded 107 boats.

The speed, simplicity and ability for exciting launching through the surf has caused a boom in catamarans, bringing into sailing many people, including former powerboaters, who might otherwise never have been tempted by conventional dinghies.

The pioneer boating journal is the magazine *SA Yachting*, which has served the sport since 1958 and promoted many of the country's indigenous class boats; it has supported a team for the Admiral's Cup and been involved in a score of other ventures.

Apart from cruising South Africa's first properly organized effort in

102

ocean racing was in 1968 when the South African Ocean Racing Trust sent Bruce Dalling to compete in the Observer Singlehanded Transatlantic Race from Plymouth to Newport.

His 50ft ketch *Voortrekker* was used during the Royal Ocean Racing Club's season on nine international races in 1969 to train South Africans in the arts of deep-sea racing. This new interest culminated in January 1971 in South Africa's own first ocean race – 3,600 miles across the South Atlantic from Cape Town to Rio de Janeiro in Brazil. This is the third deep-sea classic in the southern hemisphere, joining the Buenos Aires to Rio Race of 1,200 miles and Australia's 600 mile Sydney to Hobart Race. It was sailed for the third time in January 1976 as part of the new Le Triangle Atlantique. This long-distance circuit of the two Atlantics uses the Cape Town to Rio Race as the second of three legs, the first being from St Malo, France to Cape Town, and the third from Rio to Portsmouth. Le Triangle Atlantique is strictly under ORC rules but designed to appeal to that growing body of ocean racers who find their deepest satisfaction in true passage races, rather than taking part in marathon events like the round-the-world and ocean solo races.

The Cape to Rio Race of 1971 was the first international race to be sailed under the then new IOR rating system, and there was a remarkable entry list of sixty-nine, with fifty-nine starters from eighteen countries. That year the race coincided with the Buenos Aires to Rio Race and the Iate Club do Rio de Janeiro was overwhelmed with the great concourse of ocean racers they had to cope with at their romantic Botafogo Bay clubhouse. Consequently, it was decided to run the Cape Town to Rio every three years, like the Buenos Aires to Rio, but never in the same year.

In spite of all the talk about the South Atlantic providing fluky breezes, the line winner in 1973 averaged 7.1 knots, which was the same as the Royal Navy's sloop *Adventure* in gale-force winds in the Cape Town to Sydney leg of the Whitbread Round the World Race. In 1976, when of the 140 yachts entered 124 actually started, Huey Long's fabulous 88ft ketch *Ondine* took the line honours by two hours from Eric Tabarly's *Pen Duick VI* at an average of 8.3 knots.

South Africa has entered teams in the Admiral's Cup series, finishing sixth in 1971, twelfth in 1973 and thirteen in 1975. With the enormous increase in costs and detail sophistication the Cruising Association of South Africa has never seriously hoped to repeat Australia's fine performance. The idea has been to keep competing with the best possible boats, try hard, and at least keep abreast of the hottest competition in world ocean racing. And, generally, that sums up the state of the game south of the Tropic of Capricorn in Africa.

Part II
Practical sailing

10
The boat

Peter Cook

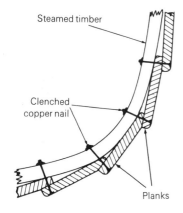

Steamed timber

Clenched copper nail

Planks

10.1 Clinker construction. The traditional method for boats up to about 20ft overall. Adjacent planks overlap throughout their length and are fastened with copper nails through steamed timbers.

Construction methods

From the time that the first yachts were built in the seventeenth century until the early 1950s most sailing craft were made of wood using the traditional construction methods employed for commercial or naval craft of similar size, the only difference being that a higher standard of finish was usually to be found in pleasure craft and, as boats were developed for racing, lighter scantlings were used.

From earliest times it has been possible to observe two broad divisions in the development of sea-going craft, especially smaller sea-going craft: a European type and a Baltic or Scandinavian type. European craft tend to be built on a skeletal structure, with a complex system of bones and ribs like most mammals. A central backbone, the keel, is the main source of strength and rigidity for the structure which is built up from the keel in a series of main ribs called the timbers or frames, and these are joined to each other by lesser 'bones', the stringers. Other main and lesser 'bones' (the stem, the sternpost, the deck beams and so on) are added, and finally the entire skeleton is given its skin, the planking. The main function of this skin is not to provide strength – that comes from the skeleton, although of course the skin does contribute – but simply to keep the water out.

The Scandinavian style of boatbuilding uses no such skeleton, but relies much more on the skin of the craft to provide strength for the structure. The craft has fewer 'bones', and sometimes none at all, even dispensing with the great spinal column of the keel and substituting a keel plank, at once part of both the bones and the skin.

Clinker

Small, open boats up to about 20ft overall in length were usually of clinker construction, that is, with overlapping planks held together by riveted copper nails and fastened to steamed timbers, as the ribs or frames are called. The planks are fitted closely together, but the seams rely upon the swelling of the wood after immersion in water to provide a completely watertight joint. Thus, when a clinker boat is first put afloat after having been out of the water for some time, it is likely that it will leak for a few days until it takes up.

A nearly completed traditional clinker-built dinghy. The overlapping solid mahogany planks are held together and to the transverse steamed timbers with copper nails. A flattish conical washer called a roove or rove is placed over the point of the nail inside, the surplus end of the nail snipped off and the end riveted over the roove. Two hanging knees tie the end of the thwart to the gunwale, and a quarter knee joins the transom to the gunwale.

Carvel

Carvel construction was usually adopted in boats above 20ft overall. The planks are fastened edge-to-edge on shaped frames or steamed timbers, thus giving a smooth outer surface to the hull. They are held to the timbers or frames with clenched (riveted) copper nails or bolts, or sometimes screws, and in the outer third of the seam between the planks a V-shape gap is left which is caulked with cotton and/or oakum and finished with putty or some other stopping to provide a watertight joint.

Very few traditionally built clinker and carvel boats are made today as more modern materials and methods have taken over, but a number of boatyards still specialize in this type of work and they are likely to survive as there is a growing demand for custom-built traditional wooden boats. In fact, in 1974 a magazine called *The Wooden Boat* was initiated in the USA dealing exclusively with the subject.

Double diagonal and triple skin

Another method of producing a smooth, wood hull is by using double diagonal planking. In this method the hull is planked with two layers of wood laid diagonally at approximately 45° to the keel, and at right angles to each other, over a temporary framework to produce the desired shape.

Double diagonal planking calls for a considerable number of fastenings as four clenched nails are used at each seam crossing as well as the fastenings holding the planking to the frames, etc. Sometimes the timbers are spaced further apart than they would be with the carvel construction method as some of the lateral strength of the hull is provided by the diagonal planking.

This form of construction became popular for building power craft and was used extensively during World War II for fast motor torpedo boats and other naval craft. Often the number of frames or timbers was reduced considerably, but a series of closely spaced stringers, running

Left Carvel construction. The main backbone of stem, keel, sternpost, deadwood and horn timber has been set up. Fore-and-aft ribbands have been fastened over a series of temporary transverse moulds. The steamed timbers have been formed to shape inside the ribbands.

Right Carvel construction. The temporary ribbands have been removed and replaced by planking. The timbers will be trimmed to gunwale level and the gunwale or beam shelf will be fitted.

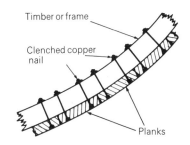

10.2 Carvel construction. The planks lie edge-to-edge.

Double diagonal construction. The first four diagonal planks have been fitted to the port side. A second layer of planks is laid over the first and at right angles to them. The framework ribbands laid over the transverse building moulds are inside the steamed timbers whereas those of the carvel boats on the preceding page are outside the timbers. When the planking is complete, the hull is turned over on top of its ballast keel. Bolts can be seen along the bottom of the keel. These hold the bottom parts of the floors in place and will be replaced by permanent keel-bolts which will also pass through the ballast keel

Double-chine plywood construction. This 11ft Gull is being built on a jig which is made to accept such parts as bulkheads, transom, centreboard case and thwart knees. The hog, chines and gunwales are attached, and this integral framework is faired in before the plywood panels are screwed and glued to it to provide a watertight hull.

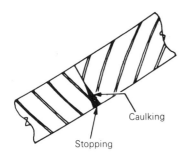

10.3 Carvel construction, seam detail.

fore-and-aft provided the main framework to which the planking was attached.

Triple-skin construction has also been used, often with the outer skin running fore-and-aft. Double-diagonal and triple-skin construction was used mainly for building specialist racing craft and fast power craft but has now been replaced by more modern methods – especially cold moulding. Many of the International Fourteens built in the 30s were of double-diagonal or treble-skin construction as it combined stiffness with light weight, but this was always a relatively expensive method.

The three methods of construction mentioned so far do not involve the use of glue, although it may be used to form laminated members of the main framework. To keep the water out double-diagonal and triple-skin construction rely upon the closeness of the seams between the planks, coupled with a waterproof layer of calico and white lead between the skins. Traditional clinker and carvel-built boats are essentially flexible and rely on the natural property of the wood to expand in water to provide a watertight hull. There are many people who will not consider any other form of construction, who gain most enjoyment from the ownership of a craftsman-built boat, and are prepared to tolerate the expenditure of both money and time needed for their upkeep. More modern techniques lend themselves to quantity production and amateur building and result in a boat requiring less maintenance.

Waterproof glue

During World War II a British aircraft, the Mosquito, was built of wood using an advanced form of construction which relied upon waterproof glue to hold it together. Waterproof glues were also used for the production of marine plywood which was used in the construction of naval patrol boats. The value of waterproof glues was soon appreciated by boatbuilders and this resulted in the first major change in construction techniques. It gave rise to three forms of glued construction – hard-chine plywood, moulded plywood, and strip planking.

Hard-chine plywood

A hard-chine boat is one in which the topsides and the bottom meet at an angle – the very simplest form having a box section in which the bottom is flat and the topsides are vertical. The main advantage of a hard-chine sailing boat is its ease of construction compared with a round-bottom boat, known as round bilge, making it more suitable for amateur building. By the same token it is an attractive proposition for yards without top quality labour.

Traditional carvel construction has been used for chine boats, the best example being the 15ft 6in Snipe, designed by American William F. Crosby in 1933, but the widespread availability of marine grade plywood saw the introduction of a large number of hard-chine boats designed specifically for plywood construction and equally suitable for building professionally on a production line basis or by amateurs from kits. In Australia and New Zealand plywood hard-chine construction has been developed to a very high state in a number of racing dinghies in which extremely low hull weights are achieved and has also been used successfully for larger boats. A later development was the double-chine hull which has three plywood panels on each side and more closely resembles a round-bilge hull form than can be produced with a single chine.

Glued clinker

Another variation of plywood construction is glued clinker in which the planks overlap as they do in a traditional clinker-built boat but are glued together at the lands, which is the term for the overlapping areas between adjacent planks. Neither frames nor steamed timbers are used, although the planks may be attached to bulkheads, floors and half

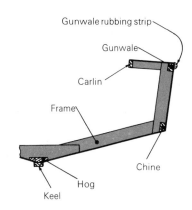

10.4 Hard-chine plywood construction. Frames, bulkheads and the transom are set up and held together with longitudinal members. This framework is faired up and planked with plywood panels.

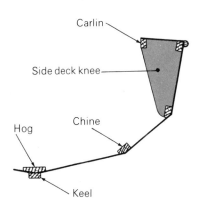

10.5 Double-chine plywood construction. Building frames, bulkheads and the transom are set up. The longitudinals are held temporarily to the frames and attached to the transom, bulkheads and stem; these are then faired up and covered with the plywood planking.

A professionally-built glued clinker hull with a kit of wooden parts ready for home completion. The boat is a 14ft Merlin Rocket restricted class dinghy. The boatbuilder has fitted the centreboard case and transverse frames on the inside of the hull to take the bulkheads. The amateur builder saves a considerable amount of money and knows that, however rough a job he makes of finishing the boat, the most important part, the hull, is soundly constructed, watertight and the correct shape.

frames. This construction method was adopted by some British racing dinghy classes, particularly the National Twelve and the 14ft Merlin Rocket whose rules required them to be clinker-built. In traditional clinker building the number of planks each side, usually ten or twelve, is dictated by the ability of the wood to resist splitting – fewer, wider planks would tend to split along their length. When plywood is used, the problem does not arise. It is possible to produce almost the same hull shape using four planks each side since the bottom and topside areas of most boats are relatively flat, most of the curvature occurring round the turn of the bilge. A glued clinker boat with four planks a side, therefore, is really a treble-chine boat, just one stage removed from a double-chine hull.

Moulded plywood
In moulded-plywood construction the hull is made up of three or more layers of wood veneer glued together over a temporary framework. As each veneer is relatively thin, it is possible to produce intricate shapes easily and lightly. Moulded plywood hulls have a high strength/weight ratio and are smooth both inside and out, while the absence of seams reduces considerably the risk of leaks and cuts down on maintenance. Examples of moulded-plywood hull designs are the 12ft Firefly one-design, designed by Uffa Fox and used as the singlehanded dinghy for the 1948 Olympic regatta at Torquay in England, the American Thistle and Luders 16 and many International Fourteen restricted class boats. Moulded-plywood construction has also been used widely for custom-built cruisers and offshore racing yachts.

Strip planking
The other form of glued construction is strip planking, in which narrow planks of almost square section are edge-glued and edge-fastened to each other over a framework of bulkheads and other structural components to which they are also attached. This produces a smooth hull without seams. It has only been used to a limited extent in Britain but, before the adoption of glassfibre construction, was more popular in the USA and was pioneered by Cyrus Hamlin of Maine.

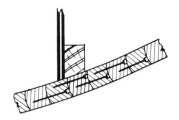

10.6 Strip planking. A framework consisting of bulkheads, transom, longitudinals and components such as bunk fronts is assembled and faired. The planks are nailed and glued both edge-to-edge and to the framework.

110

Steel

Steel has been used for yacht building but usually only in yachts over 60ft in length, except in the Netherlands where, at one time, many smaller yachts were also built in steel. The main disadvantage of building small yachts in steel is that the hull plating used is so thin that it dents easily, which is most unsightly, although the strength of the yacht may not be impaired. Another disadvantage is that the rate of corrosion of steel plating is the same for thin material as it is for thick, so a greater proportion of the plating will corrode away in a given period if it is thin rather than thick. However, there are some very reliable, if expensive, means of treating steel plating against the effects of corrosion.

Aluminium

After World War II when good boatbuilding timber was in short supply there was an interest in aluminium boats, but the material got a bad name because very often the aluminium used was surplus from aircraft construction and corroded as it was not of marine quality. Modern marine-grade aluminium alloy is perfectly suitable; advanced welding techniques have been developed which avoid unsightly riveted joints; and a very high-quality finish can be produced by yards specializing in this form of construction. Palmer Johnson in the USA, Allday Aluminium (a Camper and Nicholsons company) in Britain, and Walter Huissman in the Netherlands are leaders in the field. Although some small production craft are produced in aluminium, the use of the material is generally restricted to one-off ocean racers and larger, custom-built cruisers.

Glassfibre

(Correctly Glass Reinforced Plastics (GRP), also fibreglass and in the USA spelled fiberglass.)
Glassfibre construction has become increasingly popular since the mid 50s until today it is used in the construction of the majority of production sailing craft up to 75ft overall. A glassfibre hull is made by laying up a number of layers of glassfibre mat in a mould, impregnating each layer with resin; when the resin has cured, the moulded hull is removed.

Left Cold-moulded plywood construction. A temporary building mould is made, and the stem, keel or hog and transom fitted. A first layer of thin veneer planks is laid diagonally over the mould and stapled to it. These staples are driven through small offcuts of veneer so that they can be removed as the second layer of planking is laid at right angles to the first and glued to it. The hull is lifted off the mould and has a smooth finish both inside and out.

Right Aluminium construction. The inside of an aluminium offshore racer. The transverse frames have been formed to shape and are tied together fore-and-aft by a series of closely spaced stringers. The hull plating is fitted over this and all parts are welded together. Aluminium has become more popular recently for custom-built offshore racers because it provides a very stiff hull, well able to withstand the rigging loads and strains associated with top competition. Alterations to the shape can be made easily.

Glassfibre construction. Two stages in the building of 470 class dinghies. The boat in the background is still in its hull mould which holds the hull correctly to shape while the deck and interior mouldings are fitted. The cockpit moulding, consisting of side tanks and main bulkhead, is already in position, and the foredeck moulding is just being fitted. The dinghy in the foreground is almost completed.

The result is an integral resin structure which is reinforced with multi-directional strands of glass. Extra and localized stiffening can be achieved merely by increasing the number of layers of glassfibre in a particular area.

At first only small open dinghies were made of glassfibre and these were finished with wood trim. Later small cruisers were built of the material and they were decked and finished in wood. Today many production craft consist almost entirely of glassfibre mouldings – apart from the main hull and deck mouldings, there is often a host of sub-mouldings which result in a fully-lined accommodation with many details produced in glassfibre. The use of glassfibre has reduced the number of man-hours required to complete a boat, and the material is the most widely used for production craft the world over.

The great advantages of glassfibre construction are that it produces a smooth, seamless hull in which the only possible sources of leaks are the join between the hull and deck mouldings, the skin fittings, and around deck openings such as hatches; it requires little maintenance, at least during the first few years of its life. However, glassfibre is not as entirely maintenance free as the early builders of glassfibre boats would have had us believe. Glassfibre topsides of a boat can be left without painting for probably a period of roughly five years – less if the moulding is not of particularly good quality in the first place. Another advantage is that glassfibre can be used to produce shapes which would be difficult or impossible to achieve in wood, but intricate moulding details, although possible, are both difficult and expensive to reproduce and so are usually avoided.

In glassfibre boatbuilding the initial costs are fairly high as separate moulds have to be produced for all the component parts, and these have to be matched accurately so that the mouldings fit together on the finished job. The high initial development costs involved in glassfibre boatbuilding mean that reasonably long production runs must be assured for the boatbuilder to recover his initial outlay. These can vary from fifty units for a small dinghy down to as few as five for a 75-footer.

One of the disadvantages of glassfibre is that large, flat, unsupported areas flex rather easily. This tendency can be reduced by local internal stiffening but, in the case of the deck, this can be unsightly and, most significant in a small cruiser, can reduce the headroom in the accommodation. The most widely adopted method now used is to produce a sandwich moulding in which a layer of lightweight material (balsa wood or rigid plastics foam) is moulded between outer skins of glassfibre; this results in considerable stiffening of the panel with very little additional weight.

Sandwich

We have seen that fairly long production runs are necessary in glassfibre boatbuilding if the boatbuilder is to recover his initial costs. The normal method, therefore, in which separate moulds have to be made for each part, is ideal for the building of small one-designs and cruisers, but too expensive for individual large racing craft of which only a handful will be produced – and then only if the first boat is successful. For these boats foam sandwich construction is usually used in which a wooden framework is made of the shape of the boat and this is 'planked' with strips of rigid plastics foam on top of which glassfibre and resin is laminated. The wooden framework is then removed and the inside of the foam is coated with resin/glass laminate, thus producing a rigid glassfibre sandwich. This form of construction is popular with amateurs who are building just one boat.

C-Flex

C-Flex is a glassfibre composite reinforcing material which consists of a number of rods made of uni-directional glass fibres and resin which are themselves laid uni-directionally and incorporated into a woven glassfibre mat. The use of C-Flex enables one-off boats to be built satisfactorily from glassfibre without the need for expensive moulds.

A temporary framework is made by setting up a number of transverse wooden formers to produce the shape of the boat. The C-Flex is attached to the formers with the rigid glassfibre rods running fore-and-aft, thus producing a fair shape in the fore-and-aft direction. The shape athwartships is decided by the formers. A lamination of glassfibre and resin is then built up on the outside of the hull over the C-Flex covering. When the required thickness has been produced, the formers are removed and glassfibre and resin applied to the inside of the hull. The hull surface can then be rubbed down, filled, and painted to produce a perfect finish.

C-Flex is becoming increasingly popular for the construction of one-off racing boats and is a very suitable material for amateur use. With care a very high standard of finish can be obtained.

Stitch-and-glue

A construction technique developed with the home boatbuilder in mind is the stitch-and-glue method. It is usually used with hard-chine plywood designs, the joins between the panels and various structural members being held with glassfibre tape and resin rather than fillets of wood which have to be fitted accurately in order to ensure a watertight job.

C-Flex is popular for one-off and short production runs because no expensive glassfibre moulds are needed. C-Flex is a glassfibre woven mat with uni-directional glassfibre rods which take up the shape of the boat when the C-Flex is laid over the moulds. Resin is applied to the C-Flex, and further laminations can be built up using glassfibre mat and resin. The outer surface of the hull will not be as smooth as one from a glassfibre mould, but careful use of filler can produce an excellent finish.

113

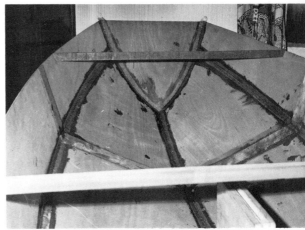

Stitch-and-glue construction.
Left The outside of the hull showing the copper wire ties which hold the hull panels together prior to taping the seams outside.

Right The inside of the hull after the seams have been taped with glassfibre and resin.

The plywood panels are cut accurately to shape and held together with loops of copper wire which are threaded through matching holes along the edges to be joined and then twisted. The inside of the join is coated with resin and one or more layers of glassfibre tape are laid over the join, thus producing a glassfibre laminate to connect the two pieces. When the glass lay-up has set, the wires are clipped off flush with the outside of the hull or removed, and a layer of resin and glass tape is applied to the outside of the join. Provided the plywood panels have been cut accurately to shape in the first place, very little fitting of the joint is called for as the glass tape and resin will ensure a good, watertight joint, even if the edges to be joined are somewhat rough. As the making of close-fitting, watertight joints is the most difficult job facing the home boatbuilder, stitch-and-glue construction is a boon to him.

Ferro-cement
Ferro-cement hulls consist basically of two layers of steel rod reinforcing laid at right angles to each other together with a number of layers of wire mesh over a temporary framework. The rod and wire mesh assembly is held together with wire ties and staples, and plastered with a strong cement mortar. The result is a strong, long-lasting structure. There are a considerable number of variations on the basic construction procedure.

Ferro-cement has been used as a boatbuilding material for many years but to a very limited extent. In fact, the first ferro-cement boat is credited to a Frenchman, Jean Louis Lambot, in 1848, and this boat can still be seen in the museum at Brignoles in the south of France. Some other early ferro-cement boats are still in existence, but generally the techniques were not wholly satisfactory. Ferro-cement has been used in ship construction, especially towards the end of World War I and during World War II, but the resulting crumbling hulks left lying round the world gave the material a bad name. It was not until fairly recently, in the 60s, that more advanced techniques were understood and adopted, and ferro-cement is now a perfectly acceptable construction material for small craft. Like any other material it has its limitations, the most serious being that it is a relatively heavy form of construction and so is unsuitable for high-performance yachts where a ratio of 40% to 50% between the weight of the ballast keel and the total weight of the hull structure is normally called for. However, ferro-cement is suitable for the construction of cruising yachts and commercial craft.

Other materials

The most recent development in boatbuilding materials has been in the field of moulded plastics. One material that has been used for small boats is high density (5lb per cu ft) expanded polystyrene which has the advantage of low cost and light weight, but its surface must be protected against petrol and other substances which dissolve it, and being very soft its impact resistance is low. While its light weight is an advantage when handling a boat ashore, it is a disadvantage afloat, as the boat floats high out of the water which causes considerable windage and makes handling of the boat extremely difficult in any strength of wind. The most successful use of expanded polystyrene has been in the construction of sailing surfboards which are skinned with glassfibre to provide a hard surface.

Vacuum-formed ABS sheet is used successfully for the production of small, open dinghies, especially in France. A sheet of ABS plastics is placed over a mould and heated while a vacuum process forms the sheet to the shape of the mould. One problem facing designers is that where the ABS is formed over a corner, which adds desirable stiffening to the finished boat, the sheet reduces in thickness which is not so desirable. But the snags are being overcome, and in France a small family cruiser is produced in ABS. With present methods, long production runs are needed to recover the quite expensive tooling costs involved, but this is one of the fields in which future changes in boatbuilding production methods may occur.

Injection moulded polypropylene

The first injection moulded polypropylene boats produced anywhere in the world were made in Britain in 1976 to an existing Ian Proctor design for a cross between a dinghy and a beach boat, the 11ft 2in Topper sailing dinghy. Polypropylene mouldings are made from matching male and female moulds under pressure in a large injection machine, one moulding being produced every few minutes.

The advantages claimed for injection moulding are that it is a low cost process; that it has high speed production – one boat every seven minutes in the case of the Topper – using polypropylene which is the cheapest of the thermoplastic materials available. Complicated features can easily be reproduced in the moulding, and strict accuracy of weight and dimensions is assured.

The planned production of the Topper was 1,000 boats a month, the level of production necessary to justify the high initial outlay of £250,000 ($500,000) compared to a mere £100,000 ($200,000) for tooling and development costs for a luxury 70ft glassfibre production cruising yacht! However, the price of the boat is very competitive, being 20% to 30% less than the comparable product in glassfibre.

Ferro-cement construction. The steel rod reinforcing and layers of wire mesh ready for plastering with cement mortar.

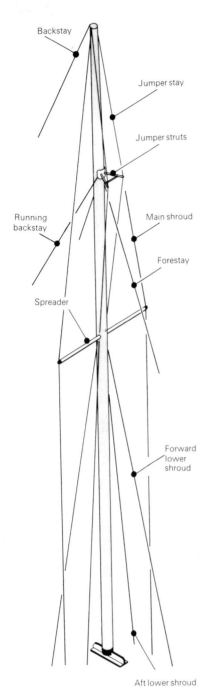

Backstay

Jumper stay

Jumper struts

Running
backstay

Main shroud

Forestay

Spreader

Forward
lower
shroud

Aft lower shroud

10.7 Standing rigging arrangement for mast of three-quarter sloop.

Opposite With her bigboy nearly dragging in the water the German Admiral's Cup team boat *Pinta* runs up the Solent during the 1975 Admiral's Cup series.

Deck construction

Deck construction usually follows that of the hull, in wooden boats a series of deck beams forming the 'main frames'. Traditionally, the deck was laid with planks running fore-and-aft or, in the best quality yacht construction, following the sweep of the deck edge. Seams between the planks are caulked, in the manner of carvel hull planking, and finished by paying them with marine glue – a black, pitch-like substance that has to be applied hot and scraped flush with the surface when hard (not to be confused with waterproof glue used for joining pieces of wood).

Laid decks are expensive to produce, and there is always the risk of leaks if the seams are not well maintained, so plywood is now used almost universally. It may be painted or, for the most attractive and hard-wearing finish, a thin layer of teak planks may be laid on top, giving the appearance of a traditional laid deck. Instead of marine glue a synthetic rubber compound is now used in the seams which is longer lasting, cleaner to apply, and unlikely to crack as it gives to the movement of the wood.

A cheap form of wood deck used before the introduction of marine plywood was tongued-and-grooved softwood boards covered with painted canvas. This is fine until the canvas rots and the ingress of water causes the deck itself to rot. Most boats have decks which match the hull material employed – they may be of plywood, glassfibre, steel or aluminium, but all can be covered with wood.

The rig

Sailing boats are frequently classified by their rig, a term which includes spars, rigging and sails. The number of masts, their relative size and position, and the type of sails vary according to the rig. Thus a bermudan sloop, the most common type of boat, has one mast stepped a little forward of amidships and sets a single headsail and a triangular bermudan mainsail, but a gaff cutter sets two headsails forward of her single mast and a quadrilateral mainsail on a gaff. Yawls, ketches and schooners all have two masts, but whereas the schooner's mainmast is as tall as or taller than her foremast, the mainmasts of ketches and yawls are stepped forward of their shorter mizzen masts. The more usual rigs are illustrated on page 123.

Spars

Solid wooden spars were used for many years but were superseded by hollow wooden masts and booms. The great advantage of hollow spars is lightness, especially up high, for weight aloft affects stability adversely. Today most masts and booms are made of aluminium alloy, strong and light, but very noisy when halyards whip against them. The making of spars has become a highly specialized business, far removed from the craftsman shipwright who earlier shaped wooden spars by eye. The shapes of masts vary greatly, round, oval and pear-shape being the most usual. In addition to light weight and strength, aerodynamic efficiency is vital if the sail is to give maximum drive. Many high-performance modern rigs call for masts which can be bent so that the

116

shape of the sails can be adjusted, and there has been a vogue for bendy booms as well. Masts can be stepped on deck, but those which are stepped on the keel are supported by partners at deck level. Other spars, such as spinnaker and jib booms, bowsprits and bumkins, are generally made of wood in older boats, but the spars of modern boats are more usually aluminium alloy.

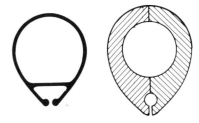

Standing rigging

Apart from some small centreboard dinghies and a few racing classes such as the Finn, masts are supported by standing rigging consisting of stays, which provide fore-and-aft support, and shrouds which provide lateral support. Some boats, such as many three-quarter rigged sloops, also carry running backstays which lead aft from the hounds to the quarters. The standing rigging of small boats may consist simply of two shrouds led slightly aft of the mast and a forestay, but the taller the mast the more complex the standing rigging, with two or three pairs of shrouds, at least one pair of spreaders and, perhaps, diamonds or jumper stays to support the top of the mast.

The tension of standing rigging is normally adjusted by means of rigging screws, the length of which can be increased or decreased. In some boats special gadgets may be fitted to enable the tension of the shrouds to be altered under way. Fittings, especially those on the mast, should be light and streamlined to reduce windage.

Running rigging

Whereas standing rigging is usually set up permanently and, apart from running backstays and boats with adjustable shrouds, is normally adjusted only when the boat is moored, running rigging controls and trims the sails under way. The halyards, which hoist the sails, may be of rope in small dinghies or, more usually, of wire, often with a rope tail. The sheets control the angle of the sails to the centreline and are usually entirely rope, but some large genoas have wire sheets with large diameter rope tails to make handling easier. The downhaul adjusts the luff tension while the outhaul controls foot tension. Vangs or kicking straps prevent the boom rising when the sail is eased out and help to control twist in a sail. Topping lifts are used to take the weight of the main boom when hoisting, reefing or lowering the mainsail.

Sails

A square sail is a rare sight nowadays but is sometimes set on an ocean cruiser for trade-wind work. Occasionally a replica of some famous old square-rigged vessel, or a sail training ship may be seen, although most of the latter are fore-and-aft rigged. Gaff sails, on the other hand, are still found in most harbours, and a certain category of sailor would not wish to own any vessel other than a traditional, heavy-displacement, gaff-rigged boat. They may be slow and cumbersome and require a great deal of maintenance, but their character and individuality give most sailors more pleasure than the sight of a dozen stock-production yachts – especially if someone else is doing the work. Today, virtually all boats are bermudan-rigged.

10.8 *Above* Cross-section of hollow spars: *(left)* an extruded aluminium section with integral track to take the bolt rope; *(right)* a hollow wooden mast made up of two pieces of wood which are hollowed out before being glued together.

10.9 *Below* The parts of a bermudan sail.

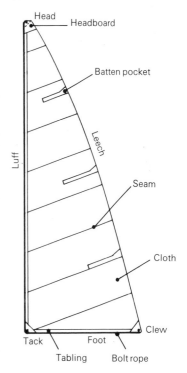

Opposite Two catamarans, a Hobie 16 (nearest camera) and a Nacara racing in a Miami midwinter regatta.

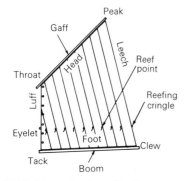

10.10 The parts of a gaff sail.

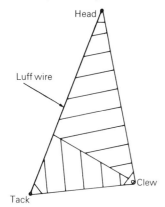

10.11 A mitre-cut foresail.

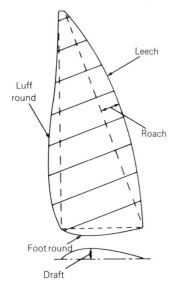

10.12 Because a sail has to set in a curve, the luff and foot will not lie in straight lines when the sail is spread out on the floor. Curvature in the sail is provided by shaping the edges of the individual cloths before they are stitched together.

Sail cloth is made in different weights and is measured in ounces per square yard of cloth or grammes per square metre. The heavier cloths are used for larger boats and for stronger winds. Lightweight cloth used for smaller boats and gentler breezes sets better in lighter winds, but is blown out of shape when the wind pipes up.

The basic sails, the working sails, are those which a boat sets when beating to windward in moderate to fresh breezes – mainsail and headsail in the case of a sloop, plus the mizzen in a ketch or yawl. They are made of moderately heavy cloth. The genoa was originally used only in light and moderate breezes, but in modern rigs a large overlapping genoa is often still set with reefed mainsail in heavier winds. The sails set for off-the-wind courses – spinnakers, tallboys, big boys, mizzen staysails and spinnaker staysails – are made of lighter cloth, while heavy weather sails – trysail and storm jib – are of much heavier cloth.

Sail cloth used to be cotton or flax, but today most cloth is woven from artificial fibres such as Dacron (Terylene) or nylon. While Dacron is favoured for fore-and-aft sails, experiments with such a stable cloth for spinnakers have not proved successful, and nylon is preferred for its elasticity. Natural fibres shrink and stretch as they get wet and dry out, and the sails require careful drying because they are subject to mildew. Artificial fibres do not rot, although they are affected by ultra-violet rays.

The sailmaker's task is to build a sail to the shape required, suitable for the conditions in which it will be set, with the desired degree of fullness in the place where it is wanted. Because the characteristics of sail cloth vary widely, he has first to select the right weight and the right type of cloth for the particular sail. There are open weave and tightly woven cloths, cloths in which the warp and weft are of different denier, cloths which are filled with chemicals and cured, and cloths with no synthetic fillers. Some cloths are more stable on the bias and will resist tension at 45° to the warp and weft; others recover their shape well after being subjected to strain. It will be no good, for example, using a cloth for a mainsail which is liable to stretch vertically along the weft, for it will not withstand the considerable tension applied to the leech. Equally, if a cloth is liable to distort on the bias, it should not be used for a jib with horizontal panels, for here much of the strain is diagonally across the sail, at right angles to the luff.

The sailmaker then has to cut the sail to the shape required. In fig. 10.12 straight lines run from the tack to the clew and head, but if a mainsail with the same dimensions is spread out as flat as possible on the floor it will overlap all three lines. The overlap aft of the line between head and clew, the roach, is extended by battens and is often generous because it usually ranks as unmeasured sail area. The overlap forward of the line between head and tack is the luff round, and that between tack and clew, the foot round. When set on the spars this spare material is pushed back into the sail behind the mast and above the boom as fullness. The greater the amount of spare material the fuller the sail. The sail will not lie absolutely flat when laid on the floor because the individual cloths that make up the sail are tapered, and this affects both the degree of draft or fullness and the position of maximum

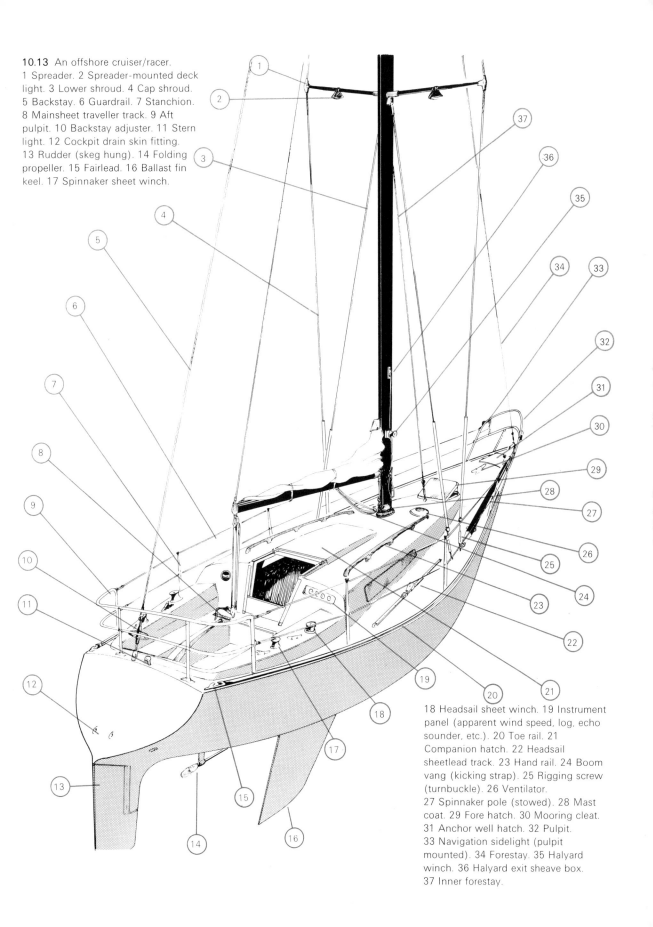

10.13 An offshore cruiser/racer. 1 Spreader. 2 Spreader-mounted deck light. 3 Lower shroud. 4 Cap shroud. 5 Backstay. 6 Guardrail. 7 Stanchion. 8 Mainsheet traveller track. 9 Aft pulpit. 10 Backstay adjuster. 11 Stern light. 12 Cockpit drain skin fitting. 13 Rudder (skeg hung). 14 Folding propeller. 15 Fairlead. 16 Ballast fin keel. 17 Spinnaker sheet winch.

18 Headsail sheet winch. 19 Instrument panel (apparent wind speed, log, echo sounder, etc.). 20 Toe rail. 21 Companion hatch. 22 Headsail sheetlead track. 23 Hand rail. 24 Boom vang (kicking strap). 25 Rigging screw (turnbuckle). 26 Ventilator. 27 Spinnaker pole (stowed). 28 Mast coat. 29 Fore hatch. 30 Mooring cleat. 31 Anchor well hatch. 32 Pulpit. 33 Navigation sidelight (pulpit mounted). 34 Forestay. 35 Halyard winch. 36 Halyard exit sheave box. 37 Inner forestay.

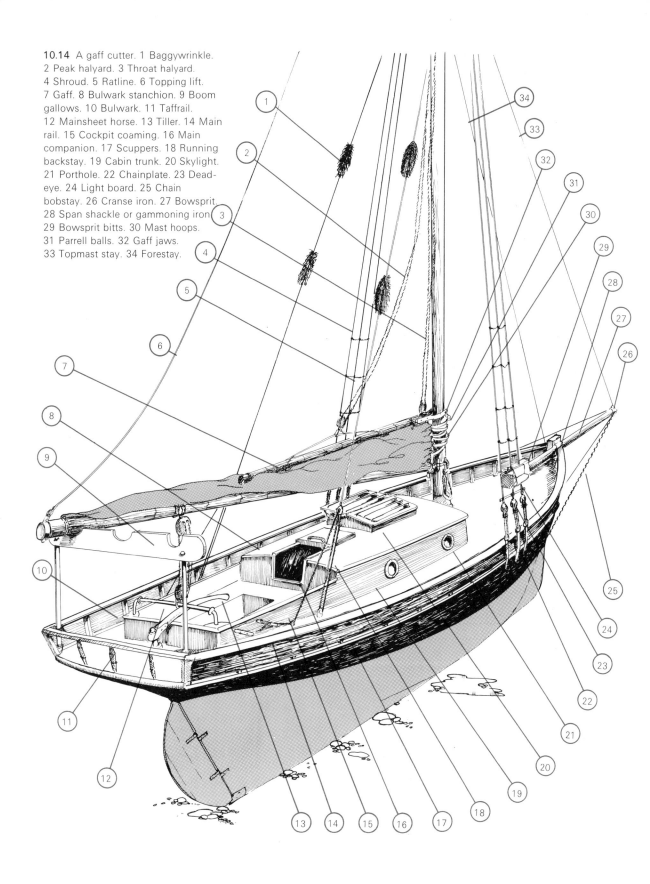

10.14 A gaff cutter. 1 Baggywrinkle.
2 Peak halyard. 3 Throat halyard.
4 Shroud. 5 Ratline. 6 Topping lift.
7 Gaff. 8 Bulwark stanchion. 9 Boom
gallows. 10 Bulwark. 11 Taffrail.
12 Mainsheet horse. 13 Tiller. 14 Main
rail. 15 Cockpit coaming. 16 Main
companion. 17 Scuppers. 18 Running
backstay. 19 Cabin trunk. 20 Skylight.
21 Porthole. 22 Chainplate. 23 Deadeye. 24 Light board. 25 Chain
bobstay. 26 Cranse iron. 27 Bowsprit.
28 Span shackle or gammoning iron.
29 Bowsprit bitts. 30 Mast hoops.
31 Parrell balls. 32 Gaff jaws.
33 Topmast stay. 34 Forestay.

draft. Broadly speaking, full sails give more drive in light airs, and
flatter sails are preferable in stronger winds. Boats, therefore, may carry
several sails, particularly headsails and spinnakers, of varying weight to
suit different wind strengths and of varying cut to suit different points of
sailing.

Whereas some boats carry a different mainsail for light and heavy
weather, others use only one mainsail and adjust its shape by altering
the tension of the controls and, sometimes, by bending the spars. Clearly,
if a sailmaker is to produce a sail which fulfils the owner's purpose,
there has to be real understanding between them as to what is required.

10.15 Rigs.

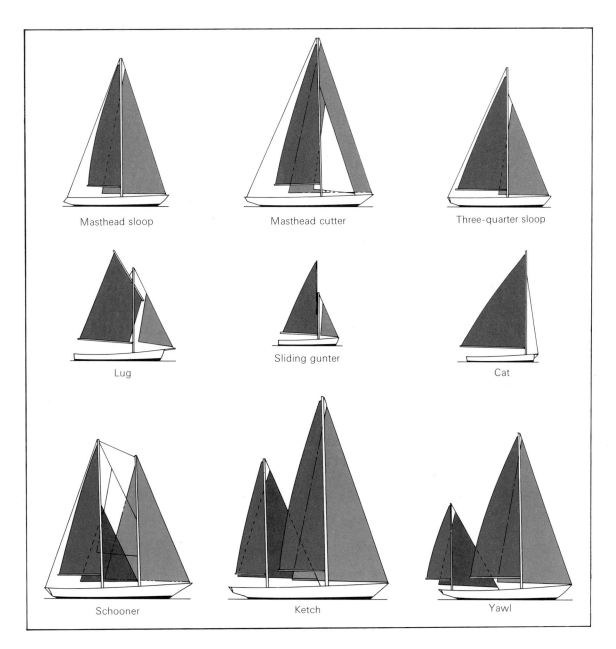

Masthead sloop — Masthead cutter — Three-quarter sloop — Lug — Sliding gunter — Cat — Schooner — Ketch — Yawl

11
Before going sailing

Barbara Webb

When invited for a first sail

Every sailor has to sail for a first time, often as a result of an invitation from a friend, and he will enjoy his first trip far more if he knows just a little about sailing beforehand. The boat may be anything from a small sailing dinghy to a large well-equipped motor sailer, so the first thing is to find out what type of boat is involved, whether there are other members of the crew, and whether the skipper knows that he is inviting a beginner. It will do no harm to offer to take food and drink, and to be prepared to contribute towards expenses. Many sailors run their boats on a shoe-string, and the skipper will not be pleased if he has to share his sandwiches.

Sailing, to the uninitiated, often conjures up visions of smooth seas and sunshine, with a bikini-clad girl reclining lazily on the foredeck; reality is usually very different. A sailing boat cannot move without wind and where there is wind there are waves. Inevitably, on many days a crew will become cold and wet – but will always be expected to work hard. Clothing must keep him warm and dry: comfortable trousers with narrow bottoms that do not catch on cleats or other parts of the boat, or shorts if it is likely to be hot (unless sunburn is a problem for the sun reflects off the water and sailors are therefore more liable to sunburn than landlubbers), a shirt and thick woollen sweaters, as well as really efficient waterproof jacket and trousers, but no long scarves or loose belts to catch in winches. Traditional oilskins are heavy and hinder movement, but modern PVC or nylon clothing is light and effective, particularly if a small towel is worn round the neck to prevent drops of water trickling down. A waterproof hood or sou'wester is recommended, and a wide-brimmed sun-hat if the sun is strong.

The right shoes are essential: smooth rubber soles are useless because they slip on wet decks and brightwork. There are several makes of sailing shoes with patterned rubber soles which grip well.

A good clasp knife with a spike or shackle spanner should be worn on a lanyard round the waist so that it is always at hand to tighten shackle pins properly. A pin that is only finger-tight soon works out of a shackle when the sails slat, and it is embarrassing, to say the least, when a halyard shackle comes adrift, for the sail falls into the water and someone has to climb to the top of the mast to retrieve the halyard.

The owner will probably provide personal buoyancy (personal flotation, PFDs) equipment for a friend sailing for the first time; if not this must be borrowed. However good a swimmer the crew may be, he should always wear a life-jacket in sailing dinghies; a thump on the head from the boom can send him flying overboard unconscious, so the jacket must be able to support the wearer face upwards in the water when concussed. Larger boats usually have bow and stern pulpits and lifelines rigged round the boat on to which the crew can hold. The golden rule is 'one hand for the ship and one hand for yourself', for a crew who falls overboard is worse than useless.

Because stowage space aboard is limited, personal gear should be kept to a minimum, although a complete change of clothes should always be taken in case of a capsize or a drenching from spray. If you are going to

A triple block. This well-designed American fitting has injection-moulded plastic cheeks and sheaves and is bound with stainless-steel side plates for strength.

124

live on board, pack your clothes in a bag – suitcases are almost impossible to stow, and, as there is little hanging room, shore-going clothes should be uncrushable. All personal belongings should be put away in the locker or space allocated and not left lying around.

Every item of equipment is stowed in a particular place so that it can be found instantly when required. For this reason it is important to find out where something lives before hiding it away.

A new crew usually feels useless at first, but if he looks willing and has learned a few basic skills, he will soon be given a job. He should know how to belay a rope on a cleat, how to coil a rope, and how to tie, at least, a reef knot, a bowline and a round turn and two half hitches (see pp. 128–30). A basic vocabulary helps him understand instructions. For a start: port and starboard – not left and right – forward, aft, amidships, windward and leeward. The parts of a sailing dinghy are illustrated in figure 1.1, and those of a keelboat in figures 10.13 and 10.14. A few verbs are essential, too – make fast, hoist, harden, or trim in, ease out, belay.

The landlubber often sneers at a sailor's insistence on using the correct word, but nautical language is not used to impress; it is precise and concise – it has to be, because events occur so rapidly. Commands are given succinctly and often vehemently. They must be obeyed instantly if the boat is to be sailed efficiently. There is time enough for questions when an emergency is over, and the boat is sailing peacefully. DO arrive on time: if the owner wants to set off at a certain time, it may be due to the time of high water. He will not like waiting about anyway, but he will be mad if he misses his tide.

DO carry out instructions instantly and without question.

DO forgive the skipper if he speaks with less courtesy than you normally expect. He has a lot on his mind and may not have time to say please.

DO keep out of everybody's way until you know how you can help or are told what to do.

DO watch other people: it is the quickest way to learn.

DON'T stand on the dinghy gunwale: the dinghy will capsize.

DON'T stand in the companionway, or you will be in the way of people coming on deck or going below.

DON'T forget to duck when the boom comes over: it is hard and it hurts.

DON'T stand on or in a coiled rope such as a genoa sheet. If the sail is let fly, you could be whisked overboard.

DON'T be tempted to stay below too long unless you are the fortunate possessor of a cast-iron stomach and are never seasick. When feeling queasy, don't watch the waves going up and down close alongside, but look at the distant horizon.

DON'T rush off at the end of a cold, wet sail to change into warm, dry clothes until you have helped to put the boat to bed.

A final warning: all sailors are individualists and hold strong opinions on the right and wrong methods of doing even the smallest jobs. A learner will find it best to imitate his skipper and will soon find out by experience which really is the best method – in his opinion. Even experts often disagree!

A snap shackle is used for spinnaker sheets and many controls that need to be attached and detached when sailing. The large eye swivels and is attached to the sheet or control, while the snap shackle is opened by pulling the plunger ring on the right. The shackle closes when the hooked part is pushed on to the spring-loaded pin which automatically engages in the hole.

A Clamcleat. A simple and effective way of jamming a line which is pulled to the left into the vee and held down. The line is guided into the vee by the angled ridges. To release, give a sharp tug upwards against the load.

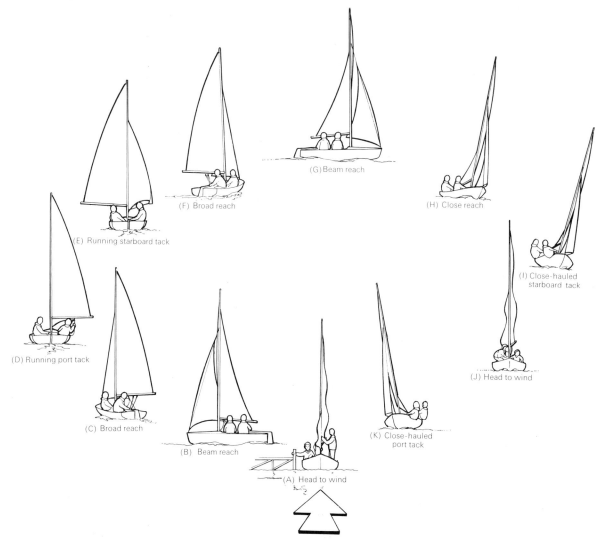

11.1 Points of sailing.

Sailing points

When standing on the end of a pier with the wind from the shore, boats will be seen sailing on the water heading in different directions, some sailing away from the land, some along the coast, some towards it. The wind is blowing from the same direction, but the boats' sails are trimmed according to their courses. Consider a two-man sailing dinghy setting off from the pier to sail a circular course.

With sails hoisted and the crew aboard the boat is held by her painter to the pier, ready to set off. The sails are slatting because she is lying *head to wind* (fig. 11.1a). The crew lets go, pushing the bow of the boat to starboard, the mainsail soon fills with wind, and the boat gathers way and answers the helm. A boat has to be moving forwards or backwards through the water before she will react to the helm. When the tiller is put to port, the rudder moves to starboard, and the water flowing past the boat meets the rudder. If the boat is moving forwards, this pushes the stern to port while the bows swing to starboard, but if the water is flowing in the opposite direction when the boat is making sternway, it forces the stern to starboard and the bows to port.

In figure 11.1b the wind is blowing from the beam striking the port side of the boat first. The boat is therefore sailing on a *beam reach on port tack* with the boom to starboard. Helmsman and crew are sitting to *windward* on the port gunwale (rail) to keep her level, and the sails are eased out about half-way.

The helmsman now *bears away* by pulling the tiller towards him which causes the bows to move to starboard; both jib and mainsail are eased and the crew sits *amidships* or to *leeward* because the pressure of the wind does not cause the boat to *heel* so much. She is *broad-reaching* on port tack with the wind on her port quarter (fig. 11.1c). Bearing away further until the wind is right aft, the helmsman lets the mainsail out as far as it will go before the boom touches the shrouds, and the jib flaps because it is blanketed by the mainsail and no wind reaches it. The crew sits to leeward to counteract the weight of the helmsman because there is no lateral pressure from the wind. The boat is *running* on port tack (fig. 11.1d).

The helmsman bears away still further, and the bows continue to turn to starboard until the moment comes when the wind strikes the sail on the opposite side, causing mainsail and boom to swing over suddenly through nearly 180° from starboard to port. The boat has *gybed* and is now running on *starboard tack*, dead before the wind. The crew leaves the jib sheeted to starboard, holding it out to windward with a jib stick (whisker pole) to catch the wind (fig. 11.1e). Helmsman and crew have changed sides so that the helmsman is sitting to starboard on the *weather* side of the boat, and the crew to port.

To continue the circle the helmsman puts the tiller down, away from him, and the boat *luffs up* towards the wind until she is on a broad reach again with the wind on her starboard *quarter* (fig. 11.1f). She is broad-reaching on starboard tack, the wind striking the starboard side first, and the crew joins the helmsman on the windward side of the boat to counteract the force of the wind on the sail.

Luffing further until the wind is abeam and hardening the sheets, the boat is soon on a beam reach, starboard tack (fig. 11.1g). The helmsman luffs again until the wind is at an angle of about 50° to the course, and the sheets are trimmed in to match. The boat is on a *close reach*, starboard tack (fig. 11.1h). The wind feels fresher and, for the first time, blows from forward of the beam.

The time has come to sail back to the pier which is some way to windward, so the boat now has to be sailed as close to the wind as possible. Sheets are hardened fully, the crew and helmsman sit out (hike out) on the weather gunwale in the gusts, and the helmsman points higher until the jib is only just full. The boat is *close-hauled* on starboard tack (fig. 11.1i). She stays on this tack for some time, but it is obvious that she cannot sail to the pier on this course. Consequently, when the pier is abeam to starboard, the helmsman *tacks*. He puts down the tiller,

127

11.2 Hauling.

11.3 Sweating up.

11.4 Belaying a rope on a cleat.

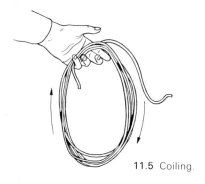

11.5 Coiling.

turning the bows to starboard towards the wind, and the crew lets the jib sheet fly. As she comes head to wind, the sails slat (fig. 11.1j), and the helmsman and crew transfer their weight to the new weather gunwale to port. With the tiller still over to port the bow continues to turn to starboard until the mainsail and jib fill, and the boat starts to gather way again, *close-hauled on port tack* (fig. 11.1k).

When he is a boat's length or two away from the pier, the helmsman luffs up head to wind, and the boat's way carries her to the pier with sails shaking, ready to tie up.

Handling rope aboard

On board a sailing boat rope has to be ready to use at any moment, and there must be no kinks or snarls to prevent it running through blocks or fairleads. It is coiled neatly by holding the rope in one hand and forming loops of similar size with the other (fig. 11.5). The landlubber's method of forcibly winding rope around thumb and elbow should never be used because it does not allow for the natural twist in the rope, and when taken off the elbow, some of the coils will cross each other. To coil rope start at the end which is made fast and work towards the loose end so that kinks shake free naturally. A very large, heavy rope should be coiled carefully on deck. All stranded ropes with a right-hand lay should be coiled clockwise and left-hand lay ropes anti- or counter-clockwise. On all ropes a single twist is required for each coil to prevent kinks. If a coil is to be hung on a cleat, the part of the rope nearest the cleat is passed through all the loops, given a twist or two, and then hooked on to the cleat, thus keeping the whole coil tidily in place (fig. 11.6).

To belay a rope on a cleat first take a complete round turn, followed by one or more figures of eight, and finally another round turn to lock the previous turns (fig. 11.4).

Handling ropes is often very hard work, particularly when sheeting in the genoa or raising the anchor, and the crew has to put his back into the job. Braced against a solid part of the boat, he can use his leg muscles and his weight as he leans back on the rope (fig. 11.2). A light crew using his weight correctly can be more efffctive than a strong man using only his biceps, and the use of leg muscles protects the back from strain. A rope being paid out must be kept under control all the time and eased out hand over hand, for a rope running fast through the hands burns them.

Many boats have no halyard winch, and the crew has to sweat up the sails, taking half a turn round the cleat with one hand and holding fast while the other hand heaves the standing part of the halyard away from the mast, thus pulling the sail higher (fig. 11.3). The slack is then pulled in round the cleat, and the process repeated until the sail is fully hoisted. In a large boat this is a two-man job, one on the tail of the halyard, the other using his weight on the standing part.

Because the load on the sheets is so great, the crew need mechanical assistance to control them. Sheet winches are used for jib and genoa sheets in larger boats, while in the bigger dinghies jam cleats are fitted to hold the sheets and take the strain from the crew. The drum of a winch rotates in one direction but is prevented from running back in the other by a ratchet or similar device. Two or three turns are taken round the winch drum, and as much of the sheet as possible is pulled in by hand. When the load is too great to continue by hand, the winch handle is inserted into its socket and the sheet is hardened home. The sheet must be led to the bottom of the drum, and each turn on the winch drum must lie neatly above its predecessor (fig. 11.7) to prevent riding turns when a later turn crosses an earlier turn above it causing the sheet to jam.

Two people normally operate a winch, one hauling on the sheet, and the other turning the handle, but the job can be done single-handed if the load is not excessive. A simple winch can be wound in only one direction at one speed, but more complicated winches used on large boats can have up to three speeds and a facility to turn the drum backwards under load. If the drum cannot be turned back, the sheet must be eased gradually by palming the turns round the drum. If they are merely flipped off the top of the drum under load, the sail will take control. After the sail has been sheeted home, the sheet is turned up on a cleat, and the winch handle removed and stowed in a safe place. If it is left in the winch, it can be knocked overboard and lost, or may fly round and hit the crew.

In a small dinghy the mainsail may be controlled by a simple sheeting arrangement. The mainsheet is attached to the transom on one side, passes through a single block on the end of the boom, down through another single block on the other side of the transom, and thence to the helmsman's hand. This gives a mechanical advantage of two to one. Larger dinghies have double or treble sheave blocks to give greater mechanical advantage, and some systems are fitted to the middle of the boom to help control the twist in the mainsail. In larger keelboats there is usually a winch for the mainsheet, but this is much smaller than that for the genoa as the loads involved are much less.

Knots, bends and hitches

There is a correct knot for every purpose on board, and the knots, bends and hitches used by seamen have stood the test of time and weather. They must fulfil several requirements: they must not come undone when the rope is shaken; they must not slip under tension; they must not jam; and they must be easy to undo.

FIGURE OF EIGHT OR STOPPER KNOT (fig. 11.8): This is tied in the end of a sheet to prevent it running out through a fairlead or block. An overhand knot should not be used as it jams.

CLOVE HITCH (fig. 11.9): A very useful hitch for attaching rope to a pole and for the burgee halyard.

BOWLINE (fig. 11.10): Used to make a loop which will not slip; it can be used for mooring lines and many other purposes.

REEF KNOT (fig. 11.11): Traditionally used for tying reef points together, for sail ties and similar purposes when rope or lines of the same size have to be joined. A granny knot should never be used; invariably it will slip or jam. A reef knot can usually be freed by pulling back sharply on one of the ends, thereby 'breaking the back' of the knot.

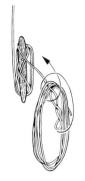

11.6 Hanging a coiled rope on a cleat.

11.7 Turns on a winch.

11.8 Figure-of-eight knot.

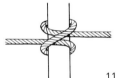

11.9 Clove hitch.

11.10 Bowline.

11.11 Reef knot.

11.12 Round turn and two half hitches.

ROUND TURN AND TWO HALF HITCHES (fig. 11.12): A useful and simple method of tying a rope to a ring or a post. The load is taken on the round turn so the two half hitches do not jam.

FISHERMAN'S BEND (fig. 11.13): This is very similar to the round turn and two half hitches, but the first half hitch is taken through the round turn as well. Used to attach a rope to an anchor.

DOUBLE SHEET BEND (fig. 11.14): A most useful bend used to join ropes of very different sizes.

These traditional seamen's knots have always been used with natural fibre ropes, but the smooth surface of modern ropes made of synthetic fibres means that they are more liable to slip and knots should be tied with particular care. For example, it may be advisable to add a half hitch to a bowline when leaving a dinghy moored for a long period.

11.13 Fisherman's bend.

11.14 Double sheet bend.

12 Sailing and seamanship

Barbara Webb

12.1 Hoisting the burgee.

A single block with swivel at one end and a single becket at the other.

A cam jam cleat. The two cams are spring-loaded so that they open when a rope is pulled over them.

Preparing for a sail

The burgee

The motive power of a sailing boat is the wind: its direction dictates where a boat can sail, and its strength dictates the speed of the boat and the amount of sail that she can carry. Before hoisting any sails it is important to know from which direction the wind is blowing, so the first job is to hoist a small flag to the masthead. This may be a triangular burgee, some other masthead fly, or in some countries a rectangular racing flag. In small dinghies the burgee may be fixed into a socket at the top of the mast or gaff, or may be fitted to the headboard of the sail, but more usually it is hoisted on its own halyard. Uncleat the halyard, ensure that it is clear of all obstructions and running freely with no twists in it, and then attach it to the burgee stick with a couple of clove hitches. The upper clove hitch should be sufficiently far down the stick to enable the burgee to stand clear above the mainsail and mast (fig. 12.1). Hoist the burgee, watching all the time to see that it does not foul anything on the way up, and secure the halyard to its cleat.

Before hoisting any sails it is usual to bend on all those that are going to be used.

The mainsail

A triangular bermudan mainsail is hoisted by a halyard attached to the head, while the tack is attached to the boom close by the gooseneck, and the clew to the after end of the boom. There are several ways of holding the luff of the mainsail close to the mast and the foot to the boom. In a simple dinghy the luff may be laced to the mast, and the sail may be loose-footed, connected to the boom only at tack and clew. The mainsail luff of some old-fashioned boats is attached to mast hoops which slide up and down the mast, while the foot is laced to the boom. Many cruising boats and some dinghies have slides sewn on to the luff and foot; these slide along tracks on the mast and boom. In most racing dinghies and sailing craft the luff and foot of the mainsail are held to mast and boom by sliding the bolt ropes into grooves in the spars which are usually metal but may be of wood.

Whatever method is used the essential is that there should be no twists in the sail. Using the track and slide system, for example, the outer slide on the foot is fed on to the track on the boom first and then the succeeding slides until the tack is reached. The tack is then attached to the boom by a pin, a lashing, or a shackle. The foot is tensioned by heaving on the clew outhaul which may be a lashing or a wire attached to a block and tackle system inside a hollow boom. The tension will vary according to the wind strength and will be decided by the skipper. In racing boats there will be a black band near the after end of the boom and near the top of the mast. The sail must not be stretched past these bands when racing – the penalty is disqualification.

Next the luff. Check from tack to head that the sail is not twisted, and then feed on the slides starting at the head, checking to see that they are the right way up. It may not be possible to feed on the lowest until the sail is hoisted, but the gate at the foot of the track must be closed so that

131

Below (top) The mast step has tangs to which blocks and the kicking strap are attached. The kicking strap consists of a wire strop from the boom, attached to a four-part tackle with the fall led to a cam jam cleat at the edge of the deck. The mainsail outhaul emerges from inside the boom. Both this and the Cunningham eye control line are attached to blocks through which lines are passed and led to both sides of the boat so that they can be adjusted on either tack. *(bottom)* The kicking strap can also be tensioned by a lever. The double-ended control line can be adjusted on either tack.

the slides do not all fall off again. The halyard is checked carefully to see that it is clear of everything aloft – it must run direct from the head of the sail to the masthead sheave – and is then shackled to the head of the mainsail. The tail is turned up on its cleat.

Battens extend and control the shape of the roach of the sail and should be marked so that each batten is slipped into the correct pocket. They are frequently more flexible at one end and this end is inserted first. They may be held in the pockets by small ties sewn to the mainsail, threaded through holes in the battens, and tied with a reef knot. Alternatively, some pockets have an offset opening above the pocket through which the battens are fed. An elastic loop sewn into the forward end of the pocket holds the batten securely to the after end.

Gaskets (sail stops) are tied around the sail and boom, and a light lashing is used to hold the head to the mast while the remaining jobs are done. This prevents the sail filling with wind and perhaps causing the boat to capsize if the wind is strong.

The mainsheet of larger boats may be left permanently rove through the blocks; otherwise it must be led through the various blocks in the correct order without passing the wrong side of the horse, tiller, or lifelines.

In dinghies and small racing boats it is usual for the mainsail to be removed after each sail, but in cruising boats and larger racing craft it is often left on the boom, usually with the battens removed and the foot tension eased off. The sail is held to the boom with gaskets, and a cover is laced over it to keep it clean and protect it from the sun whose rays cause Terylene (Dacron) fibres to deteriorate.

The headsail

First the tack is shackled either directly to a fitting at the stemhead or on deck, or to a wire strop attached to this fitting. The sail is then attached to its stay by a number of hanks. In some small dinghies and non-racing craft the headsail may be set flying without being hanked to the stay. In some offshore-racing boats the forestay carries a headstay made of metal which has a groove to take the luff rope. The sail is fed into this in the same manner as a mainsail is fed into the luff groove on the mast. After checking that the halyard is clear, it is shackled to the head and the tail is turned up on its cleat. The headsail sheets are attached to the clew, rove through the fairleads or blocks to port and starboard, and figure-of-eight knots tied in the ends. In the case of a large overlapping headsail the sheets pass outside the shrouds, but smaller headsails are usually sheeted between the mast and the shrouds. The sail is now ready and is tied down with a gasket until it is time to hoist it.

Getting under way

When a boat is at rest, either on the beach or at her berth or mooring, the mainsail may generally only be hoisted when the wind is forward of the beam. With the sheets eased, as they should be, the sails will then fly like flags and not drive the boat forward. If the wind were aft of the beam, the mainsail would fill and be difficult or impossible to hoist fully and the boat would start to gather way. It is, therefore, necessary to think ahead before hoisting the sails.

Leaving a beach

Most sailing dinghies are launched from a beach or shelving ramp, and if the wind is blowing from the shore, the boat can be held bows to wind while the sail is hoisted, the kicking strap (boom vang) tensioned, the rudder shipped, and the tiller fitted. The crew climbs on board quickly, pushing the boat on to one or other tack. If the wind is blowing onshore, the beach is a lee shore, and the crew has to stand in deep water to hold the boat head to wind – a cold preliminary to a sail – unless the boat can be paddled out and secured to a buoy some distance off the shore while sails are hoisted.

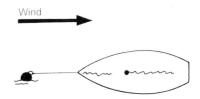

12.2 Head to wind. Hoist mainsail and headsail.

Leaving a mooring or an anchorage

A boat lying at a mooring or to an anchor in slack water will lie head to wind (fig. 12.2). If there is a current or tidal stream (tidal current), she lies either head towards the wind (wind-rode, fig. 12.3), head towards the tidal stream (tide-rode, fig. 12.4) or may well veer about between the two, especially if the wind is gusty. If the boat is wind-rode, both mainsail and headsail can be hoisted, the mainsail first.

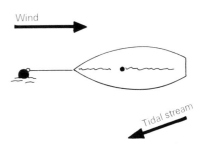

12.3 Wind-rode. Hoist mainsail and headsail.

The helmsman checks carefully on the movements of other boats nearby and decides which tack is preferable, telling the crew to back the headsail by holding it to windward on the opposite side to that on which the boat is to pay off. The crew lets go the mooring when the bow has started to swing. If the boat is at anchor, the crew hauls in the cable until it is straight up and down before backing the headsail, breaking out the anchor and getting under way. When the boat is tide-rode, the wind may well be abeam or over the quarter, and the crew then has to drop the mooring or break out the anchor with only the headsail hoisted. The boat is then luffed up into the wind as soon as possible so that the mainsail can be hoisted. Sometimes, when the boat is tide-rode but the stream or current is not too fierce, she can be turned head to wind by hoisting the mainsail a little at a time. When leaving a mooring under engine, care must be taken not to run over the buoy rope or the propeller may be fouled.

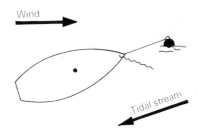

12.4 Tide-rode. Hoist headsail only.

Leaving a berth

If a boat is moored alongside a pier or marina with clear water to seaward and the wind from the shore, she can leave under sail. The mooring lines are all removed and stowed except for the bow line so that she lies head to wind while the sails are hoisted (fig. 12.5).

Leaving marinas and crowded anchorages

More and more boats are kept in crowded marinas, and there is no seamanlike alternative to motoring the boat into clear water before heading into the wind to hoist sail, with the engine running fast enough to give steerage way. As soon as the boat is under way, all mooring lines must be coiled and stowed away tidily in their lockers, together with the fenders.

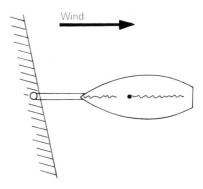

12.5 Wind from the dock. Hoist mainsail and headsail.

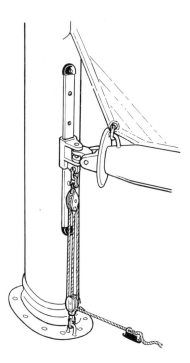

12.6a *Above* Tack tackle on a keelboat.

12.6b *Below* Sliding gooseneck on a dinghy.

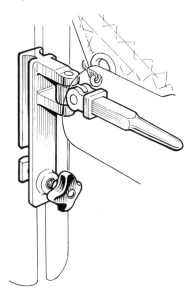

Opposite The Sydney-Hobart race fleet reaching out of Sydney Harbour at the start of the 630-mile annual classic.

Hoisting sails

As a general rule the mainsail is hoisted first when the wind is forward of the beam.

The mainsail
Aboard larger day boats and keelboats the boom is usually left connected to the mast by the gooseneck for the whole season. It may rest in a crutch to prevent it swinging about until it is time to hoist the mainsail. The boom is then raised slightly by tightening the topping lift, and the crutch is stowed. The mainsheet must be left uncleated so that it can run freely through the blocks and allow the sail to swing to the wind without filling while it is being hoisted. Gaskets are removed, and a quick check made to see that the halyard is clear.

If the mast has a groove, the sail has to be fed into it gradually as the sail is hoisted. Before heaving on the halyard, follow the luff upwards from the tack to the head to ensure that the sail has not become twisted. It is easier to have one man feeding in the bolt rope while the other hauls on the halyard.

If the mast has a track, the slides will have been fed on to it already, except perhaps for the lowest, so the sail is ready to hoist. If the boat is big enough, the crew hoists the sail from a position forward of the mast or beside it, and watches to see that the battens do not get caught under the rigging. If a halyard winch is used, the tension should be kept constant, and the turns distributed evenly over the drum. Any remaining slides are fed on to the track and the gate closed.

Most boats have a gooseneck sliding on a track on the mast. The sail is hoisted fully, or to the black band on the mast of racing craft, with the gooseneck high on its track. The halyard is then belayed, and the gooseneck hauled down so that the luff is tensioned to suit the wind of the moment. In larger boats the gooseneck is usually hauled down by a tack tackle, but in dinghies the weight of the crew pushing the boom down suffices, and the gooseneck is locked by tightening a thumb screw. The halyard is then coiled and hung on its cleat or stowed near the foot of the mast, and the topping lift is slacked off so that the boom is suspended from the sail.

Some cruising boats and simple dinghies have a fixed gooseneck, and luff tension can only be applied with the halyard. In some racing boats with a fixed gooseneck luff tension is adjusted by a line led through a Cunningham hole.

The boom of many sailing dinghies is not connected to the gooseneck until the sail is almost fully hoisted, and in this case care should be taken to see that it does not get caught under the horse or tiller while the sail is being hoisted.

If the boat is gaff-rigged, the peak and throat halyards are hauled simultaneously so that the gaff is hoisted in a horizontal position until the luff is taut. The throat halyard is then belayed, and the peak hoisted until creases parallel to the luff can be seen near the throat.

Most racing dinghies and many other high-performance craft have a kicking strap to prevent the boom lifting when the mainsheet is eased

for a reach or a run. This runs from the underside of the boom to a point near the foot of the mast, and tension is usually adjusted by a tackle, winch, or screw.

The headsail

The gasket and lashing holding down the head of the sail is removed, both sheets are left free so that the sail will not fill with wind, and the halyard is re-checked to see that it is clear. The sail is then hoisted, the crew taking care to keep clear of any shackle that may attach the sheets to the clew because this whips about violently in a breeze. The tension of the headsail luff is vitally important because a sagging luff impairs a boat's performance to windward. In cruising boats and simply rigged dinghies it is generally a case of sweating up the halyard as taut as possible, but many high-performance craft use a tack downhaul so that tension can be adjusted under way.

Before getting under way all halyards must be coiled and stowed neatly, all loose and unwanted gear put in lockers, and in larger boats a check made in the cabin that nothing that will shift when the boat heels to the wind has been left lying loose.

Windward work

More time is spent sailing to windward than on any other point of sailing because a yacht cannot sail closer than about 45° to the wind. It cannot sail a straight course to a destination to windward but has to cover more ground zig-zagging up to it. Beating is also normally the slowest point of sailing.

Although the wind is described as coming from a certain direction, such as south-west, it is in fact far from constant and will veer (clockwise) and back (anti- or counter-clockwise) continuously. To make the best use of the wind the crew has to watch for all the minor changes in direction. The burgee indicates the direction of the wind at the top of the mast, and tell-tales of light fabric or wool are often tied to the shrouds at eye-level to show its direction nearer the water.

The aim is to sail as close to the wind as possible while keeping the boat moving well through the water. The sails are trimmed with the boom nearly amidships. Hardening the boom pulls it down and flattens the mainsail, which is fine in stronger winds, but in light airs a boat will come alive and sail faster if there is more fullness in the sail, and the mainsheet should be eased enough to allow the sail to become fuller.

If the helmsman pinches by sailing extremely close to the wind, the boat moves forward very slowly and makes more leeway. Pinching rarely pays, although when racing there are occasions when ground gained to windward is more important than speed through the water. In general it is best to keep a boat footing well with sails just full.

A boat sailing to windward heads into waves and must be sailed fast enough to drive over them instead of being stopped. In strong winds and a high sea each wave should be dealt with separately, luffing through the breaking crests and bearing away on the backs of the waves to regain full speed.

Opposite An international fleet of offshore racing boats running under spinnakers on the sparkling water of the Solent during Cowes Week.

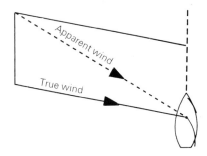

12.7 The true wind is blowing at 80° to the boat's course. Because she is sailing at 4 knots, the apparent wind blows at 60° to her course.

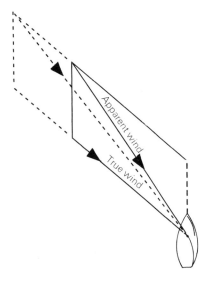

12.8 As the true wind increases from 6 to 9 knots, the apparent wind frees, and the boat can point slightly higher for a while.

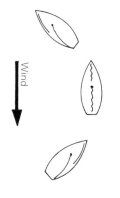

12.9 Going about smartly in a dinghy.

Because the wind varies constantly in direction and strength, the helmsman should luff slightly when it frees and bear away enough to fill the sails when it heads. The wake of a boat sailing close-hauled is a series of shallow zig-zags as the helmsman reacts to individual puffs and ensures that he is close to the wind.

The wind felt by the crew aboard is called the apparent wind to distinguish it from the true wind, which is the wind blowing across the surface of the earth. Many people believe that because it is called apparent wind there is something not quite real about it, but make no mistake, the apparent wind is the wind felt by the crew on their faces; it is the wind in which the boat is sailing, and to which the sails must be trimmed. If a boat is sailing at 4 knots with a 10 knot wind at 80° to her course, her speed through the water will cause the apparent wind to blow from further forward at about 60° to her course (fig. 12.7), and that apparent wind will be about 1 knot stronger than the true wind. When the wind speed increases in a gust, the apparent wind frees, and the boat can point higher until her speed increases to match the stronger breeze. In figure 12.8 the apparent wind frees 4° when the true wind increases from 6 to 9 knots. The reverse occurs when the wind eases, and the helmsman, therefore, luffs up at the start of puffs, and bears away in the lulls. A good helmsman watches the surface of the water to windward for early warning of gusts and slants.

The art of windward sailing lies in interpreting the clues correctly: the angle of heel, the angle of the wind on the cheek, the burgee, the tell-tales, and the luff of the headsail, plus the sound and feel of the boat as she moves through the water. If the boat is not pointing high enough, the burgee blows out to leeward of the head of the sail: if the luffs of the sails are lifting, she is too close to the wind. A skilled helmsman knows whether he is as close to the wind as he should be by the seat of his pants – the boat just feels right. But the best way for a less experienced man to check is to inch closer to the wind until the luff of the headsail just starts to lift, and then bear away slightly until the sail fills.

One of the best and simplest aids to sail trimming is a few short lengths of dark coloured wool, threaded through the headsail about 25% of the way back from the luff and knotted either side of the sail to retain them. Provided they are both streaming out smoothly in the same direction, the airflow is correct. If the windward 'woolly' flaps, the boat is being sailed too high or the sail is not trimmed in sufficiently, and, conversely, if the leeward woolly flaps, the boat is being sailed too free or the sail is trimmed too far out.

Sailing dinghies are designed to be sailed upright. When the wind increases so much that the weight of the crew cannot counteract the heeling moment, some wind has to be spilled out of the mainsail to ease the pressure. The mainsheet of a sailing dinghy should be played constantly, eased out slightly to spill the wind in gusts, and hardened again as the wind eases.

Keelboats are designed to sail at an angle of heel, and the mainsail is usually cleated, the boat heeling rather more in the gusts. Pressure can be eased by pointing slightly higher so that the luffs of the sails just lift, but the boat should not be pinched excessively or she will lose way. There is a limit, however, to the amount that a keelboat should be allowed to heel, for beyond a certain angle the weight of wind in the sails serves only to press the boat down in the water and restrict forward progress; it is then that the mainsail should be reefed or smaller sails set.

Going about

Way must be kept on the boat while she is going about so that she turns smoothly from one tack to the other. A light dinghy does not carry her way into the wind but loses and gathers way quickly. She must, therefore, be put about fairly smartly (fig. 12.9). In light airs a dinghy should be put about more slowly, and the crew should move weight stealthily from one side to the other so as not to rock the boat and stop her dead.

A keelboat, however, fetches a considerable way to windward, especially in smooth water. The helmsman should steer through a broad arc when going about, gaining at least a boat's length to windward (fig. 12.10). Some old boats are very slow in stays, especially if they have a long keel, and are reluctant to change from one tack to another. It may be necessary to help the bows round by backing the headsail, first easing it and then, when the boat is head to wind, sheeting it in on the original leeward side until the mainsail can fill on the new tack (fig. 12.11). Strong winds and choppy seas make tacking more difficult, and if there is much sea, it is wise to wait for a patch of relatively smooth water. The boat must have full way on, and the crew must be ready to back the headsail to help the boat fill on the new tack, should it be necessary.

Whatever the boat it is important not to sheet in the headsail too soon after tacking. The bows must have passed well through the eye of the wind before the sheets are hardened. If the headsail is hardened in too early, the wind will strike it on the wrong side, preventing the boat from turning further, and either force her back on to her original tack or else blow her backwards in irons.

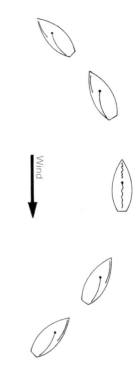

12.10 Putting a keelboat about slowly gains several boat's lengths to windward.

Off the wind

From a close reach on one tack, through running, to a close reach on the other the helmsman can select the course that he wishes to steer, and this will be as steady a course as the sea allows. It is up to the crew to see that the sails are trimmed to the optimum angle and to adjust them continuously to suit the individual slants. When reaching, the head of the mainsail should be in line with the burgee; if the burgee is blowing down to leeward of the sail, the mainsail is sheeted too close and must be eased. If the mainsail has been paid out too far, the wind will strike the lee side of the sail, first causing it to lift at the luff and then making the whole sail collapse.

The jib sheet hand must check his sail constantly because the slot between the jib or genoa and the mainsail affects the performance of the boat. If the headsail is trimmed too close, the wind exhausted from the leech backwinds the mainsail. To check the trim of the headsail the sheet is eased until the luff starts to lift and is then hardened until the sail is just full. Achieving the correct sheeting angle and optimum sail shape

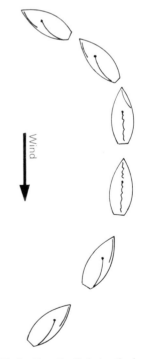

12.11 Backing the jib helps the boat to go about.

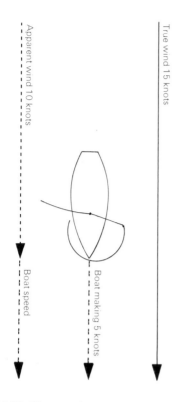

Apparent wind 10 knots

True wind 15 knots

Boat speed

Boat making 5 knots

12.12 When running, the apparent wind is blowing at 10 knots because the boat's speed is deducted from the speed of the true wind.

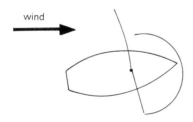

wind

12.13 By the lee. The wind is blowing from the same side as that on which the main boom lies.

are probably the most important factors in tuning a boat to sail fast and are described here only in very general terms.

A boat sails fast with sheets eased, and fastest of all on a beam reach. When broad-reaching, the waves usually travel in much the same direction as the boat, and large seas can cause her to yaw badly. The helmsman should steer as steady a course as he can, letting the boat react to the waves rather than fighting her, but always keeping her under control. The better the helmsman, the less will the tiller saw back and forth, because he anticipates the boat's movements and prevents the development of a major yaw in good time. In very heavy seas with breaking crests a boat can be picked up and carried along in a welter of foam, surfing for some distance. This is very exhilarating, but the boat will be difficult to control so it is better to reduce speed and allow the seas to overtake the boat, sailing her on the back of the waves clear of the crests.

When the wind is dead aft, the sail should be almost at right angles to the line of the burgee, the boom being eased until it touches the shroud. It should then be hardened slightly to avoid chafe, by lifting the sail off the leeward shroud, and to prevent the tendency in strong winds to lever the mast aft at the gooseneck. Although the boom may only be let out 75° or so, the mainsail will be progressively nearer to 90° towards the head, owing to the twist in the sail. Care should be taken to ensure that the sail is not eased so far that the head is beyond right angles to the centreline, because the portion of the sail eased forward will tend to force the top of the mast to windward and cause the boat to roll. This can lead eventually to broaching, to an uncontrolled gybe with breakage of gear, or to a capsize in a dinghy.

When a boat is running, the apparent wind is less than the true wind; if she is sailing at 5 knots in a 15 knot breeze, her speed through the water reduces the speed of the apparent wind to 10 knots (fig. 12.12). This fact needs to be borne in mind when sailing fast downwind with sheets eased and a following sea; the wind and sea may appear to have decreased, but this may be far from the case when the boat is close-hauled to return home and the crew is faced with head seas, more wind, and a cold wet thrash to windward.

Sailing a dead run can be very uncomfortable, especially in a strong wind and rough sea, and the boat will tend to roll from side to side, perhaps dipping boom and spinnaker boom in the water. There is also the danger of an accidental gybe (jibe) if the helmsman is distracted and bears away so that the boat is sailing by the lee – that is, with the wind blowing from the side on which the main boom lies (fig. 12.13). It is often preferable and safer to sail a very broad reach and to gybe, under control, on to the other broad reach. The disadvantage of the slight extra distance sailed is often more than cancelled out by the greater speed achieved. Sailing by the lee is occasionally justifiable in light or moderate winds when racing, but in general it is better to gybe.

Gybing

When a boat tacks, the sails are permanently under control and the boom swings over gradually from one side to the other, but when a boat gybes, the boom and sail are out on one side of the boat at one moment, and the next moment they have swung rapidly through nearly 180° to the opposite side; the crew must duck automatically to avoid being hit by the boom.

The method of gybing varies according to the way the boat is rigged. In a dinghy or racing keelboat with a kicking strap the mainsail is hauled in slightly, the helm put up, the mainsheet hauled in a little bit more, and the boom flipped over by the crew pulling on the kicking strap or boom, or by the helmsman tugging at the parts of the centre mainsheet. The boom and sail fly across the boat, and the crew balance her as the helmsman eases the mainsheet to cushion the shock of the sail filling with wind on the new gybe. The exact method adopted varies from boat to boat and crew to crew, and also depends on the wind and sea conditions. The aim is to keep the boat perfectly balanced throughout, allowing the boom to flip over easily without a struggle, and to keep moving fast through the water. If the boat wallows and slows down prior to gybing, the apparent wind will increase and make gybing more difficult, especially in strong winds.

In boats fitted with permanent backstays the mainsheet must be hauled in somewhat further than in a dinghy or small craft fitted with a kicking strap. Otherwise the boom may lift and foul the backstay which will then hold it amidships. The boat will be knocked over on the new gybe with the mainsail pinned amidships and no means of easing it.

If a boat has runners, the lee runner will be slack when the boat is broad-reaching or running. The mainsheet, therefore, has to be hauled in until the lee runner can be set up ready to support the mast after gybing. When the boom swings over, the new lee runner has to be released immediately and the mainsheet paid out as rapidly as possible. Whenever a boat is gybed with the mainsheet hauled part-way in, the helmsman has to beware the boat's tendency to broach to, rushing up to windward, and heeling violently.

Another hazard for boats with no kicking strap is the goosewing or Chinese gybe when the boom and lower part of the mainsail gybe, leaving the top half of the mainsail on the original gybe (fig. 12.14). The only solution is to gybe the lower part back again so that everything is on the same side of the mast – and then start all over again.

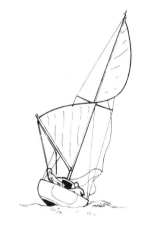

12.14 Goosewing gybe.

Returning home

The wind has to be forward of the beam when lowering the mainsail, just as it must be when hoisting. If the wind is aft of amidships, the sail is pushed forward against the shrouds and cannot be dropped. At some stage or other of anchoring, picking up a buoy, or docking, the boat has to come nearly head to wind to enable the mainsail to be lowered. Before attempting to lower sails, make sure that any halyard not on a winch drum has not become tangled, and lay the coil on deck so that, as the sail comes down, the line will run out smoothly. If the boat has a topping lift, it must be tightened just enough to take the weight of the boom when the sail is down, but not too much, or the sail will bag and the boat will not sail well at the crucial moment of picking up a mooring or coming alongside. Sails must be gathered in carefully as they are lowered so that they do not fall into the water, and gaskets must be tied round them as soon as possible to prevent them filling with wind.

Picking up a mooring

In slack water, or where there is no current, the boat will lie head to wind when moored. The aim, therefore, is to approach from downwind, shooting up head to wind with sails shaking, and to reach the mooring buoy with no way on the boat. The crew can then lean over and pick it up with a boathook, make the mooring chain fast to the mooring cleat or sampson post, drop the headsail and then the mainsail. The distance that a boat will carry her way must be judged accurately if the mooring is to be picked up perfectly. Often the boat is still moving through the water, and the headsail then needs to be dropped with alacrity before it fills and forces the bows round, causing the crew to drop the mooring buoy or to part company with the ship. The sheets should be left free so that the sails do not fill while the mooring is being picked up, and the topping lift must be tight enough to support the boom when the sail is lowered. Picking up moorings successfully is the result of good judgement arising from experience, and it is wise to practise in open water whenever possible to discover how far the boat will shoot in various wind strengths.

If there is a current or tidal stream, the skipper has to judge whether the boat will be tide-rode or wind-rode when the sails are down, and the way other boats nearby are lying gives an indication. Remember, though, that shallow draft dinghies are usually wind-rode, whereas keelboats are more often tide-rode. If the wind will be abaft the beam when the boat is moored, the mainsail must be lowered before attempting to pick up the mooring, and the headsail alone must be used to control speed when approaching the buoy. The aim is to arrive at the mooring buoy with no way on relative to the ground. If the current or tidal stream is strong, this may mean that the boat has to be kept sailing through the water, for otherwise the person picking up the mooring will not be able to secure it. Again it is all a matter of judgement and experience.

Anchoring

Sail management is the same whether picking up a mooring or dropping anchor; the chosen spot must be reached with no way on, and the sails

The luff of KA 23's spinnaker is on the point of collapse. A quick tweak on the spinnaker sheet should flip it back. If not, the pole must be eased forward, but not so far as to touch the forestay.

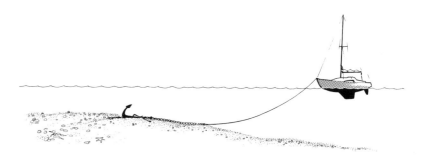

12.15 A length of chain between the mooring warp and the anchor helps to keep the pull on the anchor horizontal. The scope of cable veered should be at least four times the depth of water at high-tide.

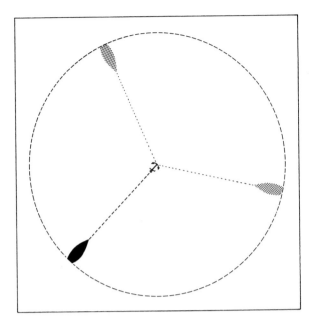

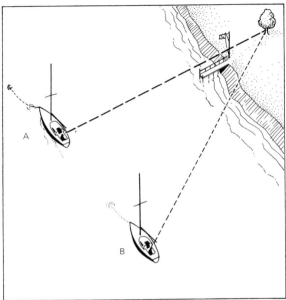

must be empty of wind when the moment comes to drop the anchor. In practice it is best to wait until the boat has just started to gather sternway before letting go, gradually veering a length of cable, snubbing the boat briefly with a turn round the sampson post or bitts to encourage the anchor to bite into the ground, and then veering sufficient cable to prevent the anchor dragging. The scope should be at least four times the depth of water at high tide, and in stronger winds more cable should be veered (fig. 12.15). Lowering the anchor when the boat is making a little sternway ensures that the chain does not land in a heap on top of the anchor and foul it.

All anchors are designed to bite into the ground and hold against a horizontal pull; they break out as a result of an upward pull. If nylon line is used, it is essential to add a few fathoms of chain between the line and the anchor ring to weight the stock down and ensure that the pull on the anchor is horizontal. Chapter 17 discusses the disadvantages of using nylon cable as opposed to chain with fin and skeg configuration.

When selecting an anchorage, the first consideration must be the weather. It is asking for trouble to anchor close to a lee shore in a rising wind, or under the lee of the land if the forecast warns of a complete change in wind direction. Beating clear of a lee shore can be a grim and dangerous business. The chart must be checked to see if the bottom is good holding ground and it will show whether the bottom is rocky, mud, sand, etc., and whether there are any underwater cables under which the anchor could become hooked. In waters where the direction of the tidal stream changes the anchorage must be selected so that a boat can swing a full circle without hitting any obstruction (fig. 12.16).

As soon as the anchor is down, the crew checks that it is holding by finding objects abeam on shore which are in line, or by taking bearings of an object lying roughly abeam. If the two objects start to separate, or if the bearing changes, the anchor is dragging (fig. 12.17).

12.16 *Left* When dropping anchor, allow enough room for the boat to swing to a change in the direction of the tidal stream or the wind.

12.17 *Right* The flagstaff and the tree are in line when the anchor is dropped at A. If the anchor drags, they will no longer be in line as at B.

143

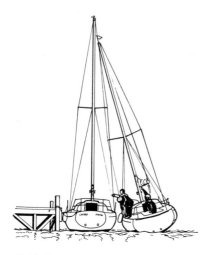

12.18 Too much weight on one side will cause the masts to clash.

Coming alongside

If the boat is to lie alongside a pier or another boat to windward, she can approach from leeward and arrive head to wind with no way on, sails slatting and ready to be lowered. If the boat or pier are to leeward, the mainsail has to be lowered in good time, well to windward of the berth, and the approach made slowly under headsail alone, dropping down gently with fenders strung out to leeward, lowering the headsail just before arrival to prevent it becoming entangled with objects on the pier. Should the wind be strong, it may be necessary to brake the speed of the boat through the water by towing a bucket or dropping a kedge over the stern.

When approaching to moor alongside another boat, the weight of the crew standing ready to fend off and moor has to be counteracted because otherwise the boat will heel towards her neighbour and their rigging will clash (fig. 12.18). Boats moored alongside each other should be so positioned that their masts are clear of each other when either boat heels.

Mooring lines

Whether alongside a pier or another boat mooring lines should consist of bow and stern lines and fore and aft springs. All four are required to keep the boat parallel, the bow and stern lines holding the ends of the boat in, while the springs prevent fore and aft movement, one running from forward to a point on the pier aft of amidships, and the other from aft to another point on the pier forward of amidships (fig. 12.19).

Crowded places

When manoeuvring space is restricted, the seamanlike approach is under engine, but if the boat has no engine, or if it is out of action, it is best to tie up to a mooring buoy or some object where there is enough sea-room, lower all sail, and either warp the boat to her mooring, or beg a tow from a passing launch.

Spinnakers

Spinnakers are used when the wind is free and they differ from other sails in that the relatively large expanse of canvas is controlled only at the three corners. A spinnaker can easily get out of control while being set if the correct technique is not adopted, but every boat and every crew have their own refinements. In dinghies and small boats the spinnaker is usually hoisted 'flying' in the lee of the mainsail, but in larger craft more control is necessary and it is set in stops – that is, held furled with rotten cotton or elastic bands so that it can be fully hoisted before the stops are broken out and the sail filled. In smaller keelboats it is usual to stow the spinnaker in a basket, bag, or turtle which may be attached to the deck or stemhead just before hoisting.

Whatever method is used the sail must first be sorted out so that there will be no twists in it when it fills. This is done by starting at the head and working down the two luffs which are matched. If the spinnaker is being stowed in a bag or turtle, the bunt of the sail is pushed in first, leaving the

12.19 Mooring lines alongside a quay.

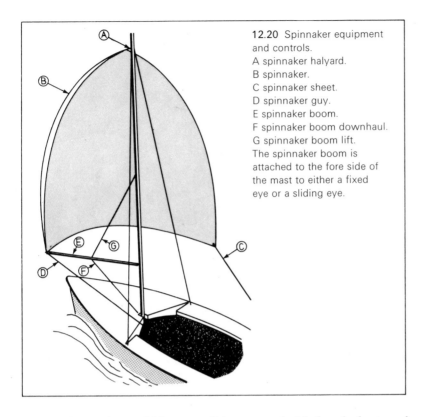

12.20 Spinnaker equipment and controls.
A spinnaker halyard.
B spinnaker.
C spinnaker sheet.
D spinnaker guy.
E spinnaker boom.
F spinnaker boom downhaul.
G spinnaker boom lift.
The spinnaker boom is attached to the fore side of the mast to either a fixed eye or a sliding eye.

head and two clews sticking out of the top so that halyard, sheet, and guy can be attached with the sail still in the bag.

Because of its size and shape the spinnaker must be set outside everything on board, so the halyard, which has a swivel fitting, runs through a block or sheave above the forestay, and the sheet and guy are rigged outside the shrouds and led through blocks on either quarter (fig. 12.20). The spinnaker pole is attached to the mast, and the spinnaker tack to its outboard end. There is a lift and downhaul to hold the pole steady at the desired level, and in many boats the spinnaker pole attachment on the mast can be raised and lowered on a track. The fore-and-aft position of the spinnaker pole is controlled by the guy (Aus: brace), while the spinnaker sheet controls the clew. When the wind is dead aft, the boom is pulled back almost to the main shrouds and the sheet eased so that the spinnaker fills roughly at right angles to the wind (fig. 12.21a). As the boat luffs nearer to the wind, the guy is eased and the lee sheet hardened so that the whole sail sets further to one side of the boat (fig. 12.21b), the limit being reached when the pole meets the forestay (fig. 12.21c).

Spinnaker trimming requires concentration and continuous attention from the crew, and every spinnaker has its own foibles. Basically, however, if the spinnaker boom is trimmed too far aft, the luff collapses; the guy has to be eased, and the sheet hardened to correct this. If the spinnaker is too far to leeward, it is blanketed by the mainsail, and the centre collapses; this is corrected by pulling back the guy and easing the sheet. As a general rule the spinnaker boom should be horizontal in order to extend the tack as far as possible from the mast and so present

12.21a Wind dead aft.

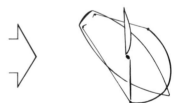

12.21b Broad reaching.

12.21c Spinnaker set shy with the wind nearly abeam.

145

An ocean racer broaching as she loses control of her spinnaker in a sudden squall. The luff of the spinnaker has collapsed. The spinnaker pole must be eased forward and the helm altered so that she bears away on to her original course after which the pole can be trimmed aft again and the sheet adjusted accordingly. K.171's spinnaker is filling properly and she maintains her course under control.

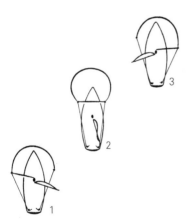

12.22 Gybing a double-ended spinnaker pole.

the greatest area of sail to clear wind. The height of the tack should be adjusted so that it is level with the clew.

A spinnaker can be gybed smoothly at the same time as the mainsail, and the system used depends on the fittings on the pole. If the pole is double-ended, it can be detached from the mast and clipped to both clews while the mainsail is gybed (fig. 12.22). It is then detached from the new leeward clew and clipped on to the mast. Alternatively, the dip pole method may be used: the pole remains attached to the mast and is dipped under the forestay after the spinnaker tack has been released before being attached to the opposite corner. This method is less satisfactory if the spinnaker pole extends beyond the forestay, as it then also has to be unclipped from the mast and this takes extra time.

A spinnaker is best lowered in the lee of the mainsail so that it is empty of wind. The tack is released from the spinnaker boom, and the sail allowed to fly out to leeward. The bight of the spinnaker sheet between the sail and the fairlead block on the quarter must first be taken in hand, or the sail will blow out from the halyard and the sheet out of reach of the crew. The spinnaker is then hauled in under the boom.

Racing dinghies often use a spinnaker chute (launching tube) through which a light line runs; this is sewn to the centre of the spinnaker. To lower the sail the crew hauls on the line, drawing the sail into the chute free of twists, and with the halyard and sheets ready for rehoisting.

Reefing

Sail can be reduced either by setting a smaller sail or by reefing which has

the advantage of simultaneously reducing sail area and lowering the centre of effort. There are three main methods: roller reefing, points reefing, and slab reefing.

With roller reefing the boom is rotated and the exposed sail area reduced by winding it round the boom. There are several methods. At its simplest the gooseneck pin that is located in the forward end of the boom has a round section at the end and a square section nearer the mast. To reef, the boom is pulled an inch or so aft and rotated. When the sail area has been reduced sufficiently, the boom is pushed forward again. It is prevented from turning by the square portion of the pin locating in a square hole in the fitting on the end of the boom. Alternatively, a ratchet system or a worm gear may be used aboard larger craft, and there are also 'through-mast' versions operated by a handle on the forward side of the mast. The leech of the mainsail must be pulled well aft while rolls are being taken in or the sail will not set well. The disadvantages of roller reefing are that the sail must be fully hoisted before rolls can be taken in, and that there is a limit to the number of rolls that can be taken because the build-up of mainsail and luff bolt rope on the boom causes the sail to set increasingly badly. The advantages are flexibility, speed, and simplicity of working which encourage the crew to make fine adjustments to suit the wind strength and keep the boat well balanced.

Points reefing is slower and less flexible because deep reefs are taken, using pennants rove through cringles at luff and leech, with reef points between them sewn to the sail parallel to the boom. The weight of the boom is taken by the topping lift when reefing. The halyard is eased so

Yeoman XIX driving to windward with a working jib and the mainsail reefed to the second batten, reducing its area by over 50%. Loa 40.9ft; Lwl 30.0ft; beam 12.2ft; draft 6.7ft; sail area 885sq ft; IOR rating 29.6ft.

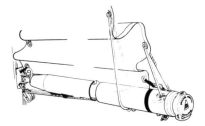

12.23 Slab reefing. The luff cringle is slipped over the hook near the gooseneck. The slab line aft, which hauls down the first reef cringle, is led internally through the boom.

147

that first the luff cringle and then the leech cringle can be pulled down and lashed to the boom (fig. 12.23).

For speed and simplicity many modern offshore-racing craft now use slab reefing (jiffy reefing) which is a development of the points reefing method. To reef, the main halyard is eased, and a cringle on the luff is attached to a hook on the inboard end of the boom. Alternatively, it can be hauled down and secured with a line. At the outboard end a line is attached to the boom and led through a cringle on the leech, round a sheave in the end of the boom, and forward where it can be adjusted either on the boom or led to a winch. The reefed portion of sail between luff and leech can be held neatly with reef points. A slab reef can be taken quickly when the sail is set or can be taken before hoisting the sail. It is gaining in popularity for use in cruisers because it is cheaper to instal than roller reefing and much quicker to operate.

Man overboard

Man overboard! The first reaction must be to throw him a lifebuoy stowed ready for immediate use close to the helmsman. It must be thrown *to* him, and not *at* him, and to show his position in the water it may have a self-igniting flare attached at the end of a line which is long enough to prevent his getting burnt (fig. 12.24).

Man overboard drill is similar to picking up a mooring and should be practised frequently, using a fender or some floating object to represent a body. The aim is to reach the man in the water as soon as possible with no way on the boat, arriving to leeward of him so that the boat does not thump down on his head. If the boat is close-hauled or -reaching when the man falls overboard, the best method is to count up to five seconds, bear away and gybe, continuously keeping an eye on the head in the water which can all too easily disappear in the waves. The boat is then brought on the wind and the man is approached from leeward, avoiding going so close to him that the bow wave sweeps him out of reach, but luffing at the right moment in order to bring him to where he can be grasped by the crew in the cockpit and secured to the boat with a line.

On the other hand, the man may fall overboard when the boat is sailing merrily downwind with the spinnaker set. It is then vitally important to detail one of the crew to do nothing except keep his eye on the man in the water, advising the helmsman where he is while the spinnaker is doused, the sails trimmed, and the boat tacked back to him.

There are two schools of thought on which is the best side to approach a man in the water, windward or leeward. If the boat is brought up with the man to windward, he is easy to see during the final approach and will not become entangled with the sheets and boom. However, the boat will tend to sag off to leeward as it loses way and, after it has been stopped, will drift downwind. The boat must be positioned really close to the man, and unless contact is made with him by line immediately, the gap between boat and man will open, and there will be no alternative to sailing off and repeating the operation – by which time he may have drowned! If the boat is stopped to windward of the man in the water, it

A well-reefed dayboat in gusty winds. The mainsail has been rolled round the boom to reduce the area and lower the centre of effort while the jib has been reduced similarly by furling it round its luff wire. The Crouch One-Design is typical of many local one-design classes that existed round the coasts of Britain. Some still survive and provide keen racing for their owners despite their age.

is not necessary to sail so close to him initially, and there is therefore less chance of running him down. The boat can be stopped a few yards to windward and allowed to drift down to him. The first action when the boat reaches the man must always be to connect him to the boat with a line. The boat should lie dormant with the helm let go and sheets eased so that the sails flap, but different boats behave differently, and it may be necessary to heave-to (fig. 12.25).

Getting him back on board is no easy matter, especially if the boat has high topsides and no boarding ladder. A thick mooring line can be attached to two stanchions so that a bight of rope hangs low in the water; this can be used as a step. The crew can help by heaving, but it is a painful business being hauled over the side, and the straps of safety harness will cut less than rope under the arms. If the man is unconscious, one line can be passed round his chest under his arms and a second around his hips, the lower ends of the lines beneath him being made fast aboard. Even a heavy, unconscious man can be rolled back on board by heaving on the upper ends of the lines and using the rise and fall of the waves.

It is important that the crew working to get him back on board should neither fall in themselves nor jump in to help him, unless instructed to do so by the skipper. They should be connected firmly to the boat by lifelines in case they overbalance.

If a man falls overboard while attached to the boat by a lifeline, the boat must be stopped quickly before he drowns as a result of being pulled under water or through the waves.

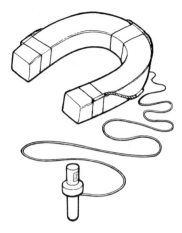

12.24 Horseshoe lifebuoy with light.

Running aground

Few skippers can boast that they have never run aground. This can lead to shipwreck or to wasted hours waiting for the tide to rise. At best, if the boat runs aground on a rising tide and a windward shore, there will only be a few minutes' delay. If the boat runs aground on rocks, she should first be inspected to establish the extent of any damage so that a decision can be made as to whether the pumps are adequate to control any leak; if not, the life-raft must be inflated or the dinghy launched.

A boat usually runs aground on sandy or muddy bottoms when the skipper is taking a short cut, and she makes a channel in the bottom as she grounds. If the boat has an engine, therefore, it is worth letting the sails fly and motoring astern flat out in an attempt to get free immediately. It can help to heel her alternately to port and starboard or to heel her as much as possible to one side only to reduce the draft slightly. Usually all attempts fail if the tide is falling, and the crew has to wait for the tide to rise again after low water.

When a boat runs aground on a lee shore, sails should be let fly or lowered immediately, whether the tide is rising or falling, so that she is not pushed further to leeward the moment she refloats. A kedge anchor is rowed out in the dinghy and dropped well to windward so that she lies to it when she refloats. In waters where the rise and fall is so great that she dries out completely she should be heeled to lie against the bank waiting for the water to return.

12.25 Heaving to. Back the headsail and lash the helm to leeward. When hove-to the boat will sail slowly making a good deal of leeway.

Capsizing

Because sailing dinghies often capsize, they carry buoyancy (flotation) bags or are fitted with watertight compartments. These enable a boat which is full of water both to float and to support the weight of the crew.

The first action to take after capsizing is to check that all members of the crew are safe and clear of the mainsail. All crew members must stay with the boat and ignore any equipment drifting away. The boat floats higher in the water than a swimmer and is often blown downwind faster than he can swim. A dinghy can be righted easily, even when she has turned turtle and is floating mast downwards. First, she must be pulled back on to her side so that mast and sail are floating on the surface. If the centreboard is still sticking through the slot, it can be used as a lever; if it has dropped through, a line is attached to a shroud near the chainplate and thrown over the bottom of the boat. Heaving on this brings her on to her side (fig. 12.26). The bow must be brought round head to wind, otherwise the sails will fill and cause her to capsize again immediately when the boat comes upright. The spinnaker must always be lowered before attempting to right her, and it may be necessary to lower the mainsail and jib as well.

Pulling or standing on the centreboard, plus a heave on the gunwale or the rope attached to the shroud, should bring her upright, and the crew can board her while she is swamped and floating low in the water. The water can then be baled out, or if she rights with relatively little water aboard, the self-bailers or transom flaps drain her while she continues to sail.

If the boat cannot be bailed out, or if the weather is very bad, a rescue launch may be on hand to tow the dinghy home. Sails should be lowered and lashed down, and the tow line given a turn round the mast, and either held in the hand or turned once round a cleat ready to let go immediately in an emergency. Never tie the tow rope to the mast but secure it so that it can be slipped instantly.

The launch should be encouraged to tow as slowly as possible, and the crew may need to sit aft to prevent the bows being pulled under.

Sailing in fog

To be unable to see where you are going but to hear the engines of other invisible vessels nearby is surely one of the most unnerving experiences for the crew of a small vessel. The importance of keeping a good lookout cannot be overstressed; eyes and ears must be open for signals made by other boats, for glimpses through patches of thinner fog, or for the sound of breakers on the shore. The only reliable indication of direction in fog is given by the compass. The true direction of sound and sound signals is difficult to determine owing to distortion and reflection of the sound waves passing through the fog, and in fog there is often no wind – what little there is can be variable in direction.

The first sign of fog may be the gradual disappearance of the coast. If it is obvious that there will not be time to put into a port, the first necessity is to check the boat's position carefully and decide where the

12.26 Righting a capsized dinghy. Pulling on a line attached to the starboard side brings the dinghy upright, head to wind.

safest place will be to wait for the fog to clear, determining the compass course to steer that will take the boat there. A busy channel should be avoided at all costs, and if the boat is small, it is usually best to anchor fairly close inshore where the water is too shallow for commercial traffic, but not so close in as to ground at low water. The look-out should be no less alert when a boat is anchored than when she is under way, and a bell should be rung at least every minute to warn other boats of her position. If no bell is carried, some other noise must be made.

A boat that cannot anchor should move very slowly in fog, ready to take avoiding action at any moment, sounding the appropriate signal with the foghorn. The *International Regulations* call for one prolonged blast followed by two short blasts at intervals of not more than two minutes.

Heavy weather sailing

It is good seamanship to avoid sailing in coastal waters in really heavy weather. Forecasts give information about local weather and also a general synopsis so that this can be viewed in a wider frame. A general forecast should be obtained before setting out to make a coastwise passage and also a local forecast if available. In many areas it is possible to obtain an up-to-the-minute recorded forecast by telephone or even to speak to a forecaster at a meteorological office. When at sea, one should always listen to regular radio forecasts, and all boats should carry a barometer. Readings taken and recorded at regular intervals will indicate when pressure falls and warns of approaching low-pressure systems and their attendant gales (see Chapter 18).

Sooner or later even the most careful skipper will be caught out by an unexpected gale blowing up suddenly when the boat is too far from port to take shelter, but usually he will have time to take appropriate action. First, he should ensure that he has sufficient sea-room to keep clear of dangers. He must avoid a lee shore, for not only does the wind try to drive the boat down on to it (a small boat with little sail set and a heavy head sea finds it virtually impossible to work to windward), but the water shallows near the shore, and this causes the seas to become steeper and more vicious with heavy breaking crests. Other areas to avoid are races, tide-rips and shoals, in all of which the seas will be more confused and dangerous.

Because the wind backs or veers as the depression passes, the skipper needs to know whether the centre is to north or south of his boat. Otherwise he may select a relatively sheltered area protected by the coast to windward only to find, when the low has passed, that the change in wind direction has turned that same bit of coast into a threatening lee shore far too close for comfort.

Boats will usually stand up to far more buffeting than the crew who become exhausted and often seasick, so if a gale has to be ridden out, it is better to reduce sail in good time, easing the motion of the boat and the work of the crew. The boat should be made as watertight as possible, with all portholes, doors, and hatches firmly closed. Older wooden boats may leak considerably in heavy weather, and a regular check should be kept on the bilges of all boats. They should be kept dry to keep the boat buoyant and to ensure that more serious leaks are not developing.

Everything should be stowed and locker doors securely fastened, while any object on deck should be lashed firmly to the boat so that it is not washed away by heavy seas. All crew members on deck should wear not only life-jackets but also safety harness and should hook themselves on to the boat. Weight should be kept low to increase stability, and no crew member should attempt to go forward without alerting another member of the crew in the cockpit.

Boats react very differently to high seas and wind, and there are various ways by which they can be helped to ride out a storm. Some boats heave-to comfortably under storm jib and a loose-footed trysail, with the jib backed and the helm lashed to leeward, sailing forward slowly, but making a lot of leeway which calls for plenty of sea-room to leeward. Some boats do better lying ahull under bare poles, broadside to the waves, and others are more comfortable heading into wind and seas, either lying to a sea-anchor or to a long mooring line streamed from the bow which not only slows the boat but discourages seas from breaking. When a boat runs before the waves, her own speed through the water encourages the crests to break over her, but a line streamed astern slows her down and helps to prevent this.

13
Safety, distress signals, flag etiquette and equipment

Barbara Webb

Letting off a distress flare from a life-raft fitted with a canopy to protect the crew from the elements. Some countries stipulate that yachts over a certain size must carry life-rafts, and yachts racing offshore are usually required to do so. Life-rafts should be serviced regularly and be large enough to take the entire crew. Flares must be renewed before their expiry date.

Safety equipment and safety on board

Some countries specify the safety equipment to be carried aboard boats, and inspectors may check to ensure that the legal requirements have been complied with. Participation in many races, both offshore and inland, is also subject to compliance with fulfilling safety regulations laid down by the organizing clubs and other authorities. Nevertheless, the provision and maintenance of safety equipment in satisfactory working order often depends only on the owner and varies according to the size of the boat and the type of sailing undertaken.

PULPITS AND GUARDRAILS: Boats that venture offshore should, at least, have a pulpit forward, but most modern boats over 25ft also carry a stern pulpit and guardrails, rigged through stanchions, along either side of the boat. A guardrail that is too low can act as a trip wire and merely serve to deposit the crew overboard, but high guardrails require a second wire half-way up the stanchions so that the crew cannot roll overboard underneath the top guardrail. Guardrails should be inspected frequently for signs of wear or corrosion.

LIFEBUOYS: The horseshoe shape is preferable to the traditional circular lifebuoy because the swimmer does not have to lift it over his head. It should be attached to the boat close by the helmsman in such a way that it can be freed immediately when required.

LIFE-RAFTS: Many boats carry inflatable life-rafts large enough to support the entire crew. They should be checked regularly to ensure that they are in a seaworthy condition and must be lashed firmly to the deck. All crew members should know how they are inflated.

PERSONAL BUOYANCY (Personal Flotation Devices, PFDs): In many countries personal buoyancy is a legal requirement, and boats may be inspected to see that they carry an officially approved life-jacket for every person aboard, designed to keep an unconscious man afloat face upwards for long periods. Life-vests, a term used in Australia and occasionally in the United States, are life-jackets which restrict movement less and are therefore more practical for the crews of sailing boats. They, too, must keep a man face upwards in the water.

SAFETY HARNESS: A webbing harness, which fits over the shoulders and around the chest, has an eye set centrally on the wearer's chest to which is attached a length of line fitted with two snap hooks – one at the end and the other in the middle. The crew attaches himself to the boat either by the end hook – which gives him plenty of scope – or by the central hook which restricts his movements but can give him support. The two hooks ensure that he can change the anchorage point when moving round the boat but always remain attached.

FIRST-AID BOX: The larger the boat and the longer the voyage, the better equipped her first-aid kit should be, and a first-aid manual should be carried aboard. Every sailor should know how to deal with bleeding, burns, fractures and concussion and, above all, how to carry out mouth-to-mouth resuscitation.

FIRE AND EXPLOSION: The shape of a boat causes flames fanned by the wind to spread rapidly, and inflammable fuels aboard explode. Fire extinguishers must be carried and positioned so that they are accessible

153

both from the cockpit and from the cabin should the companionway become impassable. In many countries the number and type of extinguishers is specified by law.

Fire prevention in small boats is far easier than fire fighting and is basic common sense: do not overfill fuel tanks; ensure that drip trays beneath engines prevent fuel and oil finding their way into the bilges; check that all electrical wiring, fuel lines and bottled gas systems are correctly installed, and properly serviced and maintained. Ban smoking and extinguish all naked lights while refuelling. When not required, turn off bottled gas supplies at the bottle, fuel at the tank, and electricity at the main switch. Make a regular check of these precautions part of the daily routine and always double check before leaving the boat.

Bottled or liquid petroleum gas (LPG) is heavier than air so leakage concentrates in the bilges and can be ignited when the engine is turned over. The result will be an explosion which will probably lift the deck off the boat and may result in fire and sinking. Some countries enforce strict regulations when LPG appliances are fitted. There are devices which detect the presence of gas in the bilges, but prevention is the best insurance of all. An excellent safety device is an extractor fan connected to the ignition switch of the engine. When the ignition is switched on, the fan extracts the air and the gases mixed with it from the bilges before the engine can be turned over.

EXHAUSTS: Exhaust fittings should be checked, because fumes blown or sucked into the cabin can cause asphyxia from carbon-monoxide poisoning.

PUMPS: Pumps must be checked regularly to ensure that they are working efficiently. All boats should carry one hand-operated pump and a bucket in addition to any other type of pump. An efficient strum box or strainer should be fitted round the bilge pump suction pipe to prevent debris lying in the bilges blocking the pump itself. The limber holes should be cleaned out regularly and the bilges kept clean at all times to ensure that the strum box does not become choked and that spilt fuel and oil do not accumulate.

SEA-COCKS: Every inlet or outlet that passes through the skin of the boat should be fitted with a sea-cock which should always be kept closed when not in use – in particular those for the w.c. and engine water-cooling systems.

LIGHTS AND SHAPES: The lights and shapes called for by the Rules of the Road should be installed or carried and used when appropriate. There should be adequate provision for keeping batteries charged.

Distress signals

Distress signals listed in the *International Regulations for the Prevention of Collision at Sea* include:
(a) Continuous sounding with any fog-signalling apparatus.
(b) Rockets or shells throwing red stars, or a rocket parachute flare, or a hand flare showing a red light.
(c) ·····--- ··· (SOS) in Morse Code made by any means, or the spoken word 'Mayday'.

154

(d) The International Code Signal flag N over flag C.

(e) A square flag with a ball, or anything resembling a ball, above or below it.

(f) A smoke signal giving off orange-coloured smoke.

(g) Slowly and repeatedly raising and lowering arms outstretched to each side.

In Australia a large orange-red rectangle bearing the letter V in black may be exhibited.

Distress flares should never be fired or ignited, nor signals made except to indicate distress and need of assistance. Flares must be kept dry and checked annually to ensure that they are ready for use in an emergency.

Flag etiquette

Flag etiquette has become less formal over the years and varies from country to country. Visiting boats should, therefore, follow local custom. Traditionally, flags are flown from sunrise to sunset, sunrise usually being taken as 8 am.

Almost all boats fly a burgee from the truck when not racing, generally that of the yacht or sailing club of which the skipper is a member. A rectangular flag is flown when racing in many countries. The flag officers of yacht clubs fly broad pennants which are swallow-tail square flags with the club emblem.

An ensign is worn aft on a staff when in harbour and when entering or leaving, and the skipper has to be sure to fly the version to which he is entitled. Traditionally, the ensign is dipped to naval vessels and to the officers of the club to which he belongs. It is flown at half-mast as a sign of mourning, and is generally recognized as a distress signal when flown upside down.

When visiting foreign countries a yacht should fly from the spreaders a courtesy flag – a small version of either the national flag or the ensign of the country she is visiting, depending on the custom (but see Chapter 4, p. 60). A personal house flag or that of a national sailing association to which the skipper belongs is also flown from the spreaders.

Some boats carry the full set of International Code of Signals flags which can be used to send messages taken from the International Code, e.g. flag 'W' means 'I require medical assistance'. When dressing ship on celebration days, the flags can be strung together and hoisted so that they fly from stem to masthead and down to the stern.

Wire rope and rope

Wire is used for the shrouds and stays, the halyards, and for other rigging linkages where minimal stretch is called for, and also for lifelines and other purposes to which its size and strength are better suited than rope.

Stainless-steel rod and lenticular rigging are too expensive for most people, as well as being inconvenient, because they have to be transported in one straight length. The most usual wire for standing rigging

13.1 Burgee.

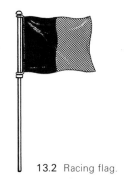

13.2 Racing flag.

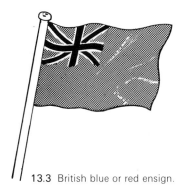

13.3 British blue or red ensign.

13.4 Ensign flown by members of US power squadron.

1 × 19

7 × 7

7 × 19

13.5 Wire rope construction.

is stainless steel of 1 × 19 construction. A single central wire has an inner layer of seven wires laid round it in an anti- or counter-clockwise direction and an outer layer of eleven wires laid in a clockwise direction. It is very strong and has little stretch and, because it is almost impossible to splice by normal methods, it must be used either with swaged-end fittings or with one of the crimped ferrule systems described below.

The other wire used for standing rigging is of 7 × 7 construction, six strands of seven wires each being laid around a central strand also of seven wires. 7 × 7 wire stretches slightly more than 1 × 19 but can be spliced by hand.

A more flexible wire is required for halyards as it has to feed round sheaves and winches. 7 × 19 construction is used in which each of the seven strands consists of nineteen individual wires. Stainless steel is usually used, but as the individual wires are so small, there is a tendency for one or two to snap after a period of use. This has virtually no effect on the strength, but the 'hot' ends can be uncomfortable to touch. Stainless steel also fatigues and therefore can snap where it is kinked. For this reason some people prefer to use galvanized wire for halyards, replacing it annually because it rusts easily.

Rope, too, is made up of a number of strands as described in the glossary. Laid rope usually has three strands, but plaited or braided rope is also obtainable and has a much smoother surface which is kinder to the crew's hands. Manilla, cotton, hemp and sisal, the traditional fibres, have now largely been replaced by synthetic fibres such as nylon, Dacron or Terylene, and polypropylene, each with its individual characteristics. A large mooring line is often made of buoyant fibres so that it floats clear of the propeller, and is sufficiently elastic to absorb the stresses which arise when a boat surges to the waves. Halyards, on the other hand, must stretch as little as possible to prevent the luffs of the sails sagging. Sheets need to be of large diameter to avoid cutting into the crew's hands.

Splicing

Wire splicing is a lengthy and skilled job. Swaged terminals or Talurit or Nicropress crimped systems are generally used for 1 × 19 wire and often for other wire, too. With a swaged terminal the wire is fed into a hole in the terminal fitting which is then squeezed over it in a special press. With the Talurit and Nicropress systems an eye is formed in the end of the wire using a soft metal ferrule which is then squeezed under pressure to grip the wire. So effective is this that the soft metal flows completely between the strands of the wire, eliminating all gaps (fig. 13.6).

Wire of 7 × 7 and 7 × 19 construction can be spliced, and this method is preferable for halyards where the use of a ferrule would cause a hard spot. 7 × 19 wire used for halyards can also be joined to a rope tail by using a wire-to-rope splice (fig. 13.7).

Rope splicing is a more frequently required skill. The long splice (fig. 13.8) is used to join ropes of equal size which have to pass through fairleads or blocks, because the spliced area has the same diameter as

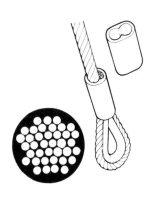

13.6 A Talurit splice.

156

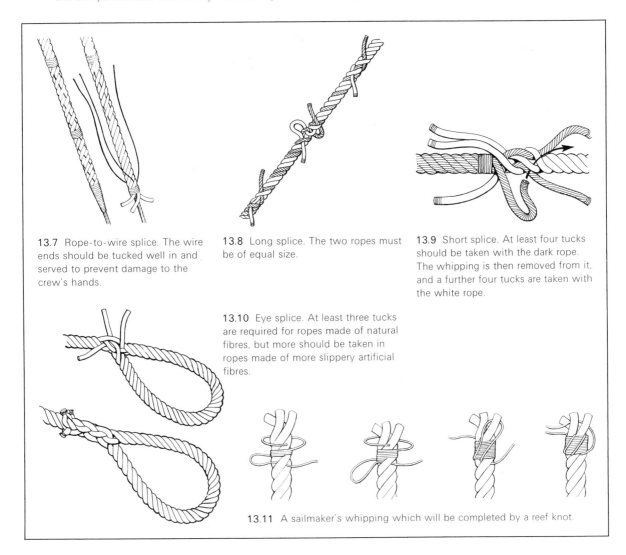

13.7 Rope-to-wire splice. The wire ends should be tucked well in and served to prevent damage to the crew's hands.

13.8 Long splice. The two ropes must be of equal size.

13.9 Short splice. At least four tucks should be taken with the dark rope. The whipping is then removed from it, and a further four tucks are taken with the white rope.

13.10 Eye splice. At least three tucks are required for ropes made of natural fibres, but more should be taken in ropes made of more slippery artificial fibres.

13.11 A sailmaker's whipping which will be completed by a reef knot.

the rest of the rope. The short splice (fig. 13.9) is used to join two ropes of equal size which do not need to pass through fairleads, the spliced area being of greater diameter than the rest.

The eye splice is used to form an eye in any size of rope or line (fig. 13.10). In natural fibre three tucks of each strand may be sufficient, but at least four or five tucks should be taken with the smoother synthetic fibres and the ends dogged by fusing them with heat.

ROPE ENDS: Once rope has been cut the ends will unlay quickly unless they are whipped. There are several methods of which one is illustrated in fig. 13.11. Since synthetic fibres melt when heat is applied, the ends can be welded together by applying a lighted match, but this should be in addition to a whipping and should not replace it.

Part III
Design, racing
and cruising

14
Design considerations

Peter Cook

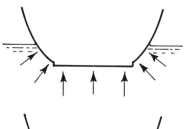

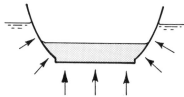

14.1 *Above (top)* An empty bowl displaces relatively little water. *(bottom)* When water is added, the bowl sinks lower in the water and displaces more.

14.2 *Below* The weight of a boat acts downwards through its CG.

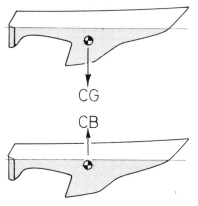

14.3 The buoyancy of a boat acts upwards through its CB.

Yacht design is an art rather than a science. Certainly scientific principles are involved, and a thorough knowledge of basic naval architecture is an asset to any budding yacht designer. Anyone trying to design a racing yacht to the International Offshore Rule will make little progress unless he can master the complexities of the various inter-related mathematical formulae involved. However, first-hand practical experience of sailing and a sympathetic understanding of the behaviour of sailing craft in a seaway, combined with a measure of artistic flair and an eye for a sweet line, are more useful attributes than a diploma in yacht design or a degree in naval architecture. This is borne out by the high proportion of successful yacht designers who have had no formal training in the subject but whose expertise has been developed from a deep involvement in sailing and a yearning for improvement.

It is possible to spend a lifetime sailing with no knowledge of hull shape or sail design. But a basic understanding of the principles involved, knowing not just how to sail but why a boat behaves in a certain manner makes one a better seaman, broadens one's interest and adds enjoyment and personal satisfaction.

A sailing boat is required to float on the surface of the water, to be stable, to move forwards, and to be controllable in a wide variety of wind strengths and sea states. First, let us look at flotation.

Displacement

The weight of any object floating in water is the same as the weight of the water that it displaces. (Remember Archimedes, the Syracusan philosopher who leapt from his bath and ran naked down the street shouting 'Eureka' when he realized this fact?) An empty bowl displaces relatively little water, but if it is partly filled, it weighs more and displaces more water. Similarly, a light-displacement boat weighs less and displaces less water than a heavy-displacement boat of similar overall dimensions.

Centre of gravity

The centre of gravity of an object is the point where the components of its weight may be assumed to be concentrated; the force of gravity acts downwards through this point.

Buoyancy

Water exerts pressure perpendicular to the immersed surface of an object, and the resultant upward force is called buoyancy. The centre of buoyancy is actually the centre of gravity of the volume displaced by and having the same shape as the immersed part of the boat.

When a boat floats freely in calm water with no external force applied, the weight of the boat acting vertically downwards through its centre of gravity is opposed by buoyancy acting vertically upwards along the same line through the centre of buoyancy.

Weight = displacement = buoyancy – this is why a boat floats. If the all-up weight is increased, the object sinks lower in the water, the upward pressure of the water on the hull increases, and buoyancy also increases. This is what happens when the crew, with their clothes and food, go aboard a moored boat. When weight exceeds buoyancy, the object sinks.

When a man moves forward, aft, or to one side, the combined centre of gravity of the boat and the man shifts, and the centre of buoyancy shifts also, vertically in line with the new position of the centre of gravity.

Stability

A boat must be stable, which means that she must float level in the water when no external forces are applied. When an external force is applied that causes the boat to heel – the pressure of the wind on the sails for instance – the position of the centre of gravity relative to that of the centre of buoyancy must be such that the weight of the boat acting downwards through the centre of gravity, and the buoyancy, acting upwards through the centre of buoyancy, tend to return her to the upright position. This is called the righting moment and the greater the horizontal separation of the centres of gravity and buoyancy, the greater the righting moment. Some boats can occasionally heel so far that the point is reached when the downward action of gravity and the upward action of buoyancy tend to make her turn turtle, in other words the boat is subjected to a capsizing moment.

In determining stability the major factor at small angles of heel with most boats is the shift of the centre of buoyancy away from the line of the centre of gravity, thus increasing the length of the righting arm. As a boat heels further, the centre of buoyancy moves less, and the major factor then becomes the position of the centre of gravity; the lower it is, the further away it will be from the centre of buoyancy, and the greater will be the righting couple. So stability depends on the length of the righting arm which is the lateral separation between the vertical lines passing through the centres of gravity and buoyancy.

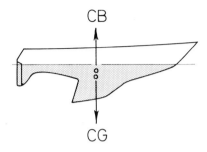

14.4 When no external forces are applied, the CB and CG lie on the same vertical line.

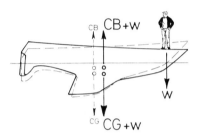

14.5 The combined CG of man and boat moves forward as he moves. The trim changes to align CB with the CG's new position.

Below The couple generated by forces acting through the CB and CG either tends to right the boat (14.6) or capsize it (14.7).

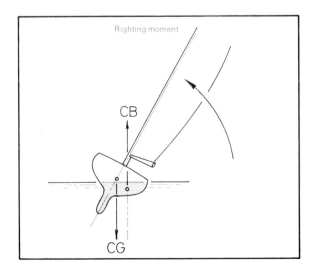

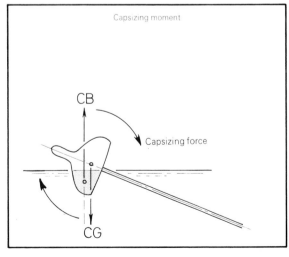

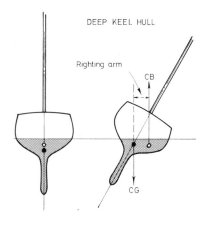

DEEP KEEL HULL

Righting arm

CB

CG

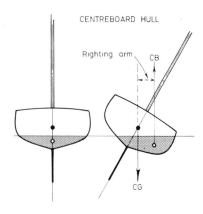

CENTREBOARD HULL

Righting arm   CB

CG

14.8 Comparison of righting arm. Initially the CB shifts further for a given angle of heel in a centreboard boat than it does in a deep keel boat. The longer the righting arm, the greater the righting moment. Increasing the beam of a boat and lowering the CG both increase the length of the righting arm. In a dinghy the weight of the crew sitting out or trapezing shifts the CG to windward and also increases the length of the righting arm.

In keelboats and cruising yachts the bottom of the keel is usually ballasted with lead or cast iron to achieve a low position for the centre of gravity. An unballasted, flat-bottomed hull will have high initial stability but the stability will drop off as the angle of heel increases, while a narrow, ballasted hull may have a very low initial stability but it will increase until it reaches a maximum when the mast is horizontal.

Figure 14.8 shows the righting arms for different hull shapes and different centres of gravity, and shows how stability can vary from one craft to another. In centreboard dinghies, and in some racing keelboats, the weight of the crew is an important factor in counteracting the force of the wind on the sails. Sitting out or trapezing moves the centre of gravity further to windward and so increases the length of the righting arm. A common fallacy is that fitting a heavy metal centreboard, in place of a wooden one, will increase the stability of a dinghy. Dinghies are designed to be sailed upright or nearly upright, and it can easily be seen by drawing a simple diagram showing the centre of gravity and centre of buoyancy that any appreciable increase in righting moment produced by the heavier centreboard will not be felt until the boat is at a considerable angle of heel. In dinghies hull shape is by far the greatest factor affecting stability.

Extreme examples of stability are, on the one hand, a narrow, deeply veed hull with a high ballast ratio giving a low centre of gravity and, subsequently, the maximum righting moment when the mast is horizontal; on the other hand, a completely unballasted catamaran with a very high inherent initial stability which reduces on heeling as the righting arm is shortened and results, ultimately, in an equally high measure of stability in the inverted position.

Forward movement

A boat is required to move forward through the water but not sideways. Any object moving through air or water meets resistance, so the aim of the designer is to reduce forward resistance to a minimum while ensuring that there is sufficient resistance to lateral movement.

The principal factors affecting forward movement can be apportioned to wave making, hull drag and skin friction. As a boat moves through the water waves form along its length. As speed increases the waves grow longer until there is one wave crest at the bow and another at the stern with a trough in between. As this point is approached there is a rapid build-up of resistance for little additional increase in speed. The hull cannot make a bigger wave owing to the limits of its length and so tries to climb out of the trough, uphill as it were, and surmount its own bow wave. The majority of displacement boats, namely keelboats, are unable to do this and have therefore reached the limit of their performance. Dinghies and fast powerboats, on the other hand, can climb out of their own wave trough, but to do this they have to surf over the surface of the water, planing. Once they are planing resistance to forward motion drops and so speed can increase rapidly.

For any hull moving through the water the maximum displacement speed as opposed to planing speed that it can achieve, in knots, is

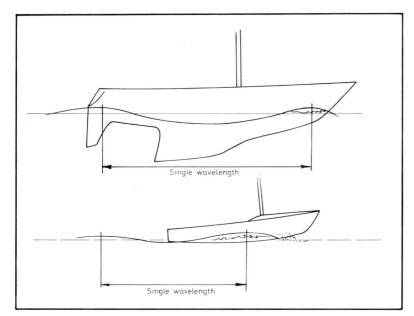

14.9 *(top)* A displacement hull sailing at maximum speed forms a wave crest at stem and stern with one trough in between. *(bottom)* Dinghies may exceed their theoretical maximum displacement speed by surfing on their own bow wave.

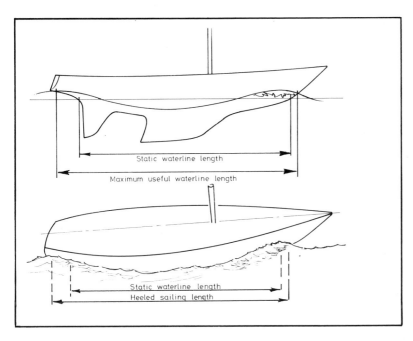

14.10 Overhangs forward and aft enable the effective waterline length to increase as the bow and stern waves build up and the boat sits lower in the water in the trough between the two crests.

around 1.4 × the square root of its waterline length (in feet). For a 16ft dinghy the maximum theoretical displacement speed will be $1.4 \times \sqrt{16} = 1.4 \times 4 = 5.6$ knots; for an ocean racer with a 36ft waterline the speed would be $1.4 \times \sqrt{36} = 1.4 \times 6 = 8.4$ knots. So the maximum displacement speed varies as the square root of the waterline length. In the examples given here increasing the waterline length from 16ft to 36ft, more than doubling it in fact, results in only a 50% increase in potential displacement speed through the water.

By giving a boat overhangs forward and aft the effective waterline

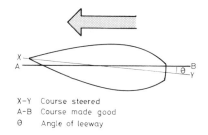

X–Y   Course steered
A–B   Course made good
θ   Angle of leeway

14.11 Except when a boat is running dead before the wind, she will always make leeway which is the difference between the course steered and the course made good through the water.

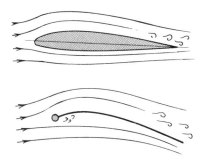

14.12 *(top)* The cross-section of an aeroplane wing. The air moves faster over the upper surface producing a drop in pressure that results in lift. *(bottom)* Similarly, wind travels faster over the leeward side of a sail than it does over the windward side producing a drop in pressure to leeward that results in forward drive.

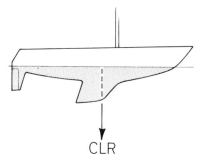

CLR

14.13 The centre of lateral resistance is the point about which a boat turns.

length is increased, for as the bow and stern waves approach their maximum height, the boat sits lower in the water, and the waves move out towards the ends of the boat. Also, the waterline length increases as the boat heels. So in calculating the maximum displacement speed of a particular hull it is the effective waterline length rather than the designed one that matters. Displacement boats whose top speed is restricted by their length in smooth water can exceed this speed when sailing in big seas as they surf down the fronts of the waves.

The majority of keelboats and ocean racers, and all cruising boats, have displacement hulls rather than planing hulls, so in the search for speed the designer will usually aim for the longest effective waterline length coupled with a hull shape that will reach its maximum speed as easily as possible. A fine lined racing boat may reach its maximum displacement speed in only 10 knots of wind, whereas a chunky cruiser of similar waterline length may need double the wind force to reach the same speed. The maximum theoretical speed of both boats is the same; all that varies is the force necessary to enable each boat to achieve this speed.

Hull drag is the resistance of the hull to forward movement caused by the shape of the immersed portion of the hull. At one time it was thought that a fast hull had to be very slim and that a beamy hull would inevitably be slow. This theory has been disproved to a considerable extent in recent years, but a discussion on the various factors of hull shape affecting boat speed is beyond the scope of this book.

Skin friction is the drag produced by the movement of water over the bottom of the boat and is in proportion to the wetted area. So another way that a designer can reduce resistance is by keeping the wetted area of the hull as small as possible.

Why a boat sails to windward

Power-driven boats and rowing boats are propelled by machinery or manpower in whichever direction the crew chooses: the driving force, be it propeller or oars, acts along or parallel to the centreline of the boat. Sailing boats, however, are propelled by the wind acting on the sails and, if the wind is blowing from the side of the boat, there is a considerable force trying to push the boat sideways through the water. This is resisted by giving a sailing boat a deep keel or a centreboard which can be lowered to provide lateral resistance.

It is easy to understand why a boat sails downwind – the wind pushes her – but a boat often needs to sail across or towards the wind and she can only do so because of the shape of the hull and the shape of the sails.

If you squeeze an orange pip against the surface of a table beneath a finger, it cannot move in the direction in which you are exerting energy because the table resists this. It therefore takes the line of least resistance and flies forward across the surface of the table. It is exactly the same with a boat: because the shape of the hull with its keel or centreboard below resists lateral movement, it is difficult for her to move sideways, and the wind's energy is converted into forward movement – the line of least resistance.

Because the table top stops the orange pip moving downwards, all the energy is converted into forward movement, apart from a small loss owing to friction, but the shape of a boat merely discourages lateral movement – it does not prevent it completely. When the boat is reaching or close-hauled, some of the wind's energy is lost in leeway, which is the sideways movement of the boat through the water. Although the boat in figure 14.11 is pointing along line XY, her course made good through the water is along line AB. The difference between these two lines, represented in the figure by the angle Θ, is known as leeway and can be seen when sailing by observing the angle that the wake makes with the heading. A boat makes most leeway when the wind is forward of the beam, progressively less as the wind frees, and no leeway when running because all the wind's energy is converted into forward movement.

The angle of leeway is decided to a great extent by the shape of the hull and in particular by the area and shape of the underwater appendages, the keel, rudder, skeg, and centreboard. If there is too little lateral area, the difference in pressure between the leeward side and the windward side is such that the smooth flow of water breaks down, turbulence is produced, and the angle of leeway and drag increase considerably resulting in a drop in speed. The cross-section of the keel and rudder is important too, for some shapes provide better lift than others and enable a smooth flow of water to be maintained – so the angle of leeway is low.

The sails are cut so that when they fill with wind they take up much the same shape as the wing of an aeroplane. The wind travels faster along the leeward side of a sail than along the windward side, and this causes the pressure to be less on the leeward side than it is on the windward side. Consequently, suction arises to leeward resulting in forward lift in the case of a sail similar to the upward lift generated by the wing of an aircraft.

Balance

If a boat is to be a pleasure to sail and capable of being controlled in all conditions, she must be well balanced. The hull turns about a point called the centre of lateral resistance, the CLR, which is the effective centre of the area of the underwater profile of the boat.

The wind force on a sail can be considered as acting through a point known as the centre of effort (CE). For a triangular sail the CE lies on a line drawn from one corner to the centre of the opposite side. If lines are drawn from two corners, the point where they cross is the position of the CE. Each sail has its own CE and the combined CE for two sails can be found by drawing a line between the two centres of effort and dividing it in proportion to the individual areas of the two sails.

If the CE is aligned exactly with the CLR, the boat will be perfectly balanced. But if the CE lies aft of the CLR, the pressure of the wind tends to turn the stern away from and the bows towards the wind. To counteract this and in order to steer a straight course the helmsman has to keep the tiller to windward, and the boat is then said to carry weather

14.14 The centre of effort of a sail is the point through which the wind forces can be considered to act. To find the centre of effort of a sail plan first find the centres of effort of the individual sails (as described in the text) and join these two points with a line. Then divide the line in proportion to the areas of each sail. In this illustration if the genoa were 400sq ft and the mainsail 200sq ft, the total area would be 600sq ft, and the line would be divided in the proportion of two to one. Note that the combined centre of effort will lie nearer the centre of effort of the larger sail than to that of the smaller.

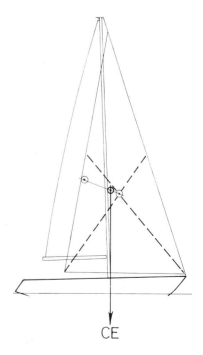

CE

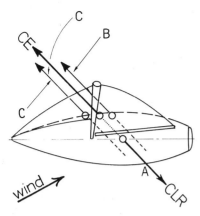

14.15 The separation of the lines of action through the CE and the CLR decide the balance of the boat. When the lines of action correspond, as at A, the boat is perfectly balanced. When, as at B, the line of action through the CE is aft of that through the CLR, the boat carries weather helm. When the line of action through the CE is forward of that through the CLR, as at C, the boat carries lee helm.

14.16 *Opposite* The lines of a 12ft general-purpose dinghy. Three views of the boat are drawn to give the shape in three dimensions. The lines must be fair and must tie up with each other. The diagonal is drawn to facilitate fairing in the area of the turn of bilge where the sections cross the waterlines and buttocks at shallow angles. In the table of offsets the heights are given above the datum line, but the heights are often related to the load waterline or datum waterline. A datum waterline (DWL), which is the approximate position of the load waterline, is shown here. The final position of the load waterline will be calculated by the designer when the lines are finished and will vary with the weight of crew.

helm. A small amount of weather helm is very acceptable; it gives a boat feel, but if it is excessive, the helmsman will tire quickly and the rudder, held well over, acts as a permanent brake. If the CE is forward of the CLR, the boat tries to bear away continuously. She is said to carry lee helm and is very uncomfortable to sail.

In most boats fine adjustments to balance can be achieved very easily by moving the position of the CE forward or aft, provided, of course, that the designer has done his sums right in the first place and produced the correct overall balance between hull and rig. Excessive weather helm can be corrected by reducing the area of the mainsail or increasing the area of the headsail, thus moving the CE forward and closer to the CLR. Conversely, to counteract lee helm the area of the mainsail must be increased or that of the headsail reduced to move the CE further aft. Balance must be maintained when sail is reduced in strong winds, and it is often necessary to set a smaller headsail at the same time as the mainsail is reefed.

The lines

The designer has to portray an irregular, three-dimensional shape on a flat sheet of paper. This is done by drawing three different views of the boat on a grid of straight lines representing vertical and horizontal planes. The body plan shows vertical sections viewed from the end of the boat, which are called sections; the profile shows vertical sections viewed from the side, which are called buttocks; and the plan shows horizontal sections viewed from above, which are called waterlines. The body plan is drawn on a grid of horizontal waterlines and vertical buttocks; the profile on a grid of horizontal waterlines and vertical stations; and the plan on a grid of vertical stations and vertical buttocks. The sections, waterlines, and buttocks are called the lines.

The designer first draws the grid of stations, waterlines, and buttocks. The stations divide the load waterline (LWL) into ten equal parts and are numbered from 0 forward to 10 aft. Two or more extra stations, at the same spacing, may be added forward and aft for the overhangs and are numbered −2, −1, 11 and 12. The reason for dividing the LWL into ten parts, rather than selecting a round figure for the station spacing, is to facilitate the use of the formulae used for calculating displacement, wetted area, centre of buoyancy, and centre of lateral resistance. If you see a lines drawing on which stations do not coincide with the limits of the LWL, or if the LWL is not divided into ten parts, be suspicious. The chances are that the person responsible for drawing the boat has not carried out any calculations to check the design, possibly because he does not know how.

The waterlines are usually numbered in sequence above and below the LWL, a minus sign being used as a prefix for those below. Buttocks are usually lettered A, B, C, etc., from the centreline out.

Before he starts to draw the lines, the designer will first have made some preliminary sketches and calculations and will have a good idea of what he is aiming for. He starts by drawing the midship section, usually station number 5 or 6. Next, he draws the outline of the boat on

166

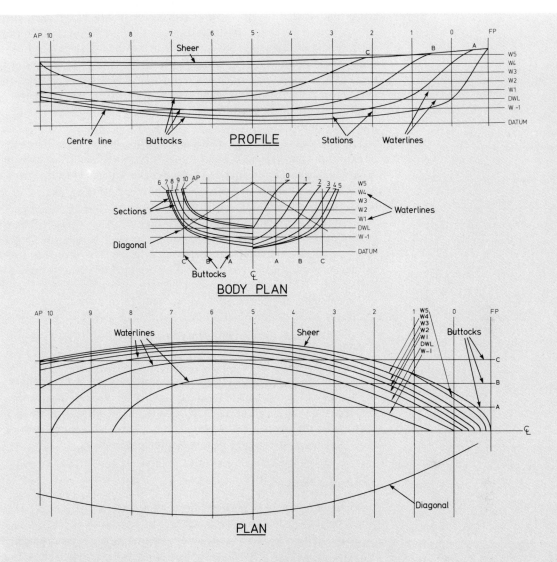

Profile — Sheer, Centre line, Buttocks, Stations, Waterlines, W5, W4, W3, W2, W1, DWL, W–1, DATUM — **PROFILE**

Body Plan — Sections, Diagonal, Buttocks, Waterlines, W5, W4, W3, W2, W1, DWL, W–1, DATUM — **BODY PLAN**

Plan — Waterlines, Sheer, Buttocks, Diagonal — **PLAN**

TABLE OF OFFSETS   Dimensions in feet, inches and sixteenths of one inch.

	Station	FP	0	1	2	3	4	5	6	7	8	9	10	AP
Halfbreadths from ℄	W5		0-11-4	1-6-13										
	W4		0-8-0	1-3-10	1-9-8	2-1-8	2-13-5	2-4-4	2-5-10	2-5-3	2-4-4	2-2-8	2-0-6	1-11-9
	W3		0-5-12	1-1-11	1-7-8	1-11-12	2-2-7	2-4-15	2-4-10	2-3-15	2-3-2	2-1-6	1-11-5	1-10-9
	W2		0-3-14	0-11-10	1-5-9	1-10-0	2-0-14	2-2-9	2-3-6	2-2-14	2-1-15	2-0-4	1-9-8	1-8-6
	W1		0-2-0	0-9-9	1-3-6	1-8-0	1-11-2	2-1-14	2-1-12	2-1-5	2-0-6	1-9-10	1-4-9	1-2-10
	DWL		0-6-10	1-0-5	1-5-1	1-8-8	1-10-7	1-11-5	1-10-6	1-8-6	1-2-0	0-0-0		
	W-1			0-2-8	0-7-0	1-0-0	1-3-6	1-5-5	1-5-5	1-2-3	0-6-12			
	Sheer		1-0-14	1-6-12	1-11-8	2-2-11	2-4-12	2-5-8	2-5-15	2-5-7	2-4-6	2-2-12	2-0-9	2-0-1
Hts. above d'm	℄	2-0-13	0-8-5	0-4-2	0-2-9	0-1-9	0-1-3	0-1-5	0-1-14	0-2-13	0-4-3	0-6-0	0-8-4	0-8-12
	A		1-8-2	0-9-8	0-5-4	0-3-6	0-2-11	0-2-11	0-3-0	0-3-13	0-5-2	0-7-0	0-9-4	0-9-13
	B			1-8-9	0-11-11	0-7-1	0-5-2	0-4-6	0-4-10	0-5-6	0-6-10	0-8-9	0-10-14	0-11-13
	C					1-5-7	1-0-5	0-9-10	0-8-11	0-9-0	0-10-11	1-1-10	1-6-9	1-9-10
	Sheer	2-0-13	2-0-1	1-11-2	1-10-4	1-9-10	1-9-6	1-9-0	1-8-13	1-8-13	1-9-1	1-9-3	1-9-8	1-9-10
Diagonal			0-8-4	1-2-10	1-7-8	1-11-5	2-1-9	2-3-1	2-3-12	2-3-4	2-2-2	2-0-1		

the profile so that at the midship station the height of the deck above the LWL and the depth of the bottom of the keel below it correspond with the dimensions used for the midship section. Then on the plan he draws the outline of the deck and the shape of the LWL, using dimensions from the midship section to determine where they cross the midship station. Further sections and waterlines are drawn in progressively with dimensions being transferred from one plan to another until the lines are complete.

The lines are drawn using either battens or curves, for each line must be fair, that is in a smooth, continuous curve without abrupt bumps or hollows. Battens, or splines as they are often called, are thin strips of wood or plastic which are held in place with lead weights; they are used to draw long sweeping lines such as buttocks and waterlines. The sections on the body plan curve too sharply for battens so curves are used. By progressively working on the three views of the boat – body plan, profile, and plan – and ensuring that each line is fair when it is drawn, the designer ends up with a full set of lines which tie up accurately with each other. He can then carry out his calculations to check that the displacement, and wetted area are acceptable, and that the centres of buoyancy and lateral resistance are correct. If necessary, adjustments will then be made to the shape until the desired result is obtained.

When designing to a rating rule the designer has many other factors to take into consideration, for his aim is to produce a hull which will be fast relative to its rating, and this may not necessarily be the prettiest or most seaworthy. This involves adjustments to the design in order to benefit from favourable allowances or to avoid penalties, and can result in aesthetically unattractive lines when a section is distorted locally in order to gain an advantage at a measurement point.

Table of offsets

From the finished lines drawing the designer produces a table of offsets which gives the dimensions of each section expressed as half breadths. These are measured along the waterlines from the centreline, and heights are measured from a datum waterline along the buttocks. The table of offsets is used by the builder who reproduces the lines full size on a scrive board or mold loft floor – a process called lofting. The designer should ensure that the lines plan is accurate and fair, but the limit of his accuracy is the thickness of the pencil he uses to draw his lines. When the lines are lofted, the designer's original drawing is enlarged. Small discrepancies may show up which the loftsman has to eliminate when he carries out the final fairing of the hull. Care at this stage will avoid time-consuming and costly work later when the boat is built, for it is much easier to adjust a drawn line than it is to cut away solid wood. The lines drawn on the mold loft floor are used to determine the shape of the various parts needed to produce the framework on which the boat will be built and, in the case of wood construction, the shape of many of the structural component parts such as the keel, stem, and rudder post.

15
Dinghy racing

Wendy Fitzpatrick

Background and development

The first sailing dinghies, as we know them today, appeared during the latter half of the last century, and nearly every boatbuilder had one or more stock designs that he produced over the years. This led naturally to the first dinghy classes – if there were sufficient boats of the same type, they would race together on level terms. To ensure that one boat did not have an unfair advantage over another, class rules were introduced governing dimensions, construction, rig and sail area.

The first truly international dinghy class was the International Fourteen which developed from the British National Fourteen class. Although an official International class today, it is active only in Britain, the United States, Canada and Bermuda. The boats have always been relatively expensive and no great number have been built, but the International Fourteen has probably had more influence on the development of dinghy design than any other class, largely because it is a restricted class in which innovation is encouraged within a set of construction and measurement rules.

The first National Fourteens of 1927 were usually clinker or carvel built and were heavy by today's standards. They were designed to be sailed through the water, and the sections were therefore rounded to keep the wetted surface low relative to the displacement. Owing to the rounded sections the underwater shape did not alter radically when heeled, and not too much attention was paid to sailing these boats bolt upright. The helmsman and crew would sit to windward in order to balance the heeling effect of the wind on the sails but would seldom sit out over the side.

In 1928 the most radical change took place. Uffa Fox from Cowes, England designed an International Fourteen that was to plane. We have seen in Chapter 14 how the maximum speed of a displacement boat is restricted by the waterline length. Uffa Fox had built fast motorboats as an apprentice and believed that the same principles could be applied to a sailing dinghy. Instead of giving his boat *Avenger* rounded sections throughout, he made the forward sections more veed and flattened the after sections to provide a planing surface. This very successful hull shape had to be sailed upright for maximum performance, and while it no more than held its own over the older designs in light winds, it was considerably faster off the wind in stronger breezes for it would get up and plane over the waves, thus exceeding its maximum displacement speed.

The basic planing hull with veed entry and flat run was developed over the years, but it was not until the early 50s that the next radical innovation affecting dinghy design was introduced. By then the dinghy planing hull, developed in the restricted classes, had a very fine entry which quickly turned into marked shoulders under the mast, intended to provide stability, before flattening out into a planing run. Boats were easily driven in light winds, but as the wind strengthened there was a rapid increase in resistance as the bow and stern waves built up, supporting the ends but leaving a trough under the shoulders, just where support was needed for stability. Provided the boat remained under

International Moth. This single-handed restricted class offers scope for experiment and development as there are few rules, the main limits being length and sail area. The strongly flared topsides resemble wings and enable the helmsman to place his weight well outboard. These boats are popular in Britain, France and Australia. Loa 11ft; beam 7ft 4in; sail area 85sq ft, weight unlimited. Over 3,600 worldwide.

control, it would climb on top of its own bow wave and plane, but as soon as it dropped off the plane it would again become somewhat unstable. The marked change in speed and handling characteristics between the displacement condition and planing meant that boats were difficult to control and easily capsized. Ian Proctor therefore introduced a different hull shape in which there was a far less marked change between the veed entry and the flat run; the shoulders beneath the mast moved aft and almost disappeared. This reduced the rapid build-up of resistance as planing speeds were approached. The boats planed earlier and faster, accelerating smoothly from displacement to planing and back again.

Ten years later came the next major development. Designs in several restricted classes had become more veed aft and hence had less initial stability, but by providing a wider floor before the turn of bilge the ultimate stability was greater. The natural progression was to flare out the topsides, especially in the area where the crew sat out, to allow them to place their weight further outboard and exert a greater righting moment. Merlins had a beam of 6ft 6in or more on a length of 14ft. Although flare allowed the crew to sit out further, the shape was difficult to handle, because if the boat rolled, the rapid shift of the centre of buoyancy as the windward or leeward topsides dug into the water tended to lead to a capsize. Within the limitations of class rules, however, most modern boats are built as beamy as possible to gain sitting-out advantage. In the International Moth class, which has very few restrictions governing the hull, the boats have wings to provide sitting-out power.

The restricted classes have influenced British dinghy design out of all proportion to their numbers. Current thinking in restricted class design has been reflected in many one-design classes – sometimes to an unnecessary or undesirable degree.

While restricted classes influenced the design of dinghies sailed in the English-speaking world, they had little or no influence over design in Europe. Traditionally, European dinghies had been designed for inland lakes or the Mediterranean where the seas are calmer and the winds lighter than on coasts exposed to prevailing winds. European dinghies, such as the Finn, 470 and 420, tend to be fuller in the bow and generally flatter than those found in the rest of the world, and only when they become International classes do they gain ground in other continents.

The IYRU held trials at La Baule in 1953 to select a new dinghy that was to replace the ageing Twelve Square Metre Sharpie as an Olympic class. The Flying Dutchman designed by Dutchman Uwe van Essen was selected. Flat and nearly 20ft long it was a shape totally different from the veed entry, pronounced shoulder and the flat-run British designs of the time, and owed its ancestry to the type of dinghy popular on Europe's inland lakes. The John Westell-designed 17ft 6in Coronet was also at La Baule, and the French Caneton Class Association asked Westell to shorten the Coronet design to 5.05 metres. The result was the 16ft 6in 505 which is now an International class, numerically stronger and more popular world-wide than the Flying Dutchman which won the trials.

On the other side of the world the reaction of the Australians to the demise of the Twelve Square Metre Sharpie was to take the design, give it a bermudan rig to replace the dated sliding gunter, and build it much lighter using thin marine plywood. The resulting boat, the Lightweight Sharpie, had a sparkling performance. Both in Australia and New Zealand lightweight, hard-chine designs have been developed, and these countries lead the world in this type of construction.

In the United States numerous one-design classes have developed over the years. Here, as everywhere, the major international classes are obtaining a stronger and stronger hold.

Design considerations

Rounded sections produce the lowest area of wetted surface and thus least surface drag for any given displacement, while flat and veed sections produce the greatest. In deciding how flat or veed to make the hull the designer must therefore strike a happy medium, bearing in mind the conditions in which the boat will be sailed. A boat that will be sailed in open water and strong winds can have moderate vee sections

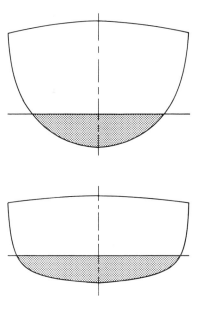

15.1 Designing is always a compromise. For a given displacement rounded sections *(top)* give less wetted surface than flat sections *(bottom)*. But the rounded section shown has little inherent stability, while the flat section provides stability and is necessary for a planing hull.

171

forward to slice through the waves; there must be sufficient beam higher up to provide reserve buoyancy so that the bow will lift when it pitches into a wave; flare is required to deflect spray and keep the boat dry; and flat sections aft are required for planing. A boat that will be sailed inland in smooth water and light winds will encounter planing conditions less frequently and can have a fine entry and more rounded sections to reduce wetted surface.

A boat that is designed for two light-weights of, say, a total of 250lb can be much flatter than one intended for two heavy-weights topping the scales at over 400lb. The designer caters for the heavy-weights by giving the boat more rocker, that is, the amount of round to the keel line, which allows for greater displacement but with the stem and transom at the correct height. Put the heavy-weights in a boat designed for a light crew, and the stem and transom will sink too far in the water causing the boat to wallow.

In restricted classes different designs are available to suit different sailing conditions and different crew weights. One-design classes, on the other hand, are usually designed with certain conditions of wind and water and weight of crew in mind. It is important, therefore, to select a class suitable for your own weight and sailing water if you are really going to enjoy your sailing. Briefly, if you and your crew are heavy, you should go for a larger dinghy – say over 16ft in length. A lightweight man-and-wife team can handle a 12–14-footer easily, while smaller boats will only perform at their optimum with less weight aboard – say a couple of youngsters.

If you are going to build a boat from scratch for the first time, choose one designed specifically for amateur construction, such as the Mirror. Otherwise, buy a professionally built hull and finish it off yourself. That way the most important part, the hull, will be right, and no matter how rough a job you make of fitting the deck and finishing it off, you will still have a usable boat.

Class rules

All class dinghies have to comply with the measurement and construction rules of their class. In restricted classes there are fewer rules and larger tolerances than in one-designs. A tolerance for a restricted class is there to allow for design variation; for a one-design class it is to allow for small variation in building accuracy, the movement of materials and variations in measurement. When taking delivery of a new boat from a builder or supplier, it is as well to have it measured beforehand, or at least soon afterwards, to ensure that it does in fact comply with the rules. If it does not, send it back, for you have not been provided with the boat you ordered but merely with one that is similar.

When building your own boat, do not build to the limit of the tolerance. Quite apart from small variations in shape and dimensions owing to changes in humidity, temperature and wear and tear, remember that different measurers will record different measurements on the same boat. A dimension that requires very careful measurement to verify that it is within the tolerance might pass when the boat is first measured in a heated workshop with good lighting, but may fail when remeasured at an important championship in a cold, damp shed in the failing light.

One last point on measurement. It is very tempting to let a measurer pass a measurement that is right on the limit or just outside it. He may feel sorry for you, but both he and you will have done yourself a bad turn if the boat is subsequently measured after a race and you are thrown out. The onus of ensuring that a boat measures rests on the owner, and it is he who will suffer if anything is out of order.

The rig

Variations in the rig and the way in which it is controlled are the most important considerations affecting performance, for the rig is the engine of a sailing boat.

For any given wind strength the greatest possible driving force must be extracted from the rig. To achieve this a smooth flow of air must be maintained which at all times produces the optimum forward drive. The responsibility for achieving this rests first with the sparmaker and sailmaker, whose products must match each other and work harmoniously together, and secondly with the crew, who must adjust and control the rig to suit the prevailing conditions.

Sails and airflow

Just as different shapes of aeroplane wing are called for to cater for different speeds and weights of aircraft, so the shape and cut of a boat's sails must suit its speed and weight, the sea conditions in which it will be sailed, and the weight of the crew. We saw in Chapter 14 how drive is produced from a single sail by the air moving faster over the leeward side than the windward side, which results in a drop in pressure to leeward. Add another sail, the jib, ahead of the mainsail, and when both sails are sheeted correctly, the airflow over the leeward side of the mainsail is directed with greater velocity and travels further before it breaks away in turbulence. This phenomenon is known as slot effect, and one of the most important factors of sail performance is achieving the correct slot effect for the rig.

Even on smooth water the wind varies constantly in strength and direction, and the rig has to adjust to this continuously if a smooth airflow is to be maintained. Changes in direction are catered for solely by the crew trimming the sheets; variations in strength by weight adjustment and sail trim. As the wind strength increases, the crew moves further to windward until they are applying the maximum righting moment possible by sitting out or trapezing in order to keep the boat level. When the heeling effect of the wind becomes greater than the righting moment that can be applied, some wind must be spilled from the sails. The normal way of doing this is for the helmsman to ease the mainsheet, but there is a risk of upsetting the smooth flow of air as the sail flogs which results in a drastic loss of drive. A far better way to spill the wind initially is to allow the top of the mast to bend away to leeward. The wind is then spilled from that part of the sail which exerts the greatest heeling moment, and leech tension is eased allowing the wind to leave the mainsail more easily, thus reducing drive and heeling effect. Further-

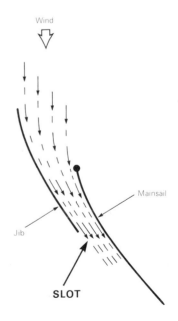

15.2 Slot effect. The jib concentrates the airflow over the leeward side of the mainsail and causes it to accelerate. This produces a drop in pressure which results in an increase in drive.

173

more, as the top of the mast falls off to leeward, the portion of mast between the deck and the hounds moves to windward thus opening up the slot, and this helps to maintain airflow in stronger breezes. By matching the cut of the sail and the flexibility of the mast to the crew weight, the rig will spill wind automatically when a certain wind strength is reached. Producing just the right degree of flexibility and matching the sail to this is very critical, for if the mast is too flexible it will bend too soon, drive will immediately be lost and the boat will become dead and slow down.

A sailing boat requires a flatter sail in stronger winds and a fuller sail in light winds. If the mast is stepped on the keel and allowed to bend forward at deck level, it will flatten the mainsail. This is achieved by the thrust applied to the boom by the vang and the mainsheet. When sailing to windward, as the wind increases in strength the helmsman applies more load to the mainsheet, which forces the boom forwards and bends the mast, thus flattening the mainsail. In order to limit the amount of bend to suit different wind strengths it is usual to have a ram or some other adjustable device just forward of the mast in the slot at deck level.

In smooth water all parts of the rig move at the same velocity, but in waves, as the boat pitches, the top of the mast is alternately accelerating and decelerating, causing not only the speed but also the direction of the wind at the top of the mast to change constantly. In these conditions a boat cannot be sailed as close to the wind and needs fuller sails to keep her moving than would be necessary in smooth water.

The art of sailmaking today calls for an understanding of the idiosyncrasies of a particular type of boat, usually by close personal involvement. The customer need do no more than ascertain which sailmaker is the most successful within his chosen class and place his order accordingly.

Spars

Very few racing dinghies today have wooden spars, the much more predictable characteristics of aluminium alloy being almost universally preferred. The bending characteristics of a wooden mast vary with humidity and eventually even the most cherished will lose their powers of recovery and feel dead.

A single metal mast will serve for a variety of wind strengths, sea states and crew weights. A given type of mast for a given design of boat will have certain bending characteristics, and a sailmaker can work to an accurate set of dimensions and figures when designing sails to suit.

Early metal masts, like their wooden predecessors, were of a pear shape. The theory that this gave the best lead to the flow of air over the mainsail is not now generally accepted because in order to be efficient the pear shape should be angled to line up with the direction of the wind, and this can only be achieved if the mast rotates. In fact, it should over-rotate so that it is angled further into the wind than the leading edge of the sail. A simple method of rotating the mast is to step it on a swivel at the bottom and slot the boom into a fixed gooseneck, but to over-rotate the mast each time the boat changes tack a special device has

A rotating mast on a catamaran. Note how the mast rotates through a greater angle than the sail so that it is set to the optimum angle to ensure good airflow over the mast and sail. The extent of over-rotation can be adjusted with a control line, seen here passing through the block at the end of the mast spanner.

to be fitted. In most dinghies rotating masts are a thing of the past, but they are used in some catamaran classes where the mast is of a particularly deep section fore-and-aft.

Modern thinking on dinghy masts favours smaller, thicker wall sections, and some are now completely circular with a tapered top mast and external sail track attached to the aft side. Because fittings attached to the mast produce turbulence which disturbs the airflow, they should be streamlined as much as possible. On many masts some fittings, such as the shroud anchorages, are internal in order to reduce windage.

With the exception of a few una-rigged single-handers most racing dinghy masts are supported by standing rigging, and this is the key to controlling the bend to suit different sailing conditions. An unstayed mast is cantilevered, held at the keel and supported at deck level. Because it carries no rigging to influence its bending tendencies, it must have built into it exactly the right degree of flexibility to match the boat, sail and crew weight. Dinghies which are designed for ease of transport on top of a car – and the Laser is a prime example – have two-part masts which sleeve together at their mid point in order to reduce overhang and to facilitate the stowage of all spars within the boat.

Aluminium alloy is used almost universally for booms, having replaced wood. In the 60s a trend developed for flexible booms that would bend off to leeward and spill wind in the gusts, but so much drive was lost that, with very few exceptions, the preference today is for stiff booms. This has brought an increase in the diameter of the extrusion. A large diameter, thin-wall boom is stiffer for a given weight than a smaller diameter, thicker-wall section, and weight in the boom is very critical for it spends most of its time to leeward of the centreline where its weight must be counteracted by the crew to windward.

International Laser. The simplicity and strict one-design character of this class make it very popular with busy people who can spend the maximum time sailing and the minimum time on tuning and maintenance ashore. Many people own a Laser as a 'second boat' and use it for evening or winter racing. Loa 13ft 10½in; beam 4ft 6in; sail area 76sq ft; weight 160lb. Over 45,000 worldwide, increasing at 10,000 annually. Designed by Canadian Bruce Kirby.

Standing rigging

Standing rigging consists, in its simplest form, of a pair of shrouds and a forestay. Few racing dinghies are fitted with backstays, but they are found on racing keelboats and are usually adjustable in order to vary jib-luff tension and influence fore-and-aft mast bend.

The shrouds are attached to chainplates which may be above deck or, where the class rules allow, below deck in order to reduce windage. They are usually provided with a means of adjustment at the lower end which may be either a rigging screw (turnbuckle) or a fitting with a vernier system of holes.

Some advanced racing dinghies have their shrouds taken to either a differential winch or a powerful tackle to provide adjustment under way. This enables the crew to vary shroud tension at will during a race and to let the leeward shroud go slack when sailing on a run to allow the mainsail to be squared off. While this refinement can add to boat speed in a highly tuned dinghy when the crew know exactly what they are doing, it is best left to the very experienced, for there is far more chance of applying the wrong setting than the right one.

Mainsail controls

The conventional main halyard that runs from the head of the sail, round a sheave on the mast and down to a cleat near the bottom is admirable for hoisting the sail but has disadvantages as a means of tensioning the luff. Even wire stretches to a certain extent, and if the length of halyard that runs down the mast stretches, luff tension will suffer. When the class rules allow, some helmsmen roll the boat on its side and shackle the head of the mainsail to the top of the mast, but this is an unseamanlike procedure for when the boat is afloat the sail cannot be lowered unless she has capsized. The best solution is to fit a halyard lock. The halyard then consists of a length of light line attached to a short length of wire fitted with a swaged ferrule. When the sail is hoisted, the ferrule engages in the lock and tension is released on the line. To release the lock the halyard is simply pulled; this lifts the ferrule out of the lock and allows the sail to be lowered. Luff tension is applied by pulling down on the tack of the sail.

The traditional mainsheet arrangement has a two- or three-part system running between blocks on top of the transom and at the extreme end of the boom, with the sheet led to the helmsman's hand from the transom. The advent of bendy masts saw the general adoption of the centre mainsheet system in most dinghies over 14ft in length. The mainsheet runs between a block or blocks on the underside of the boom about its mid-length, down to a block in the centre of the cockpit. To allow lateral adjustment the lower block is often attached to an adjustable strop or a traveller on a track or tube. The final take-off point is usually a fixed swivel jamming block mounted on the centreline aft of the traveller. A centre mainsheet requires four, five or more parts because moving the point of attachment forward reduces the leverage exerted on the boom.

With an aft mainsheet system there is no need to let go of either the mainsheet or the tiller when changing tacks as both are aft of the helmsman, but the pull of the mainsheet can tend to make him slide aft unless his feet are firmly braced. The main disadvantage is that when the boat is hard on the wind with the mainsheet pinned in the instant the sheet is eased the boom rises and the mainsail twists. On the wind a centre mainsheet assists the boom vang in its job of preventing mainsail twist. On a reach the traveller can be let out so that the pull of the mainsheet is downwards rather than inwards, and this again helps prevent twist. A centre mainsheet system calls for a different tacking and gybing technique, for the helmsman has to pass between the mainsheet and the tiller. One must be handed behind his back and he must let go of the other momentarily during the manoeuvre.

While it is unusual to cleat an aft mainsheet, centre mainsheets are cleated on a jammer fitted to the final take-off point or in jam cleats on the sidedecks. It is often convenient to have both available – the centre jammer being used when working in the cockpit and the sidedeck cleats being used when sitting out.

After the sheet the most important mainsail control is the vang or kicking strap. It is usually attached to the boom by means of a key that slots into the underside of the boom and runs to a point near the foot of the mast. Considerable power is needed to hold the boom down; in small dinghies a four-to-one purchase may be sufficient, but in larger

This well-designed swivel mainsheet jam block has a ratchet in the block which allows the sheave to turn one way only. A switch is provided for the ratchet so that the sheave can run free if desired. The mainsheet is gripped by a series of ridges in the groove in the sheave.

craft a differential winch or multi-part tackle with a mechanical advantage of up to 64:1 is required. In some boats and especially catamarans the vang may be attached to a traveller running on a curved track right across the boat and looking more like a centre mainsheet system.

Travellers for centre mainsheets and vangs must run smoothly under load or their object is defeated. The mainsail is played constantly when racing, and either the traveller or the sheet can be adjusted. Experienced helmsmen adjust the traveller more frequently than the mainsheet, but most sailors will prefer to use the sheet. Easing the traveller in a gust allows the boom to move outboard, and this releases some air from the top of the sail. Unless the vang completely prevents the boom rising, easing the mainsheet slightly allows the boom to rise which increases the fullness and power of the sail. The mainsheet, therefore, has to be eased considerably further to spill the wind from the mainsail and reduce pressure. In light airs it is usual to position the traveller to windward of the centreline on each tack to avoid flattening the sail too much.

When the mainsail is flattened by bending the mast as the wind increases, the fullness is taken out of the forward part of the sail. The maximum draft is then further aft than desirable, but this can be

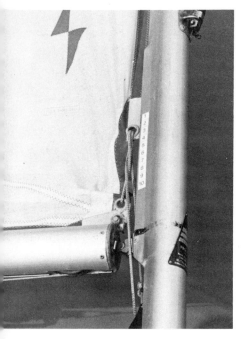

Cunningham eye adjustment. The line rove through the cringle on the luff of the mainsail above the tack enables the luff to be tensioned. This moves the draft of the sail forward and flattens it. The Cunningham is usually tensioned on the wind and released off the wind The numbered strip provides a calibrated guide for the crew.

rectified by tightening down on the Cunningham hole. This is simply a hole in the luff of the sail, a foot or so above the tack, with a length of line passing through it and led to a suitable position for adjustment. In strong winds it is usual to harden down on the Cunningham to windward, thus increasing luff tension and flattening the sail, and to ease it off the wind.

The clew of the mainsail may simply be lashed to the outer end of the boom with the clew outhaul, in which case the foot tension will be determined before the race and it will be difficult to alter. A preferable arrangement is to have an adjustable outhaul led over a sheave in the end of the boom to a tackle inside with the fall emerging through a slot at the inboard end and being taken to a cleat. Although adjustments to foot tension are not so critical as those to the luff, they are necessary if the strength of the wind changes considerably – like the luff the foot should be tightened up in stronger winds and eased off when the wind drops light.

Most dinghies have from three to five battens depending on the size of the mainsail and the number permitted by the class rules. They should be as light as possible and tapered progressively towards their inboard ends so that they merge with the natural shape of the sail and do not produce hard spots. Battens in a fully-battened sail serve a slightly different purpose in that they control the shape of the whole sail. They are tied into pockets running the full width of the sail from leech to luff at a tension to suit the prevailing wind conditions.

Black bands, or bands of a colour contrasting to that of the spars, are painted on masts and booms to indicate the limits of the mainsail. These enable other competitors and the race officials to see at a glance if anyone is using over-size sails. It is a good idea to provide limiting stops to make it impossible to pull the sail inadvertently beyond the bands. This can simply be a pin passing through the track in the mast or boom to prevent the sail going beyond the limit.

Headsail controls
A halyard hook-up is sometimes used for the headsail but more usually it is hoisted on a conventional halyard led to a lever or other means of tensioning. On some larger dinghies that carry spinnakers, such as the Flying Dutchman and the 505, the jib may be fitted with a furling device that enables it to be rolled neatly round its own luff wire once the spinnaker has been set by simply pulling on an endless line. Some jibs are provided with a Cunningham hole for adjusting luff tension under way but they are by no means widely popular in dinghies.

The lead of the jib sheets from the sail to the fairlead on the boat must be such that the tensions on the leech and the foot are balanced in relation to each other, that the angle of attack of the sail matches that of the mainsail, and, most important of all, that the line of the leech conforms with the shape of the mainsail and provides the correct slot. In a small dinghy with a small jib a simple fixed fairlead will suffice, but the larger the jib the more important it is to be able to adjust the lead of the sheet under way. Normally the fairlead is attached to an adjustable slide on a length of track running fore-and-aft. By moving the fairlead forward, foot tension is eased and leech tension increased; by moving it aft the reverse applies. Determining the final position of the fairlead is an important part of tuning.

Some large dinghies have athwartships adjustment for the jib fairlead by attaching each end of the fore-and-aft track to lengths of track running athwartships. In most dinghies, however, athwartships adjustment of the fairlead is not necessary and only succeeds in offering the crew a greater number of incorrect positions. The most usual device for altering the athwartships lead is a Barber hauler which is simply a control line with a ring on the end through which the jib sheet passes. Usually the lead of the jib sheet is taken further forward and outboard when the control line is tensioned, and this is used when sailing off the wind to prevent the leech sagging and to maintain the correct slot effect.

Small jibs of less than 25sq ft can easily be held in the hand, and cleats will only be needed in very strong winds for weak crews or for convenience to free the hands for other tasks. It is always better not to cleat the jib sheet, especially off the wind. A cleated sheet encourages the crew to be lazy and fail to make those minor adjustments to trim that are so necessary for extracting the last fraction of drive from the rig. Cleats must be provided for larger jibs, however, and cam cleats are usually used. Some crews like to fit a cleat to the weather deck, but this tends to be difficult to operate except when sitting or trapezing right out. The best position is probably on the leeward sidedeck, a little way inboard of the fairlead and set slightly off the direct line from the fairlead to the crew when he is in his normal position. This means that he can play the sheet without its jamming in the cleat inadvertently, but can cleat it when required by moving his hands slightly to one side.

Tuning and performance

Tuning a boat is not the same thing as tuning a car. A tuned car usually carries go-fast goodies over and above the manufacturer's specifications. A racing boat is not allowed to do that. Think instead in terms of tuning a musical instrument. The instrument must be at its peak so that the performer is confident of producing a perfect note. Tuning and preparation go hand in glove – an important race is no time for experimentation.

First, the boat, and the surfaces which are in contact with the water. Friction between the hull and the water is very great and must be reduced as much as possible. The hull surface must be completely smooth with all bumps, brushmarks and dead insects removed, and all scratches and hollows filled. There is more skin friction between water and a gloss or wax-polished surface than a matt surface. Place samples of each surface in water: air bubbles will attach to the shiny surface which repels water, but water will flow evenly around the matt surface. Polishes are therefore taboo, and even that perfect glassfibre or painted bottom would be better if it were rubbed down with a 400 grade wet-or-dry paper. Pay particular attention to the first few feet at the bow, as this area dictates the laminar flow over the whole hull. Having achieved the perfect finish, do not ruin it by allowing the boat to sit on a beach or

Barber hauler. The jib sheet on this Fireball is led well inboard to an adjustable fairlead on a length of track. The jib sheet passes through the nylon ring on the end of the barber hauler line, and its lead can be altered outboard by hauling in on the barber hauler. The shroud is attached to a lever, and the white plastics tube is slid up to enable the lever to be released, thus easing the shroud off the wind to allow the boom to be squared off to leeward. Shock cord through the small ring shackled to the shroud plate near the deck keeps the trapeze wires close to the shrouds when they are not in use.

slipway: float her off and on to a well-padded launching trolley and make regular checks on its condition.

The centreboard and rudder should receive the same treatment as the hull. Their ideal section is an aerofoil, thicker forward than aft, if the class rules allow it. Strips of hard rubber or plastics should be fixed to the underneath of the centreboard slot in order to close it behind the centreboard as it is lowered and cut down the drag that an open slot would cause.

If a lifting rudder is used, its cheeks must not be allowed to project below the waterline or they, too, will create drag. Obviously the helmsman cannot move aft to check whether this is happening as his weight will depress the stern. He should settle the boat on a stable point of sailing and stand up in his normal position to look over the transom for the tell-tale bubbles and turbulence.

Never pack the boat away while she is wet. She will soak up water and become heavy and less competitive against lighter boats of the same class. For the same reason do not allow water to lie in the bottom during a race but fit efficient self-bailers.

Excess weight is to be avoided, but do not sacrifice strength for weight. Through-bolt all fittings through substantial packing pads, rather than risk screws pulling out.

Think of the ergonomics of sailing the boat. Ensure that all control lines and sheets lead directly to their cleats; check, too, that those cleats are angled for ease of operation by helmsman and crew. Either fit adjustable toestraps or take great care when setting up fixed toestraps that the length is correct by sitting in the boat ashore. The same strip of toestrap should never be used for both helmsman and crew, unless it is stopped off between the two. If it is not, the one will suddenly find that his toestrap has become much longer when the other eases himself inboard.

The tiller extension must be long enough to reach the shoulder of the helmsman when he is sitting out, but not so long that it fouls the mainsheet when tacking. It should be fixed to the tiller with a fitting incorporating a universal joint so that it can be moved in any direction. Its outer end should be whipped, shaped or covered with rubber to provide a good grip.

Do not clutter a small area of the deck with myriad blocks, cleats and leads. Keep the mechanics of each control somewhere out of the way, such as the area at the foot of the mast, and lead only the fall of each control line aft. A neat row of cleats for all the controls is acceptable provided that each is labelled clearly or a colour-coded system of ropes is used for immediate identification.

Wash sand and salt from all fittings with moving parts at frequent intervals, and check that their fastenings are tight. Make a thorough check for sharp edges and eliminate them. Tape round all wire splices, split pins and safety rings with plastic adhesive tape to prevent them snagging and to keep safety pins in place.

Making the rig work
If you have bought a second-hand racing boat with a proven perform-

ance, do not alter anything until you really understand what you are doing. If yours is a brand new, untried boat, follow a few basic rules.

With the boat supported level on a trailer or trolley, step the mast raked slightly aft (about 9in for a 20ft mast), with the rigging under moderate tension. Ensure that a keel-stepped mast is held rigidly at deck level, paying particular attention to preventing sideways movement. It may be necessary later to allow the mast to move forward here to increase fore-and-aft bend.

With the boat head to wind, hoist the mainsail to the black bands. Station a friend on the windward side of the boat to control the mainsheet and move the boat's head away from the wind until she is on an approximately close-hauled course, between 45° and 55° to the wind, then sheet the sail in to the beating position.

Are there any creases in the sail? Vertical creases along the luff indicate too much luff tension, and the halyard should be eased, the boom lifted by raising the gooseneck, or Cunningham tension released. Horizontal creases on the luff show that more tension is required. If they do not disappear when the boom is let off to a reaching position, increase halyard tension until they do. If they appear only when the sail is close-hauled, apply tension by means of the Cunningham hole until they go. Use the clew outhaul to eliminate creases in the foot in the same way.

Now walk round the boat. Viewed from astern, the leech should follow the smooth curve of the sail, neither hooking up to windward nor falling away noticeably to leeward. Stand to leeward and move slowly to the front of the boat looking at the shape of the sail. The point of greatest draft should be well forward, and the sail should be fairly flat. Wait for a gust to see how far the mast bends to leeward at the top. Only the unsupported top of the mast, above the hounds, should fall away.

Then hoist the jib and sheet it in. The pull of the sheet should be approximately at right angles to the luff of the sail, and the tension of the foot and leech will indicate whether the lead is correct. If the leech is too slack, a more downward pull is required, and the fairlead should be moved forward along the deck. If the foot is loose, the fairlead should be moved aft.

When the rig looks right, launch the boat and see whether she feels right. If she has weather helm, she tries constantly to gripe up to windward, and the rudder has to be used to keep her bearing away on to a close-hauled course. There may be several causes, but the most likely are that the mast is either stepped, or raked, too far aft. Alternatively, the centreboard may be too far forward, and because the balance of a boat depends on the relationship between mast and centreboard, moving either one will pinpoint this source of the trouble. It is easier to adjust a pivoting centreboard while sailing than to move the mast, so raise the board a little (this will automatically rake it aft), and see if the weather helm decreases. Other factors which can contribute to weather helm are over-sheeting, an over-stiff mast and a jib leech which hooks to windward. The helm will also feel heavy when the boat heels or if the rudder blade is raked aft.

Mast-bend control. The screw adjustment forward of the mast limits mast bend at deck level. The pointer opposite the scale on the sliding mast chock indicates the amount of bend. Note the strong tubular mast partners and the hook plate on the mast which gives a choice of six different halyard positions.

This International 505 is perfectly balanced and sailing upright on a close reach. The helmsman is sitting well in the boat so that the crew on the trapeze can watch the luff of the jib and trim it continuously to every slight alteration in wind direction. The long tiller extension allows the helmsman to position his weight anywhere in the boat to suit the wind and sea conditions.

If the boat suffers from lee helm, she tries to bear away, and pressure has to be kept on the helm to bring her bow up towards the wind. The mast may be stepped, or raked, too far forward, the centreboard may be too far aft, or the sails may be slack or not sheeted sufficiently far inboard.

The ideal is to set up the boat so that when close-hauled on an even keel she carries just a suggestion of weather helm to enable the helmsman to feel her reactions. Neutral helm may suddenly and disconcertingly turn to lee helm when least expected. Excessive weather or lee helm not only tires the helmsman but requires the rudder to be applied at an angle while the boat is sailing, and this acts as a brake.

Once the balance of the boat is established, the power of the rig must be adjusted to suit the weight of the crew. If they are overpowered in quite gentle breezes, the top of the mast must be allowed to bend to leeward. If the crew have plenty of sitting-out power in reserve, even in a strong wind, the mast should be prevented from bending so that firm leech pressure is maintained and full drive is generated by the sail.

Spreader adjustment is the key to mast-bend control. The spreaders are attached to the mast between the hounds and the deck and, in conjunction with the shrouds, act either in compression or in tension to prevent or induce mast bend. They should be angled perpendicular to the shrouds, not the mast. A spreader which is longer than the distance between the mast and the shroud at rest will deflect the shroud outwards. When the shroud becomes the windward shroud, it takes all the strain of supporting the mast athwartships and tries to follow a straight line between the hounds and its chainplate. It therefore pushes the spreader against the mast, thrusting the middle of the mast to leeward. The top of the mast will naturally follow this induced curve and try to move up to windward, but because the mainsail tempers this tendency the effect is that the top of the mast is simply prevented from falling off to lee-

182

ward. Long spreaders are therefore used to increase lateral stiffness of a mast for a heavy crew.

A spreader which is shorter than the distance between the mast and the shroud at rest will deflect the shroud inwards. When the strain comes on to the shroud, in following the straight line to the chainplate it will pull the middle of the mast to windward, encouraging the top to fall off to leeward. Short spreaders are for lightweight crews who are being overpowered. Spreaders which are exactly the length between mast and shroud allow the top of the mast to fall off a little way before they come into compression and start to restrict mast bend.

The angle of the spreader to the mast affects mast bend in the fore-and-aft direction. If the spreaders are angled aft of the direct line between hounds and chainplate, the mast below the hounds will bend forward, flattening the mainsail, but if the spreaders are angled forward of the direct line, mast bend will be restricted.

With the rig balanced and the right power-to-weight ratio achieved, it remains only to sail against an acknowledged local expert to check for pointing ability and speed. Lack of pointing ability to windward can be traced to too wide a slot between jib and mainsail; to sails with open leeches; to a flexible centreboard which bends to windward under the pressure of water and allows the boat to sag away; or simply to the fact that the sheets or the traveller are too free.

Lack of speed can be attributed to a hundred and one faults from an over-flexible hull, to blown-out sails or plain lack of experience in the crew. Ask other helmsmen for their advice and, if possible, talk to the sailmaker who is the acknowledged expert for the class.

Bad sails are more detrimental to boat speed than a bad hull. Some faults are difficult for the layman to identify, but others are obvious and many can be rectified by the sailmaker. Sails do not last for ever. If they have been used hard for several seasons, or even if they have been abused for a relatively short time by being allowed to flog for hours, the material may have stretched between the seams. If that stretch occurs in localized areas such as the leech or jib foot, it can be corrected by re-stitching the seams in that area, or by taking in darts. An open leech can be spotted easily: it will not hold wind, there appears to be too much cloth between the battens, and it flutters or 'motorboats' while the boat is sailing. It is essential that this tendency is removed from a jib because any movement of the leech seriously disrupts the airflow through the slot and over the vital leeward side of the mainsail. Surprisingly, it is one of the least important faults when found on a mainsail, although it makes so much noise. The air disturbed by the movement has, after all, ceased to be required by the boat whose sail is motorboating, and is being passed on for re-use by the competitor astern. Other forms of stretch are more difficult to correct. Little can be done for an old sail which has scalloped between each seam, and it is as well to accept the inevitability of buying a new sail.

Leeches which hook to windward affect the airflow badly and must be remedied. The stitching on the tabling or reinforcing may be too tight and this can be corrected, but if the cause is simply insufficient material in that part of the sail to allow it to assume a smooth curve,

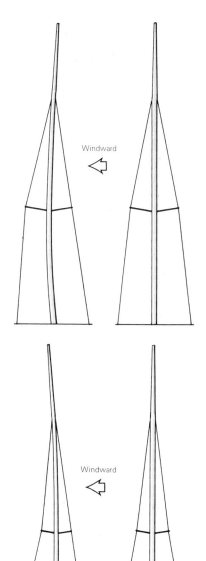

15.3 Spreader length. *(top)* The spreaders extend the shrouds. Tension on the weather shroud will tend to bend the mast to windward at the top resulting in a stiff rig suitable for heavy crews. *(bottom)* For light crews shorter spreaders are needed which cause the top of the mast to fall off to leeward when tension is applied to the weather shroud, thus spilling the wind from the mainsail.

replacement is the only cure. Faults such as too much or too little curve in the luff of a sail to match the bend of the mast are best remedied by selling the offending sail to someone whose mast it will suit and buying a new one.

Occasionally a sail looks good and sets well on the spars but does not drive the boat as fast as the rest of the fleet. The trouble may be that it is being used in the wrong conditions. There is a big difference between sailing in choppy seas and sailing on smooth, inland waters. A boat sailed on open water will use fuller sails to provide more drive through a confused sea than her smooth-water sailing cousin. A suit of flat sails used in a medium breeze at sea may not produce sufficient power.

Burgees, wind indicators and tell-tales
A burgee or solid wind indicator may be mounted at the top of the mast to register the wind direction, or tell-tales may be affixed to the sails to indicate airflow. The wind indicator registers apparent, not true, wind direction. As the boat moves forward it creates its own wind which combines with the true wind to create apparent wind, slightly forward of the true wind except on a dead run.

Tell-tales are short lengths of wool threaded through the sail in rows at regular intervals. As the air flows over the rig the tell-tales stream or stall, indicating the flow of the air at any point on the sail. The optimum sail angle is the one at which all the tell-tales, both to windward and to leeward of the sail, are streaming towards the leech. If the sail is sheeted too close, the windward tell-tale will lift and flutter. If the sail is not sheeted sufficiently hard, the leeward tell-tale will break away and begin to rotate. Thus the flow over the whole sail can be observed and adjustments made to the twist and draft of the sail to prevent the airflow breaking away.

Spinnakers
The spinnaker is a downwind sail which, with the skill acquired by practice, can be used progressively closer and closer to the wind but never on a true beat. It is much rounder in shape than the relatively flat mainsail and jib which have to drive the boat upwind as well as down. Do not think that the spinnaker is hoisted on a dead run just to sit there and catch the wind. Like the other sails there must be a flow of air around the spinnaker or it, too, will stall and cease to pull the boat along.

To set the spinnaker for optimum performance the pole downhaul should be adjusted until the tack is the same height as the clew. The pole is then brought to windward by pulling on the spinnaker guy until the leading edge of the sail begins to curl, but no further or the sail will collapse completely. Then ease the pole forward a fraction. The sail will now be controlled by the sheet until the skipper alters course or the wind shifts. Ease the sheet very gently until the leading edge of the sail threatens to curl, then pull in a small amount of sheet quickly but gently. All the time the spinnaker is set it must be encouraged to reach out for more wind. It must never be strangled but always kept on the point of collapse. Every so often try squaring the pole a little more by

Opposite A typical scene on the river Thames upstream from London in England. The figure 50 on the transom of the Enterprise indicates the trailing speed limit on British roads and is required by law.

pulling on the guy, but always let it go slightly forward when the sail starts to curl.

A spinnaker may be hoisted from a bag within the cockpit or from a spinnaker chute. If the former method is used, the bag or net must be large enough to allow the spinnaker to be packed hastily during the lowering manoeuvre.

We will assume that the spinnaker is stowed in a bag on the leeward side of the boat, with sheets attached. The halyard is unclipped from its stowage place on the mast and passed round the outside of the jib and jib sheets before being clipped to the head of the spinnaker so that the spinnaker is hoisted to leeward of the jib. The crew clips the pole to an eye on the mast and to the spinnaker guy which will be lying along the windward side of the foredeck. The tail of the halyard should be led to the helmsman so that he can hoist the sail, leaving the crew free to play the sheet and guy as the sail fills with wind and to ensure that the pole slides along the guy to the sail. If the spinnaker bag is on the windward side, the hoist must be very quick to avoid the sail being blown into the windward side of the jib, and the pole must be attached after the sail is hoisted. In this case the halyard would be rigged to windward of the jib.

Spinnaker chutes allow a spinnaker to be hoisted quickly and efficiently. A tube with a belled-out mouth is fitted beneath the foredeck with the mouth as far forward on deck as possible, preferably ahead of the forestay fitting. The spinnaker lives in this tube, the head and clews, with halyard and sheets permanently attached, just inside the mouth, the centre at the aft end of the tube or its fabric sock extension. At the centre of spinnakers hoisted by this method is a reinforcing patch and an eye to which the other end of the halyard is attached. To hoist, the pole is clipped on to the mast and the guy, and the helmsman pulls the halyard. To drop, the halyard is uncleated, pulled the other way which draws the spinnaker back into the chute centre first, and the crew removes the pole when the sail is stowed.

And so to race

Treat the progression into the racing world as a serious step but do not worry about it. Worry leads to irascibility, tension and panic decisions. Sailing is your sport, your chosen hobby, and is to be enjoyed. Learn the fundamental racing rules and stick to them. If in doubt, be prepared to give way to the other man until you are sure of your rights – but be sure that he knows that you are giving way when an alteration of course is involved. You will not win your first race, so a yard or two lost for safety's sake is good insurance. Allow plenty of time to prepare your boat and to take note of what the old hands are up to, but never copy anyone slavishly until you are certain that your efforts will result in improved performance.

Weight and windage can make all the difference to the fine tune of a boat. Unless absolutely vital, nothing must be allowed to interfere with the airflow round the sails. If the jib is hanked to the forestay, consider whether the hanks could be replaced by smaller, lighter ones. Remove any unnecessary handles or fittings which stand proud of the deck. Do

Above The spinnaker chute or launching tube on a 505. The spinnaker is drawn into the soft fabric tube seen in the lower photograph.

Opposite (top) Over 100 Lasers starting in the 1974 World Championship held in Bermuda. *(bottom)* Trying to coax life into the sails of Spearheads in light airs in Table Bay.

not leave the spinnaker halyard or pole downhaul line flapping and causing turbulence in the slot. Fair in all mast fittings with rubber sealer or epoxy filling compound, paying particular attention to the spreader roots. Try to find somewhere other than the mast to stow the spinnaker pole. Check whether the mainsheet blocks could be replaced by smaller ones or mounted on wire strops to lower them to deck level.

Are you and your crew wearing baggy clothing, huge anoraks and cumbersome life-jackets? Throw them away or compress them beneath an all-in-one stretch nylon suit. In light airs to present as little windage as possible the helmsman should sit as low as possible in the boat on the windward side while the crew should curl up, out of sight, to leeward. In a breeze helmsman and crew should sit close together. Windage is an advantage only on a run.

Even if a boat is down to minimum weight, the distribution of her payload is important. At all costs keep weight out of the ends of the boat; the rudder assembly should be as light as possible and an anchor, if carried, should be stowed on the centreline amidships. Spare clothing should be kept to a minimum and not stowed in the forward buoyancy tank.

Keep a note of how the rig is set up each time you race. Self-adhesive numbered strips can be used for calibration of control lines. After each race record in a notebook the strength of the wind, the sea condition, the sails used and the settings which were used for their controls, adding your position in the race and any notes on your performance, speed and tactics. Eventually a performance pattern will emerge, and it should be possible to select exactly the right equipment and the correct settings for any given set of conditions.

Fitness is important. The average club sailor sails to keep himself in

188

trim, but the race winner keeps himself fit to sail. An unfit crew will tire during a long race. When tired, concentration lapses and mistakes will result. Too much to eat or drink before going afloat is as bad as too little, but it is sensible to eat a cooked breakfast. You may be on the water for six hours; at a big international regatta when the course may be many miles from land and, perhaps, a long postponement is followed by a slow race in light weather, this time can be doubled. In heavy weather a concentrated glucose drink taken shortly before the start will feed instant energy into the blood stream, and chocolate, an apple and soft drinks should also be available.

A cap with a peak, or sunglasses, can prevent the headaches which are caused by squinting into the sun across water. The crew of a boat with a spinnaker should never be without his sunglasses.

Light airs

In very light airs the sails should be very full, with luff and foot tension eased. The boat can be heeled to leeward so that the sails fall into shape instead of collapsing. To reduce friction wetted surface should be kept to a minimum and, depending on the design, this may mean heeling the boat slightly or moving the crew forward a little to raise the broad, flat aft sections of a planing dinghy just clear of the water. Movement in the boat will slow her down, so avoid all jerky actions; tack, gybe and alter course as gently and smoothly as possible, avoiding excess use of the helm which will act as a brake.

On the wind

Except in very light airs the boat should be sailed upright, using crew weight to counteract wind pressure. You should sit roughly amidships so that the boat sails on an even keel with neither stem nor transom digging into the water. In moderate breezes crew weight will probably suffice, but if the boat is to be kept upright as the wind increases, the mainsail may need to be flattened and the mainsheet played to spill the wind in the gusts.

Off the wind

The boat will sail fastest when upright, but you generally need to move crew weight further aft to help her on to a plane and to prevent the tendency for the bow to be pressed down into the water. Weight should never be so far aft as to cause the transom to drag.

On all points of sailing the centreboard can be raised progressively as the wind frees, thus reducing the wetted surface, but the boat should always be kept balanced so that movement of the rudder can be kept to a minimum. When planing fast in strong winds on a broad reach or a run, only a corner of the centreboard should be lowered to provide a small skeg to assist directional control. This allows the boat to skid sideways slightly in the water when a strong puff hits her and helps to avoid a capsize. Too much centreboard down in these conditions provides too much grip on the water and the boat will be over in a flash.

16
Offshore racing

Jack Knights

The background

There has always been ocean racing of one kind or another, whether it was a French frigate chasing – and usually overtaking – a British man-of-war, a pilot cutter trying to be first out to an incoming ship, or a tea clipper risking her spars to be home to catch the best of the market.

Ocean racing as a sport is comparatively recent, its growth following the progressive taming of the oceans and lesser waters. What only fifty years ago was thought of as an epic voyage has now come to be regarded as almost routine. The ability of ever smaller craft to complete ever longer voyages is now limited mainly by the time at the disposal of the voyagers. Over 120 yachts completed the third race from Cape Town to Rio de Janeiro in 1976 across 3,500 miles of the Southern Atlantic and many of these were less than 40ft overall. In the fifth Singlehanded Transatlantic Race in 1976 from Plymouth, England to Newport, Rhode Island 125 single-handed sailors started.

The Atlantic has now been crossed in both directions by boats of less than 12ft in length: it has been rowed several times, it has been crossed by folding canoe, by drifting inflatable and by amphibious jeep. Yet, according to Humphrey Barton, it had not been crossed by any small sailing boat of any description until 1866 when the 26ft iron lifeboat *Red, White and Blue* sailed from New York to Deal in Kent.

It can be assumed that from the very earliest days long voyages must have been attempted in small open craft. They must have had a better chance of success in warmer latitudes, particularly in the Pacific and the Mediterranean, yet in northern waters the Vikings ranged far and wide. The history of ocean sailing and, later, of ocean racing parallels the story of human technology. A start was made only comparatively recently, but once some momentum was gained, acceleration has been progressive.

'Offshore' would be a more accurate term than 'ocean' though it lacks something in romance. The word ocean came into use because the Atlantic Ocean was the first and most obvious course. At first it was the clipper ships that made the running, and then in the middle of the nineteenth century the new breed of large yachts owned by wealthy sportsmen began to make its presence felt. Before formal races were instituted, lone yachts recorded fast times which became targets for others. Kelley's book on American Yachts published in the USA in 1884 lists twenty-nine individual crossings made by sixteen different yachts between 1851 and 1874.

The first event resembling a modern yacht race came in 1866 when, stung by a newspaper article criticizing New York yachtsmen for venturing no further than the sheltered waters of the Hudson River and Long Island Sound, two wealthy sportsmen agreed to race their yachts *Vesta* and *Fleetwing* across the Atlantic in the dead of winter for a wager of $30,000 a side. The next day twenty-five-year old Gordon Bennett Jr persuaded them to let him race his *Henrietta* for the same entry fee. Bennett won, which was only fair, since the other two owners neglected to ship aboard their vessels.

The German Kaiser Wilhelm had taken up yachting around the turn of the century and proposed a race from New York to Cowes in 1905. This attracted eleven entries, a magnificent fleet comprising two- and three-masted schooners, a topsail schooner, a barque, a fully rigged ship and a yawl. The race was won by the American three-masted 187ft schooner *Atlantic* owned by Wilson Marshall and skippered by the legendary Charlie Barr. Her time for the crossing from Sandy Hook to the Lizard was 12 days 4 hours, a time which has yet to be equalled by a sailing vessel of any description.

After that fast race between those mighty vessels there could be no turning back; ocean racing had arrived. Of course, the great yachts were doomed, mostly by World War I, but partly by Thomas Fleming Day who preached the gospel of small yachts which could be managed by amateurs. As early as 1904 he had organized a race of 330 miles from New York to Marblehead for yachts of less than 30ft on the waterline. Two years later three yachts, all less than 40ft, took part in the first race to Bermuda, won by *Lila* in spite of her being dismasted first day out.

The history of ocean racing is the history of the innovators such as Fleming Day having to overcome the instinctive resistance of established experts. The idea of ocean racing was imported to Britain from the USA, mainly by an adventurous English sailor and wonderful writer, Weston Martyr. As a result of his efforts the Fastnet course was agreed upon, and the first race took place in August 1925.

Most of those who had become acknowledged experts in yacht racing before ocean racing amounted to anything were either patronizing, critical, doubtful or, at best, ambivalent. Sherman Hoyt writes: 'For many years I avoided ocean racing on the ground that it was not racing *per se* as I understood it, and I considered that going to sea in moderately small craft, with attendant discomfort, exhibited a mild form of insanity.' Nevertheless from the late 20s on the story is one of steady and then accelerating progress, with races at first held either annually or even less frequently, attracting the more experienced cruising man with his well-found cruising yacht.

By 1938 there were no less than ten races in the British Royal Ocean Racing Club's calendar, and Kristiansand in Norway, Copenhagen in Denmark, Kingstown (Dun Laoghaire) in Ireland and Bréhat in France all saw fleets of offshore racers. In 1938 there were forty-nine starters in the Bermuda Race, and in 1939 twenty-seven yachts started in the 2,000 mile San Francisco to Honolulu Race. The Honolulu Race, now called the Transpac, was run biennially from 1906 to 1912, in 1923 biennially from 1926 to 1936. In 1939 it was agreed to hold the Bermuda Race on even years and the Transpac on odd years.

The post-war period in ocean racing has been one of internationalization, expansion, and intensification; no limit to the sport's growth can yet be visualized. Nothing could prevent offshore racing spreading from country to country. Only two factors were needed – a sympathetic club and an individual enthusiast. John Illingworth, as an engineer officer in the Royal Navy, was posted to all corners of what was then the British Empire and, like a diligent gardener, he sowed the seeds of offshore racing wherever he went. The Royal Hong Kong Yacht Club already had its own cruiser races in the 20s; in 1938 he was already getting the

Royal Malta Yacht Club offshore-minded; and Boxing Day morning 1946 found him off Sydney Heads, bound for far-away Hobart along with ten others in the first of what was to become the classic of the southern hemisphere. One nation after another started its deep-water races and usually its offshore racing associations – Argentina and Brazil, South Africa and more recently, Japan.

In 1957 the knot that joined the inshore keelboat racers with the offshore fleet was finally tied when the RORC and the Royal Yacht Squadron invented the Admiral's Cup, awarded for the highest-scoring national team of three yachts over a series of races. This competition has flourished and brought to ocean racing a new internationalism, a new racing intensity. In less than no time the Americans had set up their own Onion Patch series for Bermuda Race years, and soon after the Australians set up their Southern Cross.

Although ocean racing soon came to be conducted on handicap under a variety of rating systems, it actually began under the elemental system – first home, wins. In 1965, after forty years of handicap racing, the French advocate and sailor Jean Peytel brought level racing back to the sport by arranging a series of long and short races for yachts rated at the same level, 22ft (RORC), for the One Ton Cup. So successful was the idea that other competitions for other sizes of level raters had to follow.

Only one type of racing is still missing from the 'ocean' seascape which now runs from round-the-world races for 80ft ketches to fifty-mile coastal hops for boats shorter than many an American car: nobody has yet been able to organize one-design racing offshore. But this last and most obvious development is bound to come soon; its accomplishment only awaits the congruence of a sympathetic institution and the right personality.

The development

The large yachts which competed in the few ocean races held before the end of the nineteenth century, and the yachts which raced in that famous transatlantic race of 1905 were the ultimate examples of half a century of development, crewed by tough and skilled professionals who mostly had yacht-hands for fathers and salt in their blood. American big yacht tradition managed to stay comfortably ahead of the British tradition from well before 1851 when the schooner *America* humbled the best of the British fleet in British waters.

The reason, it seems, is that the American yacht designers were able to borrow from a richer, healthier strain of commercial sailing vessel. The schooner was an American invention. Howard I. Chapelle, in his book *The History of American Sailing Ships*, says 'By 1790, if not earlier, the schooner was the national rig of both the United States and Canada.' At that time square rig was the rule everywhere else, and the word 'schooner' meant more than rig. It soon came to define a hull type too – finer in the bow, with a greater rise of floor in the midship section, a more pronounced keel and, in the smaller sizes, a beamier, more shallow form.

The schooner *America* was nothing special – to the Americans; she

192

was simply a good example in the mainstream of this development, and so, later, was the Grand Banks schooner *Bluenose*. The three-masted schooner yacht *Atlantic* was very close to this model too. American designers of the turn of the century had something to lean on.

Early British yacht designers were not so lucky; the cod's head, mackerel-tail shape of men-of-war, and the lumbering squareness of our trading ships were not much help to them. Britain's first rating rules for yacht racing encouraged depth in the hold, which was a way of measuring merchant ships, and this led to freakishly deep and narrow shapes, while the scantlings of craft built specially for racing became so light that they could only be used inshore. As a consequence the more serious cruising yachtsmen used the fishing boat and the pilot boat as their models, for at least they had proved their seaworthiness.

In a nutshell this is why American yachtsmen found it easy to hang on to their America's Cup and why, when they began to interest themselves in Britain's Fastnet Race, they tended to win it in most cases. It also explains why it was not until 1972 that a yacht from anywhere but the USA had ever won their Bermuda Race – but then she was the British-owned and -sailed *Noryema*, built in Finland to the American design of Sparkman and Stephens. Only in the last decade have ocean racing techniques become so internationalized that these deep-seated traditions can be said to have become impotent.

It was several years after the first reconstituted Bermuda Race and the first Fastnet before yachts were designed for the purpose of winning such races. Since then, of course, more and more have been designed in an increasingly specialized manner to win offshore races. It is unthinkable today that anybody should hope to win any major offshore event without a boat that had been designed specifically – and recently – for that purpose. It has become increasingly apparent that it is no longer possible to design a dual-purpose yacht – that is to say, one that will provide both comfortable short-handed cruising and truly competitive racing.

The impetus that has led to the creation of the offshore racing machine, good for little else, has been simply the desire to win. The various handicapping rules have had and are having their influence on the exact type and shape the racing machines takes. The factors that make for pure speed – lots of sail, light structural weight, canoe bodies with short deep keels, sophisticated sail-handling machinery – have been developed because of the need for greater speed in all conditions.

Offshore rating rules have always kept a looser rein than the rating rules of the inshore classes. Their purpose was to equalize the racing chances of existing boats of differing types, and as far as it was possible it was hoped to be able to rate boats without hauling them out of the water, weighing them, or referring to their original drawings which often no longer existed. The rating rules of inshore classes, on the other hand, were created to foster close racing among yachts which were yet to be built, and whose competitiveness was to be preserved for as long as possible. For this reason inshore rules have led to much more clearly pronounced types and pure speed-producing innovations which have

193

A long, deep keel hull form. This old Six Metre has now been converted into a fast cruiser. This type of hull form, with the rudder hung on the rudder post at the aft end of the keel, was common until recent years when a separate fin and rudder form was generally adopted.

often been proscribed. Offshore they have been given much greater scope – until somebody has persuaded his fellows that a particular development has gone too far and needs to be penalized.

The story of ocean racing rating rules has been one of action and re-action. Some reactions have been so emphatic that there has been dis-affection, and a new start and new rule have become necessary. Ocean-racing yachts, meanwhile, have become steadily faster but not necessar-ily 'racier' in the sense of being slimmer and sleeker – these are only our conditioned ideas of the features that make for speed. For decades inshore racing yachtsmen were able to say, smugly, that their yachts would outsail the ocean racers which were, by insinuation, slow. This is no longer true since 90% of recent design development has been made under the more open offshore rating rules. By contrast the inshore classes have either been stalemated by their one-design rules or inhibited, like the Metre boats, by old-fashioned rules conceived when a now outdated type was reckoned to be the ideal. And although present off-shore rating rules do not insist upon accommodation and have, there-fore, produced very spartan yachts, the measurement requirements have ensured that the hulls are internally roomy, wide and accom-modating.

For the first transatlantic race boats raced without handicap. For the early 'informal' races to Bermuda from 1906 to 1910 only length was measured, and this was translated into time handicaps by the award of so many minutes per foot for the course. For the formalized early Bermuda Races from 1923 to 1926, which followed the founding of the Cruising Club of America, very much the same system prevailed, but since overall length was measured, boats with long waterlines were favoured.

Britain's Ocean Racing Club, later Royal, adopted a simple formula which takes into account length, sail area and displacement with a bonus for ample freeboard. After only one year, the displacement factor

A fin and skeg hull form with the rudder hung on the skeg. This Quarter Tonner photographed in 1973 has a relatively small fin keel, merging into a vestigial skeg beneath the cockpit before it fairs in to the skeg proper on which the rudder is hung. A rudder hung as far aft as possible can be smaller and works more effectively than one hung further forward.

was replaced by a beam times depth requirement which was found to be a much more practical if rougher, method of obtaining an approximation of the displacement of existing boats. In 1928 the CCA borrowed this British rule, modifying the length measurement and adding rig allowances. From then on, however, the American and British rating systems drifted apart until a single universal rating rule was hammered out, the International Offshore Rule (IOR), which came into effect in 1970.

The 1923 Bermuda Race was won by the John G. Alden-designed schooner *Malabar IV*. The first Fastnet Race in 1925 was won by *Jolie Brise*, a Le Havre pilot cutter designed and built in France by Paumelle and owned by Lieutenant-Commander George Martin who once said: 'It seems to me to be far more important to be steady and comfortable in rough water than to sail very fast.'

Jolie Brise was light years behind *Malabar IV* according to any rational assessment of offshore sailing efficiency. With her long bowsprit, fidded topmast, heavy gear and rough-hewn construction it is very doubtful that the pilot cutter would have emerged from an ocean storm in better shape than the schooner yacht. One thing to be noted is that the Fastnet organizer banned the entry of yachts designed to inshore racing rules, judging they would be unseaworthy and, perhaps, unfair.

Probably the first yacht designed anywhere for offshore racing was the Scottish 70ft overall *Hallowe'en* which was designed by Will Fife for Colonel Blaxendale as a more robust 15 Metre and equipped, to begin with, with a large bermudan mainsail. She was ahead of her time and had so much trouble with her main in the 1926 Fastnet that she went over to gaff rig.

The first yacht designed for ocean racing to make a real impact was the 58ft *Nina*. Designed by Starling Burgess and built in 1928, she won the transatlantic to Spain and then the Fastnet of the same year. Shrill criticism greeted her Fastnet win, but in fact she was in the true American schooner yacht tradition. *Nina* continued to win, regardless of rule changes, until in 1962 she won the Bermuda Race. This stresses the fact that crews matter at least as much as the boat and the rating rule. It could be said that *Nina* marked the end of the road, for she was one of the very last of the ocean racing schooners. Inshore racing experience had taught that windward ability wins races, and the windward ability of the bermudan-rigged single-sticker was soon shown to be superior.

The yacht which really pointed the way ahead in ocean racing design was *Dorade*, designed by the young Olin Stephens in 1929 and well sailed by Olin and his brother Rod. Although a yawl, *Dorade* was heavily influenced by current design in the Metre-boat classes. She was slim with a cutaway profile, fine in the ends, and carried a great deal of lead in her clearly defined keel. Interestingly, schooners beat *Dorade* to Bermuda in both 1930 and 1932, but was able to walk off with the Fastnets of 1930 and 1931. Olin Stephens's run of six consecutive Bermuda wins did not begin until 1934 with *Edlu*, which was followed in 1936 by *Kirawan*, and in 1938 by *Baruna*. After the war Stephens won in *Gesture* in 1946, *Baruna* again in 1948, and *Argyll* in 1950.

Nobody has yet influenced ocean racing to anything like the same extent as Olin Stephens. He has fathered more winning boats and influenced more rating rules than any other man. Yet *Dorade* was no revolutionary; his boats have been developments, refinements, evolutionary adaptations of ideas that have already shown promise. Everything about a Stephens boat is moderate – displacement, ballast ratio, sail area and rig height. Others are left to innovate, and only when their innovations work do the Stephens designs begin to reflect their influence. But Stephens is certainly no plagiarist; he merely knows that races are won conservatively by gradual improvement.

Another feature of Stephens's work is that he has never played the rating rule game to the extremes shown by others. This means that as rating rules have chopped and changed his boats have been able to remain competitive. Rating rules are like income-tax regulations – they are supposed to ensure universal fairness but by their very existence they act as a constant temptation to the keener operators to exploit them. No rating rule can be perfect, and the more nearly perfect, the more complicated they become. Rating rules tend to take rough and ready assessments of a boat's true features. Thus displacement used to be assessed by multiplying beam and depth at one point in the boat. It is not difficult to see that if you maximized your boat's dimensions at this one point and shaved it away elsewhere, you would obtain a hull which measured as if it displaced more water than it actually did.

The RORC's original, simple method of measuring the depth part of the displacement equation, by taking the depth of hull from deck to the bilges, was exploited most successfully by Captain John Illingworth who was not attracted to the careful accretion of small advantages that might be said to characterize Olin Stephens's cautious approach. Illingworth's *Maid of Malham*, designed in 1936 by Jack Laurent Giles to his ideas, was more advanced in her tall masthead fore-triangle rig than in her hull. She won her first Dinard and came third in her first Fastnet, but she was not a breakthrough.

Myth of Malham, Captain John Illingworth's famous ocean racer designed in 1946 by Jack Laurent Giles, won the Fastnet Race in 1947 and 1949. Designed to take advantage of the RORC Rule with her light displacement, high freeboard, snubbed ends and straight sheer, she influenced the design of ocean racing yachts greatly. She was a good sea boat despite her light construction. Loa 23ft 9in; Lwl 33ft 6in; beam 9ft 4in; draft 7ft; sail area 620sq ft; ballast ratio 50%.

When Illingworth had returned from Sydney after the war in 1946, he decided to build *Myth of Malham* and this time he masterminded the hull form as well as the rig. He had decided on very short ends and light displacement, reasoning that he could preserve a good hull depth measurement by giving the boat plenty of freeboard and by removing the conventional concave sheer. Most of the 'depth' was in the air. The *Myth of Malham* was the most radical and successful ocean racer up until that time anywhere in the world. Those who criticized her looks were being subjective; those who criticized her seaworthiness were simply prejudiced. Had she been given more beam, she would have remained completely competitive in spite of harsh rule changes aimed against her and the breed she fathered which thrived until the coming of the fin keel and separate rudder. If she had a weakness, it was sailing off the wind, and in this respect one should realize that British sailors were always keener on, and thus better at, windward work, and tended to take off-wind techniques and spinnaker work too casually.

Myth of Malham won her first two Fastnets, the first in light and the second in heavy weather, and then went to the USA to win a couple of Off Soundings Club Races before doing poorly in the Bermuda Race. Her lack of beam and high, 52% ballast ratio was not at all what was required under the CCA rule, although she might have shown had there been more windward work.

Right This typical medium-size ocean racer of the 50s, built of wood to the old RORC Rule, would have been comfortably fitted out below for cruising. Narrower in the beam than boats built to the IOR, they had relatively narrow sidedecks and less space below. Compare this deck layout with that of *Frigate* below.

Below Frigate, a modern out-and-out IOR ocean racer, was designed by American Dick Carter and built in 1973. She was in the British Admiral's Cup team in 1973 and in the South African team in 1975. Her clear decks provide easy working area and low windage. The majority of sail controls are led to a bank of winches mounted on the bridge deck at the forward end of the cockpit. The reinforcing at the clews and reefing clew points shows up clearly. Loa 39.0ft; Lwl 33.0ft; beam 12.8ft; draft 6.0ft; sail area 725sq ft; IOR rating 30 4ft.

The newcomer to sailing tends to think that light boats must be faster than heavier ones, but that is not necessarily so. Any ballasted yacht needs the ability to stand up to her sail. Although a light boat needs less sail to propel her at a given speed, she needs enough stability or power to resist the heeling effect of the hard wind, and this calls for weight on the keel if not in the hull. Rating rules always say that you can have a lighter boat if you like, but you will not be allowed as much sail to drive it. These proportions may be fine in firm breezes, but in light airs the lighter boat tends to suffer because it may well have as much immersed hull or skin area in the water as the heavy boat. In light airs skin friction is the biggest contributor to overall drag, and the lightweight boat has less sail power to overcome this drag. Most offshore sailors tend to go for fairly heavy boats instinctively just as, when given the choice between a light and heavy car, most people will choose the latter because it feels safer.

A few designers, in their younger years at least, have crusaded for lightness in boats. One such was the Dutchman Ricus van de Stadt whose sleek designs, often built out of plywood sheets, proved beyond doubt that seaworthiness and lightness are by no means incompatible. Such boats as *Black Soo* and *Zeevalk* led the way in this respect, although they failed to find a big following. They led in another respect, too, by heralding the big revolution in yacht design with their very short keels and separate rudders. The first prominent designers to follow this lead were the Californian Bill Lapworth and the Bostonian Dick Carter, both of whom came to yachts from racing dinghies. It is no exaggeration to say that the biggest advance in keelboat design since the invention of the ballast keel has been the realization that the most effective yacht form is that of the dinghy with its wide and shallow-bodied hull, a fin-like ballast keel attached beneath and a separate rudder hung from the stern. This type, which is now general in offshore racing, would have evolved with or without rating rules. The rating rules have often been blamed for it, but their effect has been neutral.

Dick Carter had his big, fat, dinghy-like *Rabbit* built of steel in the Netherlands because steel appeared to be favoured by the RORC scantling rule. Her 1965 Fastnet Race win boosted the dinghy style of boat, but it should not be overlooked that *Rabbit* was considerably heavier than either *Myth* or the van de Stadt designs. She was too heavy to surf like a dinghy, but she did prove that a fat, shallow hull could be fast to windward, provided it was kept upright and provided the keel was an efficient shape. 1965 was also the first year of the One Ton Cup.

Throughout the 60s the CCA and RORC gradually worked towards the adoption of a single rating rule. Olin Stephens was largely responsible for co-ordinating the work which had the support of the IYRU who were at that time hankering after having offshore racing in the Olympics. Agreement was eventually obtained by broadly adopting the RORC method of hull measurement, the CCA method of sail measurement and then adding the vital new ingredient – an inclining test to measure stability and, through stability, to safeguard structural strength.

The International Offshore Rule was introduced in late 1970 and used for the first time on an international scale for the 1971 Admiral's Cup

The flat decks and no-compromise racing layout of *Jiminy Cricket*, a light displacement One Tonner designed by New Zealander Bruce Farr sailing in the One Ton World Championship at Marseilles in 1976. Her tiller extension allows the helmsman to sit on the side of the deck to obtain a clear view of the jib or spinnaker. Note the simple block and tackle arrangement for tensioning the backstay.

which was won by Britain – a fact which may help to show that the new rule encouraged a shape of hull with which the British were already familiar.

Olin Stephens made separate rudders respectable when he put one on his America's Cup defender *Intrepid* in 1967. Gradually his offshore racers were being given shorter and shorter keels, and the rudders were placed further and further aft. Carter was making his boats bigger and bigger for the same rating, as were most designers. It is amazing how familiarity with a rating rule teaches designers how to contrive a bigger hull which does not actually measure any bigger. The trend in the first few years of the IOR was 'bigger is better'. Soon owners were grumbling that the cost of One Tonners had multiplied four times in six years.

Then, at the 1973 One Ton Cup held at Porto Cervo in Sardinia, one new boat appeared which caused a stir by being smaller. Her name was *Ganbare*, owned and skippered by her as then unknown Californian designer, Doug Peterson. If she had not turned the windward mark of the long-distance race in the wrong direction, she would have won the series easily. In 1974 another Peterson design, *Gumboots*, slightly larger admittedly, but then she was designed for the heavier breezes of the English Channel, did win the One Ton Cup and confirmed Doug Peterson as the 'in' designer of offshore yachts up to about 40ft. His boats were not unlike those of Dick Carter in their flatness, great width above the water amidships, fine bows and narrow sterns, but at any given rating the Peterson boat had a smaller hull and larger sail plan than the equivalent Carter design of that time, and the new proportions paid off.

The Peterson style was soon reflected in the work of his rivals. He designed larger boats, but not always with the same success. This type of boat reigned supreme until, once more, really light displacement began to win prizes. Throughout the short history of ocean racing very light boats have enjoyed sporadic success, and the little Quarter Tonner *Robber* from Sweden won her world championship at La Rochelle with a keel weighing hardly more than 500lb. Even her successes were only

Kialoa, An American Maxi rater. The limit for most offshore races is 70ft IOR and *Kialoa* actually rates at 67.4ft IOR. She is one of a number of expensive large yachts that move round the world from one major ocean race to the next. This photograph gives an idea of the number of crew needed to race a yacht of this size — at least eighteen can be counted on deck.

Jack Knights sailing his Quarter Tonner *Odd Job* in 1974, a somewhat extreme design by Stephen Jones. Like most modern offshore racing boats when on the wind the crew sit inside the guardrails with their legs over the weather gunwale to provide righting moment. The stern is left open to reduce weight at the ends of the boat and this also provides the most effective self-draining system for the cockpit.

occasional, and her many imitators were usually beaten by heavier boats. Then, from distant New Zealand, came a pair of Quarter Tonners designed by Bruce Farr who had built his reputation with 18ft skiffs. One, *45 Degrees South*, won the Quarter Ton World Championship at Deauville in 1975, and the other was only a few places behind. At the same time Farr's larger *Gerontius* surprisingly beat far more expensive boats to win a place in New Zealand's Admiral's Cup team for 1975. Then at the end of the year the Bruce Farr-designed One Tonner *Prospect of Ponsonby* won every trial race to lead the New Zealand Southern Cross team and followed this by emerging the top-scoring yacht of the 1976 Southern Cross series. *Ponsonby* displaces 8,500lb compared to the 13,500lb of the Peterson type, and in spite of the rule that is said to encourage narrow sterns, *Ponsonby*'s stern, like all Farr-designed sterns, is wide and flat – more like a racing dinghy.

One quite different trend was distinguishable in ocean racing in the early 70s – the so-called Maxi, designed to rate at 70ft under the IOR, which happens to be the upper rating limit for most offshore races. Such craft measure nearly 80ft overall. Their sail plans are nearly always divided between two masts, usually in the manner of a ketch. Even so, the large headsails and spinnakers are big enough to have caused serious physical injuries when wires and ropes have parted. In 1976 there must have been a round dozen of these magnificent yachts around the world, each crewed by eighteen or so hands, some professional, some amateur and some in between. Their owners commonly keep them in commission all the year round, having them sailed from one major race or series to the next. In many ways they mark a full-circle return to the beginnings for, with their ability to reel off daily runs of 200 miles and more, they are coming close to the speeds put up by the great schooners of the end of the nineteenth century. In sailing from regatta to regatta they are following the traditions of the big British yachts up to World War II, but, instead of following the regatta circuit around the British coast, they follow the season globally.

That is the measure of the advance of ocean racing; that is the extent to which the oceans, once feared by every yachtsman, have now been tamed and become their playground.

The sport today

The outline history of offshore racing handicapping has already been described. Every factor that makes a boat fast and every factor that makes it slow is assessed, entered into a formula and the boat's rating calculated. The rating is expressed in feet since the speed at which boats travel through the water is regulated by their length. If you try to drive a boat faster than its length dictates, the waves made will be so large as to create obstacles which seriously obstruct further speed increase.

The rating is converted into the handicap by another formula. Unlike the IOR, which is now almost world-wide, handicapping systems still vary from country to country, and even from club to club. Broadly speaking, the USA prefers to handicap its ocean races on the length of the course, and all the longest races are normally handicapped in this way too. The British and most Europeans prefer to handicap on the length of time a race takes, reasoning that if the wind is light, the race will be slow, and hence the slower boats will need more compensation. This is not quite true since in the lightest of winds all boats are likely to be moving equally slowly, and so the slower craft, by which is usually meant the smaller craft, may be over-compensated under this time system.

There have been attempts to combine both the distance of the course and the time taken into a system which will equate every eventuality fairly. The practical objections so far have been great complexity, so that during a race a competitor is unlikely to know how he stands. The truth is that if ever a perfect handicapping system is devised, one which equates every factor, human and physical, with complete impartiality, then all the competitors will end up with equal corrected times.

In all rating rules those factors are taxed which create speed: length,

Opposite The Italian Admiral's Cup boat *Guia III* owned by Giorgio Falk flying her spinnaker and bigboy. She was designed by Australian Bob Miller.

sail area, lightness, depth of keel and stiffness (meaning, essentially, a heavy keel on a light boat). The features that slow a boat are width, depth of hull, smallness of sails, weight of structure, comprehensiveness of the accommodation, size of the propeller, weight of the engine and high freeboard. These features, therefore, all receive benefits.

The IOR in its Mk III form first of all arrives at a so-called Measured Rating (MR). This is then multiplied by the Engine and Propeller Factor (EPF) evolved from a calculation of the propeller. Thus, if MR was 30ft and your EPF was 0.98, your actual rating (before the Centre of Gravity Factor was applied) would be 29.4ft. To guard against abuse the EPF cannot be smaller than 0.96.

The Centre of Gravity Factor, and with it the Inclining Test, attempt to assess the all-important matter of stability. In light winds a yacht does not require much stability for the wind has little heeling effect, but when the wind blows fresh, the yacht will not cover the course fast if she heels so much that the keel lifts and slides over the water and the boat drifts sideways.

Measuring an offshore racing boat for its IOR certificate. Some measurements are taken ashore. When the boat is afloat, more measurements are taken and the inclining test is carried out to determine the stability factor.

The Centre of Gravity Factor (CGF) is found by heeling the boat sideways, first to one side, then to the other so that the two sets of readings can be averaged. The weight required to heel a boat to a given angle and the distance of that weight from the boat's centreline are both taken into account. The water must be calm and the wind light when this important test is conducted. The more easily a boat will heel, the smaller will be its CGF fraction, but to avoid freakishly unstable designs this fraction cannot be less than 0.968. Thus, if your MR was 30ft, your EPF 0.98 as above, and your CGF happened to be on the maximum of 0.968, your final actual rating would be 28.5ft (ratings are rounded out to the nearest one tenth).

The CGF principle has caused more argument than any other aspect of the IOR. There are wild stories about unscrupulous owners who have resorted to dodges in order to make their boats heel easily – such as hoisting lead weights up inside their masts. It is certain that many owners sail close to the wind in trimming their boats down by the bow before measurement, for most boats lose their natural stability when their broad after sections are lifted out of the water and their narrower forward ones are more deeply immersed.

Although this new test could be improved, it has the makings of being a more accurate assessment of one very important factor than any other previous system. There is no real evidence that it has caused freak designs, but it is complicated and its calculation is, at the moment, subject to error.

This is the IOR Mk III:

$$MR = \frac{0.13L\sqrt{S}}{\sqrt{B \times D}} + 0.25L + 0.20\sqrt{S} + DC + FC$$

S is the sail area and its square root is always taken. The sail-area part of the rule runs into many pages: there are complex balances to encourage mainsails and discourage over-large jibs and spinnakers and to assess double-masted rigs according to their real efficiency.

Opposite Carrying spinnakers on a shy reach. In these conditions the spinnaker has to be watched and trimmed continuously to ensure that it remains filled with wind.

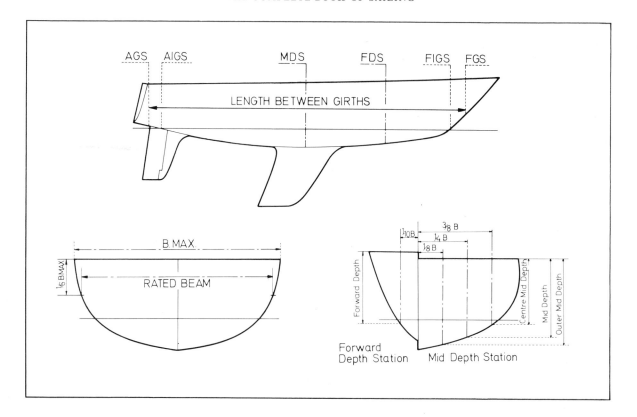

Labels in figure: AGS AIGS MDS FDS FIGS FGS

LENGTH BETWEEN GIRTHS

B MAX.

RATED BEAM

⅙ B MAX

$\frac{3}{8}$ B
$\frac{1}{10}$ B
$\frac{1}{4}$ B
$\frac{1}{8}$ B

Forward Depth
Centre Mid Depth
Mid Depth
Outer Mid Depth

Forward
Depth Station

Mid Depth Station

16.1 IOR measurement points. The measurements for length (L), beam (B), and depth (D) are taken from points defined by the rule and do not represent the simple maximum values for each dimension. L in the rule is the 'Length between Girths'; B is the 'Rated Beam'; and D is determined by measuring sections at different positions. The abbreviations used are: FGS Forward Girth Station; FIGS Forward Inner Girth Station; AGS After Girth Station; AIGS After Inner Girth Station; MDS Mid Depth Station; FDS Forward Depth Station.

L is length, by no means simple length measured along the waterline or along the deck; such simple dimensions would lead to wholesale rule evasion. L is measured between girths which are the circumferences of the hull at predetermined points at bow and stern. The idea here is that if the hull endings are small, the boat will be slower than if they are wide and full. The smaller, more pointed ending will enable the girths, whose length is related to the beam amidships, to be brought closer together, and hence L is reduced. There are all manner of complex checks and balances to regulate the girth measurements points or stations.

B is beam which not only decides girths but is one factor in displacement, depth being the other. Here again, B is not just the width across the deck amidships or even the width across the floating waterline. It is basically the width of the boat somewhere between the water and the deck, though with small additions and subtractions.

D, depth of hull below water, is even more complex. It is measured amidships and half-way between the bow and amidships. It is also measured at several points, laterally speaking, between the centreline and the extreme beam.

DC and FC are small corrections for variations from normal draft (not depth) and freeboard.

The rule already fills over sixty pages and is growing year by year – always trying to keep one jump ahead of the unscrupulous and the ingenious.

Design has advanced so quickly recently that older ocean racers have become outclassed after as few as two or three seasons of racing, and as a result, entries for the big events in both Europe and the USA have declined. To encourage owners of older boats and owners of the true dual-purpose cruiser-racer – the sort of yacht the sport was intended to cater for in the first place – various measures have been taken. Many clubs operate their own 'old age allowances' which take the form of a percentage reduction of rating (more accurately the handicap factor deduced from rating) calculated according to the date of the boat's launching.

In addition, the Offshore Racing Council at the end of 1975 took a more controversial step; they invented a new rule, IOR Mk III(a) which applies only to yachts built before 1973. The rule follows the style of the normal IOR but helps those features such as large mainsails, smaller rigs, heavier displacements, less beam, which tend to characterize older boats. Clubs and associations are not compelled to adopt this second rule, but if it is adopted, it operates alongside the original rule, in the same races. This experimental move was prompted by a widespread feeling of dissatisfaction, emanating mainly from the USA, with the way ocean racing was developing. It was felt that racing was falling into the hands of a minority of exceptionally keen, tough men, a large number of whom were professionally involved with sailing as designers, sailmakers and boatbuilders. They were prepared to build new boats every year, if not more often, and could devote more time to the sport than the normal yachtsman with his family commitments.

Whether ocean racing can rule against this trend remains to be seen. It is a trend seen in all other sports, two of which are motor racing and skiing. Many believe that the answer lies in stratification, separating the top competitors into their own 'Grand Prix' fleet and making new provisions for the weekend racers, the owners of stock-production cruiser racers. The sport is certainly large enough for this kind of development; it now awaits the necessary organization.

A backstay tensioner. The wheel fitted to a rigging screw arrangement enables the tension on the backstay to be adjusted under way by hand.

The rig

The rigs of offshore racers have developed at least as fast as the hulls. Modern ocean racing came in with the bermudan rig, and two or three years before the invention of the genoa jib. The bermudan mainsail rapidly became universal, and soon the genoa jib was to become the biggest influence in offshore rig development. Sven Salen, the Swedish shipowner and yachtsman who invented the genoa jib, so called because he first set it on his Six Metre *Maybe* at the Genoa Week regatta of 1927, has much to answer for! The mistake was in the rule and has yet to be properly rectified. Instead of measuring actual sail set ahead of the mast, the geometrical fore triangle made by the forestay, the mast and the deck between mast and the point where the forestay meets the deck, was taken. Salen realized that he would gain unmeasured area if the jib over-lapped the mast and came aft of it.

The fore triangle became still more important when spinnakers were developed which were many times bigger than the actual triangle. These, too, were developed first by Sven Salen.

Since the mid-30s the story of offshore rigs has been of bigger and

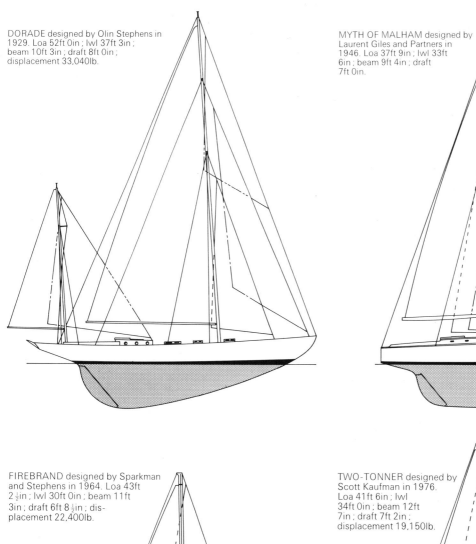

DORADE designed by Olin Stephens in
1929. Loa 52ft 0in ; lwl 37ft 3in ;
beam 10ft 3in ; draft 8ft 0in ;
displacement 33,040lb.

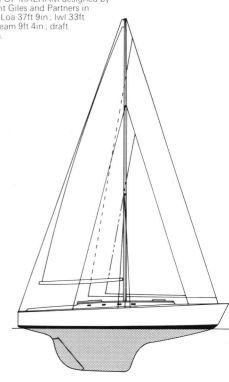

MYTH OF MALHAM designed by
Laurent Giles and Partners in
1946. Loa 37ft 9in ; lwl 33ft
6in ; beam 9ft 4in ; draft
7ft 0in.

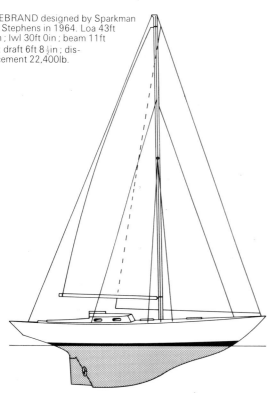

FIREBRAND designed by Sparkman
and Stephens in 1964. Loa 43ft
2½in ; lwl 30ft 0in ; beam 11ft
3in ; draft 6ft 8½in ; displacement 22,400lb.

TWO-TONNER designed by
Scott Kaufman in 1976.
Loa 41ft 6in ; lwl
34ft 0in ; beam 12ft
7in ; draft 7ft 2in ;
displacement 19,150lb.

bigger fore triangles and correspondingly smaller mainsails which have become taller as technology has developed stiffer alloy masts, less stretchy stainless rigging and more rigid hulls. At the same time the rating rules have endeavoured to preserve the *status quo* by taxing fore triangles, overlaps and oversize spinnakers ever more severely.

In spite of the rating rules, the sails set forward of the mast become continuously more effective in ever wider weather conditions. Spinnakers, first used only for running square to the wind, were soon being developed to set with the wind on the quarter. More recently came the very flat starcut spinnaker which could be set with the apparent wind on the beam. This invention by the British sailmaker Bruce Banks was soon copied and developed. Then the New Zealand sailmaker Chris Bouzaid discovered a novel way of setting a big jib alongside a spinnaker. This soon developed into an entirely new sail called the blooper by the Americans and the big boy by most others. This sail can only be used with the wind well aft of the beam. For closer sailing other special jibs are now set inside the spinnaker called tall boys and spinnaker staysails.

The genoa jib is now made in a variety of fabric weights and cuts for different wind strengths. Well-found ocean racers will carry one full-size No. 1 genoa in light cloth for light airs, and another full-size in heavy cloth for moderate conditions. Then there will be a slightly smaller No. 2 genoa, a No. 3, smaller still, and an ordinary working jib for heavy weather. There will also be a lightweight, big sail with the clew cut high for reaching and ghosting in near calms.

This same well-found boat will have at least three spinnakers, probably four. One will be a lightweight, full-size runner of fabric weighing around $\frac{3}{4}$oz per square yard. Then another of much the same cut of $1\frac{1}{2}$oz cloth for normal use, plus a flat-cut sail of $1\frac{1}{2}$oz for reaching – either a starcut or one of the newer cuts such as triradial. The fourth spinnaker will either be a spare or take the form of a small, heavy-weather sail cut from heavier fabric.

The quest for better windward ability has led to rigs becoming taller and slimmer. The theoretical aerodynamic advantages of high aspect ratios appear to have been borne out, but there are signs that a mainsail three times as high as it is wide on the foot is about as high as is practicable, given the present rating tax on high aspect ratios. At least one designer is actually coming down to well under 3:1 (aspect ratios of 3.3:1 have been used with success) in the search for more offwind speed.

Rating rules permit a maximum overlap of half the fore-triangle base before big rating penalties are levied. All modern ocean racers go to this limit and many accept the penalties and go further. Such big sails, which are in almost all cases hoisted to the masthead, need immensely powerful sheet winches to handle them. These quite often have three-speed gear-boxes and may be cross-linked so that two sets of winch handles turn a single drum. If these genoa jibs are to set effectively, their luffs must be kept taut and straight. Sag can only be prevented by very stiff masts, hulls which do not bend and rigging which does not stretch. Spars today are universally of light alloy. One of the reasons why so many hulls are now made of welded alloy is to reduce the tendency for

Above A bigboy in use. Larger headsails and smaller mainsails are rather inefficient when running, the spinnaker providing drive and the small mainsail contributing relatively little. This led to the development of the bigboy or blooper, a headsail set flying between the stemhead and the masthead which is allowed to fly out to leeward balancing the pull of the spinnaker. It catches wind even with full mainsail set, but here the mainsail has been reefed right down to give an uninterrupted flow of air to the bigboy.

16.2 *Opposite* Sail plans and hull profiles of four ocean racers spanning nearly fifty years *Dorade* won the Fastnet Race in 1931 and 1933 and the Bermuda Race in 1932. *Myth of Malham*, a light-displacement boat with straight sheer, short ends and high freeboard, won the Fastnet Race in 1947. *Firebrand* is typical of the early 60s. The 1976 Two Tonner, designed to the IOR, has a large, dinghy-like hull with a small fin keel, and the rudder is hung on a separate skeg.

the mast heel to push the middle of the hull down and the forestay and backstay to bend the ends up. Rigging is always of high tensile stainless steel and is quite often in the form of solid rods. A recent sail-handling development is the twin-groove forestay; the jibs are provided with thin luff ropes which slide in keyhole grooves formed in the forestay. With two such grooves it is possible to hoist a second jib while the first is still in use. Thus, headsail changes may be carried out without any loss of speed, and with so many headsails to choose from an ocean racing yacht needs to change frequently to match the ever-changing wind. Mainsails are now reefed much more quickly than before, roller reefing having largely been discarded in favour of 'jiffy' or slab reefing.

Double-masted rigs are usually confined to larger craft where the large size of individual sails becomes the limiting factor. The most popular two-masted rig is the ketch. The tall mizzen of a ketch permits spinnaker-shape staysails to be set ahead of it, while genoa and reaching jib are set from the mainmast. Like them, most of the actual area of sail fabric goes unmeasured.

The modern sail plan has made the ocean racer what it is today – fast, challenging and expensive, demanding a numerous and powerful crew, complex deck gear, large and costly sail inventories – and all this came about because it was decided about the time of World War I that the fore triangle should be measured and not the real area of the jibs and spinnakers.

The hull structure

Modern technology has been exploited to make hulls more monolithic, more of a piece. Not so long ago all hulls consisted of separate planks fastened to timbers. Under stress the planks were sometimes forced apart and leaks started. New waterproof glues were used to join the planks together more strongly. Then came new techniques for laminating multiple layers of thin planks or veneers into a homogeneous monocoque, sometimes with the framing omitted altogether. Well executed, this remains one of the best strength for weight methods, but it is extravagant in man-hours. Glass-reinforced plastic laid up by hand has quickly become the norm for production yacht building and, again, the effect is a one-piece structure, but because the plastic is inherently elastic, special techniques are needed to increase hull rigidity. In search of more lightness foam or sometimes balsa wood cores are used to form a sandwich of increased stiffness. Lightweight welded steel was used when the RORC scantlings rule encouraged it, but when scantling rules were replaced by the Inclining Test, light alloy, also welded, became popular and remains so. The material is expensive, and such boats can be noisy and cold, but they are strong and stiff and that is what matters.

Since there are at present no rigid requirements governing internal accommodation, the insides of top-class ocean racers have become progressively more spartan. Some owners seem to believe that to cut out the luxuries and even the simple comforts is, of itself, speed-producing, but often the weight thus saved has to be put back in the form of lead blocks attached quite high in the hull. If crews are to be at their best, they

The spartan interior of an out-and-out racing yacht, a Three-Quarter Tonner built of wood by McGruer. The engine box doubles as a companion step and the berths each consist of a thin mattress on a tubular-framed canvas base. When their racing days are over, these modern racing yachts can be converted to comfortable fast cruisers as there is plenty of internal volume.

must be able to sleep soundly, eat well and stay as dry as possible. Navigators must be able to use their charts, radios and instruments effective, and the skipper must plan his tactics without distraction.

The racing

Amateur ocean racing began as a cruise in company, with sea-keeping qualities and survival uppermost. In fifty years it has become as intensive a form of yacht racing as any other. The only difference is that crews need to maintain concentration and keenness for two or three days over the normal events of around 225 miles, and for as long as three weeks for ocean marathons.

It is in the sustaining of concentration that the best ocean racers are revealed. When, on a chill grey dawn in driving rain, two days out, others are beginning to take it easy, the potential winners are detecting a slight easing of wind which will enable them to reset their biggest spinnaker.

It is also true to say that ocean racing calls for better team-work and a more comprehensive range of talents than any other type of yacht racing. Navigation, tactics, strategy, helmsmanship, sail trimming and weatherlore are all critical factors, and so is sheer luck. All ocean races used to be conducted on a two-watch system, watch on and watch off with probably the owner, skipper, navigator and cook (who might be one man or four) not working a watch. Nowadays the crews of most top yachts race as one watch for the normal-distance races, a couple of men snatching time for a cat-nap below when sailing permits. In the old days most of the crew would take a trick at the wheel; today most yachts use two or, at most, three steering specialists. It is normal for one man to navigate. His job is to trace the yacht's position, assess tidal currents, ingest weather information and plan ahead. Usually the all-important question of tactics will be discussed between him, the skipper and possibly, in a small yacht, the whole crew. In ocean racing, yachts soon become spread out over many miles and begin to encounter differing conditions and even different weather zones. Tactics will depend upon these conditions and their interaction. This is why luck will always play a part, for often the weather will do the unexpected. No forecasting is completely accurate on the small, local scale of an offshore race.

Ocean racing is not for everybody. If you are prone to motion sickness, you had better put it out of your mind. Nevertheless, there are people, owners mostly, who have raced regularly for years and been seasick regularly for years.

You need to be at home on the high seas, in good weather and bad; you need to be able to suffer physical discomfort happily; you need to be able to make do with a minimum of sleep; and you need the will to operate at close-to-peak efficiency for a continuous two or three days. The true ocean races sailed over thousands of miles are different because you then break into a watch-on, watch-off rhythm.

Frankly, only a few really enjoy bad weather at sea; the others endure it for the sake of the real pleasure that offshore racing brings. It is, after all, the most testing, most profound form of yacht racing. Some will say it is the only true yacht racing.

Yankee Girl changing headsails in rough conditions. When racing, sails must be changed frequently to keep the yacht moving at her best speed, and considerable care is needed when working on a wet foredeck, pitching up and down in a sea. Here one crew member by the mast is manning the halyard, three are handing the sail, another unhanks the luff from the forestay and, to windward, another waits holding the sail that will be hoisted.

211

17
Cruising keelboats

Malcolm McKeag

Cruising is the broadest word in the yachtsman's vocabulary; it can mean almost any activity from a simple spin down the river, with no particular end in mind, to half a lifetime spent roaming the oceans of the world in search of anything from daring adventure to peace of mind. Between those two extremes is a whole range of waterborne activity: weekends spent exploring the creeks and shallows of the local coast, a fortnight's holiday sailing to some not far distant island or another country, or a year off work to cross the Atlantic and try to get that bug out of the system once and for all. At its simplest cruising is sailing which is not racing, with the proviso that the crew lives on the boat each night. Above all, cruising is sailing for the fun of it.

What sort of person takes up cruising? Enthusiasts can be found from every profession and trade and at every age. Nor is cruising confined to those who are uninterested in other branches of sailing like dinghy, keel-boat or offshore racing; many racing men happily find relaxation cruising. It is sea-going cruising that calls for the widest range of abilities and knowledge – the skills of the cruising man are those of the complete seaman. He must master the art not only of sailing but also of living aboard a small yacht; he must be housewife, rigger, administrator, engineer, cook, plumber, navigator, electrician, personnel manager and much more, for all these things are required when a yacht leaves port for a voyage of even a few days.

Nowadays there is often a spirit of friendly badinage between racing and cruising men, instead of the utter antipathy that once existed. The first cruising men wanted nothing to do with yachting and yacht clubs – indeed, the very term yachtsman was an anathema to them. They called themselves 'amateur seamen' and ventured offshore in their yachts often with the aid of just one paid hand, a longshoreman or inshore fisherman, who knew both the ways of small craft and the coastal waters in which they were sailing. The amateur seaman went to sea either in a converted working craft or in a yacht built 'on the lines of' a suitable working craft such as a Colchester smack, a Gloucester schooner or a Bristol Channel pilot cutter, built not for the sheltered waters of a yachting resort on a fine summer day, but for whatever the sea could throw at her, night or day, calm or storm. Even today when sailing working craft have all but disappeared, modern motor sailers and motor yachts are designed along the lines of small fishing vessels.

Running parallel with the influence of working craft has been the influence of the yachts being built to the various rating rules. These have swayed general fashion so subtly that cruising yacht shape has, per-force, tended to follow suit. The blessings of this state of affairs are mixed. The latest rating rule, IOR Mk III, has done a service to cruising yachts in generating a breed with an almost unprecedented amount of room below without prejudice to performance. Whether other charac-teristics, like the stereotype masthead sloop rig with its tiny mainsail and large headsails, the cut-away underwater profile, widely adopted fin keel and separate rudder are quite so desirable, is more debatable.

A cruising yacht is a sailing craft on which the crew can live for greater or lesser periods, and almost any yacht can be fitted with bunks and some sort of makeshift cooker and be used for cruising. Although

The relaxation of cruising under sail. The cushion on the starboard side of the cockpit would not even be considered in a racing boat. The windward runner on the far side is set up while the leeward runner level has been thrown forward to release the runner and prevent it fouling the mainsail. If the boat were sailing off the wind, the end of the whip, the runner purchase wire, could be unhooked and led forward to ease it off still further.

many racing yachts and working craft have been converted successfully for living aboard, the best cruising yachts are those designed and built for the job they will be asked to do.

Cruising yachts may be divided into three broad categories: those that are used almost as a waterborne country cottage, frequently based on a marina; those that are used within sight and easy reach of land and sheltered water; and those for which the open sea is home – the offshore and ocean cruisers that can safely put to sea for days, weeks, or even years on end.

Marina cruisers

The marina cruiser often takes to sea for a brief spell, an afternoon sail out and back perhaps, or even a hop along the coast to another marina, but most of its life is spent alongside while the owner and friends relax and watch the world go by. In Britain a rather sarcastic name – floating caravan – is sometimes used for such a yacht, but at least she provides her owner with the relaxation he wants. It is, all the same, an apt description, for usually the designer and builder of such a craft will have paid rather more attention to the interior fitments than the gear on deck, and rugged seafaring may be something that would suit the boat no more than it might suit her owner. Although the layout may lack sea-going practicality, her interior is likely to be well upholstered and appointed, lavishly equipped with deep-freeze, portable television, stereo or hi-fi, hot and cold running water, electric cooker with split-level grills and all the conveniences of modern life – run from the marina's shoreside electricity supply. Such a yacht might come in any size, but 27ft is usually the minimum, for their owners would find anything smaller too cramped for comfort.

The galley and chart table of a small cruiser. The chart table is angled and can be seen easily from the main hatch. There is a shelf outboard for navigation books and instruments, and a quarter berth beneath the chart table. The stove is in gimbals so that it can swing and remain level when the boat heels.

Estuary cruisers

The smallest yachts used for real cruising are sometimes known as estuary cruisers – a polite term which might mean that estuary cruising is what their owners wish to do, or it might mean that the boat is not fit to be taken further to sea save in the most settled of weather. These little ships – and some of them can be game little boats indeed – may have a couple of berths, a cooker, a tiny w.c., a chart or two, lead line or sounding pole and a compass – and little else. For auxiliary power there might be a small outboard motor to shatter the evening calm with its busy, noisy rattle, or the skipper, if he likes doing things in the old way, might use that traditional aid of the coastwise sailor, the sweep, or long, single oar. In such a boat a couple of young people or a small family, who do not mind being a bit cramped and getting wet, can spend happy summers without going more than ten miles from home, exploring new beaches, and working into coves where bigger yachts cannot go, or visiting old haunts. Many have relatively large cockpits, and in the warmer months of an English summer, or even all the year round in such places as Florida or California, an awning can be rigged in the evening, greatly increasing the available living space. This canvas or nylon tent is lashed along the rails and supported by the boom when the boat is at anchor and, depending on the weather, provides somewhere to sit and enjoy the evening calm – or somewhere to leave wet boots and oilskins – or prevents the evening rain penetrating below. Such boats usually draw very little, probably about three feet at most, and even less if the boat has twin bilge-keels or a lifting centreboard. This allows her to creep to the head of a shallow creek and sit more or less upright on the ground when drying out at low tide, with only the sea birds and the waders for company as the kettle begins to sing on the stove, and the yellow light of the oil lamp in the cabin takes over from the golden rays of the setting sun.

Coastal cruisers

The distinction between the coastal cruiser and the sea-going cruiser is vague and indistinct, being really one of equipment rather than size.

214

A typical tidal creek in the West Country of England, Portnavon, on the Helford river. The south coast of Devon and Cornwall is laced with many picturesque creeks like this that provide sheltered anchorages and delightful cruising.

A 33ft cruising boat with bilge keels that enable her to be sailed in shallow waters and to take the ground on a level keel.

Ocean voyages have been made in very small boats – like the 19ft *Willing Griffin* and the 20ft *Trekka* – while many 30ft coastal cruisers are not really properly equipped to venture out to sea. The coastal cruiser will tend to be bigger than the estuary cruiser. Apart from having to cope with more open water, she can expect to stay at sea longer – perhaps not for days on end, but certainly long enough to require meals to be cooked and eaten while under way, serious navigation to be carried out and the occasional night passage with the watch below able to sleep under way. In her the cruising family will graduate from exploring known areas to visiting completely unfamiliar anchorages and harbours. Charts and pilot guides are needed to provide information about the approaches, the off-lying dangers, the buoys and landmarks. Yet another pleasure is experienced: that half expectant, half apprehensive feeling as the yacht shapes her course to make a tricky entrance for the first time. Again, the

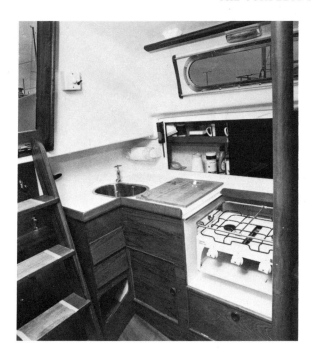

Left The galley area in a Contessa 32 is positioned to port just inside the main companion where fumes and heat can easily escape and where the cook has full standing headroom. The two-burner, gimballed, butane gas stove has a fiddle rail all round to prevent pans sliding off.

Right The well-thought-out area for the navigator in a Contessa 32. He occupies the starboard quarter berth, conveniently close to the cockpit, and can sit on the forward end of his berth when working at the chart table. Instruments are fixed to the half-bulkhead above, and the charts stow beneath the hinged top of the chart table. The main switch panel is conveniently to hand.

tide table is checked. Yes, we'll have enough water to see us safely over the bar and a fair tide to take us up river. The fairway buoy slips past. . . . Where are the leading marks? The book said two orange posts in line – there are only trees and a house and – oh, there they are, we're right on. . . . Safely in and anchored, there is a feeling of satisfaction at finding somewhere new, another anchorage to revisit, and next time it will be a familiar favourite holding no unexpected terrors – but there is always somewhere new to try.

The coastal cruising boat carries more equipment to make her self-reliant: below – bunks that hold the occupant secure at sea and do not need to be used as anything but bunks, a gimballed cooker, and a clear surface to spread the charts; on deck – guardrails and stanchions for crew security when working in the open sea, a radar reflector in case she is caught at sea in fog where she might be run down by coasting steam-ships, an inflatable dinghy to save towing a rigid dinghy everywhere, and probably an inboard auxiliary engine, say an 8hp diesel, rather than that less handy outboard.

Offshore cruisers

For more than a day or two at sea the offshore-cruising yacht must have sound gear and adequate, although not necessarily elaborate, equipment. Although a well-found small yacht can be cruised offshore, between 30ft and 35ft is a handy size. Extra space is needed for that extra gear, and the waves remain the same size for the little boat as for the bigger boat. Above 35ft finding sufficient crew can be a problem, unless special arrangements are made to enable the rig and the sails to be handled by only a couple of people. Since speed is closely related to size

in sailing yachts, bigger boats offer more scope for offshore cruising. A 35ft yacht, able to average 5½ or 6 knots on passage, can range surprisingly further afield than a 25-footer making about 4 knots.

Whereas the racing man is interested primarily in sailing his boat as fast as possible, the sea-going cruising man takes a broader view. He need not be a hedonist, but comfort on board, which is itself conducive to efficient sailing, will be as important as sheer speed. He requires a boat that is reasonably dry, has an easy motion in a seaway and can be handled safely and efficiently by a smaller crew than is to be found on a racing yacht. Often speed will be sacrificed deliberately for the sake of easing the strain on the yacht or the crew. Sail is shortened earlier as it comes on to blow, and the yacht sailed freer when on the wind to ease the motion and keep the watch on deck dry. While seconds count for the racing man, cruising is for fun: it is better to arrive an hour later in comfort and good shape than to make port shattered, exhausted and eager to buy a farm.

The offshore cruiser must be as near self-reliant as possible, a veritable small ship. Unlike her coastwise sister, where the charts can be put away before the evening meal is served with the yacht safely at anchor, she must have a permanent place for the navigator to ply his trade. She will probably have a great deal more navigational equipment: a radio direction finder, possibly a remote compass with electronic repeaters sited about the ship, a proper marine radio receiver for listening to weather forecasts, shipping bulletins and the navigational warnings put out by marine coast radio stations. As advances in solid state electronics make such sets less expensive year by year, more and more small yachts are being fitted with radio telephones. In short, she must be equipped to cope with any situation she might meet, including the ultimate when all

Left The saloon of a Nicholson 43 – a comfortable, high-performance cruising yacht. The galley to starboard has pressure-fed hot and cold fresh water as well as sea water. The settee forward of the galley provides one berth while the upper pilot berth is ideal for use at sea. Stainless-steel pillars provide convenient handholds to grab in a seaway, and the folding saloon table has a well in it to hold bottles and glasses securely.

Right The aft end of the small cruiser on p. 214. The folding table has holes to take bottles, and the stainless-steel pillar doubles as a handhold and table support.

on board must take to the life-raft which must be ready for use packed in its valise on deck.

The most marked difference between the serious cruising yacht, designed and used for offshore passage making, and her marina-hopping country-cottage sister is in her layout below decks. On the seagoing yacht narrow sea berths that hold their sleeping occupants secure, plenty of solid grab handles and serious efficiency are the order of the day. The U-shaped dinette, so useful for sitting six people for dinner, can be a real curse at sea, and as for double berths – a single bean hurled down a flight of steps in a dustbin has an easier time of it than the sailor condemned to spend a night at sea in too wide a berth.

Desirable properties

The qualities that are needed in a sea-going cruising yacht, be it 23ft, 43ft, or 63ft long, are much the same. While we can forget speed, that goal of the racing man, for its own sake, it does bring benefits in a broader sense. Speed, perhaps, is not quite the word: efficiency, or even performance would be better. Best of all is the seaman's word – weatherliness. The cruising yacht rarely needs the ultimate in speed, and her owner, given the choice, will opt for a fair-wind passage rather than one to windward, but she must sail efficiently to windward. The cruising yacht which cannot make progress to windward in a stiff blow is a serious liability to her skipper and crew, perhaps depositing them upon a lee shore at night in a gale – an unenviable fate which can have the most tragic of consequences.

It is all very well having a comfortable car with an excellent heater and eight-track stereo, but it is not much of a car if it cannot go round corners without skidding off the road. Equally, comfortable berths, electric cabin lights, a separate heads and a four-burner cooker with oven and grill are all very desirable in a boat, but not much good if, at the crucial moment, the design of the hull proves unseaworthy. This is the basic fundamental necessity. Other important considerations are the ability to self-steer, an easy motion (taking the seas without slamming and pounding), and a measure of stiffness so that the boat does not lie on her ear at every fitful gust, requiring constant vigilance and attention to the trim of the sails. Add to these dry decks; a sheltered and not over-large cockpit for the watch on deck to remain dry but still alert and able to keep a proper look-out; a layout below that can be worked just as well at 20° of heel as upon an even keel in harbour; a chart space that does not require the navigator to grub around on hands and knees; lockers that keep their contents dry, intact and in place; berths that give the watch below a good night's rest; settees that allow the crew to relax in comfort at anchor or in harbour; and a construction that does not have the skipper checking the bilges every five minutes to see how much of the ocean remains outside. These are just some of the qualities of the complete cruising yacht.

Before the prospective owner becomes too embroiled in details, the two fundamental questions of hull form and rig have to be considered. Unfortunately, more than one owner, impressed by a gleaming bank of winches or an array of instruments at a boat show, has found himself possessed of an undeniably fast but singularly flighty little boat, when what he really wanted was a stolid, stable platform on which to spend the weekend with his young family, introducing them to the pleasures of sailing when the weather was kind and the wind fair.

Hull form

The choice nowadays normally falls to deciding between light and heavy displacement, and between fin and skeg and straight keel configuration. In the broadest of terms we can say that fin and skeg is faster, heavy displacement is more comfortable, but such generalizations have to be treated with caution. (See illustrations on pages 194–5.)

That the vast majority of racing yachts, whether they are designed to a rating rule or not, now take the fin and skeg configuration speaks for itself when it comes to the matter of speed and performance, especially to windward, but the configuration is something of a mixed blessing. While the performance advantage cannot be denied, it comes at the expense of directional stability – that is, the tendency of the yacht to maintain a straight course and not wander off in response to the slightest change in trim or helm angle. The manoeuvrability of the short-keel yacht, her ability to tack quickly and to place herself surefootedly just where the helmsman wants her, is a great blessing when racing, but when cruising her persistent refusal to stay on course and not shy away like a frightened pony while a short-handed crew try to cope with the dual problems of steering and taking a fix, or brewing a cup of tea, can drive the most patient of souls to distraction. At anchor, or sailing in coastal waters, fin and skeg yachts have a most unendearing trick, which their long keel sisters are physically incapable of emulating, of catching stray warps and buoy ropes under the hull between the keel and the rudder.

Although fin keel yachts can dry out against quay walls, greater care is required than with a long-keel yacht. To be able to dry out easily is a valuable asset for any yacht, especially one which sails in shoal waters; not only can she visit harbours which dry, but she can be scrubbed and painted by her owner which is a good deal cheaper than paying a yard to lift her out.

The disadvantages of the long keel are the usually poorer performance, especially upwind, and the fact that building costs are very much a function of displacement. A straight keel 27ft yacht has a much heavier displacement than a fin keeler of similar length and will be proportionately more costly to build.

Rigs

Hand in hand with considerations of hull form go those affecting choice of rig. On the production cruiser of today below 30ft in length the sloop rig predominates, but there are alternatives. On racing yachts the sloop rig, like the fin keel, is virtually universal, and, again, both builders and buyers of stock-production cruisers follow this trend. Apart from being

219

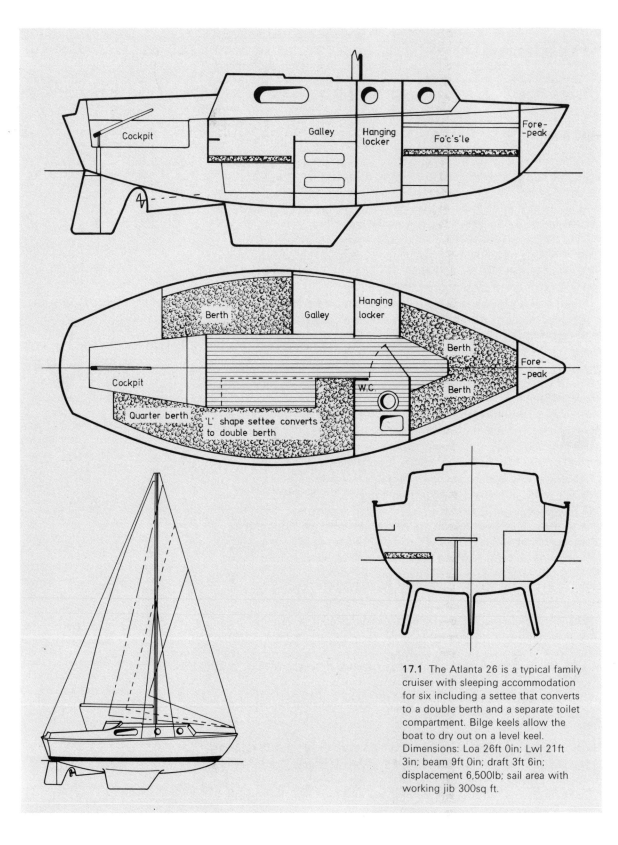

Cockpit

Galley

Hanging locker

Fo'c's'le

Fore--peak

Berth

Galley

Hanging locker

Berth

Cockpit

W.C.

Berth

Fore--peak

Quarter berth

'L' shape settee converts to double berth

17.1 The Atlanta 26 is a typical family cruiser with sleeping accommodation for six including a settee that converts to a double berth and a separate toilet compartment. Bilge keels allow the boat to dry out on a level keel. Dimensions: Loa 26ft 0in; Lwl 21ft 3in; beam 9ft 0in; draft 3ft 6in; displacement 6,500lb; sail area with working jib 300sq ft.

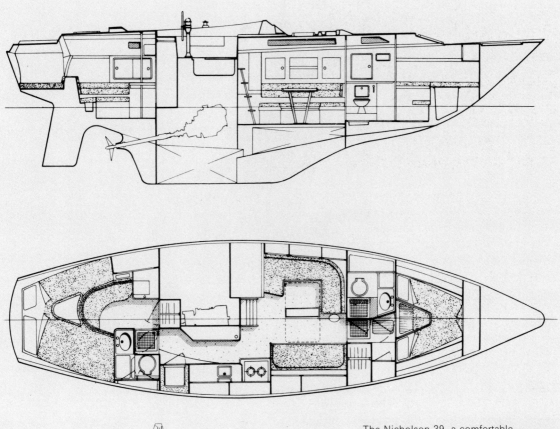

The Nicholson 39, a comfortable cruising ketch capable of sailing anywhere in the world. In this size of boat three separate cabins can be provided. The owner's stateroom is aft with its own shower and toilet compartment, and there is another double cabin forward also with its own shower and w.c. The centre cockpit with wheel steering gives the helmsman a good view and allows a passage down the starboard side for access aft without going on deck. Outboard of the passage is a good-size galley equipped with cooker, refrigerator and freezer. The saloon provides comfortable seating for ten or more, and there is a full-size chart-table to port. The ketch rig is ideal in a cruising boat of this size as it splits the sail area up into easily managed individual sails. Dimensions: Loa 39ft 0in; Lwl 30ft 2in; beam 11ft 6in; draft 5ft 6in; displacement 20,160lb; sail area 878sq ft.

Right A gaff-rigged ketch designed by the famous Norwegian, Colin Archer. She has a topsail set, her mainsail and mizzen are both loose-footed; the jib has a jib boom, and its sheet is led to a horse so that it can be left unattended when tacking. The gap above and below the bulwarks allows water to run quickly off the deck. Norwegian lifeboats were of this type and some have been converted, making ideal cruising boats as they are seaworthy and strongly built.

Below Sheet winches. The larger winch in the foreground is for the genoa sheet, the other for the spinnaker sheet which can be seen led through the large turning block on the quarter. Sheets can be turned up easily and securely on these good-size cleats. The winch handles are stowed correctly in special pockets.

more efficient to windward than other rigs, the sloop with its single mast and only two fore-and-aft sails set at a time, is also the cheapest. The cat rig is more than a little unsuitable for a cruising boat.

Cheapest of all the variants is the masthead sloop. For the twin reasons of imitativeness and economy this rig is found on a great many stock cruising boats – boats which will never take part in a serious race in their lives – although the masthead rig is far from ideal for cruising. With its tiny mainsail and disproportionately large overlapping genoa, such a rig is not particularly efficient once the sheets have been eased and a course shaped across the breeze. Although contrary winds are the most readily remembered, a cruising yacht spends much of her time other than hard on the wind, and on these points it is the mainsail which provides the greater drive, not the headsail. How much better then to have a rig in keeping. Being constrained on two of its sides by the mast and boom, the mainsail is more easily controlled than the genoa, and a 500sq ft mainsail can be trimmed easily by one normally strong adult using an inexpensive four-part purchase on the sheet. Multi-purchase headsail sheets with more than two parts can be a great nuisance, and any headsail bigger than about 200sq ft will normally require the use of a sheet winch, a money- and labour-consuming device. A 30ft yacht, masthead-rigged, will carry a largest genoa of about 600sq ft that will almost certainly require the combined efforts of two people each time the yacht is tacked.

The masthead rig has another disadvantage in that more headsails, and consequently more frequent headsail changes, are needed to cope with a range of weather conditions, whereas by keeping more of the sail area in the mainsail the smaller headsail need not be changed as the wind increases, the main being reefed instead. Particularly with roller reefing, or better still slab reefing, reefing the main is an easier and less exhausting task than changing the headsail.

If the headsail is taken anywhere other than to the top of the mast, the staying of that spar becomes more complex than the simple forestay, backstay and shrouds of the masthead rig. Running backstays are needed to take the load on the mast at the hounds and, opposing the forward pull of the forestay as they do, they must be led as far aft as is practicable. This means that the leeward backstay often fouls the now enlarged mainsail with its consequently longer boom, and the running backstays require attention every time the yacht is tacked or gybed.

It is a delusion beloved of boat salesmen that a sloop is ready for sea with only a mainsail and one headsail, especially if that headsail is a large genoa, but no cruising yacht should venture far without her storm canvas – in this case a small, stoutly made jib to be worn when life becomes really troublesome. Since this tiny sail will not provide enough drive in a normal breeze, a working jib is needed to cover average conditions and a large headsail, usually a genoa of lighter cloth than the working jib for lighter conditions. Although the sloop sets only two sails at a time, the usual wardrobe of even the most modest sloop is four.

The cutter is the favourite rig of the traditionally-minded small-boat cruising man, especially in Britain. Her second headsail is often carried on a bowsprit, the tack taken outboard on a traveller ring which is hauled to and from the bowsprit end by a block and tackle, enabling the yachtsman to handle the sail from on deck. The inner headsail (the staysail) is normally hanked to the forestay and is sometimes set on a short boom, sheeted to a traveller across the foredeck. Once the sheet has been trimmed, the sail looks after itself as the yacht goes about, and the cutter becomes no more complicated to tack than the sloop.

The serious cruising man has an inbred preference for what he calls a broken-up sail plan: a number of little sails, each easily managed by one person even in a hard blow. This avoids constantly changing sails as the wind alters in strength, or being caught out with a sail which is too large to be handled easily. This is the most often quoted advantage of the cutter over the sloop. Furthermore, it is a good deal easier, when on watch, to see round two small headsails than a single deck-sweeping big one.

When a masthead-rigged racing sloop is sailing just free of close-hauled, she sets a cutter staysail inside her big genoa. Much cruising is done on this point of sailing, and it is here that the cutter comes into her own, her two headsails being more efficient than a single genoa.

There is much argument about the precise difference between a yawl and a ketch. A traditional British ruling states that the yawl has her mizzen mast stepped aft of the rudder post and the ketch has hers forward thereof, whereas one American rule relies on the sail area of the mizzen relative to the sail area of the main.

223

A better means of definition is to rely on the function of the mizzen. In the yawl the mizzen is essentially a trimming sail, used to balance the yacht. It can serve also to help the yacht sail herself with the wind on or forward of the beam. With the yacht on the required point of sailing and with the mizzen sheeted 'just so', as the yacht begins to bear away the mizzen fills and pushes the stern away from the wind and the bow towards it, but as the yacht luffs up, the mizzen spills completely, the headsails take charge and pull the vessel's head away from the wind.

In the ketch the mizzen is an integral part of the working sail plan. Under plain sail she may carry two headsails, main and mizzen. As the wind pipes up, she begins to reef the main, then the mizzen, then maybe hands the jib and still remains well balanced under shortened canvas of, say, reefed mizzen and staysail only. In the yawl the mizzen is almost always the first sail to come off as dirty weather closes in.

Two masts involve extra expense and gear, but although the vast majority of cruising yachts sail all their lives without ever coming near losing a mast, two masts are arguably safer than one provided they are stayed independently. Yawls and ketches can also use the lovely mizzen staysail, set on a beam reach from the mizzen mast head, and tacked down somewhere near the foot of the mainmast. The mizzen staysail not only looks good but can pull like a train.

The schooner, with two or more masts and the mainsail carried on the aftermost mast, is much more popular in America than in British cruising grounds. There is, of course, a long and great tradition of American schooner sailing, and the schooners of the Grand Banks hold much the sort of place in American sailing folklore as do the smacks of England's east coast in British tales.

The rig is at its best when not hard on the wind, and a schooner sweeping along with everything set in a quartering breeze makes not just a brave sight but a very difficult boat to catch. To make the best use of the sail plan a largish vessel is required (there have been schooners under 35ft overall but below this size a ketch rig makes more sense), and this could be another reason for the rig's greater popularity in America where just about everything seems to be that little bit larger.

The fortunate mortal who can have his cruising yacht designed and built to his own specification is in a position to specify precisely her hull form and rig, but most of us will buy an existing boat, either a second-hand craft or a new, stock-production boat, and must therefore be prepared to accept the best compromise we can find. Once the boat is ours, however, much can be done to make life easy and pleasant while cruising.

Sail handling

The delights of the broken-up sail plan for cruising have already been mentioned. About 250sq ft is the maximum area that can readily be handled by just one person – above that size it becomes too easy for the sail to take charge. One person must be able to trim the sail alone, and should be able to set and hand the sail as well. On boats over, say, 30ft overall the distance between the mast and forestay may be such that one

17.2 Fisherman anchor.

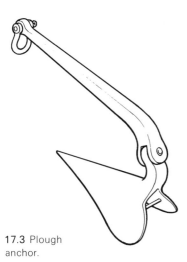

17.3 Plough anchor.

17.4 Danforth anchor.

Ras Mus Tas, a comfortable sailer, has a centre cockpit and deckhouse which provides good shelter. Horseshoe life-belts are ready for instant use, stowed in canvas pockets on the guardrails. The dinghy's outboard motor is carried on chocks fitted to the aft pulpit where any spillage or leaking fuel will go overboard.

person has to tend the halyard while another brings down the sail, but in any boat the fewer people required to handle a sail the better. Sail-handling techniques vary from boat to boat, but certain principles always apply. Never allow the sail to blow over the lee side into the water where the bow wave will quickly fill and can readily tear even the most stoutly made jib. Off the wind the sheet is eased to allow the clew to be taken forward, and then, with the foot safely gathered in, the halyard is eased and the sail pulled down the forestay and gathered in. With the wind forward of the beam the sheet should not be let go – instead, the helmsman gives a gentle luff as the halyard is let off its winch or cleat, and the fluttering sail falls neatly down the forestay unaided if the manoeuvre is timed correctly. If it sticks, it is the work of a moment to give the luff a tug at the forestay to bring the sail on deck.

The sail must then be secured quickly. It can be stopped to the guard-rail with some sail ties or bagged *in situ* by taking the clew, with the sheets still attached, right forward to the tack, thus doubling over the foot of the sail and then, beginning at the mid point of the foot, tucking the sail into its bag. Because a halyard swinging loose is a considerable nuisance, it should be unclipped and set up taut attached handily to the pulpit.

Equipment

Anchors and cables

One of the most important items on board, and one which regrettably often receives insufficient attention from the builder, is the ground tackle. We must at once distinguish between ground tackle adequate for holding the boat in any weather in an overnight anchorage – the bower anchor – and ground tackle used for brief afternoon picnic stops, when there is normally someone on deck or ready to act if the yacht needs attention. The latter can be lighter than the main anchor and can

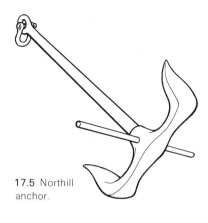

17.5 Northill anchor.

This self-draining anchor stowage well in the foredeck of a glassfibre cruiser has a hatch which clips over it. This practical arrangement avoids having to stow the anchor below or lash it on deck where it gets in the crew's way.

safely be laid with a rope cable. In tidal waters there are several reasons why the only satisfactory cable for the bower anchor is chain rather than nylon warp with a fathom or two of chain at the seabed end.

It is not the anchor which should hold the yacht, but the cable; the anchor merely holds the bottom end of the cable in place. In still water the yacht lies with her cable straight up-and-down, most of it lying on the seabed, and uses only a length of chain equal to the depth of water. As the tidal stream, current, or wind tries to pull the boat away from her anchor, the angle between the cable and the seabed decreases, bringing more chain – and therefore more weight – into use. As the pull on the cable increases, so does the pull exerted by the greater weight of the chain increase in response.

No such self-adjusting mechanism operates in the case of a rope cable, and the pull of the yacht is transmitted direct to the anchor. Indeed, with the variety of seabed and weather conditions encountered in even modest coastal cruising, sooner or later the anchor alone will not be able to hold that pull and the yacht will drag. With overnight ground tackle there is no substitute for weight.

A further disadvantage lies in the fact that nylon, the most common material for anchor warps, is neutrally buoyant and will not hang straight up and down when there is no pull on it. In tidal waters the tidal stream usually changes direction every six hours. A yacht lying to chain first turns around the chain and then, reacting to the pull of the new stream, drags as much of her cable as she needs across the seabed after her, until equilibrium is again reached. Only the quiet rumble of the chain disturbs the sleeping crew, and this noise can be prevented by taking the weight off the cable between the stemhead and the water with a length of line, allowing the chain to hang in a bight. The fin-keel yacht, however, lying to her unsinking nylon warp, stands a good chance of looping a bight around the keel. And it is more than likely that, if you habitually lie overnight in a tideway to nylon warp, sooner or later you will end up anchored by the keel, athwart the tidal stream, and dragging through the anchorage like a ship under full sail.

A fairly modern innovation on small yachts is the anchor well on the foredeck, a recessed locker where the anchor and cable can be stowed, leaving the foredeck clear of obstructions while sailing. This can be a useful arrangement provided it has an independent drain, so that water can return where it belongs after washing mud and weed off the anchor and lower end of the cable.

Worst of all is the small yacht with no well and a cambered foredeck, seemingly designed with the express intention of depositing anchor and chain back overboard every time the boat heels. Whatever the arrangement, be in no hurry to make all sail before the anchor is on board and safely stowed. Usually, the mainsail alone should be set, leaving the foredeck clear for working, and the yacht can be jilled along quietly under main until everything forward is secure.

Leaks and pumps

In a wooden yacht it is probable that small leaks at the plank seams and other hull joins, will result in the accumulation of water in the bilge.

Glassfibre yachts have no seams to leak, but most auxiliary yachts will let in some water at the engine stern gland and a good bilge pump is essential. Ideally, two pumps are needed, one operated from below, and one from the cockpit. Most modern pumps work on the diaphragm principle with a central chamber, the volume of which expands and contracts as the pump handle extends and compresses a rubber diaphragm. The older, barrel-type pumps are more prone to being choked by scraps of rag, paper, or cordage which have found their way into the bilges, and which cause the pump to stop drawing water, usually at the worst possible moment.

Cooking

Cooking on board at sea requires a gimballed cooker, so that pots and pans remain horizontal even though the yacht is heeled. The smaller the yacht, the simpler must be the galley arrangements to allow the cook to cope with the quicker motion of a small boat, and the simpler should be the meals prepared.

Self-steering gear

Modern cruising yachts with their short keels and tendency towards a lack of directional stability need more constant attention to the helm than many of the older designs. The long, straight-keel yacht is less manoeuvrable, but she will hold her course better if the helm is left unattended and can often be left to look after herself for quite long periods with the helm lashed, or perhaps allowed to swing between two peg stops pushed into holes in a specially made rail below the tiller.

Ways and means of making a vessel steer herself are as old as seagoing itself, but by the modern expression self-steering we mean mechanical contrivances designed to make the yacht hold a steady course relative to the wind. Devices which enable the yacht to hold a steady compass course are more properly called auto-pilots.

There are two basic types: those which use a wind-vane to move the yacht's helm, and those, usually found on larger yachts, where the wind-vane itself cannot generate sufficient power to alter the yacht's course and which are therefore fitted with a small servo rudder. This is used for fine alterations of trim and also makes use of the force of water rushing past it to generate more power to move the main rudder.

Watch keeping

On all but the shortest coastal passages some established watch-keeping routine should be followed to ensure that all on board have adequate rest. Those off watch do not have to be in bed and asleep, but they should relax and rest, leaving those on watch to sail the boat, trim the sails and cook the meals. Good lee cloths or boards are needed at sea to prevent the slumbering occupant of a narrow bunk being rudely dumped out of bed when the yacht puts about. It is on these occasions that the importance of watertight decks, secure hatches, and leak-proof ventilators makes itself firmly and wetly felt. The remorseless steady drip of water on to the victim's face is one of the oldest tortures devised by man.

A diaphragm bilge pump is less liable to choking than the barrel-type pump and shifts water quickly.

A lee cloth keeps the occupant safely in this pilot berth when the yacht is at sea.

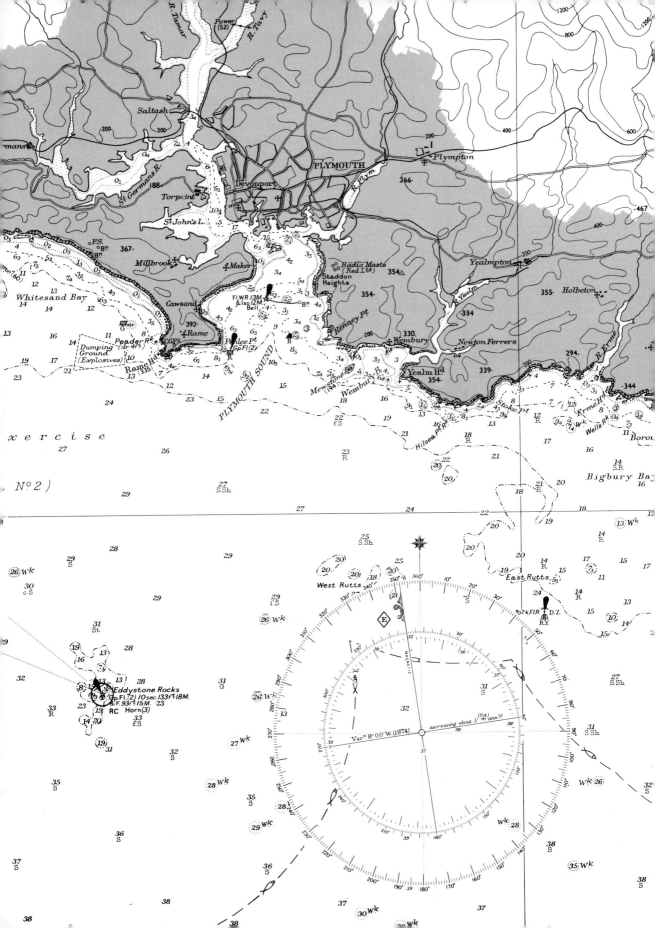

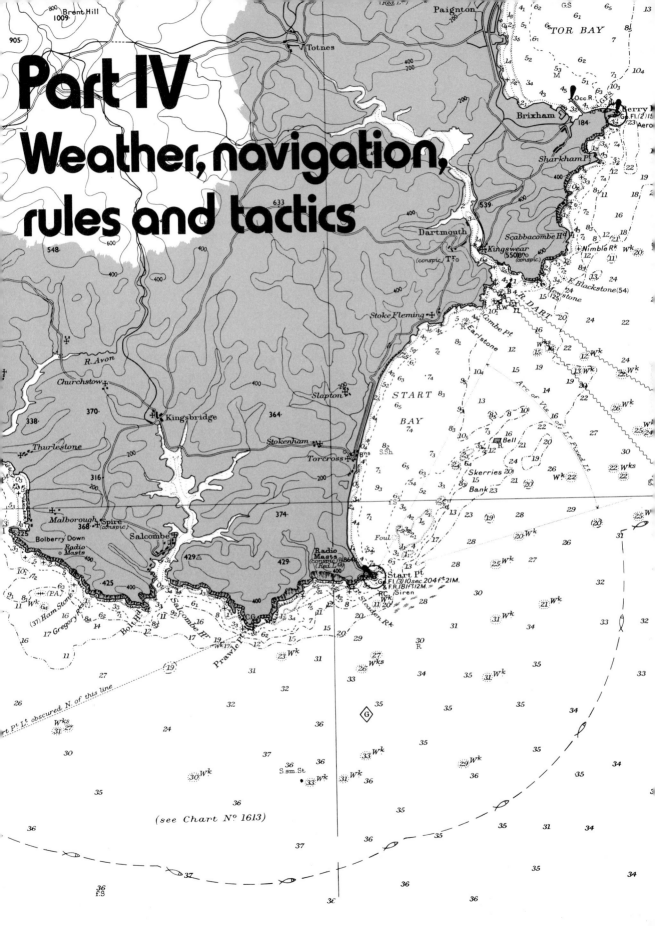

Part IV
Weather, navigation, rules and tactics

18
Weather

Ingrid Holford

The weather, to a competent seaman, is not just a facile topic of conversation, but a very pertinent issue in the whole business of getting afloat. The weather can be a friend or a foe, and it can change from the former to the latter in an uncomfortably short time, so that it is imperative to assess future events realistically in relation to the size of the boat and the helmsman's skill. There is no absolute demarcation between 'safe' and 'unsafe' weather, but an inexperienced sailor in a small boat, who attempts to combat weather which is proving tough going for a large cruising yacht, is obviously courting the sort of trouble from which he may not return. It shows common sense, not faint-heartedness, to remain ashore if the elements are likely to prove too much. Nevertheless, there will be occasions when weather deteriorates while one is already afloat, and then a lot will depend upon knowing the tricks of the enemy.

Professional meteorologists issue forecasts at all times of the day, all over the world, and in a blessedly uniform kind of language. But no forecaster is given enough time on the radio nor space in the newspapers to spoonfeed all the details which make weather in one locality slightly different from that in another. Nor is meteorology an exact science able to come up with precise answers, and though a forecaster makes the best prediction possible on the basis of known data, the unexpected can always happen. That is why it is so important to watch the weather as closely as you would a sick child for any symptoms showing deterioration, and to add your own local detail to what can only be a general summary forecast for a large area. It is impossible and unnecessary to learn by heart the local characteristics of weather in every part of the world because weather always forms for the same basic reasons. If you can master just a few elementary principles of science, you will be surprised how skilful you can become at anticipating the foibles of the weather wherever you go.

Local winds

The simple fact that *cold air is heavier than warm air* determines that there is wind, without which there would be no sailing. Wind is moving air, a familiar phenomenon even inside the home when cold outside air pours as howling draughts through badly fitting windows into nicely warmed rooms. Outdoors the sun is the major source of heat and warms the surfaces of the world according to the materials of which they are made. Tarmac heats faster than soil, bare soil heats faster than a grassy field, and a sea surface warms only very slowly because its ration of heat spreads through a considerable thickness of transparent water. Any surface heats more quickly when the sun's rays impinge at right angles than when they strike at a low angle and therefore cover a greater area. Air itself is not warmed directly by the sun's rays, but by contact with other warming surfaces. On any day, therefore, there are local differences of air temperature producing winds which can be useful to a sailor.

Air in contact with a rapidly heating road beside a river will warm, become lighter and rise, and then be replaced by colder, heavier air drifting off the river. It is surprising how well a river helmsman can

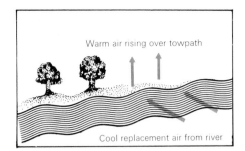

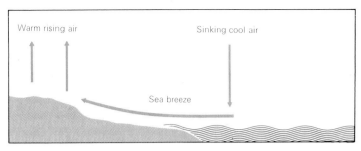

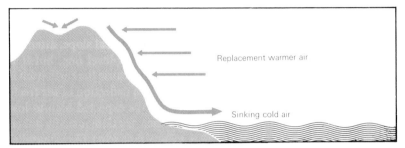

18.1 *Above left* River zephyrs. Warm air rising over the towpath and cool air replacing it from the river.

18.2 *Above right* Sea breezes. Warm rising air over the land is replaced by cool air from the sea.

18.3 *Left* Land breeze and katabatic wind. Cool land causes sinking cold air down the mountainside to flow off the land as a strong night-time breeze.

progress with tiny zephyrs like that. On the coast the wider expanse of water makes more decisive impact. As air rises over the rapidly heating land, a plentiful supply of cool air pours in from the sea as a wind called the *sea breeze*, which may penetrate many miles inland by mid-afternoon. Hence, no coastal sailor need be unduly depressed about the breathless early morning of a heat-wave, but can prepare for an onshore wind by the middle of the morning.

There is, however, the other side of the coin. Materials which heat up rapidly under the sun also cool rapidly when the sun goes down, but water cools slowly because of constant movement within the liquid as individual layers of water cool and sink. By the end of a cloudless night, during which heat has been radiating away from the earth, the land may well be colder than the adjacent sea, and air flows as an offshore wind. In particular, if the shoreline is mountainous, the cold air clinging to the steep cooling land sinks under gravity, causing a strong down-slope wind called a *katabatic* wind, which may extend several miles out to sea. With very simple reasoning about the topography of the area in which you are sailing you can, therefore, anticipate where wind will be, even though you cannot see it.

Pressure winds at 2,000 feet above ground

The same sort of temperature considerations which produce the shallow river zephyrs and the stronger sea breezes also produce the major wind systems of the world. Warm air rises over the tropics, cold air sinks over the poles, but the straightforward movement of air between the two is complicated by the fact that the major land masses are adjacent to seas of contrasting temperatures. Moreover, exchanges of heat on such a scale produce repercussions throughout the whole depth of atmosphere so that, at any one time, air which is cold near the surface may be

231

relatively warm aloft and vice versa. Fortunately, the nightmare complexity of vertical temperature structure can be summarized by one very useful factor at the surface – *the pressure which that depth of atmosphere exerts*. Pressure varies from day to day and from place to place, but if values at any one moment are plotted on to a map in the appropriate situations, they give a pressure contour picture analagous to a geographical contour map. Lines, called *isobars*, can be drawn joining places having equal pressure, and these form closed concentric patterns round centres of high and low pressure. The pressure readings are made strictly comparable by adding to each the pressure of an imaginary column of air equivalent to the physical height above mean sea-level at which the readings are made.

Air, like any other liquid confronted with a physical slope, attempts to move from a high-level contour line to a low-level one, but it is thwarted from achieving this direct movement because the earth itself is spinning on an axis. The rotating forces cause a deflection of the freely moving air so that it flows at right angles to the expected high-to-low direction when it is undisturbed by surface friction, usually taken to be 2,000ft above the ground. This means that wind blows parallel to the isobars on the appropriate part of the weather map. The apparent direction of movement round pressure centres is opposite in the two hemispheres of the world for the same 'upside down' reason that clock hands appear to be moving in opposite senses when viewed from the front and from the back. But the wind rule is just as simple in either hemisphere and must be learned by heart – only read the version you need so that you do not get muddled!

Northern hemisphere: The wind at 2,000ft blows parallel to the isobars so that, when blowing on one's back, *low pressure is on the left hand*. This means it blows anti- or counter-clockwise round low pressure and clockwise round high pressure.

Southern hemisphere: The wind at 2,000ft blows parallel to the isobars so that, when blowing on one's back, *low pressure is on the right hand*. This means it blows clockwise round low pressure and anti- or counterclockwise round high pressure.

Pressure winds at the surface

The wind which interests yachtsmen is that at the surface rather than that at 2,000ft above, but the two are closely related. The drag of friction prevents the full 90° deflection of surface air from the high-to-low direction, making it more like a 60° deflection over the land and about 80° deflection over the sea. Again this gives a different directional rule for the two hemispheres in terms of the isobars.

Northern hemisphere: Surface wind is *backed* from the wind at 2,000ft by about 30° over land and about 10° over the sea.

Southern hemisphere: Surface wind is *veered* from the wind at 2,000ft by about 30° over land and about 10° over the sea.

In both hemispheres this gives the result that surface air flows in towards the centres of a low-pressure circulation, called a *depression*, and outwards from the centre of a high-pressure circulation, called an *anti-*

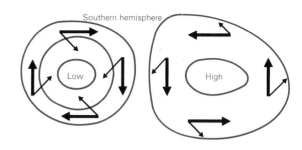

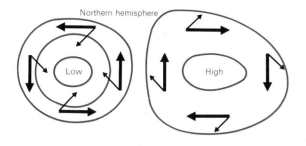

cyclone. In both hemispheres friction slows up surface wind speed by about 30% over the land, but rather less over the sea. However, there is usually enough vertical movement of air to bring down to the surface from higher levels momentary gusts of wind with speeds and direction more like those at 2,000ft level. The force which wind exerts is proportional to the square of its velocity, which means that, if a gust is twice as strong as the average speed, it will exert a force on sails four times as great as the average. If wind is already strong, this sort of gustiness can add enough 'weight' to the wind to make a boat as hard to handle as a bucking bronco. The strength of the wind at 2,000ft can be gauged from the distance between the isobars – the closer together, the stronger the wind. Hence, an isobaric chart is a kind of super eye-piece enabling you to see at a glance what the wind is doing all over the country.

Northern hemisphere	Southern hemisphere
← 2,000′ wind anticlockwise round low, clockwise round high	← 2,000′ wind clockwise round low, anticlockwise round high
← Surface wind backed from 2,000′ wind (in a counter-clockwise sense)	← Surface wind veered from 2,000′ wind (in a clockwise sense)

18.4 and **18.5** Direction of airflow at the surface and at 2,000ft above ground around centres of pressure, northern and southern hemispheres.

Wind behaviour

Since wind is invisible it is important not only to know where it comes from but how it behaves, and you cannot do better than to picture it moving in the same way as that familiar visible liquid, water, because they both behave similarly. When air meets an obstacle it must surmount it or make a sideways detour, and if two obstacles are close together, the passage-way between becomes the popular by-pass. The result is an increase in the volume of air flowing over a ridge, round a corner, or down a passage, and wind speed must increase in order to get through (just like the water forced through the constricting nozzle of a hose). The principle applies whatever the size the obstruction. Wind funnelling down a passage between sail sheds gives a totally unrealistic idea of wind speed some distance away; wind down a street of houses may burst out as a capsizing slam for boats sailing on the river at the end; and wind down a mountain valley may emerge with extreme ferocity, like the northerly wind funnelling down the Rhône Valley in France as the local mistral to churn up the Mediterranean.

18.6 *Below left* Wind increasing in speed over the top of a mountain (cross-section view).

18.7 *Below right* Wind increasing in speed between two mountains (plan view).

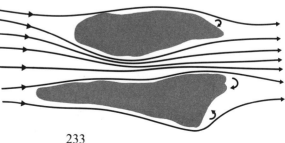

Nor can one bank on complete peace and quiet to leeward of solid obstacles like harbour walls or headlands. As air pours swiftly over the top or round the corners, it often slams back as a contrary eddy into the relatively empty space to leeward – rather like eddies swirling backwards to the lee of bridge pillars in a river. This can be quite a useful thing to remember when wind is fairly light, because it sometimes enables a sailing boat to make progress along a windward wall which at first glance appears devoid of wind.

Condensation

Apart from all this imaginative know-how of wind behaviour, clouds often serve as tell-tale indicators, provided you understand how they form. *All air contains water vapour*, even on a clear day. The supply is obtained by evaporation from the seas, rivers and lakes of the world (not forgetting all the wet washing on countless lines!), and the specially moist airstreams are those which have had a long journey over the sea. But at any particular temperature air has a maximum capacity for this invisible water vapour, and the capacity gets smaller as temperature falls. Visualize this in the more tangible terms of tankards in the bar. A half pint goes into a pint tankard with ample safety margin even for an unsteady hand. Pour that half pint into a half-pint tankard, and it needs a steady hand to prevent spillage. Cut the tankard capacity still further to a quarter pint, and some of the liquid must overflow. Obviously, the fuller the tankard in the first place, whatever the size, the less the reduction in size required before spillage occurs. It is the same with air when temperature decreases, and *dew-point* is the level at which air is full to the brim with vapour. Any further reduction in temperature results in condensation – dew, mist, fog, cloud, rain, or snow. The moister the air, the greater the risk of these forms of visible weather with even small falls in temperature. It is therefore important to understand how natural cooling occurs.

Cooling by contact

(1) Air may cool because a cloudless sky allows heat to radiate away from the ground into space. When there is little or no pressure wind to stir up this cooling, the cold, heavy air squats low on level surfaces, or drains by gravity down slopes into hollows. Any cooling beyond dew-point results first in *dew* (as on the outside of a jug of iced water taken from the refrigerator into a warm room), and later, as cooling is transferred through a greater depth of air, in *mist or fog*. A hot summer sun will clear all of these over land next day, but they often persist throughout the day in winter.

(2) A moving airstream cools when it journeys over colder surfaces, for instance when a mild airstream suddenly gains precedence after a bitterly cold winter. Indoors the air blooms as dew over cold furniture in unheated rooms. Outdoors fog forms temporarily over snow surfaces until the snow itself melts in the warm air, but this takes time. *Sea fog* occurs when an airstream cools over a particularly cold sea current, or

when it travels into progressively colder latitudes. The longer the sea track taken by the airstream, the more moisture it will have acquired *en route*, and the more rapidly will dew-point be approached, with the danger of fog. If wind is fairly strong, fog may be lifted off the surface to form, instead, a low ceiling of grey formless cloud called *stratus*. Because the temperature of the sea surface changes only imperceptibly during any one day, it requires a radical change in airstream before sea fog or stratus over the sea clear. The sun alone has little chance of doing it. Over land, however, a hot sun will burn off any sea fog or stratus which drifts onshore during the summer. Sea fog or stratus can occur even during a heat-wave if the airstream is particularly moist, but evasive action is possible if local geography permits. Search for a length of coastline which is in the lee of a sizeable headland over which the airstream can dry out, and you may find bright sunshine although there is thick fog only a few miles upwind.

Sea fog drifting across a shore line in summer. One mile inland there is bright sunshine, but there is little chance of fog clearing here. The best tactic would be to load the boat on a trailer and travel to some other beach to leeward of a sizeable stretch of warming land.

Cooling by reduction in pressure

When air is lifted above the ground, the column of air above it becomes less, and it therefore suffers a reduction of atmospheric pressure, expands, and thereby cools. This is why a soda-syphon cartridge becomes so exceedingly cold once the compressed air inside has been released into the syphon. To understand cloud formation, therefore, means looking for the methods by which air is lifted into regions of reduced pressure.

Cumulus forming over mountain tops because of intense heating over the slopes facing the sun and because air also has to surmount the obstacle in its way. The clouds dissolve on the leeward side as the air sinks down again and warms.

(1) Air lifts and cools when it is forced to surmount *hills or mountains*. This often causes a cloud to form over a mountain top when the sky nearby is clear, or it produces a lower cloud base over the mountain than already exists nearby.

(2) Air lifts in *thermal upcurrents* whose embryo stage has been described when explaining about the zephyrs along a river towpath. Air near the ground warms, rises, is replaced by air from above which warms in turn, rises, etc., etc. – a continuous process leading to a rising air current. In this thermal air cools at known fixed rates. The air mass in which the thermal is rising has a vertical temperature pattern which is a reflection of its previous history, and varies each day. Air in the thermal may, therefore, have a different temperature from the surroundings in which it is rising, but so long as it is warmer than the surroundings, the thermal air will be buoyant and continue to soar. On days when the air mass is particularly cold aloft (e.g. of polar origin, but moving towards the Equator) thermals may reach several miles high. When the air mass is relatively warm aloft (e.g. air moving from somewhere in the region of the Equator towards the poles), cooling air in the thermal soon meets a lid of air warmer than itself, and it rises no more. The strongest thermals occur over land in spring and summer during the daytime, and when the sun sets, thermals cease. Thermals also occur when cold air travels over a sea, and in that case thermals may continue into the night because sea-surface temperature does not change.

At some point in the upward journey of a thermal air cools beyond dew-point, and the base of a cloud forms. Condensation continues in the thermal and produces a *cumulus* cloud with a crisp billowing top. If thermals are shallow, cumulus remains no more than modest tufts of fleece. If thermals are deep, towering castles in the air called *cumulo-nimbus* develop, which give showers of rain, snow or hail, sometimes with a dramatic accompaniment of thunder and lightning. That alone can be a hazardous weather deterioration, but the disturbance of wind in the vicinity of such a cloud is of much greater importance to boats afloat. A cumulonimbus replenishes its violent upcurrents by sucking in air from below like a giant vacuum cleaner, and a yachtsman must prepare for wild fluctuations of surface wind, both as to direction and speed. Do not be lulled by any impression that the cloud, previously travelling towards you, is now travelling away. A cumulonimbus has no

236

Cumulus over land are being held back from drifting across the sea because of a sea breeze blowing on shore.

Cumulus development over land is accompanied by an offshore pressure wind which causes cumulus clouds to drift over the sea. These clouds are not of a height to produce showers, and the rather diffuse tops suggest that the lack of thermals over the sea is causing them to disperse.

Small cumulus spread evenly over the sky because the expanse of river is insignificant compared with the area of land by which it is surrounded. When such a sky occurs in early morning, watch for development of cumulus upwards during the rest of the day and possible increase in gustiness. When a sky has progressed no further than this by early afternoon, weather will continue fine and there should be little gustiness.

It is enough to see the tops of these cumulonimbus, without seeing their full depth, to know that they contain showers, perhaps hail, thunder and lightning, and to know that there will be violent fluctuations of wind strength and direction in the vicinity of their base. The cloud on the left is on the wane, and its upper layer of ice crystal cloud is streaming along in the upper winds to give the characteristic anvil shape. The cloud on the right is still soaring upwards and continued to do so for another ten minutes after this photograph was taken.

reversing gear, and it travels on the pressure wind of the day, but it has an abundance of power with which to take temporary control over surface wind.

(3) Air lifts into regions of lower atmospheric pressure when two air masses of different temperature and humidity characteristics confront each other from different directions. Like coffee and cream they cannot mix together at once, and as a temporary expedient, cold air undercuts warm air, giving violent upcurrents and a line of showers at the surface boundary called the *cold front*. Warm air, pushed by cold air, may be forced to slither upwards over cool air ahead, giving a more extensive sheet of *flat cloud*. It starts as a thin veil of high ice cloud, which gradually obscures the sun, and thickens to a solid looking grey, without the characteristic billows of a cumulus cloud. At that stage rain starts to fall and continues for several hours until the arrival of the surface boundary called the *warm front*, after which rain ceases. These clouds, too, bear messages to the yachtsman about the future behaviour of the main pressure winds.

Pressure patterns

The biggest shortcoming of the isobaric charts is that it shows the picture at only one moment, whereas weather is changing continually. However, the isobars arrange themselves in certain classic patterns which indicate a fairly standard type of weather sequence. If you can recognize these patterns you are half-way to being able to predict the weather that will follow.

Anticyclones are sluggish systems, slow to establish themselves by persistent but gradual rise in pressure, often reluctant to depart, and they decorate the weather charts with widely spaced isobars often arranged asymetrically. The charts tend to look empty, and thermals grow to shallow heights only because the outflow of air near the ground causes air above the centre to subside and warm. The weather is fine in summer but foggy or frosty in winter, and pressure winds are often maddeningly light. Sailing becomes difficult on rivers, lakes and reser-

238

voirs inland, but coastal sailors are better off because of sea breezes. Wind direction may change in haphazard fashion as the pattern re-orientates itself, but the difficulty of forecasting such a change should not constitute a danger, because the wind is light. Strong pressure wind does occur in fine, anticyclonic weather, but usually in the bordering *ridge of high pressure* between the centre of the anticyclone and a deepening depression elsewhere.

It is the passage of *depressions* which gives wind troubles to yachts-men, not only because of the risk of gales, but because of the changing wind directions as well. The particular nightmare in relatively confined waters is that a safe windward shore can suddenly become a dangerous leeward shore from which it is not possible to escape.

There are two broad types of depression pattern. First the busy, almost circular, pattern of closely spaced isobars which indicates an active, travelling depression. It has probably been born along the

Cumulus clouds flattening as thermals are cut off because of increasing and thickening frontal cloud. Watch for deteriorating weather and frontal changes of wind.

Sun almost obscured by warm front sheet cloud. Rain imminent.

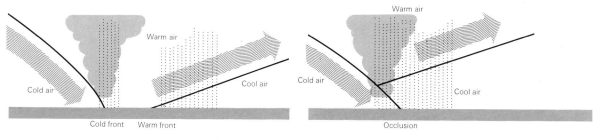

18.8 Cross-sections through a typical warm front, cold front and occlusion.

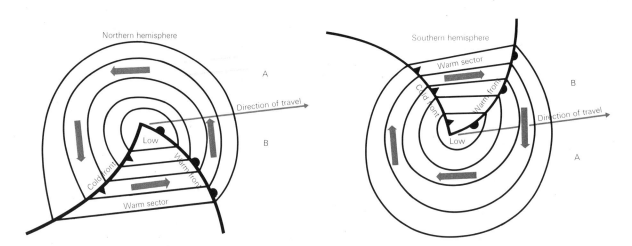

Manner of wind change as depressions pass overhead, northern and southern hemispheres.

18.9a *Above left* As the depression moves eastward, wind at A *backs* smoothly from S-E-N and wind at B *veers* from S-W-N with abrupt changes at fronts.

18.9b *Above right* As the depression moves eastward, wind at B *backs* from N-W-S with abrupt changes at fronts and wind at A *veers* smoothly from N-E-S.

boundary between two air masses, and the circulation carries with it a wave of contrasting air and well-marked surface fronts. The depression announces its approach in the sky by the flat sheet cloud of a warm front, and confirms its progress by a message on every barometer along its line of approach. Pressure starts to fall at a rate commensurate with the speed of approach of the depression, proximity to the path of the centre, and the rate at which the system itself is deepening. Pressure always falls more quickly at the centre than on the periphery, leading to a steeper pressure gradient, more isobars on the chart, and more wind in the boat's sails. *Rapidly falling pressure* ahead of warm front cloud, and *rapidly rising pressure* behind the cold front as the depression passes indicate a risk of *gales*.

Figure 18.9 shows how these warnings also indicate changes in wind direction. The abrupt manner in which the isobars change direction at the warm and cold fronts is not artistic licence, but an indication of real fact. Assuming a boat is on the same side of the depression centre as the fronts, the following rules apply:

Northern hemisphere: Pressure falls, and wind backs ahead of the warm front. Pressure steadies, and wind veers behind the warm front. Pressure rises, and wind veers still further behind the cold front.

Southern hemisphere: Pressure falls, and wind veers ahead of the warm front. Pressure steadies, and wind backs behind the warm front. Pressure rises, and wind backs still further behind the cold front.

If a boat is on the opposite side of the path of the centre from the fronts, wind direction changes from the one extreme to the other but in the opposite manner. Hence, the importance of knowing your position relative to the travelling centre so that you can make a reasonable estimate whether a nearby shore will be to windward or to leeward.

Cyclones, hurricanes and typhoons are all names of low-pressure circulations of greater violence, though smaller cross-section area, than depressions. They occur over subtropical seas, feed on a diet of warm, moist air, and generally revert to ordinary depressions once they reach land. No one in their senses would want to be anywhere near a hurricane, but for those who unfortunately find themselves in the vicinity, the wind follows the same directional behaviour as in depressions. Wind blows in almost circular fashion, perhaps as strong as 200mph near the centre, but at the centre there is a relatively calm 'eye' where wind drops to about 10–15mph. It affords a brief respite to effect repairs or batten down more securely, but the wind always returns just as fiercely – although from the opposite direction.

After a brief maturity active depressions start to wane, central pressure rises, pressure gradients decrease, and wind drops. The depression

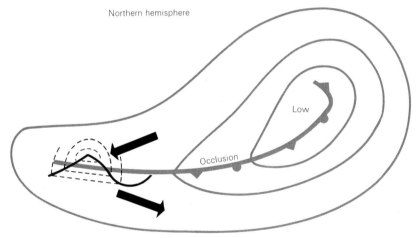

18.10a Filling depression and trailing occlusion liable to wave and generate another depression.

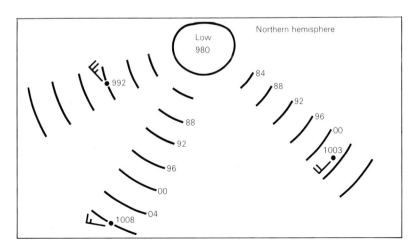

18.10b How to draw a complete isobaric pattern with only a few given pressure values. To make your own weather chart plot the given position of the pressure centre and draw an isobar around it. Plot the three pressure and wind observations, with wind shafts drawn on the side of the station *from which* wind is coming and half a barb indicating one strength of the Beaufort scale. Draw the isobars at those stations (veered from surface wind in northern hemisphere). Space off isobars from these given positions, closer together where wind is stronger. Complete the lines to make concentric patterns.

drifts or grinds to a halt, and by that time the pressure pattern has changed. The centre will have travelled faster than the outer edge where the cold front may be trailing behind and becoming extinct. Near the centre the cold front will have overtaken the warm front and lifted the warm sector off the ground, at which stage the fronts are said to be *occluded*. The weather chart may look as empty of isobars as in an anticyclone, but there is one important difference. Surface winds, being backed from those at 2,000ft, blow slightly inwards towards the centre of the depression, and this convergence forces air above the centre to lift and become cooled. Cloud and rain may therefore continue, particularly if the isobars change direction in strongly marked fashion and bring together airs of contrasting nature. Such a V of isobars is called a trough, and when it is as extreme as that shown in figure 18.10a, makes the pattern look as insecure as a stretched water drop about to separate from a dripping tap, and that is precisely the danger. The area becomes the possible birth-place of another depression which may make a take-over bid from the parent depression. Forecasters can only stress the probability of this happening; they cannot pinpoint the actual centre until it has formed, or a vital clue is reported by which time, if you are sailing in the vicinity, weather may deteriorate with little warning. Always distrust a sloppy-looking depression with troughing isobars, and watch carefully for cloud and barometer clues for the formation of a secondary depression.

The composite wind

Every aspect of wind and weather is simple to understand after the event. The difficult thing is to combine the various considerations in such a way that it gives a true forecast before the events happen. It is a complicated kind of mental arithmetic but without quantitative ingredients or answers. The best thing is to develop the habit of detective reasoning, and you will find that with practice the answers become more accurate. Look at an isobaric chart every day, even if not sailing, so as to be familiar with the air mass encompassing your area.

Is it cold or warm? Dry or moist?

Is it cooling in the lower levels and moist enough for fog?

Is it warming in the lower levels and likely to give thermals?

Is it cold aloft, are there deep thermals, gusty winds, showers? Or is it warm aloft because of subsiding air over an anticyclone, and likely to give only small clouds and little gustiness?

Are there any fronts marked on the charts?

How quickly are they advancing? (Following winds push them along with greater effect when they are at right angles to the line of the front.)

Will frontal cloud obscure the sun and cut down thermals?

How will the pressure wind change?

Are you in the path of any depression?

How fast is it advancing? (Approximately the speed and direction of the isobars in the warm sector.)

Is there any trough whose innocuous appearance could belie its capacity for making trouble?

Is the sun high enough to give sea breezes?

Will they operate in the same direction as the pressure wind and therefore increase the joint effect?

Will they counteract each other and decrease the joint effect?

This sort of question, weighted according to season and time of day, leads with practice to that indefinable know-how called weather wisdom.

Barometers

If you are going to take the weather seriously, the minimum equipment needed is a barometer. Dinghy owners will find a decorative model for the home is adequate, but any boat large enough to make long cruises should have a barometer aboard, provided it can be protected from the elements. Mercury barometers have long ceased to be popular for general use, and aneroid barometers are used which measure pressure by the movement in a capsule partially evacuated of air. These are quite suitable, even for a wildly plunging boat, and need not be expensive to be reasonably accurate. Precision reading is less important than a reasonably sensitive movement, because it is this *tendency* which indicates future weather developments. Do not rely upon any dictatorial message painted on the dial face like 'fine', 'dry' or 'storm' because these weathers can occur at most levels of pressure. Rely more upon the following code language.

Falling pressure: Deterioration of weather

Rapid fall: Strong winds, perhaps gales, and bad weather

Rapid rise: Strong winds, perhaps gales, improving weather but probably only temporarily

Slow persistent rise: Decreasing winds, fine weather in summer, fog or frost in winter.

The major snag with this warning language is that, although noticeable movements of pressure give positive weather indications, the absence of pressure movements does not necessarily indicate that all is well. A stationary depression may give continuous rain for several days with absolutely no wind to send the system on its way, and without a flicker of movement registered on the barometer. And since it needs two pressure values to determine a gradient and wind speed, one boat on the edge of an anticyclone experiencing obstinately steady pressure may, nevertheless, find wind increasing to gale force simply because pressure is tumbling many miles away with the advance of a deepening depression. Despite the snags a barometer is a most helpful instrument.

Because of the importance of tendency, choose your barometer carefully for its design. The figures on the dial face should be easy to read even in a dim cabin, and there should be a pointer, movable by a central knob, to serve as a memory aid. Set this pointer above the pressure hand when you take a reading, and then, at the next reading, you can tell immediately if pressure has fallen or risen. But the memory pointer must be clearly distinguishable by shape or colour from the pressure hand to avoid confusion between the hand which records present pressure and the pointer which reminds you about earlier pressure. Most dials of sensible size have room for two unit scales, one being the traditional

BEAUFORT WIND SCALE

Beaufort No.	Velocity in knots	Description	Sea state
0	Less than 1	Calm	Sea like a mirror.
1	1–3	Light air	Ripples with the appearance of scales are formed but without foam crests.
2	4–6	Light breeze	Small wavelets, still short but more pronounced. Crests have a glassy appearance and do not break.
3	7–10	Gentle breeze	Large wavelets. Crests begin to break. Foam of glassy appearance. Perhaps scattered white horses.
4	11–16	Moderate breeze	Small waves, becoming longer; fairly frequent white horses.
5	17–21	Fresh breeze	Moderate waves taking a more pronounced long form; many white horses are formed. Chance of some spray.
6	22–27	Strong breeze	Large waves begin to form; the white foam crests are more extensive everywhere. Probably some spray.
7	28–33	Near gale	Sea heaps up, and white foam from breaking waves begins to be blown in streaks along the direction of the wind.
8	34–40	Gale	Moderately high waves of greater length; edges of crests begin to break into spindrift. The foam is blown in well-marked streaks along the direction of the wind.
9	41–47	Strong gale	High waves. Dense streaks of foam along the direction of the wind. Crests of waves begin to topple, tumble and roll over. Spray may affect visibility.
10	48–55	Storm	Very high waves with long, overhanging crests. The resulting foam in great patches is blown in dense white streaks along the direction of the wind. On the whole the surface of the sea takes a white appearance. The tumbling of the sea becomes heavy and shocklike. Visibility affected.
11	56–63	Violent storm	Exceptionally high waves. (Small and medium-sized ships might be lost to view behind the waves.) The sea is completely covered with long white patches of foam lying along the direction of the wind. Everywhere the edges of the wave crests are blown into froth. Visibility affected.
12	64 +	Hurricane	The air is filled with foam and spray. Sea completely white with driving spray; visibility very seriously affected.

'height of mercury' in inches or millimetres. The other ought to indicate units of atmospheric pressure called millibars because that is what is used internationally by meteorological offices.

The fascinating instrument to have in the home, if you can afford one, is a *barograph*. This is a barometer with a connecting pen which records a continuous trace of pressure on a chart wrapped round a rotating drum driven by clockwork. The see-sawing movement gives a cross-section view of what happens in the atmosphere. A barograph is not suitable for small boats because movement takes the pen off the paper, but it can be helpfully revealing to make your own graph in worsening weather by plotting frequent pressure readings. There is something more imperative about a plunging graph than there is in a list of decreasing numerals!

Self-made isobaric charts

Obviously there are no newspapers or television screens in small boats to flash you the latest isobaric chart. The solution is to make your own, and this is not such an outrageous suggestion as you might think. Although it needs a vast network of weather reporting stations, information from the upper air, and satellite photography to enable meteorologists to pinpoint centres of low and high pressure and fronts, it only needs a few words on the air to relay the information to the public. The actual pattern of isobars which accompanies these main features can be drawn with extraordinary accuracy with only a few actual or forecast values of pressure and wind, because of one simple fact which the haphazard contours of a landscape do not give to a physical contour map. Pressure gradient changes smoothly from one area to another except at fronts, and, therefore, one can interpolate isobars between known pressure values with confidence of accuracy. It is only necessary to orientate the isobars by backing or veering them from the observed surface winds, according to which hemisphere you are in, and to space the lines according to where the fastest wind speeds are. Since the convention is to draw isobars at even intervals of pressure, an actual pressure value reported in a weather bulletin need not have an isobar drawn through it, but it serves as a spacing value to determine the next isobar.

It is easier to take down a bulletin and make a chart than it is to understand an explanation in words, but the time to practise is not when you most need a chart, afloat in deteriorating weather. Buy a supply of outline maps, which include wind scales, plotting symbols, and simple instructions, and practise taking down a weather broadcast in the comfort of your own home. The reader of the bulletin may be rationed for time and have to read quickly, so listen and take down what is said like an automaton without trying to interpret anything. Try not to panic if anything is missed; leave it and concentrate on what the reader is saying next. The time to start thinking and plotting is when everything is down on paper. Mark in all centres of pressures and fronts, plot all known pressure values and reported wind speeds and directions, sketch in the isobars, and see how your efforts compare (and improve!) with the version published next day in the paper.

19
Navigation
Barbara Webb

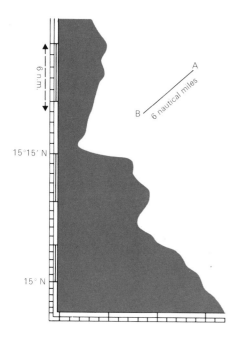

19.1 Measuring distances on a chart. One minute of latitude along the side margin of a chart equals one nautical mile. On a Mercator chart the scale varies from top to bottom so measurements must be taken from the side margin at the same level as the distance being measured.

The navigator's art is to determine his position as accurately as possible and to establish the course to his destination. In theory he should be able to point to a spot on the chart and say, 'We are there.' Sometimes he will be right, but in most cases he can only say, 'This is where we are to within a couple of miles.' So the art of navigation is really that of knowing at any given moment how close to one's calculated position one can reliably expect to be.

Coastal navigation is used when a boat is within sight of or close to land, the boat's position being checked by reference to features marked on a chart. Astro-navigation is used when a boat is out of sight of land on long passages, and the position is determined by taking sights of celestial bodies – by measuring the angle of a celestial body above the horizon (its altitude), and by referring to navigation tables. Radio navigation is used in all waters by taking bearings of radio transmitters, or by interpreting radio transmissions.

All sailors require some knowledge of coastal navigation which is covered briefly in this chapter. Astro-navigation affects a relatively small number of small-boat sailors, and good books on the subject are readily available. The different radio-navigation systems are mentioned later.

Equipment required

The following list of equipment is desirable in even the smallest cruiser, undertaking a short coastal passage: charts, steering compass, hand-bearing compass, tide tables, tidal-stream atlas, sailing directions, echo sounder or lead and line, log book, nautical almanac, log, and publications relating to navigational aids. Some boats also carry direction-finding (DF) radio or radio-navigation apparatus and a sextant. Charts and steering compass are essential and, in tidal waters, tide tables and details of the tidal streams or currents.

The navigator needs a flat surface, big enough to take a spread-out chart, on which to work. In smaller cruisers, where space is limited, he may have to fold the chart once and use the main saloon table. There should be adequate lighting over the chart table for night work and convenient stowage for charts, books, and equipment. Because the navigator has to draw straight and accurate lines, stowage space is needed where charts can be kept flat and folded as little as possible – a shallow drawer beneath the chart table or under a berth are often satisfactory places.

Charts, particularly of local waters, will be used time and time again, and so a soft, black pencil and a soft rubber to erase notes and lines are needed. Dividers, used to measure distances, should be rust-free and steady – tight enough not to alter their setting when transferring distances across the chart. A magnifying glass can be useful for reading small print.

Charts
A chart is a map of an area of water giving information about those features on land which are of use to the sailor, together with details of

246

the coastline, the seabed, anchorages and aids to navigation, warnings of special dangers, and many other matters of interest to the mariner.

SCALE: Small-scale charts cover vast areas of water and are usually only used for ocean passages or planning long-distance cruises. Medium-scale charts cover fairly large sections of coast and are used for plotting courses and positions on shorter passages. Large-scale charts cover small areas in very great detail and are used for harbours and areas where navigation is particularly tricky. Every boat should carry medium- and large-scale charts covering not only her intended passage but waters and ports nearby into which she may be forced by bad weather.

MARGINS: The top and bottom margins identify the lines of longitude, while the side margins identify the lines of latitude. Because the lines of longitude converge at the poles, the distance between two lines of longitude 1° apart reduces from 60 miles at the Equator to nothing at the North and South Poles. On the other hand, the distance between two lines representing minutes of latitude is constant – one sea mile, whether at the Equator, New Zealand, or Nova Scotia. Therefore, the side margins only can be used as a scale measuring distances: 1′ equals 1 nautical mile. They must be used at the same level as the distance being measured because in the Mercator charts normally used there is a variation in scale between the top and bottom of a chart (fig. 19.1). Some charts used in the Great Lakes are based on statute rather than nautical miles.

SOUNDINGS: The depth of water is shown on charts by isolated figures giving soundings below Chart Datum (fig. 19.2), while contour lines join points of equal depth and indicate the shape of the bottom. Soundings may be given in fathoms, fathoms and feet, feet alone, or metres, and it is important to be aware of the units used. These are usually indicated below the title of the chart together with information as to what level has been selected for chart datum. This can be Mean Low Water (US), Low Water Ordinary Spring Tides (UK feet and fathoms charts), Lowest Astronomical Tide (UK metric charts) or a certain number of feet above sea-level for such areas as inland waters. To determine the depth of water at any particular time the height of the tide must be worked out and either added to or subtracted from the sounding shown on the chart.

19.2 Soundings are given in feet, fathoms and feet, or metres below chart datum. Drying heights are given in metres or feet above chart datum and are underlined. Clearance under bridges, overhead power cables, etc., and heights on land are given in metres or feet above high water.

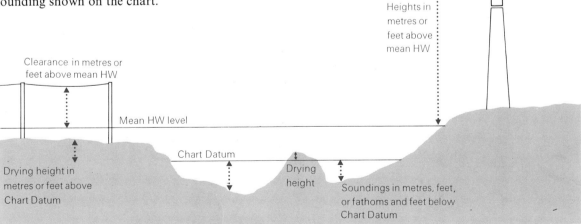

DRYING HEIGHTS: The height of some objects such as sand-banks and rocks, which are covered at high water but visible at low water, is given in either feet or metres above chart datum (fig. 19.2). The figures on the chart are underlined to differentiate them from soundings.

HEIGHTS ON LAND AND CLEARANCE: The heights of features or objects on land which are permanently above water level, and the heights of cables or bridges are given in feet or metres above mean high water (fig. 19.2).

CORRECTIONS: Charts must be amended at least annually and before every cruise into strange waters to include all alterations given in *Notices to Mariners*. A note is made outside the margin of the chart giving the serial number of the correction.

ROSES: At least one compass rose is printed on almost every chart and this is based on true north. There is usually a second rose inside the first, based on magnetic north, or alternatively an arrow pointing to magnetic north at the time the chart was printed.

TIDES AND TIDAL STREAMS (tidal currents): Many charts give details of the set and rate (drift) of tidal streams at various places, together with basic facts about tides at certain ports on the chart.

SYMBOLS AND ABBREVIATIONS: So much information is printed on charts that symbols and abbreviations have to be used if the chart is to be legible. Many countries use internationally agreed symbols; others use their own, but all publish charts or booklets giving the meaning of the symbols. The navigator must have at hand the publications relating to all charts carried on board (*US chart 1, Admiralty chart 5011*). Particular attention should be paid to the symbols used for dangers such as rocks, wrecks, eddies and tidal rips.

Compass

The magnetic compass used in small boats consists of a bowl in which a card pivots around a central point. The bowl contains a liquid to damp the motion of the card. There are magnetic needles on the card which are attracted towards magnetic north, and the face of the card is marked in degrees or points. Many sailing boats carry two magnetic compasses – a steering compass which is a permanent fixture and a hand-bearing compass for taking bearings. Alternatively, a pelorus or dumb compass can be used to take relative bearings.

Close to the rim of the card of a compass is the lubber's point or line, and the compass-card reading directly opposite the lubber's point shows the direction in which the boat is pointing or, in the case of a hand-bearing compass, the direction of an object from the boat. The compass card points to magnetic north all the time while the bowl and the boat turn around it.

A magnetic compass is always attracted to magnetic north, not to the North Pole which is true north. Magnetic north is not stationary but moves a small, but predictable amount each year. The difference between true north and magnetic north varies from place to place and is called variation. Details of local variation are found on charts, usually inside the compass roses: for example, 'Var^n 15°E (1965) decreasing about 5' annually' means that in 1965 magnetic north was 15° east of

Below (top) A gimballed steering compass with a cover which can be rotated to align with magnetic north for the course to be steered. It is easier for the helmsman to keep the north pointer of the compass card aligned with the arrow on the cover than to keep a particular bearing lined up with the lubber's line. *(bottom)* A small steering compass suitable for a dinghy or small cruiser. It is mounted on a fixed bracket, but the compass card will operate satisfactorily at small angles of heel. The cover can be turned to align with magnetic north.

true north at that spot, and that each year the figure is reduced by about five minutes.

A compass is also influenced by ferrous metal situated nearby, such as an engine, cooker, or the rigging, and instead of pointing to magnetic north it will often be a few degrees out and will point to compass north. The difference between magnetic north and compass north is called deviation. The amount of deviation varies according to the course the boat is steering. In order to know what deviation to allow on each course a deviation table is drawn up for each individual boat, giving the deviation to allow on a number of headings. Once the table has been established, it is essential not to alter the deviation by placing an object such as a beer can or knife close to the compass.

Variation is due to natural causes and will be the same for all boats in one area. It is determined by the geographical location of the stretch of water and the year. Deviation is due to the magnetic field of the individual boat and remains the same for any particular course – wherever that boat may be sailing. The combined effect of variation and deviation is called compass error and must be applied to magnetic north to obtain true north, and vice versa (fig. 19.3).

Whereas a deviation table can easily be drawn up for a steering compass which is a permanent fixture, a hand-bearing compass is held by the navigator, often in different positions on board so that he can see an object clearly. To reduce deviation and obtain a magnetic bearing he should hold the hand-bearing compass as far away as possible from magnetic influences in the boat, such as rigging or guardrails, and always take bearings from the same place if he can. It is worth while checking the bearing of the hand-bearing compass against that of the steering compass to verify that large errors are not present.

Just as there are three 'norths' of interest to the small-boat sailor, so can every line on the chart, every bearing taken, and every course steered be expressed in three ways, true, magnetic and compass.

Log

Boats may carry either an electronic log fitted to the hull to record both distance sailed through the water and the speed of the boat, or a patent log (taffrail log) which has a spinner towed at the end of a long line, and this turns a register attached to the stern.

Echo sounder and lead and line

Echo sounders record the depth of water beneath a vessel by sending a signal to the bottom and measuring the time it takes for that signal to echo back to the vessel. The traditional methods of measuring the depth of water are a lead dropped overboard on the end of a marked line or, in shallow waters, a sounding pole dipped in the water alongside.

Radio aids

The amount of radio equipment carried varies according to the size of the boat and the depth of the owner's pocket, but few boats should put to sea without a simple radio with which to listen to weather forecasts. Some boats carry radio telephones and radar equipment.

Above Hand-bearing compass.

19.3 *Below* A magnetic compass points to magnetic north; the difference between magnetic north and true north is called variation. A magnetic steering compass is influenced by objects on board and points to compass north; the difference between magnetic north and compass north is called deviation.

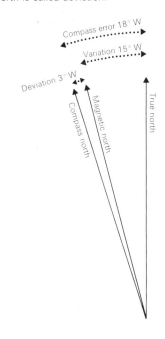

Compass error 18° W

Variation 15° W

Deviation 3° W

Compass north

Magnetic north

True north

This chart table can take a standard-size chart folded once. Radio direction finder, speedometer and echo sounder are on the half-bulkhead.

RADIO DIRECTION FINDERS (RDF): These are radio receivers with a means of taking the bearings of a signal transmitted by a radio beacon, each beacon having its own identifying call sign. The aerial is turned until the signal fades out, and this null indicates the bearing of the radio beacon from the vessel. As there are two nulls, 180° different, care must be taken to use the right one. Radio bearings are subject to error owing to various causes such as sky-wave effect.

CONSOL: The beacon transmits a radiating pattern of dash sectors and dot sectors which are marked on a special Consol chart. The navigator counts the number of dots or dashes to establish his position.

LORAN: Pairs of stations transmit radio pulses, timed so that there is a delay between the master transmission and the slave transmission. The receiver on board measures the difference in time and so establishes the distance of the boat from the transmitter. The resulting position line is a hyperbola, and these hyperbolas are superimposed on a normal chart, each marked with its delay. To obtain a fix a second position line is required from a second pair of stations, or from the master and a second slave.

Publications

The navigator needs to refer to books giving full details of all aids to navigation covering buoyage, lights, fog signals, and radio beacons.

NAUTICAL ALMANAC: A good nautical almanac compiled for small-boat sailors gives all this information and much else besides such as the International Code of Signals, the Rules of the Road in various waters, tables for astro-navigation, distress signals, times of weather forecasts and tidal information.

TIDE TABLES AND TIDAL-STREAM ATLASES: Tide tables are issued annually and give the predicted times and heights of high water for various ports. Tidal-stream atlases (current charts) give the rate and set of tidal streams around the coasts.

SAILING DIRECTIONS: Pilots are printed which give details of such matters as ports, tides and tidal streams, dangers, and the coastline, but they are produced for commercial and naval shipping. There are many excellent books of sailing directions written by small-boat sailors for small-boat sailors which give details about waters where commercial traffic seldom ventures, and the good ones are invaluable. Many include plans of small ports and harbours, anchorages and matters which concern small cruising boats such as where water and fuel can be obtained.

LOG BOOK: The navigator needs to note all the details of the voyage such as courses, bearings, fixes, weather, barometer readings and speed.

SEXTANT: A sextant is needed to measure angles and, although it is used mainly for taking sights on heavenly bodies, it can also be used to obtain a fix by measuring angles between objects on land or to establish distance off an object the height of which is known (fig. 19.5).

Tides, tidal streams (tidal currents) and currents (non-tidal currents)

The word tide relates to the vertical movement of water caused by

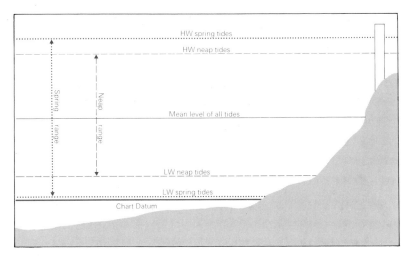

19.4 The range of a tide is the difference in the height of the water between succeeding high and low tides. The range is greatest at springs and decreases gradually to a minimum at neap tides.

changes in depth as quantities of water move across the surface of the earth in response to the horizontal pull of the moon, and to a certain extent, the sun. The level of water is highest at high water (HW), lowest at low water (LW), and the half-way mark of all tides is called the mean level (ML) (fig. 19.4). Tides are semi-diurnal when there are two cycles of high and low water daily, or diurnal when there is only one. Because the pull of the moon varies according to its position in relation to the earth and sun, the range of some tides is greater than that of others. Those with great range are called spring tides, and those with least range are called neap tides.

On many charts chart datum is at the level of mean low water springs (MLWS), but on the metric charts being introduced in many parts of the world it is the level of the lowest astronomical tide (LAT). On inland and non-tidal waters another level is defined as chart datum. The actual datum used for the chart is of little practical consequence to the small-boat navigator, but it is important to ensure that the tide tables referred to have predictions related to the same level as the chart, as small differences can exist.

The times and heights of tides are predicted and published annually. Generally HW times and heights are given for major ports, and sometimes LW heights and times are included. Tidal differences based on these major ports are given for neighbouring harbours and areas, and are applied by adding or subtracting the given number of hours and minutes to or from the times given for HW at the major port.

Horizontal movement of the water is due to the tides or various other natural causes such as weather, salinity, the shape of the seabed, or a combination of any of these factors. In the UK the word current is used only in respect of horizontal movement of water owing to natural causes, excluding the tide, and the US term is non-tidal current. The term tidal current is used in the USA for horizontal movement of water owing to the tide, but according to UK usage this would be a contradiction of terms; the UK equivalent is tidal stream. Like tides tidal streams are least vigorous at neaps and achieve their maximum rate at springs.

The navigator has to take both the set and rate (drift) of tidal streams

19.5 Vertical sextant angle.

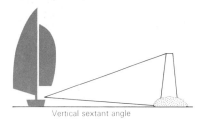

into account when plotting courses. This information is printed on charts and contained in tidal stream atlases. Figures are given for the mean neap and spring rates, but to find accurately the rate at a particular time it is necessary to determine the range of the tide – the difference in height between the previous and subsequent high and low waters. The set is indicated either in degrees or by arrows for each hour before and after high water at some neighbouring port. Tidal streams do not flow flat out in one direction and then reverse in an instant to flow equally rapidly in the opposite direction. Instead there is a gradual easing of the rate, say of the flood stream, followed by a period of slack water when the water barely moves and set is often uncertain until the ebb stream sets in. With a normal ebb and flow pattern the maximum rate is achieved half-way between the two periods of slack water. In some areas tidal streams are rotary and their set changes hour by hour through 360°.

The rise and fall of tides varies, too, in pattern. In many areas of semi-diurnal tides the rise lasts six hours, followed by a six-hour fall, and, like tidal streams, the rate of rise is greatest near half-tide, whereas just before and after high and low water both rise and fall are slight, often with a stand at HW and LW when the level remains virtually constant. In other areas there may be a double high water, or an extended period of low water. The rise may last five hours, followed by a three-hour stand and a four-hour fall. The more unusual the pattern, the more details will be available from the authorities.

Both tides and tidal streams are affected by the weather conditions prevailing at the time: the figures in the tide tables are only predictions. A strong wind can delay or accelerate the time of high water, can increase or decrease the rate of a tidal stream, and can cause the water to build up or be held back so that the level may be several metres different from that predicted.

Aids to navigation

Whether built on shore or anchored in open water all aids to navigation are positioned so that they inform vessels where it is safe to sail and where dangers exist. A symbol on the chart marks the position of the object on land, and a small circle shows the position of the anchor to which a buoy is moored. Abbreviations and symbols are used on charts to show such details as colour, shape, character of the light, sound signals, radar reflectors and topmarks.

Buoys
These vary in shape and colour and are laid in accordance with an agreed system so that the vessel knows where the danger lies in relation to the buoy. The most usual shapes are:
Can buoy: flat top
Nun buoy: conical with the top cut off
Conical buoy: pointed top, cone shape
Pillar buoy: a buoy with a vertical structure above it
Spherical buoy: round
Spar buoy: a buoy with only a spar showing above water

Opposite Uniform System of Buoyage.

252

LATERAL MARKS

PORT HAND
Lights white, 2, 4 or 6, or red 1, 2, 3, 4 fl.
Can be chequered red and white

STARBOARD HAND
Lights white 1, 3 or 5 flashes
Can be chequered black and white

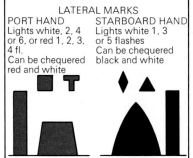

WRECK MARKS
also lightvessels and floats — lights green

ISOLATED DANGERS
Light red or white fl.

SAFE WATER MARKS
Mid channel or landfall, striped vertically or painted distinctively
Lights distinctive
Any shape

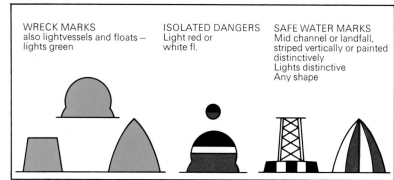

MIDDLE GROUND MARKS

Inner end of middle ground

Outer end of middle ground

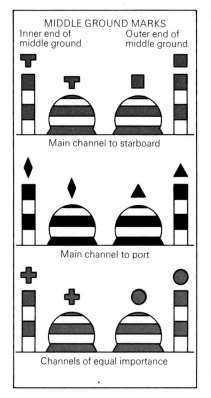

Main channel to starboard

Main channel to port

Channels of equal importance

Cardinal Marks

NORTH CARDINAL MARK
Light white   1 or 3 flashes

THE DANGER

WEST CARDINAL MARK
Light white
2 or 3 flashes

EAST CARDINAL MARK
Light white
VQF (3) ev. 5 secs
or QF (3) ev. 10 secs
SE

SOUTH CARDINAL MARK
Lights red   2 or 4 flashes

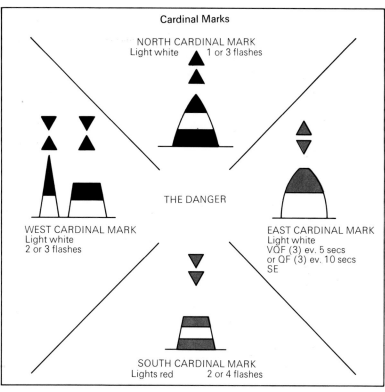

PORT SIDE

Marks port side of channel and obstructions which must be passed on the port hand
Colour : black
Numbers : odd
Light : white or green
Shape : can or as below

Bell

Lighted

MID-CHANNEL
Lighted

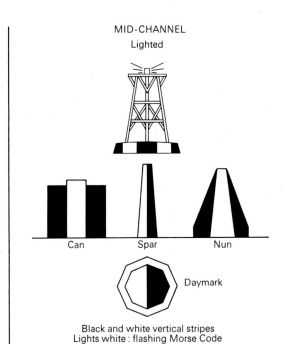

Can   Spar   Nun

Daymark

Black and white vertical stripes
Lights white : flashing Morse Code

STARBOARD SIDE

Marks starboard side of channel and obstructions which must be passed on the starboard hand
Colour : red
Numbers : even
Light : white or red
Shape : nun or as below

Bell

Lighted

JUNCTION

(entering from seaward)
Colour : red and black horizontal bands
Light : white, red or green, interrupted quick flashing
May be lettered

Preferred Channel to Starboard
Topmost band black

Lighted

Preferred Channel to Port
Topmost band red

Lighted

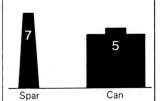

Spar   Can

Whistle

Pointer   Daymark

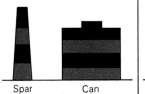

Spar   Can

Daymark

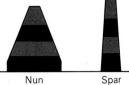

Nun   Spar

Daymark

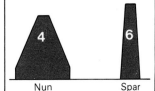

Nun   Spar

Whistle

Daymark   Pointer

Buoyage systems

Over thirty different buoyage systems have been in use in various parts of the world – nine in north-west Europe alone. In some cases more than one system is used in a single country so the notes that follow must, of necessity, be very general. Currently the situation is further confused because the Uniform System of Buoyage in use until 1977 in many waters, including Australia, New Zealand and much of Europe, is to be replaced by Maritime Buoyage System A which combines cardinal and lateral systems with red to port. System A will cover Europe, Africa, India, Australia, New Zealand, and parts of Asia, and a period of five years from 1977 has been allowed for the change-over. In Britain replacement will be completed in 1979, the first section, the busy Dover Strait area from Brighton to Orford Ness, being tackled over three or four months commencing April 1977 concurrently with the French and Belgian coasts opposite.

Maritime System B (lateral only, red to starboard) more nearly approximates to the North American buoyage systems, but was still under discussion in 1976, and no date can be given for its introduction. It will apply to North and South America, the Caribbean, and parts of Asia not covered by System A.

Several systems use combined cardinal and lateral marks; others use only lateral. The cardinal marks, as their name implies, relate to the cardinal points of the compass. They are called north, south, east and west cardinal marks, and are used to indicate the position of dangers. The south cardinal mark, for example, indicates that the danger lies somewhere in the quadrant between north-west and north-east, safe water being found to the south, and the vessel must pass south of the mark. Lateral systems, on the other hand, indicate to which side of the boat the mark must be left if she is to keep clear of a danger. When used in combination with cardinal marks they mark channels, estuaries, harbour entrances, etc. The lateral system uses port-hand and starboard hand-marks. Every lateral system states the direction in which a vessel is sailing when she leaves a port-hand mark to port; obviously, when she is sailing in the opposite direction, she will have to leave a port-hand mark to starboard.

UNITED STATES AND CANADIAN WATERS

Direction: red starboard hand buoys are left to starboard when entering harbours and estuaries, when sailing upstream in rivers, when sailing southwards down the Intracoastal Waterway and when sailing clockwise round North America from north to south down the east coast, westward across the Gulf of Mexico, and northward up the west coast.

Port side: black can or lighted buoy, square daymark, odd numbers, lights white or green.

Starboard side: red nun or lighted buoy, triangular daymark, even numbers, lights white or red.

Preferred channel to port: red and black horizontally striped nun or lighted buoys, topmost stripe red, triangular daymark, lights white or red interrupted quick flashing.

Preferred channel to starboard: red and black horizontally striped can or

Opposite United States buoyage.

lighted buoys, topmost stripe black, square daymark, lights white or green interrupted quick flashing.

Mid channel: black and white vertically striped can, nun or lighted buoys, octagonal daymark, lights white flashing Morse Code.

Marks used on the Intracoastal Waterway are similar but incorporate a yellow edge to daymarks and a yellow stripe on the buoys. The unlit marks on western rivers have white tops so that they can be picked out more easily by search light.

UNIFORM SYSTEM OF BUOYAGE (p. 253; some countries do not use cardinal marks)

Direction: port-hand marks are left to port when sailing with the main flood stream and when entering harbours, estuaries, etc.

Port hand: red or red and white chequered can: flat-topped can or T-shaped topmarks, lights red or white.

Starboard hand: black or black and white chequered conical: pointed topmarks (conical or diamond), lights white.

Mid channel: black and white or red and white vertical stripes, shape optional but not conical, can or spherical.

Middle ground, main channel to port: black and white horizontally striped spherical: pointed topmarks (outer end conical, inner diamond).

Middle ground, main channel to starboard: red and white horizontally striped spherical: flat topmarks (outer end can, inner 'T').

Middle ground, channels of equal importance: red and white horizontally striped spherical: topmarks, outer sphere, inner cross.

Wrecks: all navigational marks are green, with green lights.

North cardinal mark: black with white band, conical, topmark two black cones above each other, points up.

East cardinal mark: red over white, ogival, topmark two red cones above each other, base to base.

South cardinal marks: red can with white band, topmark two red cones above each other, points down.

West cardinal mark: black over white, can or needle, topmark two black cones above each other, point to point.

N.B. There are minor variations in individual countries.

IALA MARITIME BUOYAGE SYSTEM A (p. 271)

Direction: port-hand marks are left to port when entering harbours, estuaries, etc., and generally when sailing clockwise round land masses.

Port hand: red can or spar, topmark red can, lights red.

Starboard hand: green conical or spar, topmark green conical, point up, lights green.

North cardinal mark: black over yellow pillar or spar, topmark two black cones above each other, points up, lights white quick flashing (QF) or very quick flashing (VQF).

East cardinal mark: black with yellow band pillar or spar, topmark two black cones above each other base to base, lights white QF (3) every ten seconds or VQF (3) every five seconds.

South cardinal mark: yellow over black pillar or spar, topmark two black cones above each other points down, lights white QF (6) plus long

flash every fifteen seconds or VQF (6) plus long flash every ten seconds.
West cardinal mark: yellow with black band pillar or spar, topmark two black cones above each other point to point, lights white QF (9) every fifteen seconds or VQF (9) every ten seconds.
Isolated dangers: black with red horizontal band(s) pillar or spar, topmark two black spheres, light white group flashing (2).
Safe water marks: red and white vertical stripes, pillar, spar or spherical, topmark single red sphere, light white isophase, occulting or single long flash every ten seconds.
Special marks: yellow of any shape perhaps with single yellow X-shape topmark and yellow lights with a rhythm different to those above.
N.B. Topmarks are not always fitted, except in the case of the four cardinal marks and marks for isolated dangers; in these cases the topmark is the most important feature.

Lighthouses
Because lighthouses are stationary, the directions in which their lights shine are accurately fixed, whereas buoys move constantly in the water and their lights shine all round the horizon. Many lighthouses exhibit lights which shine only over a specific sector, and some show lights of different colours over different sectors. The range of visibility of lights exhibited by lighthouses is given in the *List of Lights* and is sometimes shown on charts.

Beacons and daymarks
These supplement buoys and vary immensely in purpose and shape. Whereas in UK parlance a beacon can be lit or unlit, in the USA a beacon is lit, and a day-beacon is unlit.

Leading marks
Frequently two marks are sited on shore so that when a vessel entering or leaving a harbour holds them in line she is kept clear of all dangers. The bearing of leading lines is given on charts in true notation.

Lights
The character and colour of lights is selected to enable the sailor to identify with certainty which buoy or navigational aid he is observing. The main abbreviations are:
F   Fixed: unbroken continuous light
Fl   Flashing: the light period is shorter than the dark period
QF or Qk Fl   Quick flashing: a light which flashes sixty times a minute
VQF or V Qk Fl   Very quick flashing: a light which flashes 100 or 120 times a minute
F Fl   Fixed and flashing: a continuous steady light with occasional flashes of greater brilliance
Gp Fl   Group flashing: a light which flashes in groups of two, three or more, followed by a period of darkness
Occ   Occulting: the light period is longer than the dark period
Gp Occ   Group occulting: a light which eclipses twice or more at regular intervals

The 143ft granite tower of Bishop Rock Lighthouse in the Scilly Isles. The light flashes twice every fifteen seconds and has a range of twenty-nine miles. Lighthouses are positioned on headlands and outlying rocks.

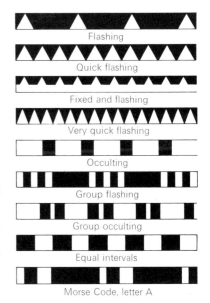
19.6 Characteristics of lights.

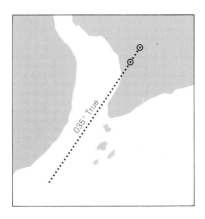

19.7 Two conspicuous marks on shore, which may be lit at night or in poor visibility, lead a vessel clear of all dangers when they are kept in line. The bearing is given on the chart in true notation.

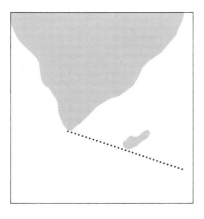

19.8 Two points are in transit when they are seen to be in line. The boat's position will be somewhere along the extension of the line drawn through the two points.

E Int   Equal intervals: the light period is the same as the dark period
Morse Code: a light in which flashes of different duration are grouped to produce a Morse Code character or characters (see fig. 19.6)

Sound signals
These are made by buoys, lighthouses and light vessels to indicate their position when visibility is poor. There is a great variety of sounds, such as bells, whistles, gongs and diaphones.

Chart work

Chart work is based largely on angles and straight lines. The lines of longitude on Mercator charts run true north and south and are drawn parallel to each other so that any straight line will intersect all of them at the same angle. Suppose a line is drawn representing the course the navigator wishes to steer and that the angle that line makes with the lines of longitude is 215° (true). To convert from true course to magnetic course variation must be applied, say 12°W, and to convert from magnetic course to compass course deviation must be applied which is found in the boat's deviation table to be 3°E for this course. The rule is:

TRUE to MAGNETIC to COMPASS: add westerly variation and deviation: subtract easterly variation and deviation

True course	215°
Add westerly variation	12°
Magnetic course	227°
Subtract easterly deviation	3°
Compass course	224°

A second rule applies when a bearing or a course has to be converted to true:

COMPASS to MAGNETIC to TRUE: subtract westerly variation and deviation: add easterly variation and deviation

In the case of a compass bearing 134°, deviation 2°W, variation 7°E:

Compass bearing	134°
Subtract westerly deviation	2°
Magnetic bearing	132°
Add easterly variation	7°
True bearing	139°

The navigator can choose from a variety of plotting instruments with which to enter a bearing or a course on a chart. He needs to know the angle between a line and true north; he can carry the line over to the true rose on the chart with a parallel ruler, reading the figure on the outer rose; he can use a rule attached to a swivelling rose or grid which is lined up on the lines of longitude and/or latitude, finding the answer where the ruler cuts the rose; he can use a ruler marked in degrees, or a set-square marked as a protractor, which measures the angle between the line and any line of latitude or longitude.

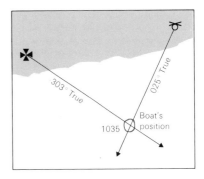

Position finding

A position line (line of position or LOP) is a line drawn on the chart from some object, and the boat is known to be somewhere along that line. To obtain a fix two or more position lines are obtained. The boat's position will be where they intersect. The time must always be noted on the chart against a fix. There are many ways of obtaining position lines.

TRANSITS (ranges): When two objects marked on the chart are seen to be in line, the boat must be somewhere along the line through them extended to seaward (figs. 19.7 and 19.8).

BEARINGS: A bearing can be taken of any object marked on the chart or of any light that it exhibits, and the bearing line is drawn on the chart to pass through the object.

CROSS BEARINGS: Two bearings of different objects give two position lines and thus give a fix. In practice taking bearings from the unsteady platform of a small boat is liable to error, and to minimize this objects should be selected carefully, as close to the boat as possible, and so that the bearings meet as near to right angles as possible (fig. 19.9).

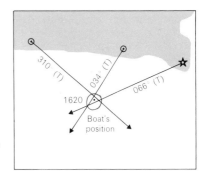

19.9 The boat's position will be where bearings taken of two objects marked on the chart cross.

COCKED HAT: If three objects are available, three bearings can be taken and, when entered, they usually make a small triangle called a cocked hat: the boat's position is taken as the centre of the triangle or the side of the triangle nearest the danger (fig. 19.10).

HEIGHT: If a sextant is carried and the height of an object above sea-level is known, a circular position line can be obtained by measuring the angle between sea-level and the line from the observer to the top of the object, thus finding the distance off the object by reference to tables. A fix is obtained by taking a bearing of the same object which gives a second position line (fig. 19.5).

19.10 *Above* Cocked hat.

RADIO BEARINGS: Radio bearings give position lines in just the same way and can be used in conjunction with other position lines.

SOUNDING AND BEARING: Where depths change fairly quickly, a sounding can sometimes be used to obtain a position line. The sounding must be adjusted according to the height of the tide. A bearing is then taken of an object marked on the chart, and the position of the boat will be where that bearing meets the appropriate contour line.

19.11 *Below* Tide triangle.

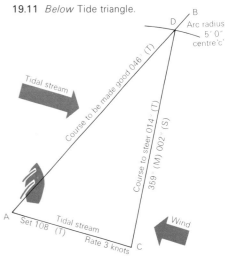

Plotting courses

In order to give the helmsman a course to steer which will take him to his destination the navigator has to take into account the set and rate of the tidal stream, the anticipated speed of his boat through the water, and the leeway she will make.

In figure 19.11 he intends to sail along the line AB, 046° true, and finds that the set and rate of the tidal stream during the next hour is 108°, 3 knots. From A he draws a line 108° true (all information as to set is given in true notation) to point C, three miles from A. Anticipating

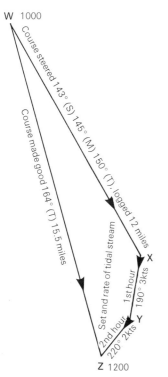

19.12 *Above* Estimated Position (EP).

19.13 *Below* Running fix.

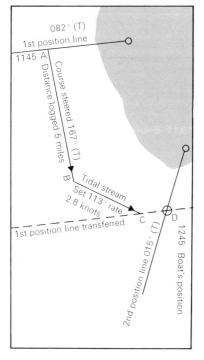

that with an easterly wind on his starboard beam the boat will make 5 knots through the water, he marks point D on line AB, five miles from C, and joins CD, 014° true. Now he has to convert this true course to a compass course for the helmsman, so he allows for variation, 15°E and deviation 3°W.

True course	014°
Subtract easterly variation	15°
Magnetic course	359°
Add westerly deviation	3°
Compass course	002°

From past experience he reckons that his boat will make 2° of leeway, so he will have to sail 2° closer to the wind if the boat is to follow the course he wishes: 002° + 2° = 004°. Although the boat will be pointing 004° according to her steering compass, her course made good over the ground will be along the line ADB that he has drawn on the chart.

Estimated position

Frequently the navigator has to estimate his position because there are no objects in sight on which to take bearings. He bases his estimate on the rate and set of the tidal stream, the distance logged, which is the distance the boat has sailed through the water, and the leeway she has made (fig. 19.12). Suppose that he left position W at 1000 and that he has been steering a compass course of 143° for two hours. With a following wind he made no leeway. Deviation is 2°E, so his magnetic course is 145°, and variation of 5°E brings his course to 150° true. During those two hours the boat logged twelve miles, so from his 1000 fix he draws a line WX, twelve miles long, 150° true. During the first hour the set of the tidal stream was 190° and the rate 3 knots; during the second hour it was 220°, 2 knots. From X he draws XY, three miles long, 190°, and from Y he draws YZ, 220°, two miles long. Z is his estimated position at 1200. He now joins WZ, and this is the course made good, 164°, distance made good over the ground, fifteen and a half miles.

RUNNING FIX: It may be that only one position line can be obtained because there is only one object in sight which is marked on the chart. The bearing of this object is noted and the time taken. The boat is then steered carefully on a given course for a period, after which a second bearing is taken of the same object, or of another object that has come into view (fig. 19.13). From any point A on the original position line the navigator draws a line AB, representing the course steered and the distance logged during the time between taking the bearings. From B a line BC is drawn to represent the rate and set of the tidal stream during the same period. The first position line is now transferred to run parallel to the original bearing through point C. The second bearing is then entered on the chart, and the boat's position is where the second position line cuts the transferred first position line at D.

20
Rule of the road

Peter Cook

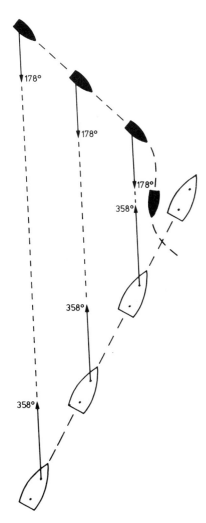

20.1 Converging courses. If the true bearing of another vessel remains the same, both vessels are on a collision course. The giving-way vessel must alter course.

Although the sea is so vast, there are many occasions when boats large and small sail on courses which converge, or negotiate narrow channels in close company with other vessels. Regulations have been laid down which make quite clear the action that is to be taken by each vessel to avoid collision and the lights that vessels must exhibit at night. It is essential to find out which rule of the road is in force in those waters where the boat will be sailing, and to obtain a copy of them to keep on board for reference purposes.

The *International Regulations for Preventing Collisions at Sea* apply to all vessels upon the high seas and in all waters connected to them and navigable by sea-going vessels, but rule 1 states that nothing in the rules is to interfere with special rules in force in harbours, lakes, inland waterways, etc. In the USA, for example, different rules govern vessels sailing on Inland Waters, on the Western Rivers, and on the Great Lakes, and although these rules have much in common with the *International Regulations*, there are many minor differences.

The internationally agreed rules described here were redrafted in 1972 and are due to come into force on 15 July 1977. The main changes affecting yachts are in their lights and in the rule stipulating that they must now give way to vessels restricted by their draft. Certain words are defined precisely. 'Vessel' includes every type of water craft, air cushion vehicles, and seaplanes, too, while 'sailing vessel' means any vessel proceeding under sail alone. Whether her sails are hoisted or not, the moment that a sailing vessel uses her engine she is classed as power-driven, like all vessels propelled by machinery. A vessel 'making way' is moving through the water, whereas a vessel 'underway' is not at anchor, made fast to the shore, or aground.

All vessels are instructed to keep a proper look-out 'so as to make a full appraisal of the situation and of the risk of collision'. A proper look-out means all round the boat, not just to windward and ahead, but also to leeward and in the area hidden by the deck-sweeping genoa. What is seen has to be interpreted correctly – perhaps a white flash as the sun catches the bow wave of a large ship moving at speed some miles distant, or a can shape hoisted in the rigging of a large vessel showing that she cannot manoeuvre freely due to her draft.

When another vessel is travelling at a very different speed, it is not always easy to tell whether there is likely to be a risk of collision. If the shore can be seen behind her and she remains in line with any particular feature on shore, collision is likely because the boats are on converging courses. Alternatively, a bearing of the converging boat can be taken periodically; if the compass bearing remains the same, the vessels are on collision courses.

As soon as it is evident that a collision situation might arise, action must be taken quickly by the vessel that has to give way, and that action must be so substantial that it is apparent to the vessel standing on. The latter vessel, which does not have to give way, must not alter her course or speed.

If it appears that the give-way vessel is not taking action to avoid a collision, the stand-on vessel may then alter her course or speed, and, if the give-way vessel approaches so close that no action of hers alone can prevent a collision, the stand-on vessel *must* take appropriate action and do all she can to avoid a collision.

Responsibilities between vessels
In days gone by steam gave way to sail because the sailing vessel was less manoeuvrable. Common sense still applies today: the more manoeuvrable gives way to the less manoeuvrable vessel. The modernized rules evaluate the relative manoeuvrability of vessels realistically. Bottom of the list, the least manoeuvrable, are those not under command, those restricted in their ability to manoeuvre, and those constrained by their draft: everybody has to give way to them. Then come vessels engaged in fishing because they are hampered by their nets and gear; sailing and power-driven vessels give way to them. Next come sailing vessels, and, top of the list, are power-driven vessels which give way to all other classes.

Sailing vessels, therefore, are obliged to keep clear of those types of vessel which cannot manoeuvre so well as themselves. Most sailing men will also do their best to keep out of the way of larger power-driven vessels both from courtesy and because the wash of some large, fast-moving vessels can be quite unpleasant. Furthermore, those on the bridge of a vast supertanker cannot see the sea immediately beyond the bows which can easily hide a small yacht from view.

When appraising a situation, and before a risk of collision exists, a man sailing may decide that his boat is more manoeuvrable than the vessel that would have to give way in a close-quarters situation, perhaps a motor boat having difficulty in heavy seas, but action must be taken very early before any possibility of collision arises. Equally, it is common courtesy to keep well clear of racing boats, or of another sailing boat to leeward on the same tack fighting her way to windward against a strong tidal stream or current, or otherwise manoeuvring with difficulty.

Narrow channels
The *International Regulations* state that vessels in narrow channels shall keep as far to the starboard side of the channel as possible, and that vessels under 20m in length must not impede the passage of vessels which can only navigate within the channel or fairway. Provided the water is deep enough, the small-boat sailor would do well to keep to the shallower water beyond the edge of the channel where he can sail without anxiety, knowing that the deeper draft vessels will be safely out of his way in the channel.

Lights

Lights are exhibited at night by all vessels so that they can be seen by other vessels, and they shine over specific arcs to indicate to other vessels the course being steered. In the USA's Inland Waters, Great Lakes, and Western Rivers there are many minor differences between the various rules of the road, especially in the requirements for the masthead and sternlights of small power-driven craft, but the basic principle is similar to that of the *International Regulations*. See page 272.

20.2 *Opposite* Steering rules.

262

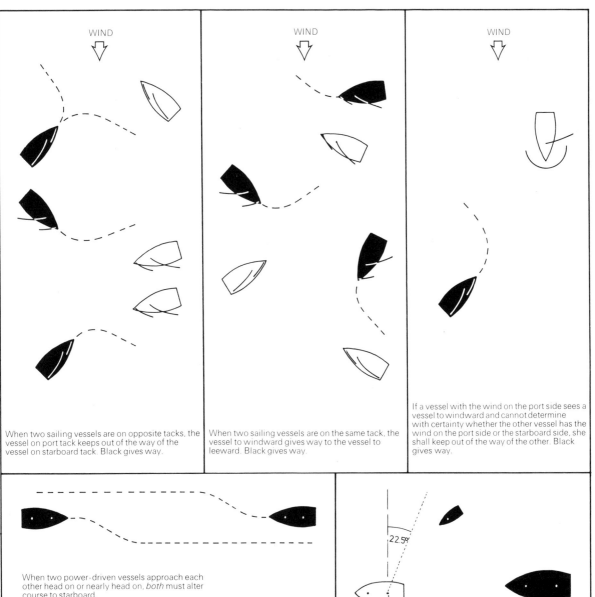

WIND

WIND

WIND

When two sailing vessels are on opposite tacks, the vessel on port tack keeps out of the way of the vessel on starboard tack. Black gives way.

When two sailing vessels are on the same tack, the vessel to windward gives way to the vessel to leeward. Black gives way.

If a vessel with the wind on the port side sees a vessel to windward and cannot determine with certainty whether the other vessel has the wind on the port side or the starboard side, she shall keep out of the way of the other. Black gives way.

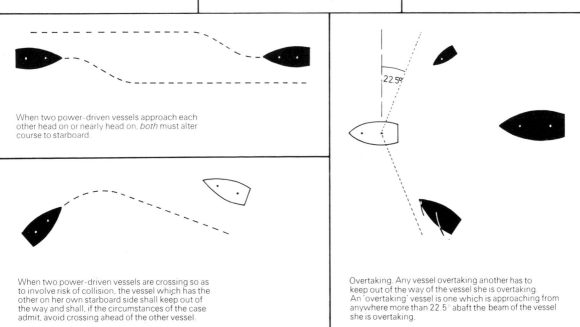

When two power-driven vessels approach each other head on or nearly head on, *both* must alter course to starboard.

22.5°

When two power-driven vessels are crossing so as to involve risk of collision, the vessel which has the other on her own starboard side shall keep out of the way and shall, if the circumstances of the case admit, avoid crossing ahead of the other vessel.

Overtaking. Any vessel overtaking another has to keep out of the way of the vessel she is overtaking. An 'overtaking' vessel is one which is approaching from anywhere more than 22.5° abaft the beam of the vessel she is overtaking.

	TYPE OF VESSEL	SHAPE CARRIED IN THE RIGGING (all shapes are black)	LIGHTS EXHIBITED AT NIGHT a/r = all round light m/h = masthead light	ALL VESSELS EXCEPT THOSE MARKED ARE UNDERWAY (G=green, R=red, W=white, Y=yellow)		
				SEEN FROM AHEAD	SEEN FROM ASTERN	SEEN FROM A VESSEL TO PORT
	Vessels towing or pushing If tow is under 200m	None	Underway: side and stern lights and towing light Two white m/h forward above each other	W W G R	 Y W	W W R
◆	If tow is over 200m	Diamond	As above, but three white m/h forward	W W W G R	 Y W	W W W R
⧗	*Vessels engaged in fishing*	Cones or a basket	Underway: side and stern—no anchor lights	G W	G W	G W
	When trawling		a/r green over a/r white	G R	W	R
	Other than trawling If gear extends more than 150m also	Black cone, point up, in the direction of the gear	a/r red over a/r white a/r white in the direction of the gear	R W W G R	R W W W	R W W R
● ●	*Vessels not under command*	Two balls above each other	Underway: side and stern lights plus two a/r red above each other	R R G R	R R W	R R R
▮	*Vessels constrained by draft*	Cylinder	Underway: m/h, side and stern lights plus three a/r red above each other	W R R R G R	 R R R W	W R R R R
● ◆ ▶	*Vessels restricted in ability to manoeuvre (except minesweepers)*	Ball over diamond over ball	Underway: m/h side and stern lights: or anchor light, plus a/r lights red over white over red	W R W R G R	 R W R W	W R W R R
● ◆ ● ◆ ● ◆	If an obstruction exists: On the side of the obstruction On the side on which a vessel may pass	Ball over ball Diamond over diamond	NOT UNDERWAY a/r red over a/r red a/r green over a/r green	R W R R G R G	R W R G R G R	R W R G G
● ● ●	*Vessel engaged in minesweeping*	Three balls, one near top of foremast and one at each end of the foreyard	Underway: m/h, side and stern lights plus three a/r green, one near top of foremast and one at each end of the foreyard	W G G G G R	 G G G W	W G G G R
●	*Anchored*	Ball	NOT UNDERWAY a/r white where it can best be seen	W	W	W
●	over 50m long	Ball	NOT UNDERWAY a/r white forward and lower a/r white aft	W W	W W	W W
● ● ●	*Aground*	Three balls over each other	NOT UNDERWAY As for anchored vessel plus a/r red over red	R R W W	R R W W	R R W W
▼	*Sailing vessel using engine*	Cone, point downwards	As for power-vessel under way	W G R	 W	W R

Sailing vessels

Sailing vessels are permitted to combine all three lights in one lantern carried at or near the top of the mast. This is more satisfactory than lights sited near deck level where they can be masked by the sails and the waves. Alternatively, sailing vessels may exhibit two all-round lights high on the mast, red above green, but not in addition to the combination lantern. They supplement normal side and sternlights. An all-round light shows an unbroken light over an arc of the horizon of 360°.

Sailing vessels and rowing boats too small to carry these lights should have a powerful torch which can be shone on to white sails to attract attention. The diagram on page 272 illustrates the situation at night, and, of course, the same steering rules apply by day. Whereas the lights of a vessel can be seen from a considerable distance at night, a fast-moving merchant ship can approach a small sailing vessel surprisingly quickly by day, so the look-out should be equally sharp by day as by night, especially if visibility is at all restricted.

Sound signals

When vessels are manoeuvring in sight of one another, they give signals on their whistles or sirens to inform other vessels of their actions. In all waters one short blast means 'I am altering my course to starboard'; two short blasts mean 'I am altering my course to port'. Although not universally specified, three short blasts mean 'I am operating astern propulsion'. Five short blasts may be sounded as an emergency or danger signal, or to indicate that the signal another vessel has given has not been understood.

If visibility is restricted, all vessels are expected to move at a speed suited to the situation. Sound signals are given, either on the whistle, foghorn, or bell, but the signals inland and in some harbours and docks may differ from those given below which are laid down in the *International Regulations*. Power-driven vessels making way through the water sound a long blast at least every two minutes; if they are under way but stopped, they sound two long blasts. Sailing boats and all those classed as less manoeuvrable than a power-driven vessel sound three blasts in succession at least every two minutes – namely, one long blast followed by two short blasts. A vessel being towed, or the last vessel of a tow, sounds one long blast followed by three short blasts at least every two minutes. Vessels at anchor ring a bell rapidly for about five seconds every minute.

Special vessels

Vessels engaged in certain activities, or whose manoeuvrability is restricted for some reason, exhibit special lights by night and carry shapes in their rigging by day. These warn other vessels nearby to keep well clear. There are many minor differences between the various rules of the road. Those shown opposite are the lights and shapes specified by the *International Regulations*.

20.3 *Opposite* Lights and shapes.

265

21
The racing rules

Eric Twiname

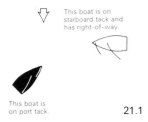

This boat is on
starboard tack and
has right-of-way.

This boat is
on port tack.   21.1

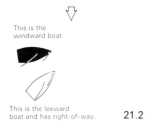

This is the
windward boat.

This is the leeward
boat and has right-of-way.   21.2

This boat is tacking
and must keep clear.

This boat is
on a tack.   21.3

This boat was clear
astern so should
have kept clear.

This boat was
clear ahead.   21.4

Racing without even a basic grasp of the rules would be like driving in a country you had never visited before where the driving rules were totally different from those to which you were accustomed. However careful you were, ignorance over who gives way to whom and when would inevitably lead to collisions or hair-raising near misses. It would be silly to drive without first finding out the basic right-of-way rules. The same is true of sailboat racing.

The big difference between the way the sailing rules work and the way the rules of other sports work is that it is the competitors who see that the rules are implemented. There are no referees, line judges or umpires standing by to spot fouls. Fouls – usually collisions between boats or right-of-way boats having to avoid boats that should have kept out of the way – are dealt with through a protest by a competitor and settled after the race by an independent committee which holds a hearing over the incident and disqualifies a boat that is found to be wrong.

Alternatively, a helmsman who has committed a foul can take a voluntary penalty which is less severe than disqualification. The traditional voluntary penalty is retirement by dropping out of the race immediately after committing the foul. In a points series or team race a boat that retires receives a slightly better score than a disqualified boat, but slightly worse than the last boat to finish the race.

Recently, less severe penalties for conceding a foul have been introduced. In offshore racing time penalties are the most usual (when a prescribed time is added to the finishing time), or percentage penalties in which the rule breaker drops 20 % down the finishing order. This percentage system may also be used for small-boat racing, but the more popular system is one which requires an acknowledged foul to be penalized by a 720° turn – two complete circles. The main advantage of these alternative penalty systems is that all boats continue to race.

The right-of-way rules are dealt with in only ten pages of the rule book, but they cause racing sailors more trouble than half a gale of wind. Coming to terms with ten pages of rules is not too difficult provided you are prepared to make some effort. The first two pages are devoted to definitions – words like 'tacking', 'windward', 'overlapped', 'proper course' have precise meanings which are defined in this section. These defined words appear in the rules printed in bold type and the definition should always be referred to when reading the rules; otherwise the rules themselves will often seem too vague to mean much. That leaves eight pages of right-of-way rules.

The rest of the book is devoted to the management of races, entering races, the procedure for protesting, rules to do with sailing the course, and what crews may or may not do to their own boats, including such obvious matters as not being allowed to propel the boat with a paddle. All these sections are secondary to the right-of-way rules because what you need to know when you are on the water is whether you, or the boat you are just about to hit, is in the wrong. There is no time to look up rule books – the collision is just about to happen.

The basic right-of-way principles are these:

1 A boat on port tack keeps clear of a boat on starboard tack.

266

2 A windward boat keeps clear of a leeward boat.

3 A boat which is tacking or gybing keeps clear of one that is not.

4 A boat clear astern of another keeps clear of the one ahead.

5 When a boat has to round a mark or avoid an obstruction, boats which are overlapped outside her must give her room.

6 A boat which holds right-of-way must not alter course to hinder another boat which is keeping clear.

7 A boat which newly gains right-of-way must do so far enough away from other boats to enable them to keep clear.

8 A leeward boat has the right, within limits, to protect her wind by a sharp alteration of course to windward – luffing.

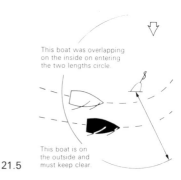

21.5

This boat was overlapping on the inside on entering the two lengths circle.

This boat is on the outside and must keep clear.

These principles are essentially simple, but there are situations – quite common ones at that – in which two basic principles are in direct conflict. It is important to learn when these conflicts are likely to arise and which basic principle governs each situation. For example, it is quite common to have two boats approaching a mark on a run, the inside boat on port tack, the outside one on starboard. Principle 1 above says the starboard tack boat has right-of-way, while principle 5 says exactly the opposite. Which is right? We will come back with an answer shortly.

Fortunately, you do not have to learn every situation in which two of the basics contradict each other. Most of the contradictions arise at marks and obstructions, and you need only to remember that, when rounding marks or obstructions, the overlap principle 5 overrides any conflicting principle when rounding on a free leg of the course – a reach or run – and when overlapped boats on the *same* tack are rounding at the end of a windward leg. When boats at a windward mark are on opposite tacks, the port and starboard rule 1 governs, and when they are on the same tack, but one is clear ahead of the other, principle 3 governs.

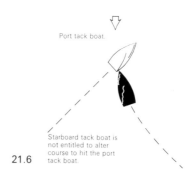

21.6

Port tack boat.

Starboard tack boat is not entitled to alter course to hit the port tack boat.

One other important point is that some special right-of-way rules apply before and at the start. The way in which one boat can luff another is radically different, and a boat which is about to start is not entitled to ask for room on a starting mark surrounded by water. The other right-of-way requirements before the start are essentially the same as after the start.

There, briefly, you have the basis of the racing rules. Certainly they have been simplified in distilling out the essentials, but if you learn these essentials, you will be adequately equipped with rule knowledge for starting to race and well equipped for learning and understanding the detail of the rule book later on.

The rules themselves are subject to change and minor modification every four years. They apply world-wide with only minor local differences, and none of these is in the right-of-way section. Changes are mostly the result of difficult appeal cases (you can usually refer a protest committee decision to a national appeal committee) which have been resolved and which expose ambiguity or unexpected contradictions in the meanings of the rules.

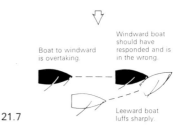

21.7

Windward boat should have responded and is in the wrong.

Boat to windward is overtaking.

Leeward boat luffs sharply.

22
Tactics

Eric Twiname

Without tactics racing would be dull in all but the heaviest weather. Tactics represent the chess-like side of the game, the whole range of moves available to crews to make the most of the natural conditions and to outwit opponents in the boat-to-boat involvement of close racing. When sailing speeds are equal, it is the master tactician who will win; in fact, he will often win when his sailing speed is marginally slower than that of an opponent.

Tactics play the biggest part when sailing to windward because one tack is always liable to be more favourable than the other. A successful helmsman will put a lot of effort into working out which tack is favourable at any moment, and will be on that tack. In variable winds this requires frequent tacks, but in steady winds many fewer tacks will be required to sail the fastest route up the windward leg.

Tactically, there are two goals when sailing to windward fast: use the natural elements to drive the boat to the windward mark in as short a time as possible, and sail the course which cuts down to a minimum the adverse effect of other boats. For simplicity's sake we shall consider the two separately before discussing how best to make the necessary compromise between them. In the first place, the ideal route up a beat, when considering only the natural conditions, could be ruined by disturbed wind from boats ahead if the other boats were totally ignored. On the other hand, it is easy in the middle of a fleet to be so aware of all the other boats that the advantages offered by the wind are ignored. Tactics are always a compromise, but by being aware of the two sides of the gamble a helmsman takes each time he tacks, he greatly shortens the odds against being wrong.

It is always easiest to sail a race when lying clearly in the lead. Then there is only the wind, the water and your own boat speed to worry about – no disturbed wind from nearby sails, no water churned into a turmoil of quarter waves by boats ahead. In the lead you sail against the

22.1a *Left* On a mile-long beat with wind shifts of 5° each side of the mean direction, using the correct shifts will give you a 150yd advantage over a boat sailing in steady wind (shown by the dotted outline) and a 300yd lead over a boat sailing in the wrong shifts (white).

22.1b *Right* A mountain or headland can bend the wind in much the same way as it curves round the leeward side of a sail but on a bigger scale. The boat that tacks first towards the centre of the curve, gains.

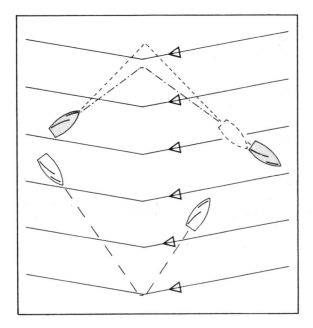

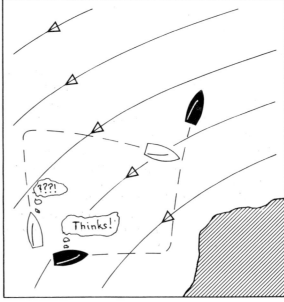

22.2 The importance of having inner berth at a mark is shown clearly in this photograph of Stars racing in Switzerland. The mark is hidden behind A (sail number 3837). The sketch below left shows the relative positions of the boats at the time the photograph was taken and the sketch on the right how it could develop. Although A rounded inside B, B was far enough ahead to keep her wind clear. C rounded third but on the outside and received dirty wind first from A and B and then from D, E and F sailing through to windward. G had clear wind and ended up in second place.

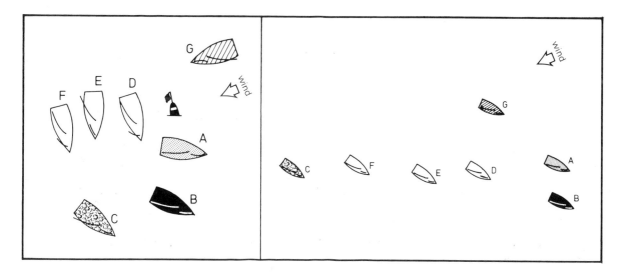

clock and, if not closely threatened from astern, can work all the wind shifts untroubled and concentrate on sailing the boat fast.

Put yourself in this happy position for the moment. How, in the absence of other boats, are you to get round the course in the shortest possible time? In offshore winds and on inland waters wind shifts play a big part. The more a wind shifts about its mean direction, the less distance a boat needs to sail to the weather mark. If the helmsman always tacks at the right moment, he will make a better course than he would in a steady wind (shown in figure 22.1a). If he picks the wrong shifts he sails further to the weather mark than he would in a steady breeze. If the wind shifts 10° (5° each side of the mean direction, which is quite usual), the good shifts give an 8% advantage over steady conditions and a 16% advantage over the wrong shifts. And 16% means a difference of 300 yards on a mile-long beat.

Learning how to pick the right shifts is obviously essential for winning races. Wind which passes over land always changes direction and shifts are nearly always predictable; the wind swings one way a few degrees and back the other way a little later. Sometimes the changes are small, at other times large, but a big shift is usually followed by an equally big one which swings the wind to the other side of the mean direction. More races are won on small lakes, rivers and reservoirs by working these shifts properly than by any other single skill.

The shifts to tack on for the ideal route up the beat are the heading shifts – the ones which force the helmsman to bear away to keep the sails drawing properly. The biggest headers are easy to recognize; the moment you sail into one, the jib backs appreciably at the luff. On the other hand, in a lift the flag at the masthead swings more across the boat, but to see this you do have to be looking at the top of the mast, which in most cases you are not. A better way is to sail to windward pinching slightly, in such a way that you edge the boat all the time up to the point where the jib begins to tremble at the luff (a movement of no more than a degree or two towards the wind). You can tell when the lift comes because the luff of the sail does not tremble immediately as you ease the boat a touch into the wind. You then continue luffing until the jib begins to tremble again, almost anticipating the point at which the tremor comes and preventing the jib backing too much.

The smaller shifts are harder to spot but they are worth using. On still water small shifts are comparatively easy to pick out because the boat moves fairly steadily forward in a straight line, but among waves the jiggling about of the rig hides the momentary big tremor that tells of a header. There are other clues to check if you have just been headed; your angle to the nearby boats and to the shore changes, and these changes can be recognized with practice. In recent years a sensitive compass has become an essential instrument for recognizing the wind shifts on even quite small dinghies.

Just how small a wind shift to tack on depends upon the ground lost in the act of tacking. If the gain you make on the good shift only equals the amount you lose when tacking, there is no point in tacking – the tack only has to be a bad one and you lose ground. Bigger boats tack less well than dinghies and so cannot take advantage of the quite small and short-

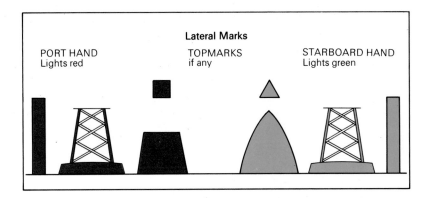

Lateral Marks

PORT HAND
Lights red

TOPMARKS
if any

STARBOARD HAND
Lights green

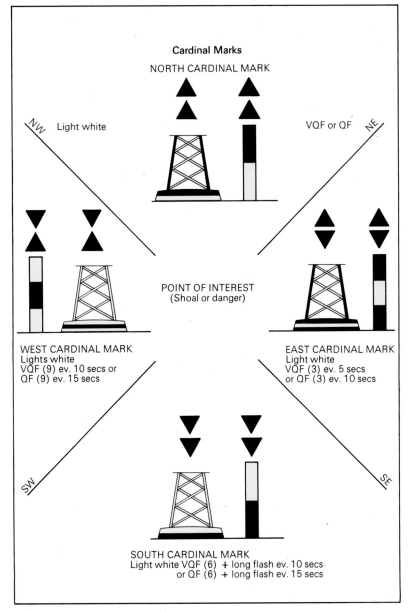

Cardinal Marks

NORTH CARDINAL MARK

Light white

VQF or QF

NW

NE

POINT OF INTEREST
(Shoal or danger)

WEST CARDINAL MARK
Lights white
VQF (9) ev. 10 secs or
QF (9) ev. 15 secs

EAST CARDINAL MARK
Light white
VQF (3) ev. 5 secs
or QF (3) ev. 10 secs

SW

SE

SOUTH CARDINAL MARK
Light white VQF (6) + long flash ev. 10 secs
or QF (6) + long flash ev. 15 secs

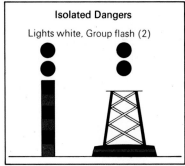

Isolated Dangers

Lights white, Group flash (2)

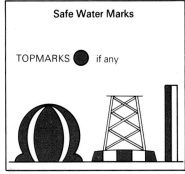

Safe Water Marks

TOPMARKS if any

Special Marks

TOPMARK
if any

All sailing vessels over 7m in length must exhibit:
Stern light: white, visible from right aft to 67.5° to either side of the boat
Side lights: a red light visible from dead ahead to 112.5° to port and a green light visible from dead ahead to 112.5° to starboard
Vessels under 7m should exhibit these lights if possible.
All three lights may be combined in one lantern at or near the top of the mast.

Alternatively sailing vessels may exhibit two all-round lights high on the mast in addition to side and stern lights, but not in conjunction with the combined lantern.

SAILING VESSELS

Lights exhibited when under way, using sail only. When the auxiliary engine is being used the lights of a power-driven vessel are exhibited.

Power-driven vessels exhibit a white masthead light forward, visible from dead ahead to 112.5° to either side of the boat.

Power-driven vessels over 50m in length must exhibit a second masthead light further aft and higher, but in practice many vessels under 50m exhibit two masthead lights.

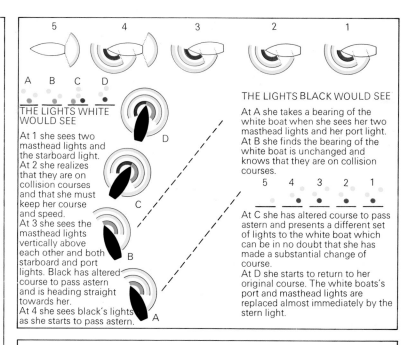

THE LIGHTS WHITE WOULD SEE

At 1 she sees two masthead lights and the starboard light.
At 2 she realizes that they are on collision courses and that she must keep her course and speed.
At 3 she sees the masthead lights vertically above each other and both starboard and port lights. Black has altered course to pass astern and is heading straight towards her.
At 4 she sees black's lights as she starts to pass astern.

THE LIGHTS BLACK WOULD SEE

At A she takes a bearing of the white boat when she sees her two masthead lights and her port light.
At B she finds the bearing of the white boat is unchanged and knows that they are on collision courses.

At C she has altered course to pass astern and presents a different set of lights to the white boat which can be in no doubt that she has made a substantial change of course.
At D she starts to return to her original course. The white boats's port and masthead lights are replaced almost immediately by the stern light.

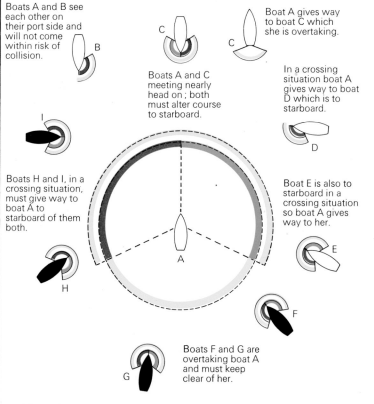

Boats A and B see each other on their port side and will not come within risk of collision.

Boats A and C meeting nearly head on; both must alter course to starboard.

Boat A gives way to boat C which she is overtaking.

In a crossing situation boat A gives way to boat D which is to starboard.

Boats H and I, in a crossing situation, must give way to boat A to starboard of them both.

Boat E is also to starboard in a crossing situation so boat A gives way to her.

Boats F and G are overtaking boat A and must keep clear of her.

All vessels are power-driven and exhibit side, stern and masthead lights. The colours indicate which lights would be seen by boat A. A must keep an especially sharp look out ahead and in the sector covered by her green light; she has to give way to power-driven vessels in this sector. She also gives way to sailing vessels and those less manoeuvrable than herself, wherever they may be.

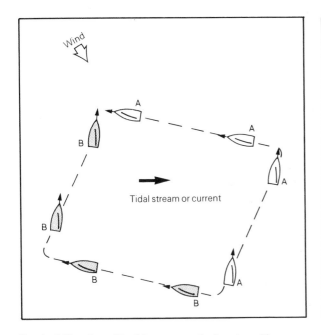

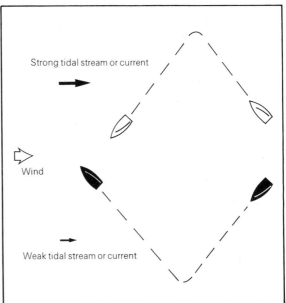

lived shifts that dinghies can gain by, but if you can tack your boat without losing much, even the smallest shifts are worth using.

The wind shifts so far described swing to and fro so that you can tack on the headers time and time again, but this is not the only mode of shift: sometimes the wind bends round in a steady curve. A hill or a valley can bend the wind in much the same way that wind curves round the back of a sail, but on a much larger scale. When the wind curves like this, the boat will gain that takes the tack carrying her first towards the centre of the curve. The boat going the other way has to sail appreciably further. (See fig. 22.1b.)

Even with this kind of shift the wind is almost certain to be doing its little fluctuating shifts as well. If they are fairly small, they are probably not worth bothering about as you will reach the weather mark more quickly by first taking the tack towards the inside of the wind curve as the black boat does in the diagram, but there comes a time when the shifts may be worth using if they are big enough. The best plan then is to work towards the centre of the wind curve but tack on the biggest headers you come across on the way.

In a shifting wind a good helmsman can be at the front of the fleet in a relatively slow boat provided he takes the trouble to spot and use the shifts, which means keeping his eyes wide open. It is often said that some helmsmen pick the wind shifts with a sixth sense. This may be so, but they learned how to spot them with the other five first.

The other natural phenomenon that affects tactics is water movement – tides and currents. When a current is running at constant speed and in the same direction over the whole sailing area, no one can gain any advantage from it since a uniform current gives the same advantage or disadvantage to everyone, whether it is under the weather or lee bow. This is often misunderstood. In figure 22.3a boat B is lee-bowing the tide at first and A has it on her weather side, but they will both travel the

22.3a *Left* In a uniform tidal stream or current neither boat gains an advantage; they are both pushed back the same amount.

22.3b *Right* When the tidal stream or current varies in strength, select the tacks that take you to windward by sailing the least distance through the water. Both boats have sailed the same distance through the water, but black has made most ground to windward.

Opposite Lights exhibited at night by vessels under way.

273

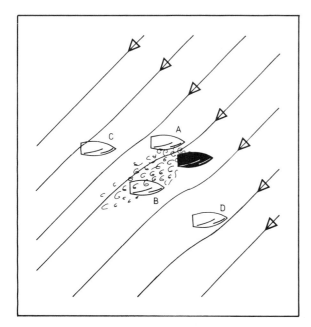

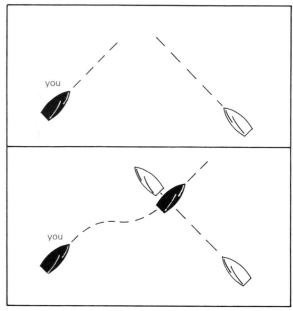

22.4a *Left* A boat at position B sails in disturbed, heading wind. At position A the wind heads seriously. Boats at C and D are unaffected by the black boat.

22.4b *Right (top)* As helmsman of the black boat you should have made up your mind before this stage whether to tack to lee-bow the white boat or to bear away and cross astern. *(bottom)* If port is the favoured tack, bear away to cross astern of the starboard tack boat. When the wind shifts again and you are headed, tack and you will clear her.

same distance to the weather mark – the tide will push them both to the right by the same amount. This is best understood by putting knives, representing boats, on a table-cloth, representing the surface of the water, and pulling the table-cloth over the table, the seabed. If the knives are beating towards one corner of the table, you will see that the only thing that matters is their relative positions to each other on the table-cloth.

Things are very different, of course, if the current flows in a curve or is faster at one part of the course. Then there is definitely something to be gained by sailing up one side of the beat. The rule is simply to take the tacks which get you to the weather mark by travelling the least distance through the water. In figure 22.3b, for example, the best route is that of the black boat. Near the shore the current is usually slacker, and there are often back eddies which can be extremely useful. By going closer inshore boats can take advantage of them, making great gains on their less astute opponents plugging away against the adverse current.

We will now leave the effect of variations in the natural elements, switching from a race against time, with no other boats about, to tactics employed specifically to deal with the other boats in the fleet – this time ignoring any variations in wind and current.

Nearby boats are a constant nuisance because they can only hinder you: unlike wind shifts, tides, and other natural phenomena they cannot help your progress. Tactics related to other boats are designed, therefore, first to keep you clear of those ahead and secondly to help you hinder those behind. The rest of the fleet turns what would otherwise be a sprint into something of an obstacle race, and your aim should be to retain as much of the sprint element as possible while avoiding the intricacies of the obstacle race. Make use of the wind shifts, tidal streams, and every other natural aid to get round the course fast while altering this ideal route so that you are not too seriously slowed by the other boats nearby.

A sailing boat on the same tack can slow you down when it comes within about five lengths and can slow you down drastically when within half a length. How much you are slowed depends on your position in relation to the other boat (fig. 22.4a). There are two positions that no one should tolerate for a moment. The first is the lee-bowed position A, the second is position B. The worse-off of the two is A because, after travelling five lengths you will lose at least one length, fall into dirty wind and be headed off until you end up in position B. Unfortunately, it does not stop there, for in position B you are in turbulent wind and will very soon lose at least two more lengths, even if you can sail the same speed as the windward boat in clear wind. So the ground thrown away in position A by holding on would be at least five lengths and probably more.

If a boat to windward prevents you tacking when you find yourself in position A, the best plan is to pinch hard and fall back astern and slightly upwind to position C, clear of the heading wind pattern. Alternatively, you could bear away with sheets eased fractionally and break through the wind shadow to leeward to position D.

When sailing in close quarters with other boats, last-minute panicky avoiding action is excessively wasteful. It helps, therefore, to keep a good look-out so that you see a boat coming and have ample time to work out the best way to deal with the situation. You then make decisions rather than having them forced upon you.

As port tack boat in figure 22.4b you obviously have two choices: you can either tack or bear away to cross astern. If you see the starboard tack boat late, there is no decision to make; you have to throw in a hurried tack to avoid hitting her. But if there is time to think about the best move, you can weigh up your decision: 'It was a good header I tacked on a moment ago so this is the right tack, and I want to stay on it. I do not want to be forced about. I'll bear away round her stern . . . fine, I'm still on the right shift, and he is on the wrong one. When the next header comes I'll tack and I've got him.'

If you had tacked close to white into a lee-bow position, she would have been forced to tack off on to the good wind shift and would have ended up comfortably ahead when you next crossed tacks. When you are clearly on the favoured tack (that is, on a lifting shift), the best move is to make a detour round the stern of a starboard tack boat. The exception comes when you would almost cross her bows; then tack really close under the lee bow to force her off on to the other tack immediately. Soon after she has tacked, you tack too, far enough away to remain outside the area of her backwinding (fig. 22.5). When the heading shift comes, you are free to tack on it and continue to sail the fastest course.

So far a boat's wind influence has been seen as wholly bad, but it can be used as an extremely powerful tactical weapon. Imagine yourself in the black boat of figure 22.4a and your closest rival is the white boat B. So long as he sails in your dirty wind, there is no way he is going to overtake you; he is bound to drop back further behind you. This method of defending your position is known as covering and can be extremely valuable late in a race in order to hold a lead or retain a position when approaching the finishing line.

Covering should usually be reserved for the last beat and is not a

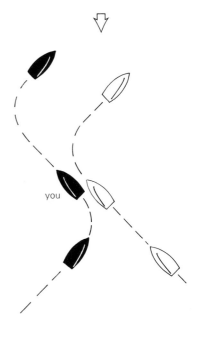

22.5 When port is the favoured tack and you can almost cross the bows of a starboard tack boat, tack on to starboard close under her lee bow to force her to tack on to port. Then sail on for a few lengths to clear your wind before tacking back on to port yourself.

you

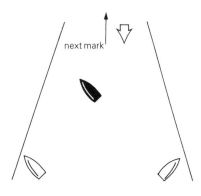

22.6 You cannot cover both boats. The best way to defend your lead is to stay within the triangle formed between the two following boats and the next mark and to sail as fast as possible.

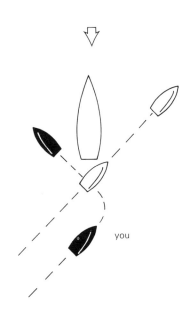

22.7 Obstacles can be used to gain a clear wind. Wait until the boat covering you is committed to passing one side of the obstacle, then tack to pass on the other side.

tactical ploy to overuse, especially not in the middle of a fleet. The snag when covering is that you are not sailing your own tactics; they are dictated by the boat whose wind supply you are affecting, because every time he tacks you tack. The chances are that this duel will mean that he is taking little or no notice of the favourable wind shifts, yet other boats in the fleet will be, so both boats in the duel, therefore, drop back in relation to the rest of the fleet. In a covering contest you may not be overtaken by the boat you are covering, but unless there is a big gap astern the chances of other boats doing so are increased.

Defensive tactics become particularly difficult when there are two boats astern to be covered; if you cover one, her skipper will tack frequently to escape, you both slow down, and the chances are that the other man will overtake. The strategy is to stay within the triangle formed between the two boats and the windward mark and make the best speed you can to the mark, sailing within this triangle (fig. 22.6). By staying within the triangle and covering loosely you reduce the danger of one boat tacking off to a flank and coming back with a winning shift. You cannot guard against this completely but, if you are working the shifts well, you should be close enough to take advantage of the good shift and still stay ahead. As soon as one of your pursuers drops well back, you can take a more immediate interest in the remaining challenger.

The nearer the front of the fleet you are, the more likely you are to find yourself at the dirty wind end of a covering match, and the choice will not be yours; the boat ahead tacks on you. Until you are within about five lengths of her, there is no point in taking any notice – just sail as fast as you can, because every time you tack on a heading shift she tacks a little after the header has passed her and loses; every time you pick the best wave on which to tack she has either to go about immediately, maybe on a nasty wave, or hold on and let you gain clear wind. Once you are within five lengths, she begins to slow you down so you should concentrate on how to overtake.

The greatest advantage when at close quarters with another boat of the same speed is the ability to tack better than she does. When you are behind, you will close the gap on every tack, and when ahead, pull away on each tack and avoid being drawn into a wasteful tacking duel.

If the helmsman ahead tacks badly, make him tack often. If he gets annoyed with his crew because the jib is not pulled in fast enough, make him tack so often that he gets really mad and the crew tacks even worse. If the helmsman wears waterproofs with weak elastic and his boat has non-slip decks, his trousers will need pulling up after each tack – don't give him time to, for when they are round his ankles he cannot cover you so well.

You can use moored boats, obstructions, and even other boats in the race to gain clear wind when someone is intent on covering you. Among moored boats you simply wait until the man is committed to pass on one side and you tack off to the other (fig. 22.7).

When beating through a running fleet, you can arrange to tack so that the boat covering you will have to take action to avoid a running boat, or at least be heavily blanketed. Make covering you a sufficiently diffi-

276

cult, unpleasant, and hazardous experience and your opponent will stop doing it. But never forget that there are other boats in the race which, if you ignore them in the preoccupation of a duel, may slip by.

We have seen how important tactics can be when sailing to windward. On a free leg of the course, that is, one in which the next mark can be laid without tacking, the aim should usually be to sail the shortest distance through undisturbed water in clear wind, gaining the maximum help from any current or avoiding its adverse effects, and to approach the mark with right of way over other boats.

In light and variable winds it often pays to luff up gently in the lulls and to bear away in the puffs – by luffing, boat speed usually increases, and the boat will reach the next puff earlier; bearing away means that the boat stays in the puff longer and returns to her original track. This luffing and bearing-away tactic can also be employed in marginal planing conditions to keep the boat planing longer. By luffing to increase boat speed when the wind is lighter, the boat may be coaxed on to the plane, and by bearing away when there is sufficient wind she keeps on planing on the freer course.

Off the wind, unless you happen to be in the lead, you will inevitably find boats ahead of you sailing the shortest distance between the two marks of the leg. If you are sailing faster than a boat ahead and attempt to pass to windward, he may luff to prevent you doing so. If you try to pass too close to leeward, you will be slowed by his wind shadow and will not be able to pass on that side either. The answer is to plan your tactics well in advance. If you find that you are sailing faster than the boats ahead, either luff gently out to windward in plenty of time aiming to pass well clear of them – if your wind shadow is not going to affect them, they will be less likely to try to luff you – or bear away and pass far enough to leeward of them to avoid being affected by their wind shadow.

Luffing matches are generally best avoided for the boats involved will be delayed and this can often allow other boats to pass. Only when seeking to establish an advantage before rounding a mark, or maintaining a position just before the finish is luffing really worthwhile.

On a broad reach or a run a boat astern can take the wind of a boat in front, but unless it is to gain a particular tactical advantage, it is best not to 'sit' on boats ahead or they are likely to do exactly the same to you, should you succeed in passing them. All that this achieves is to allow the boats ahead to go further away and those astern to catch up.

When two or more boats round a mark close together before a reach or a run, they tend to luff out higher than the course between the two marks as each boat seeks to establish clear wind. They may go far off course as they alternately sail through to windward and then drop back as other boats astern come up and take their wind. Some boats may break free from the bunch, but the majority will spend the leg fighting their own private battle while other boats in the race, sailing faster and a shorter distance, pass them. Another disadvantage is that boats that luff out too far to windward have to bear away on to a slower point of sailing during the final approach to the next mark. If you round a mark at the beginning of a reach or run in close company with other boats, it will often pay to bear away immediately and keep well clear to leeward. You will then be able to dictate your own tactics, will not be slowed by other boats, and will approach the next mark sailing a higher, faster course. The only thing to avoid, however, is bearing away too quickly in the lee of other boats, rounding the mark and thus losing the wind.

Approaching the leeward or wing mark at the end of a reach or run you should normally aim to be on the inside of the turn. The rules do not allow you to establish an overlap when the leading boat is within two of her lengths of the mark. If it appears that you will be the outside boat of a group rounding the mark at the same time, it will often pay to drop back and move in astern of the inside boat so that you round close to the mark. You will then start the next leg of the course behind the leaders of the group but ahead of those who rounded on the outside. If a beat follows, you are free to tack when you wish.

Tactics at the start of a race depend on several factors. If the start is to windward, the first essential is to establish which end of the line is more advantageous. Although the starting line is frequently laid at right angles to the wind, the wind often shifts before the starting gun, causing one end of the line to be more favourable (see fig. 22.8a). It may be obvious which end of the line will pay but, if not, sailing along the line in both directions before the start and trying first one tack and then the other will given an indication. A compass is helpful, noting the course on each tack, and the bearing of the starting line shows which is the better tack.

If there is a tidal stream or current, the best use must be made of a fair current, or the worst of a foul one avoided, not only when the gun goes but during the first part of the ensuing beat.

If the fleet is small, you will be able to start where you plan and make small, last-minute alterations if other boats have chosen the same place. In a large fleet there is usually bunching at the ends of the line, and it can

22.8a *Left* This starting line is angled at 80° to the wind so that a boat that starts at the port end will have a shorter distance to sail to the first mark than a boat starting at the starboard end.

22.8b *Right* In a large fleet there is usually bunching at the ends of the starting line so it can often pay to start in the middle where there is less congestion.

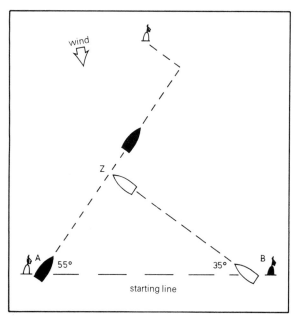

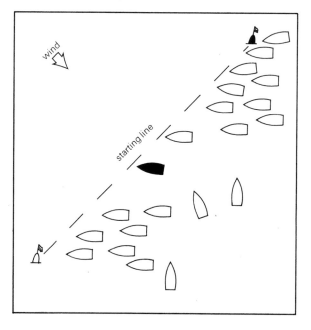

often pay to start nearer the middle in clear wind to avoid the crush. After the start it is often worth bearing away under the sterns of several boats in order to sail fast in an area of clear wind and smooth water, for places lost at this stage of the race may be impossible to make up later when the leaders have drawn away.

If the start is off the wind, you must determine which end of the line is closer to the first mark and where you will find clear wind. The obvious place, the windward end, may be overcrowded, but, after a reaching start, if one boat sails past you to windward and takes your wind, there is little that you can do to prevent a stream of others following him. If the wind is forward of the beam, the leeward position can often be best, provided you hit the line on the gun, as you can then luff up gently and should pull ahead of those to windward. However, if you once lose your wind from another boat, there is little you can do, for tacking will only put you behind all those to windward of you.

With all this emphasis on tactics there is a danger of ignoring boat speed and this must be avoided. Sailing races are won by tuning a boat to sail at least as fast as anyone else's, learning how to make her go as fast as possible through the water, and getting the tactics right consistently. It is not so easy and it takes time, but it is not impossible.

Although the leading boat is two or three lengths ahead of N1903, she may lose her advantage if 1903 can sail sufficiently high to prevent the leader clearing her bows when she tacks on to port tack. N1903 is just clear of the leader's lee-bow backwinding effect, but if she drops into the dirty wind area, she will be unable to tack to clear 1901 astern of her. 1901 is in a bad position; she is already being backwinded by 1903 which is why the helmsman is sitting in and the boat is not pointing so high as those ahead.

279

23
Team racing

Eric Twiname

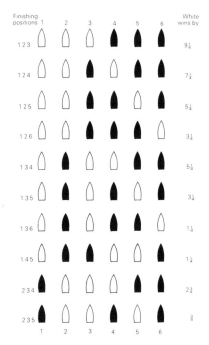

23.1 *Above* Team races take place between two teams of three boats each. Usually the first boat takes $\frac{3}{4}$ points, second 2, third 3 and so on down to 6. The team with the lowest score wins. This diagram shows the possible winning combinations for white when neither team is penalized for rule infringements.

23.2 *Right* White are losing by $1\frac{1}{4}$ points. Instead of gaining the lead by sailing faster than black, white boat A can slow down the black boat lying third and let team mate B overtake which gives white a $\frac{3}{4}$ point lead.

Team racing started life as individual racing with the one difference that half the individuals sailed for one team and the other half for another team. At first this teaming-up of helmsmen did little to alter the style of the racing, but later team racing virtually became a sport in its own right, with a range of unique and subtle tactics of its own.

The usual racing rules apply with a few minor additions, and, ideally, the races should be sailed in one-design boats with three boats on each side. Matches are normally of two races, but representative international matches can run to as many as seven races.

What is the great attraction of team racing? It is by far the best way for two clubs to sail against each other because matches are extremely easy to arrange. Most inter-club matches are held on the waters of one of the two clubs in the home club's boats which are lent by the keener sailing members, so there is no need for the visitors to go to the trouble of packing up three boats and towing them to strange waters; they simply drive to the club, taking only their sailing clothes and their expertise. On the water the game is attractive to the advanced helmsman because the special team tactics and manoeuvres called for often mean that, in practice, the fastest team does not win.

If the winning team was the one that sailed round the course in the least aggregate time, there would be no difference in tactics between team and individual sailing – every boat would sail the course as fast as possible and there would be no scope for giving help to team mates. But the winning team is decided by the places in which the boats finish, and this means that a team member can often sacrifice his own position to help a team mate. The usual scoring system is $\frac{3}{4}$ point for first place, 2 points for second, 3 for third, and so on down to last (sixth) place. A boat receives 3 additional points for each acknowledged infringement and 6 additional points for a lost protest. These penalty points are cumulative and are added to her finishing score. An acknowledged infringement is signified by tying a green streamer to a shroud, a protested infringement by a red one. The winning team is the one with the lower points aggregate. Figure 23.1 shows all the winning combinations for White using this scoring system.

To understand how team-work can win a race, which cannot be won by fast sailing alone, we can look at a team which is losing with second, fourth and fifth positions (fig. 23.2). The white boats are unable to improve their position by sailing quickly because boat A is too far behind the leader, and B is too far behind the second black boat. So instead of winning by speed the white boats try to make one of the black boats go more slowly, and the black boat that can usefully be slowed lies

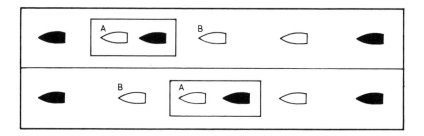

in third place. If A now slows this boat down, allowing team mate B to overtake, White gain a winning combination which they would not have achieved by sailing at full speed to the finish.

As team racing has evolved, many methods of slowing down opponents have been introduced, all of them permitted by the standard racing rules. To windward the most obvious method is for the white boat in the example above to cover an opponent closely so that he sails in constant turbulent wind; the opponent is delayed, and the white boat's team mate sailing in clear wind overtakes.

More intensive covering is necessary when the team mate is a long way behind, and this is achieved by sailing exactly upwind of the opponent and slowing down by letting the jib flap. Both boats then sail more slowly with the opponent in even greater turbulent wind. If he tacks frequently to escape wind shadow, the windward boat tacks to cover, and they both go even more slowly, allowing the team mate from astern to catch up and eventually overtake.

A quicker way of stopping someone and a very effective way of gaining a place is to force an opponent to overstand a windward mark by preventing him tacking for the mark and so enabling a team mate to overtake. The photographs above illustrate the procedure. In the first picture sail number 10017 is sailing on to prevent 10011 under her lee tacking. This allows team mate 10010 to sail through and round the mark first (second picture). 10017 then tacks for the mark and will end up well clear of 10011 which has borne away and is about to gybe in order to break clear.

An opponent can also be delayed from what in individual racing is the worst possible position – in his wind shadow. The white boat in figure 23.3 is in this position. The leader can be slowed because team racing is essentially a game of attack and defence; the leading team defends its position while the losing team attacks. An important part of the leaders' defence is the use of wind shadow to cover opponents and prevent them overtaking. Every time the white boat in figure 23.3 tacks the black boat tacks to cover. The white boat, therefore, dictates the route that the black boat sails to windward, and by tacking often or sailing deliberately on the least favourable wind shifts the black boat will sail the windward leg slowly. A second white boat, picking the best

Left Number 10010 is heading for a windward mark, off picture right. His team mate, in the boat on the right, has positioned himself upwind of an opponent whom he is preventing from tacking towards the mark.

Right The result – boat 10010 comes through from behind to round the mark ahead of team mate 10017 who has sacrificed his own first place to help his team mate.

23.3 As long as black persists in covering her, white dictates the tactics and can slow black to let another white boat overtake her by forcing black to tack frequently or by sailing deliberately on unfavourable windshifts.

A team race between the United States of America and Britain in International Fourteens in 1975. Note the mast bend on US 85 and the 'woollies' on her jib.

route from astern, will gain and probably overtake. Once this second white boat is ahead, she can assist her team mate to escape from behind the black boat.

The game resembles chess in that if it helps the overall plan, a man can sometimes help team mates by sacrificing his own position, just as a piece may well be sacrificed in chess. The pieces can make certain moves: each piece, however brilliantly moved, cannot win without the support of the others. The moves on the water are simpler but follow each other more rapidly than in chess. The game is fast, and when the best teams are opposed, one mistake can be enough to lose a match.

Much shorter courses are usually set for team racing than for individual competition, often providing a race lasting no more than half an hour. The start lines are short too, ensuring that the fleet of six boats is thrown together immediately. As in any team game selection of sides of fairly equal standard is important – for a weak team will be left on the first beat by a good side, and the match ceases to be a competition.

Although the windward leg is the one on which tactics play the biggest part, there is some scope for helping team mates on the downwind legs. When an opponent attempts to overtake to windward, he can be luffed sufficiently to allow a team mate to overtake by sailing the straight line course to the next mark. Of course, an opponent does not necessarily overtake, but he will if the leading boat lets the sails flap and waits. If

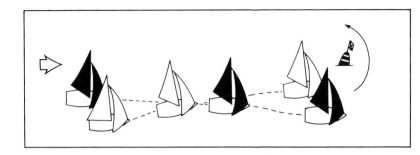

23.4 To gain the inside berth to leeward of black at the next mark white slows herself by sheeting in the mainsail, falls behind black, lets her mainsail out and blankets black. When black slows down as a result of the blanketing, white wins the overlap and rounds the mark on the inside.

the opponent decides to pass to windward, he can be luffed way off course, and if he attempts to overtake to leeward, he can be slowed down seriously by the windward boat sheeting in the sails too hard, creating a wall to the wind and a highly disturbed wind pattern to leeward.

The dead run gives a side which is losing narrowly the best chance to gain places. When an opponent ahead is placed exactly in the wind shadow, he will sail more slowly and can often be overlapped and forced to sail round the next mark on the outside. The wind shadow of one boat is effective, but when two team mates sail side by side, the shadow is considerably increased. For this reason an opponent in the turbulence downwind can be slowed from further astern.

The inside berth when rounding the mark at the end of the run is so important that it is usually worth sacrificing a length or so to secure it. A mark is to be rounded to port by the two boats in figure 23.4, and if they maintain their positions, the black boat will gain the overlap and round inside. The white boat prevents this by pulling in the mainsail hard to slow down, and then letting it out again when astern of the black boat so that her wind is taken. This delays the black boat, and the white boat gains the overlap.

The aggressive moves – the slowing manoeuvres – are usually made by a losing team anxious to pull back the places they need to win, while the defensive ones – covering and luffing to defend a position – are used mostly by the race leaders. A team's view of the race changes immediately the race leadership changes: the team that had a position to defend now has to undermine the opposing team's position. The helmsmen of both teams, therefore, need to know all the time whether their team is leading or losing because this affects many of their tactical decisions.

The white team in figure 23.2, for example, said to themselves: 'Unless we change things we lose.' The black team's attitude was: 'This is the way we want to finish – let's hold these places.' Once the positions had been changed by the team-work of white boats A and B, it was White who wanted to retain the position, while Black had to do something to change it. Black's move would be to drop the last white boat (lying fifth) behind the last black boat to give Black first, fourth and fifth places – a winning combination. White, of course, would work to prevent Black doing this and, in their favour, have three boats to deal with two black ones, because the leading black boat is isolated from her team mates by two white boats and cannot help.

It is sometimes sensible, therefore, to allow the most experienced opposition helmsman to go ahead and win the race, leaving only two opponents astern to be dealt with by the whole team. The most successful teams are well balanced, with no one man much better than the other two, although where one member of the team is a little weaker, his stronger team mates try to arrange for him to sail clear and take first place while they deal with the opposition.

The most exciting matches are between top-flight helmsmen who sail at much the same speed and have to use the tactical side of the game to win. These matches are also excellent to watch, and when a commentary is provided to explain some of the finer points, team racing can be an unexpectedly good spectator sport.

Because the game involves more close manoeuvring than regatta sailing, the rules are more important. No one can decide that he is going to keep out of everyone's way and sail a lone course, or expect to keep clear of other boats all the time. His opponents are unlikely to leave him alone – particularly if they are losing. A working knowledge of the rules is essential when deciding on the best course of action and the rights and wrongs of a hundred events. A good knowledge of the rules tends to limit the number of incidents settled by protest meetings, and there is probably no better way to learn regatta racing tactics and rules than by team racing regularly.

The crucial and most difficult part of a team race is the start. A side that plans its start and draws away from the line well placed has the vital first initiative. When two members of a team make good starts and the third starts ahead of at least one opponent, the team starts well. Practised teams arrange to have their three boats spread along the line so that they do not interfere with each other. White makes this sort of start in figure 23.5a where A makes the perfect start at the starboard end, C makes a clear wind start to leeward, and B has a fairly clear position in the middle of the line. The moments after the start are then used by White to drive home the advantage by using wind shadow.

Ideally, White wants C to take the lead, and they work towards this through A and B pinching instead of sailing at top speed. Twenty seconds after the start C noses into the lead through the pinching policy of her team mates (fig. 23.5b). The tack by the black boat E should not be ignored by A, although she must hold on for a length or two to avoid tacking straight into a lee-bowed position. If A maintains control of the starboard flank, White will continue to dominate Black.

Once they are firmly in control of the race, the white boats continue to work together, defensively covering Black's every move and at the same time attacking with wind shadow and lee-bow influence. The fleet will split into three pairs, with White controlling each pair.

To retain the lead each white boat also has to keep clear of her team mates and avoid putting any of them in wind shadow. Right-of-way rules may be waived between team mates provided no opposition boat has to take avoiding action as a result. Therefore, in a port and starboard encounter the starboard tack boat will sometimes lose least in taking avoiding action. Rather than force an unnecessary tack she bears away behind her team mate.

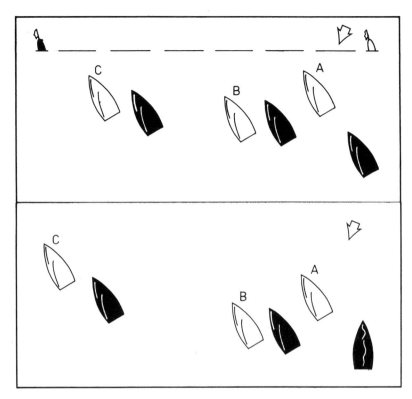

23.5a *(top)* White makes a good team start, spread along the line to ensure clear wind.

23.5b *(bottom)* Twenty seconds after the start the white boats drive home their tactical advantage, but the black boat tacking off must be covered by white boat A if white are to be sure of retaining their advantage.

Helmsmen in experienced teams frequently waive rights among themselves, very rarely forcing each other to tack. They also strictly avoid tacking in a position which will give a team mate disturbed wind.

Among team mates the finishing order is unimportant: it is the overall position of the team that counts. Although alien to every principle of individual competition, the sacrifice of a personal advantage and the forfeit of first place, or even several places, to help a team mate and ultimately the team as a whole is the essence of team racing.

So far international competition has been mainly between representative student teams in Europe and America, and through less formal links between clubs and classes in the western world. Team racing in Britain takes place in just about every competitive dinghy class and club and in many keelboat classes as well, with over 250 teams competing in the annual British National Team Championship. Interest in America has increased considerably, and full-scale international competition is probably not far off. In the meantime the number of sailors who get pleasure and excitement from this branch of sailing is growing every year.

Appendix I
Glossary

ABACK: said of a sail which is sheeted to windward; the wind strikes what is normally the leeward side of the sail, pushing it towards the centreline.

ABAFT: on the after side of.

ABEAM: to one side or the other of a vessel, and at right angles to the centreline.

ABOUT SHIP: an order to prepare to tack (cf. ready about).

ABREAST: alongside, side by side.

ADRIFT: anything broken away from moorings or fastenings.

AFT: towards or near the stern.

AGROUND: touching the bottom.

AHEAD: beyond the bows of a vessel, in front of.

AHULL: no sails set, helm lashed to leeward.

ALEE: to leeward, used particularly of the helm in US and AUS as 'hard alee'.

ALOFT: above the deck, usually up high.

ALONGSIDE: in line with or made fast to a jetty, boat, etc.

AMIDSHIPS: central part of a boat, both in the fore-and-aft and athwartships directions.

ANCHOR: metal object used to hold a vessel in position by dropping it to the bottom (see figs. 17.2–5).

ANCHORAGE: a place where a vessel may anchor.

ANCHOR BUOY: buoy attached to the crown of an anchor to indicate its position on the bottom.

ANCHOR LIGHT (also RIDING LIGHT): all-round white light exhibited at night by vessels at anchor.

ANCHOR RODE (US & AUS): anchor cable.

ANEMOMETER: instrument used for measuring wind velocity.

ANTI-FOULING: paint used on the bottom of boats to discourage marine growth and organisms such as barnacles and borers.

APPARENT WIND: direction and strength of the wind as felt aboard a moving vessel.

APRON: an additional wooden piece fastened inside the stem of a wooden boat to provide adequate landing for the planks.

ARCHBOARD: solid chock of wood which provides the transom and ties the deck to the hull planking on a long, fine counter.

ASPECT RATIO: ratio between the height and width of a sail (high aspect ratio = tall and narrow, low aspect ratio = low and broad).

ASTERN: (1) in the direction of the stern; (2) aft of the vessel.

ASTRO-NAVIGATION: navigation by means of celestial bodies.

ATHWART, ATHWARTSHIPS: at right angles to the centreline.

AUXILIARY: (1) a boat propelled by both sail and power; (2) the engine used in a sailing boat.

BACK: (1) the wind backs when it changes direction anti-clockwise (opp. veer); (2) a sail is backed when it is sheeted or held to windward.

BACKSTAY: stay which supports the mast from aft to prevent it bending forward.

BACKWINDING: when wind from a sail or a surface is exhausted on to the leeward side of another sail, thus affecting the smooth flow of air over the sail.

BAIL: remove water from the bilges using a scooping action.

BALANCED RUDDER: the stock around which the rudder pivots is placed so that pressure on the part of the rudder forward of the stock balances some of the pressure on the after part.

BALANCE LUG: a lugsail, the boom of which projects forward of the mast.

BALLAST: weight, usually of metal but can be of concrete, placed low in a boat to provide stability.

BALLAST RATIO: the ratio between the weight of the ballast and the total displacement.

BANK: a part of the seabed which is higher than the surrounding area.

BAR: shallows at the entrance to a harbour or river caused by silting.

BARBER HAULER: a line, taken from the bite of the jib sheet between the clew and the fairlead, which can be adjusted to alter the angle of the lead of the sheet.

BARE POLES: no sails set, but under way.

BAROMETER: instrument which measures atmospheric pressure.

BATTENS: strips of wood, plastics, or metal inserted in pockets in the leech of a sail to extend it. (Fully-battened, the battens run from luff to leech.)

BEACON: navigational aid (US: beacon is lighted, day-beacon is unlit).

BEAM: (1) the extreme breadth of a vessel; (2) a transverse support for the deck; (3) on the beam = abeam.

BEAM-REACH: to reach with the wind abeam.

BEAM WIND: blows at right angles to the fore-and-aft line.

BEAR: direction of an object from an observer, as 'the lighthouse bears 215°'.

BEAR AWAY: put the helm up so that the boat alters course away from the wind (opp. luff up).

BEAR DOWN: approach from windward.

BEARING: direction of an object from an observer.

BEATING: work to windward close-hauled.

BEAUFORT WIND SCALE: see p. 244.

BECALMED: unable to move owing to lack of wind.

BECKET: loop or small eye in the end of a rope or on a block.

BEFORE: forward of.

BEFORE THE WIND: running with the wind coming from over the stern.

BELAY: (1) make fast a rope; (2) an order to cease.

BELAYING PIN: a pin on which ropes may be made fast.

BELLY: camber, draft, or fullness of a sail.

BELOW: beneath the main deck.

BEND: (1) attach or fasten; (2) a knot used to fasten two ropes together or a rope to an object.

BERMUDAN RIG (US: MARCONI RIG): triangular fore-and-aft rig.

BERTH: (1) the place occupied by a vessel in harbour; (2) to berth is to secure alongside; (3) sleeping place.

BIGBOY (AUS: BLOOPER): full headsail set flying to leeward of a spinnaker when running.

BIGHT: (1) any part of a rope between the ends; (2) shallow bay.

BILGE: the part of the hull where sides and bottom meet.

BILGE KEELS: (1) strips of wood or metal fastened to the bilge of a boat to protect the planking; (2) shallow keels attached to the bilge to provide lateral resistance and a measure of stability, usually in place of a fin keel.

BILGES: the area inside the boat between the port bilge and the starboard bilge; lowest part, usually under the region beneath the floorboards or cabin sole.

BINNACLE: the case in which a ship's compass is housed.

BITTER END: end of a piece of rope.

BITTS: (1) vertical pieces of timber to which a rope may be attached; (2) inboard anchorage of a bowsprit.

BLANKETED: when the wind is taken from the sails by an obstruction to windward, such as another boat, land, or a building.

BLOCK: wood, metal, or plastics case, with a sheave around which a rope runs. Double block, two sheaves side by side. Fiddle block, two sheaves one above the other. Snatch block, one side open or hinged to take a bight of rope without reeving. Swivel block, with a swivel eye or hook. Foot block, usually fastened on the rail, leads a sheet from the fairlead to the winch.

BLOW UP: increase in wind strength.

BOARD: (1) a single close-hauled leg or tack, a long or short board (see also STERNBOARD); (2) go aboard a boat.

BOARD BOAT: centreboard sailing dinghy with very low topsides and virtually no cockpit.

BOATHOOK: pole with a hook on the end used for fending off or for picking up something from the water.

BOATSWAIN'S or BOS'N'S CHAIR: plank or canvas seat on which a man sits when being hoisted aloft.

BOATSWAIN'S LOCKER: compartment or locker in which spare gear such as blocks, ropes, hanks, etc., are kept.

BOBSTAY: stay which runs from the bowsprit to the stem.

BOLLARD: (ashore) post to take mooring lines; (on board) fitting which takes mooring lines.

BOLT ROPE: rope sewn to the edges of a sail to add strength and discourage fraying, as 'luff rope'.

BOOM: spar which extends the foot of a sail, as 'main boom'.

BOOT TOP: narrow strip of paint applied between anti-fouling and topside paint.

BOTTLESCREW: see RIGGING SCREW.

BOTTOM: (1) all the exterior part of the hull of a vessel that is below the waterline; (2) seabed.

BOW: forward part of a vessel.

BOW LINE: line securing the bows to a jetty, boat, etc.

BOWLINE: knot used to make a loop in the end of a rope (fig. 11.10).

BOWSPRIT: a spar projecting from the bows.

BRACE: (1) rope used to trim a yard in square-rigged vessels; (2) AUS: line which controls the fore-and-aft position of the spinnaker pole (see GUY).

BREASTHOOK: wood chock at the top of the stem which binds the sides of the boat together and to the stem.

BREAST ROPE: rope from a vessel to a jetty or another vessel, at right angles to the vessel's side.

BRIDLE: a line made fast to the centre of another line which is itself made fast at both ends.

BRIGHTWORK: varnished parts of the boat.

BROACH: slew round towards the wind dangerously.

BROAD-REACH: to reach with the wind coming over the quarter.

BULKHEAD: partition which divides a boat into compartments.

BULL'S EYE: round, hardwood, plastics or metal eye used to alter the lead of a rope.

BULWARKS: the extension of a vessel's topsides above the level of the deck.

BUMPKIN or BOOMKIN: spar projecting from the stern to which a backstay, mainsheet, or mizzen sheet is attached.

BUNK: fixed sleeping place.

BUNKBOARD: canvas or wood used to prevent the occupant falling out of his bunk.

BUNT: middle part of a sail.

BUOY: floating object anchored to the seabed. Navigational aids are defined on p. 252. Mooring buoy: buoy to which a vessel can moor or which can be picked up and made fast on board. Dan buoy: small buoy with a spar through it, often used as a racing mark marker.

BUOYANCY: upward thrust exerted by the water on a vessel that supports its weight. Reserve buoyancy is provided by extra hull volume available above the waterline to support any increase in displacement anywhere along the hull.

BUOYANCY AID (PERSONAL FLOTATION DEVICE, PFD): jacket or separate garment with positive buoyancy worn to help someone float.

BUOYANCY BAGS, BUOYANCY TANKS, or BUOYANCY COMPARTMENTS (US: FLOTATION BAGS, etc.): fitted to a boat to enable her to float when full of water.

BURGEE: triangular or swallow-tailed flag flown at the masthead.

BUSTLE: bulge in the after body which produces an unfair run of the buttocks. Adopted as a method of improving performance without incurring penalty in racing yachts rated under the IOR.

BUTTOCKS: the buttocks on a lines plan of the hull of a vessel are the fore-and-aft sections of the hull parallel to the centreline. Sometimes the after underbody is referred to as the buttock.

BY THE LEE: running with the wind blowing from the same side as the main boom.

BY THE WIND: close-hauled.

CABLE: (1) rope or chain made fast to the anchor (see RODE); (2) one tenth of a nautical mile, about 200 yards.

CAMBER: (1) athwartships curve of the surface of the deck; (2) fullness or draft of a sail.

CANVAS: (1) material of which sails are made, such as cotton or artificial fibres; (2) general word for sails.

CAPSIZE: turn over (a boat, or a coil of rope).

CARDINAL POINTS: north, east, south, west.

CARLING, CARLINE, or CARLIN: member of the deck structure which runs fore-and-aft or at an angle to the centreline.

CARRY AWAY: break or part company.

CARVEL: edge-to-edge planking giving a smooth hull surface.

CAST OFF: let go a line.

CATALYST: agent which produces chemical change in other bodies such as the hardening agent used with resin in glassfibre construction.

CATAMARAN: boat with two hulls joined by cross-beams.

CAT BOAT: boat with one or two masts carrying no staysails but a single sail set on each mast. Usually a shallow draft, beamy boat with a single mast stepped right in the bows.

CATSPAW: light puff of wind.

CAULK or CALK: fill the seams of a boat to prevent leaks.

CAULKING COTTON: strands of soft cotton used for caulking the fine seams in small boats.

CAVIL: piece of wood attached to two or more bulwark stanchions to which ropes may be attached, often fitted with belaying pins.

CEILING: inside lining of the sides of a hull.

CENTREBOARD or CENTREPLATE: wooden board or metal plate lowered through a slot in the bottom to reduce leeway.

CENTREBOARD CASE (US: CENTERBOARD TRUNK or WELL): box in which the centreboard is housed.

CENTRELINE: see FORE-AND-AFT LINE.

CENTRE OF EFFORT: the place where the effect of the wind on the sails may be considered to act for purposes of calculation.

CENTRE OF LATERAL RESISTANCE: the centre about which a boat pivots when changing course.

CERTIFICATE OF REGISTRY: official document giving the vessel's measurements and confirming her registration with the national authority.

CHAIN LOCKER: where the anchor cable is stowed.

CHAIN PIPE: pipe on the foredeck through which the chain passes.

CHAIN-PLATES (UK also SHROUD-PLATES): metal plates bolted to the vessel's sides to which rigging is attached.

CHANDLERY: items of equipment needed to fit out a vessel.

CHART DATUM: level to which soundings on a chart are reduced. See page 247.

CHECK or CHECK AWAY: ease out carefully.

CHEEKS: sides of a block or rudder stock.

CHINE: (1) line of intersection between flat portions of a hull; (2) structural member joining flat panels of a hull.

CHOCK-A-BLOCK: when two blocks of a tackle are so close together that they are touching.

CHRONOMETER: time-measuring instrument used in navigation, essential when determining longitude.

CHUTE (US): sl. SPINNAKER. See also SPINNAKER CHUTE.

CLAMP: doubling member placed inside the frames and below the shelf, often to provide additional strength in way of mast and shrouds.

CLAW OFF: beat up to windward, usually with some difficulty, from a dangerous shore or area to leeward.

CLAW RING: C-shaped ring slipped over a spar, to which a sheet or other control line may be attached. The sail passes through the slot in the ring.

CLEAR: (1) not entangled (opp. foul); (2) sail past a head, etc.; (3) pass customs in and out.

CLEARANCE: (1) certificate from customs; (2) space between two objects or parts.

CLEAR WIND: free of interference from boats or obstructions.

CLEAT: fitting to which a rope or line is made fast.

CLENCH: fasten a nail, rivet or bolt by turning the end or riveting it over a roove or washer.

CLEW: (1) lower, after corner of a fore-and-aft sail, where foot and leech meet; (2) lower corners of a square sail.

CLINKER-BUILT or LAPSTRAKE: hull construction in which adjacent planks overlap each other.

CLINOMETER: instrument measuring the angle of heel of a vessel.

CLIPPER or SCHOONER BOW: the profile of the stem is concave (opp. spoon bow).

CLOSE-HAULED: sailing as close to the wind as possible.

CLOSE-REACH: reaching with the wind forward of the beam, but not so close as close-hauled.

CLOSE-REEFED: all reefs taken in.

CLOSE-WINDED: said of a boat which will sail very close to the wind.

CLOTH: a sail is made up of cloths sewn together.

COACH ROOF (US: TRUNK): raised part of the cabin top above deck level.

COAMING or COMBING: raised portion round the edge of an opening in the deck; it helps prevent water entering.

COCKED HAT (UK, AUS): triangle formed when three lines of bearing which do not pass through a common point are plotted on a chart.

COCKPIT: a well lower than deck level in which the helmsman and crew work.

COFFEE GRINDER: powerful winch controlled from a separate pedestal having two handles which rotate about a horizontal spindle.

COIL: (1) rope formed into rings; (2) form rings with rope; (3) rope can be bought by the coil.

COLLISION COURSES: when two vessels are on courses that will bring them within risk of collision.

COLOURS or COLORS: (1) national ensign; (2) ceremony of hoisting national flags in the morning (US: making colors, lowering the national flags at sunset).

COMMISSION: provide a vessel with a full crew and stores.

COMMITTEE BOAT: vessel from which the race officers operate and give instructions such as course and starting signals.

COMPANION or COMPANIONWAY: main hatch and the immediate surrounding area giving access below from on deck.

COMPASS: instrument which indicates the direction of true north (gyro compass), or magnetic north (magnetic compass).

COMPASS BEARING: direction of an object from an observer as indicated by a compass.

COMPASS COURSE: course to be steered by a vessel allowing for variation and deviation.

COMPASS ERROR: total deflection of a compass from true north owing to the effects of variation and deviation.

COMPASS ROSE: circle(s) printed on a chart, marked in degrees and/or points, related to true and magnetic north.

COMPOSITE CONSTRUCTION: construction using more than one type of material. Usually refers to a vessel with metal frames and wood planking.

CONSTANT BEARING: compass bearing which remains the same.

CORED CONSTRUCTION: see SANDWICH CONSTRUCTION.

COUNTER: overhang aft produced by the continuation of the hull lines beyond the aft end of the waterline.

COURSE: direction in which a vessel is steered.

COVERING BOARD: outermost deck plank.

CRADLE: frame in which a vessel stands ashore or when being launched.

CRAZING: tiny cracks in the gel coat or in varnish.

CREW: (1) entire ship's company; (2) member of a ship's company; (3) to be a member of a crew.

CRINGLE: (1) eye or rope around a thimble, usually in a sail; (2) eye in a sail or canvas.

CROSS-LINKED WINCH: winch connected by rods and gearing to another winch so that power can be applied to one winch drum from more than one position.

CROSSTREES: see SPREADERS.

CROWN: highest point of the camber of the deck.

CRUTCH (US: also BOOM CROTCH): removable support in which the main boom is stowed (cf. gallows).

CUDDY: small shelter in a sailing vessel.

CUNNINGHAM EYE or HOLE (US: also OOKER): eye in the luff of a sail above the tack through which a line may be passed to increase tension on the luff and thus reduce the camber of a sail.

CURRENT (UK): horizontal movement of water owing to various natural causes, but specifically exclusive of tidal influences (cf. below).

CURRENT (US): horizontal movement of water, non-tidal currents being due to various natural causes, tidal currents being due to tidal influences (cf. above).

CURRENT TABLE AND CHART (UK: TIDAL-STREAM ATLAS): table and chart giving the set (direction) and drift (speed) of tidal currents.

CUSTOM-BUILT: one-off vessel (cf. stock production).

CUSTOMS: duties imposed by law, and the officials who implement the law.

CUTTER: single-masted sailing vessel with

more than one headsail, gaff-rigged or bermudan-rigged.

DAGGER BOARD: centreboard which does not pivot but is raised and lowered vertically.

DAVITS: posts of wood or metal which project over the sides or stern, used for raising and lowering small boats.

DAYMARK: see TOPMARK.

DEADEYE: block of wood with holes in it which take a lanyard; used in old sailing vessels for tensioning shrouds, etc.

DEADLIGHT: (1) metal cover which can be fastened over a port; (2) porthole which does not open.

DEAD RECKONING: position of a vessel based on the course steered and the distance run through the water.

DEADRISE OR RISE OF FLOOR: the amount of rise of the bottom between the top of the keel and the chine or turn of the bilge.

DEADWOOD: member which binds the sternpost to the keel.

DECK: covering over the cabin, etc.

DECKHEAD: underside of the deck.

DEPTH SOUNDERS: see ECHO SOUNDERS.

DEVIATION: difference between the direction indicated by the compass needle and the magnetic meridian, caused by ferrous metal, etc., aboard the vessel.

DEVIATION CARD: card giving the figure to be allowed for deviation for a number of different headings, established by swinging the vessel through 360°.

DIAGONAL PLANKING: planking at an angle to the centreline or waterline, usually with a second layer at right angles to it.

DIAMONDS: stays giving lateral support to the mast, running from a point on the mast, over spreaders and back to a lower point on the mast.

DINETTE: table bordered by settees which can be converted into berths.

DINGHY: small open boat for sailing, rowing, fishing, etc.

DISMAST: break the mast.

DISPLACEMENT: weight of water displaced by a floating vessel, which is the same as the weight of the vessel itself.

DOCK (US): berth where a vessel may moor alongside or stern on to the shore or a pontoon connected to the shore.

DODGER: canvas screen fitted to protect the crew from spray, etc.

DOGHOUSE: raised area aft of the cabin.

DOLPHIN STRIKER: strut extending downwards from the bow over which the bobstay passes.

DOUBLE ENDER: vessel with pointed bow and stern.

DOUBLING: (1) turned-over edges of a sail; (2) patch fitted to strengthen a sail.

DOUSE OR DOWSE: drop sails quickly.

DOWNHAUL: rope fitted to pull down a sail or spar.

DOWN HELM: put the tiller down so that the boat points closer to the wind.

DOWNWIND: (1) running, with the wind aft; (2) to leeward.

DRAFT OR DRAUGHT: (1) vertical distance from the waterline to the lowest point of the hull; (2) camber or curvature in the cross-section of a sail.

DRAG: a vessel drags when the anchor does not hold.

DRAW: (1) a sail draws when filled with wind; (2) a vessel draws x metres (draft x metres).

DRIFT: (1) float with the current, stream, or wind; (2) US: the velocity of a current in knots (UK: RATE); (3) US: a vessel's leeway.

DROGUE: open-ended canvas bucket shape used as a sea anchor or to slow a boat.

DROP ASTERN: (1) leave or be left behind; (2) move an object such as a dinghy nearer to the stern.

DRYING FEATURES: areas of the seabed covered at high water, but exposed when the tide falls.

DUTCHMAN'S LOG (US: CHIP LOG): traditional method of establishing speed by measuring the time a vessel takes to pass a piece of flotsam thrown overboard at the bow.

EARING: line bent to the cringle of a sail.

EASE: (1) slacken a line gradually; (2) lessen, of wind.

EBB: falling tide (opp. flood).

ECHO SOUNDER OR DEPTH SOUNDER: electronic device for sounding.

EDDY: circular or contrary movement of water flowing across or against the direction of the main stream.

ENGINE BEDS OR BEARERS: the structural members to which an inboard engine is attached.

ENSIGN: marine version of the national flag, flown at or near the stern to show the vessel's nationality.

ESTIMATED POSITION: position of a vessel calculated by allowing for the distance run, tidal stream, and leeway.

EVEN KEEL: a vessel floating upright is on an even keel.

EYE BOLT: bolt with an open eye.

EYELET HOLES: small holes sewn or clinched in canvas, through which a lacing may be passed.

EYE OF THE WIND: direction from which the true wind is blowing.

FAIR: line or surface which is smooth and without abrupt or awkward changes of direction, bumps, and hollows.

FAIRLEAD: fitting through which a line runs; it guides or alters the direction of the lead of the line.

FAIRWAY: main channel navigable by vessels in restricted waters.

FAIR WIND: allows a boat to sail from one place to another without tacking, usually

used for a wind abaft the beam.

FALL: (1) of a tide, the ebb; (2) the rope used for a block and tackle.

FALLING OFF: when the vessel's head drops to leeward of the required course.

FALSE KEEL: usually, pieces of wood used to complete the underwater form at either end of the ballast keel.

FALSE TACK: when racing, to pretend to go about to mislead an opponent but to pay off on the original tack.

FASHION PIECE: a doubling piece round the edge of a bulkhead or transom to increase the thickness and thus provide more landing for the planking.

FAST: secure.

FATHOM: 6ft, measurement used for depths and lengths of rope.

FENDERS: soft objects hung outboard to prevent damage to topsides.

FEND OFF: push a boat clear of another object.

FETCH: (1) sail some distance close-hauled without tacking; (2) to achieve an object, as 'fetch the mark'.

FIBREGLASS: see GLASSFIBRE.

FID: tapered tool, usually of wood or steel, used for splicing.

FIDDLE: a rail fitted to the edge of a horizontal surface to prevent objects sliding off when the vessel heels or rolls.

FILL: fill the sails with wind.

FIN KEEL: a keel which does not form an integral part of the hull shape; usually attached after the hull is completed.

FINE ON THE PORT (OR STARBOARD) BOW: just to port (or starboard) of a line dead ahead.

FINE LINES: narrow boat with a high length-to-beam ratio.

FIT OUT: prepare a boat for sea at the start of a season or prior to a voyage.

FIX: the vessel's position established on the chart by means of two or more position lines.

FLAG: rectangular piece of bunting.

FLAGSTAFF: mast on shore from which flags are flown. On board the ensign is flown from the ensign staff.

FLAKE: a rope is flaked down when it is arranged on a surface so that it will run out easily without becoming tangled.

FLARE: increase in beam above the waterline (cf. tumble home).

FLAW (US): gust or stronger puff of wind.

FLOAT: be waterborne.

FLOOD: (1) rising tide; (2) fill a vessel, or part of a vessel, with water.

FLOORBOARDS: bottom boards of a boat.

FLOORS: the bottom, vertical, transverse members which, in a wooden boat, connect the timbers to the keel or any transverse strengthening member beneath the cabin sole.

FLOTATION BAGS (US): see BUOYANCY BAGS.

FLUSH: level.

FLY: (1) horizontal length of a flag; (2) the part of the flag furthest from the hoist; (3) small pennant at the masthead to indicate wind direction.

FOG SIGNALS: signals made by vessels and navigational aids to indicate their position in fog and restricted visibility.

FOLLOWING SEA: a sea that runs with the vessel.

FOOT: (1) lower edge of a sail; (2) to foot well is to sail fast.

FORCE (OF WIND): number given to classify wind strength according to the Beaufort Scale (see p. 244).

FORE: in, or towards, or nearer the bows.

FORE-AND-AFT: lengthwise.

FORE-AND-AFT LINE: centreline from stem to sternpost.

FORE-AND-AFT RIG: not square-rigged, sails set in the fore-and-aft line.

FORECASTLE or FO'C'S'LE: area forward of the mast below decks.

FOREDECK: deck forward of the mast.

FOREFOOT: where the stem joins the keel.

FOREMAST: forward mast of two or more.

FOREPEAK: furthest forward compartment of a vessel.

FORE-REACH: shooting ahead in stays.

FORESAIL: (1) in schooners, the fore-and-aft sail set aft of the foremast; (2) US: in boats with two sails the sail forward of the mast.

FORESHORE: the part of the shore which is covered at high water and dry at low water.

FORESTAY: any stay led forward of a mast.

FORE TRIANGLE: the area bounded by the foremost forestay on which a sail is set, the forward side of the mast, and a line between the foot of the same forestay and the mast at deck level.

FORWARD or FORRARD: (1) forward part of a vessel, near the bows; (2) nearer the bows, as 'forward of'.

FOUL: (1) opp. clear or fair; a foul anchor has something wound round the flukes; (2) when racing, to collide with another boat or illegally cause her to alter course.

FOUL GROUND: anchorage littered with obstructions which may cause the anchor to become foul.

FOUL-WEATHER GEAR: see OILSKINS.

FOUL WIND: wind blowing from the direction in which the vessel wishes to sail.

FOUND: a well-found vessel is well fitted out.

FRAME: (1) transverse structural member to which the hull planking or shell is secured; (2) skeleton of a vessel.

FRAP: secure something with a rope tied round it.

FREE: (1) the wind frees when the direction from which it is blowing moves towards the stern (opp. the wind heads);

(2) 'sailing free' is not close-hauled; (3) free wind (opp. head wind).

FREEBOARD: height of a vessel's sides above the waterline.

FRESHEN: (1) the wind increases when it freshens; (2) US: luff up when sailing downwind; (3) freshen the nip, to adjust a line, sail, or anchor cable so that chafe occurs in a different place.

FULL: (1) a sail is said to be 'full' of wind; (2) sail with plenty of draft, as opposed to flat.

FULL AND BY: sails set and drawing with the boat as close-hauled as possible.

FULL SAIL: all sails set and not reefed.

FURL: roll or gather up sail or canvas.

GAFF: spar to which the head of a fore-and-aft sail is bent.

GAFF-HEADED: any sail with which a gaff is used.

GAFF-RIGGED: fore-and-aft rig, the sail(s) set on the mast(s) being quadrilateral and attached to a gaff.

GAFF TOPSAIL: triangular sail set on a topmast.

GALE: strong wind, force 7–10, 28–55 kts.

GALLOWS: permanent support in which the main boom is stowed (cf. crutch).

GARBOARD STRAKE: the plank next to the keel on either side.

GASKETS, TYERS, or SAIL TIES (US: SAIL STOPS): bands with which to secure the sails.

GATE START: used to avoid congestion on the starting line when a racing fleet is very large. One boat, the pathfinder, sails close-hauled on port tack away from the committee boat, with a motorboat following close astern. Other competitors start by passing astern of the motorboat on starboard tack. Finally, the pathfinder bears away and gybes on to starboard tack to pass behind the motorboat.

GATHER WAY: begin to move through the water.

GEL COAT: first coat of resin applied to a mould when producing a glassfibre moulding. If a coloured moulding is required, pigment is added.

GENOA: a large headsail which overlaps the mainsail.

GHOSTING: making way under sail in very little wind.

GILGUY (US): lanyard used to prevent the halyards slatting against the mast.

GIMBALS: system by which an object is suspended and pivoted in one direction, or two directions at right angles to each other in the horizontal plane, so that the object remains horizontal regardless of the attitude of the vessel; usually used for the compass and cooking stove.

GIVE WAY: take action to prevent a collision.

GLASS: often used for the barometer, as 'the glass is rising'.

GLASSFIBRE or FIBREGLASS, GRP (US: FIBERGLASS): fine threads of glass, matted or woven, which are impregnated with resin to make a glassfibre and resin laminate.

GO ABOUT: change from one tack to the other.

GOOSENECK: universal joint which connects the boom to the mast.

GOOSEWING: sail with jib on one side and mainsail on the other side of the mast.

GREEN SEA: solid water taken aboard, as opposed to spray.

GRIPE: (1) a boat gripes if she carries excessive weather helm; (2) hold in to a vessel's side by means of ropes or strops.

GROMMET: (1) rope ring; (2) eye in a sail or canvas; (3) ring of boat cotton or oakum placed under the head of a bolt or the washer beneath a nut to prevent water passing through the bolt hole.

GROUND: touch the bottom.

GROUND TACKLE: anchors, cables, etc.

GROWN FRAMES: frames sawn from solid timber selected so that the grain of the wood follows the shape of the frame.

GUARDRAILS or LIFELINES: safety rails fitted around a boat through stanchions to prevent the crew falling overboard.

GUDGEON: a fitting with a hole in it which takes the pin of a pintle on which the rudder pivots.

GUNKHOLING (US): exploring shallow waters.

GUNTER RIG: a gaff slides up a short mast and forms an extension of the mast. The sail has four sides but appears to be triangular.

GUNWALES or GUNNELS (US: also RAIL): upper edge of the sides of a vessel.

GUST (US: also FLAW): sudden, brief increase in wind.

GUY: steadying rope for a spar, etc. Spinnaker guy (UK & US) controls the fore-and-aft position of the spinnaker pole (AUS: BRACE); foreguy holds the spinnaker pole forward and down.

GYBE (JIBE): change tacks with the wind aft.

HALF BEAMS: beams which run between the gunwale and a carling.

HALF-TIDE: half-way between low and high water.

HALYARDS or HALLIARDS: ropes used to hoist sails, flags, etc.

HAND: (1) lower a sail; (2) crew member.

HAND-BEARING COMPASS: magnetic compass which is held in the hand, fitted with sights for taking bearings.

HANDICAP: time or distance factor applied to enable boats of different types to race fairly against each other.

HANDSOMELY: gradually, with care.

HANGING KNEE: a vertical bracket, usually of wood or metal, which ties the deck and hull structure together.

HANK: a fitting to attach sails to a stay.

HARD (not US): a firm part of the foreshore, a landing place.

HARD ALEE: (UK: more commonly LEE-O): the helmsman's warning that he is putting the helm down to go about.

HARD CHINE: as opposed to round bilge, the topsides meet the bottom at an angle instead of a curve.

HARDEN IN: trim the sails closer to the centreline.

HARDEN UP: sail closer to the wind, point up.

HARD OVER: when the rudder is as far over to port or starboard as it will go.

HARD UP and HARD DOWN: when the tiller is over as far as possible to windward (up) and leeward (down).

HATCH: opening in the deck giving access to the interior.

HAUL: pull on a rope.

HAUL OUT: take a vessel out of the water.

HAWSE HOLE: the hole through which the anchor cable passes.

HAWSER: heavy rope used for mooring, towing, etc.

HEAD (n.): (1) upper corner of any triangular sail; (2) upper end of a spar; (3) bow of a vessel; (4) upper edge of a quadrilateral sail; (5) US: W.C. or toilet.

HEAD (v.): (1) aim in a particular direction; (2) the wind heads (opp. frees) when it comes from nearer the bow of a close-hauled boat, forcing her to bear away to fill the sails. Such a change in wind direction can be described as a header (US & AUS: also KNOCK).

HEADBOARD: a piece of stiffening, usually of wood, metal, or plastics, sewn into the head of a sail.

HEADING: direction in which a vessel is going.

HEADROOM: the greatest distance between the cabin sole and the deckhead underneath the beams.

HEADS (UK): toilet or w.c. compartment.

HEADSAIL: any sail set forward of the foremast.

HEAD SEA: a sea approaching from the direction in which the boat is moving.

HEAD TO WIND: when the bows are pointing right into the wind.

HEAD UP: luff (opp. bear away).

HEADWAY: forward motion of a vessel through the water.

HEAD WIND: the wind is coming from the direction in which the boat is moving (opp. fair wind).

HEART: central core of a rope.

HEAVE TO: (1) stop; (2) back the jib and lash the tiller to leeward.

HEAVING LINE: light line suitable for throwing and used to make connection with the shore or another vessel. Often attached to a messenger or heavier line which is pulled in afterwards.

HEEL: (1) lower end of a mast or spar (US: also butt); (2) after, lowest part of a keel; (3) when a boat lies at an angle to the horizontal owing to wind pressure (see STIFF and TENDER).

HEELING ERROR: error in the compass caused by the vessel heeling.

HELM: tiller or wheel controlling the rudder (not the person).

HIGH AND DRY: a vessel which has grounded and is left clear of the water when the tide recedes.

HIGH WATER: the highest level reached by a rising tide.

HIKE OUT (US & AUS); SIT OUT (UK): keep a dinghy or small boat level by sitting on the rail (gunwale), side deck or edge of the boat and leaning outboard.

HIKING BOARD (US); HIKING PLANK or SWINGING PLANK (AUS); SLIDING SEAT (UK): board which slides across the crew's quarters to enable him to place his weight as far outboard as possible to keep the boat level.

HIKING STICK (US): see TILLER EXTENSION.

HIKING STRAPS (US); SWINGING STRAPS (AUS): TOE-STRAPS (UK): straps under which the crew can hook their feet so that they can sit or hike out.

HITCH: used to make a rope fast to another rope or some object.

HOG: (1) fore-and-aft timber over the keel of a small boat; (2) drop at the ends (applied to the hull of a vessel).

HOGGED: (1) a vessel higher in the middle because the ends have drooped with age; (2) a vessel designed in this way (see also REVERSE SHEER).

HOIST: (1) raise or lift; (2) the rope used to raise or lift something; (3) the vertical edge of a flag or ensign nearest to the mast; (4) the length of a sail's luff.

HOLD: (1) the anchor holds when it digs firmly into the ground, as opposed to dragging; (2) the place where cargo is stowed in commercial vessels.

HOOD ENDS: ends of the planks.

HOOK: anchor (coll.).

HORN TIMBER: piece of timber forming the continuation of the keel along the counter.

HORSE: a bar, wire, or piece of track which runs athwartships and takes a traveller to which the lower block of a sheeting system is attached.

HOUNDS: the point on the mast below the masthead where forestay is attached.

HOVE TO: see HEAVE TO.

HULL: the structure, the body of a vessel.

INBOARD: as opposed to outboard; (1) within the vessel; (2) nearer to amidships; (3) inboard engine.

INBOARD-OUTBOARD: inboard engine coupled to an outboard drive unit.

IN IRONS: when a sailing vessel has come head to wind and has no way on, so cannot fill on either tack without going into a sternboard.

INSHORE: on, near, or towards the shore.

IN STAYS: when a vessel is changing tacks.

IN STOPS: a sail is set in stops when light line is knotted around it to prevent it filling while being hoisted.

IN WAY OF: lying in the same athwartships plane.

ISOBAR: line drawn on a weather map which links points of equal barometric pressure.

JAWS: the horns which project from a gaff and fit either side of the mast.

JIB: triangular sail set furthest forward, commonly used to describe the headsail of a small boat with two sails.

JIB SHEET: sheet, attached to the clew, which controls the jib.

JIB STICK (US: WHISKER POLE): a stick inserted into the clew to wing the jib out to windward when running.

JIB-HEADED: triangular sails.

JIBE: see GYBE.

JUMPER STAYS: stays led over jumper struts, angled forward to give both lateral and fore-and-aft support.

JURY RIG: a temporary arrangement to enable a sail to be set, usually after damage. Similarly jury rudder, etc.

KEDGE: (1) light additional anchor; (2) to kedge off is to lay out the kedge away from a vessel so that she can be moved by hauling on the line attached to it, esp. after running aground.

KEEL: centreline backbone of a vessel to which the frames, timbers, and floors are attached.

KEELSON: an inner keel fitted over the floor timbers.

KETCH: two-masted sailing boat with the smaller mizzen mast stepped forward of the rudder post.

KICKER: (1) AUS: the line which controls the up and down movement of the spinnaker pole; (2) US: outboard or inboard auxiliary engine; (3) UK: abbr. kicking strap.

KICKING STRAP: see VANG.

KING POST: a vertical post between the bottom of the hull and the deck.

KING PLANK: centre plank of the deck running fore-and-aft down the centreline.

KNEES: brackets joining structural members such as deck beams, thwarts.

KNIGHTHEADS: the chocks fitted right forward which take the forward ends of the bulwark planks.

KNOCK (US & AUS): see HEAD, vb, (2).

KNOT: (1) measure of speed, one knot = one nautical mile per hour, used as 'one knot', never 'one knot per hour'; (2) method of securing a line to another object.

LACING: line used to bend on sails, canvas dodgers, etc.

LANYARD: small line used to make something fast.

LAPSTRAKE: see clinker-built.

LASH: secure or bind with light line.

LASH DOWN: secure something in position with a lashing.

LATEEN: a sail bent to a yard which is set obliquely on a mast.

LATITUDE: distance north or south of the Equator measured in degrees, minutes, and seconds.

LAUNCH: (1) put a vessel in the water; (2) small powerboat.

LAUNCHING TUBE: (1) US: see SPINNAKER CHUTE; (2) tube in the stern in which an emergency dan buoy is stowed for marking the position of a man overboard.

LAY: (1) a vessel can 'lay' a course when she is able to steer the desired course; (2) of a rope, the direction in which a rope is twisted (see ROPE).

LAY UP: take a vessel out of commission.

LAZARETTE: small stowage compartment forward or aft (US: aft only).

LEAD AND LINE or SOUNDING LINE: a lump of lead on a marked line used for sounding. The base is hollowed so that it can be filled with grease to bring up a sample of the bottom.

LEADING LINE: marks on land sited to guide vessels clear of dangers.

LEE: (opp. weather). In the lee, sheltered from the wind.

LEEBOARDS: boards lowered on either side of a flat-bottomed vessel to reduce leeway.

LEE-BOWED: a boat that is slowed because its sails are backwinded by another sailing boat to leeward and slightly ahead.

LEECH (US: also LEACH): (1) after edge of a triangular sail; (2) the two side edges of a square sail.

LEECHLINE: light line threaded into the leech which gives some control over the way the sail sets.

LEE-O (not US): as HARD ALEE.

LEE SHORE: shore to leeward of the vessel (to be avoided in bad or threatening weather).

LEEWARD: (opp. windward). (1) downwind; (2) the direction to which the wind blows; (3) away from the wind.

LEEWAY: sideways movement of a vessel caused by wind blowing on one side. Often expressed as the angle between the course steered and the course made good through the water.

LEGS: spars used to keep a boat upright when she is aground or out of the water.

LENGTH BETWEEN PERPENDICULARS: abbr. LBP, length from fore side of stem to after side of sternpost at deck level.

LENGTH OVERALL: abbr. LOA, the extreme length of a hull, or the hull, bowsprit and bumpkin.

LET FLY: let the sheet go.

LEVEL-RATING CLASS: class in which boats below a certain rating level race against each other without handicap.

LIFEBUOY: floating ring or horseshoe capable of keeping a man afloat.

LIFE-JACKET: jacket worn to keep a man afloat for long periods.

LIFELINES: (1) lines attached to safety harness so that a crew can attach himself to the boat; (2) see GUARDRAILS.

LIFE-RAFT: inflatable raft capable of carrying the entire crew.

LIFE-VEST (US & AUS): less bulky than a life-jacket, worn by small-boat sailors to keep them afloat in the water.

LIFT: (1) rope from the mast used to suspend a spar, such as spinnaker-pole lift, topping lift; (2) UK: a sail lifts (US: luffs) when wind strikes the leeward side of the sail near the luff; (3) freeing wind.

LIMBER HOLES: gaps left at the lower end of timbers or frames above the keel, or holes in the floors, to allow water in the bilges to drain to the lowest point.

LINE: correctly, rope of less than an inch diameter, but commonly used for most ropes aboard a small boat.

LINE OF POSITION, LOP (US): see POSITION LINE.

LINES OF A VESSEL: drawings showing the shape of a vessel (body plan, sheer plan, and half breadth plan), also used descriptively as 'sturdy lines'.

LIST: a vessel lists if she leans to one side owing to disposition of weight (cf. heel).

LOAD WATERLINE: abbr. LWL, the length of a vessel along the waterline at her designed displacement.

LOCKER: compartment in which articles are stowed.

LOG: apparatus for measuring distance sailed through the water and recording speed.

LOG BOOK: book in which all details of a voyage are recorded.

LONGITUDE: distance east or west of the meridian of Greenwich, expressed in terms of degrees, minutes, and seconds.

LOW WATER: lowest level of a tide, abbr. LW.

LUFF: (1) forward edge of a sail; (2) alter course towards the wind; (3) US: see LIFT (2).

LUFF UP: put the helm down so that the boat points nearer to the wind.

LUG: (1) fore-and-aft sail with a yard, part of which extends forward of the mast; (2) US: carry too much sail.

MAGNETIC BEARING: bearing of an object in relation to the magnetic meridian allowing for variation.

MAGNETIC COMPASS: standard compass used in vessels.

MAGNETIC COURSE: course with variation applied.

MAGNETIC MERIDIAN: magnetic north-south line as indicated by a compass which is not diverted by local attraction.

MAIN: (1) prefix used to indicate the larger of two or more similar objects; (2) coll. mainsail.

MAIN BOOM: spar to which the foot of the mainsail is attached.

MAINSAIL: sail set on the mast, or the main mast if there is more than one mast.

MAINSHEET: sheet which controls the mainsail.

MAKE FAST: secure.

MAKE HEADWAY: move forwards through the water.

MAKE SAIL: set the sails.

MAKE STERNWAY: move through the water stern first.

MAKE WATER: leak.

MAKING WAY: moving through the water (cf. under way).

MAN OVERBOARD: shout made by any member of the crew when someone falls overboard.

MARCONI RIG (US); BERMUDAN (UK): triangular fore-and-aft rig.

MARINE RAILWAY (US): tracks at a boatyard used for launching or slipping.

MARK: object used to guide vessels.

MARLINE: light, two-stranded line.

MARLINE-SPIKE or MARLINSPIKE: tapered spike used for splicing.

MAST: spar on which sails are set; it is stepped approximately vertically and is usually supported by standing rigging.

MAST COAT (US: also MAST BOOT): a canvas, plastics, or rubber cover lashed to the mast just above deck and secured to a chock on deck; prevents water finding its way below round the mast.

MASTHEAD: top of the mast.

MASTHEAD RIG: fore-and-aft rig with the forestay extending to the masthead.

MAST HOOPS: wood loops, to which a sail is attached, which slide on a mast.

MEAN: average.

MEASURED MILE: distance of one nautical mile measured between buoys or as indicated by markers (US: ranges) ashore.

MEET HER: check the swing of a vessel.

MERIDIAN: an imaginary line encircling the earth, passing through North and South Poles and cutting the Equator at right angles.

MESSENGER: a medium-sized rope which is passed to the shore or another vessel after a heaving line, and which is strong enough to pull in a heavier rope or wire.

MIDDLE GROUND: shoal in the middle of a channel or fairway.

MISS STAYS: fail to go about and fall back on to the original tack.

MITRE or MITER: seam in a sail from which cloths run in different directions.

MIZZEN or MIZEN: fore-and-aft sail set on the mizzen mast.

MOLE HILL (US: ANT HILL): remote drive position for a winch.

MONOHULL: vessel having one hull as opposed to a catamaran (two hulls) or a trimaran (three hulls).

MOOR: fasten a vessel so that she is not adrift.

MOORING ALONGSIDE: tie up a boat alongside a pier, dock, another boat, etc.

MOTOR SAILER: boat designed to perform reasonably well under sail or power.

MOULDED or MOLDED HULL: a hull constructed by laying a number of skins of thin wood in succession.

NAUTICAL ALMANAC: publication containing tables relating to stars, sun, tides, etc.

NAUTICAL MILE: measurement of distance equal to one minute of longitude at the Equator (6,080ft).

NAVIGATIONAL AIDS: buoys, lights, marks on land, etc., placed to indicate where a vessel may sail safely.

NEAP TIDES: tides of least range (cf. spring tides).

NULL: when using RDF, the point at which the sound emitted by the radio beacon is least.

OAKUM: tarred, unstranded fibres used for caulking seams.

OFF THE WIND: (opp. on the wind) not close-hauled, with the sheets slacked off.

OFFING: a position at a distance to seaward.

OFFSETS: the measurements of the shape of a vessel.

OFFSHORE: away from the coast.

OFFSHORE WIND: blowing from the land.

OILSKINS or OILIES (US: also OILERS or SLICKERS): waterproof clothing.

ONE-DESIGN CLASS: class in which the boats are so closely restricted that they are virtually identical.

ONSHORE: towards the land.

ONSHORE WIND: blowing towards the land.

ON THE WIND: close-hauled (opp. off the wind).

OPEN: (1) an open boat is not decked; (2) two marks or features are said to be open when they are not in line.

OUTBOARD: (1) a portable engine which is clamped on to the boat, usually over the stern, but sometimes on a bracket over the side or through a special trunk aft so that it protrudes through the bottom; (2) outside the vessel; (3) towards the side of a vessel.

OUTHAUL: line used to extend the foot of a sail.

OUTPOINT: point closer to the wind than another vessel.

OVERBOARD: over the side.

OVERFALLS: disturbed water caused when a strong tidal stream or current passes over a rough bottom or one where the depth varies considerably.

OVERHANGS: the parts of the bow and stern which extend beyond the waterline.

OVERSTAND: stay too long on a tack before going about for a mark or object to be rounded; consequently, sheets have to be eased to sail back to the mark.

PAINTER: line by which the dinghy is made fast or towed.

PALM or SAILMAKER'S PALM: leather band with a metal insert used for pushing a needle when stitching canvas, rope, etc.

PARCEL: cover a rope with marline to protect it from chafe.

PARREL: short rope that attaches a yard to a mast.

PART: (1) break; (2) bight of a rope between the two blocks of a block and tackle.

PARTNERS or MAST PARTNERS: the framing which runs fore-and-aft between the deck beams and supports the mast at deck level.

PATENT LOG (US: TAFFRAIL LOG): a spinner towed at the end of a line works a register on the stern, indicating distance sailed through the water.

PAY A SEAM: run marine glue (similar to pitch) into a caulked seam.

PAY AWAY or PAY OFF: fall off to leeward.

PAY OUT: ease out a rope.

PEAK: (1) upper, outer corner of a sail attached to a gaff; (2) upper end of gaff.

PENDANT or PENNANT: (1) long, narrow or triangular flag; (2) hanging rope.

PERMANENT BACKSTAY: backstay which is not released when sailing, although the tension on it may be adjusted.

PERSONAL FLOTATION DEVICES, PFDS (US): see LIFE-JACKETS and LIFE-VESTS.

PILE: wooden or concrete post embedded in the bottom to which a vessel may moor or which supports structures.

PINCH: sail too close to the wind.

PINTLE: a fitting with a pin which locates in a hole in a gudgeon and on which the rudder pivots. Attached to the stern or rudder post and to the rudder.

PITCH: (1) plunging up and down of the bows; (2) angle of the propeller blade.

PLANE: high-performance dinghies plane when the lift generated by forward motion exceeds part of the force of gravity, so that the boat skims along the top of the water rather than pushing through it.

PLANK: strip of wood used to cover the outside and deck of a vessel.

PLAY: adjust a sheet continuously so as to trim the sail to the wind.

PLOT: apply position or course to a chart.

POINT: (1) a point of the compass; (2) a place where the line of the coast alters abruptly; (3) point well is to sail close to the wind (opp. point badly).

POLE: (1) true north and south; (2) the spinnaker pole is a spar used to extend the spinnaker to windward.

POOPED: a vessel is said to be pooped if she takes a large sea over the stern.

PORT: (1) the left-hand side of a vessel when looking forward; (2) harbour; (3) opening in the side of a vessel, as 'porthole', 'gunport'.

PORTSMOUTH YARDSTICK: a measure of performance for use in handicap races. A Portsmouth Number is allocated by a club to a boat, based on its performance in local races, or, when several clubs agree, can be allocated to a one-design or restricted class. Primary Yardsticks are awarded to popular classes whose Yardstick number has been attested by many clubs.

PORT TACK: a vessel is on port tack when the wind strikes the port side first and her main boom is to starboard. A vessel on port tack gives way to one on starboard tack, and to a sailing vessel approaching from windward if she is in any doubt as to whether the windward vessel is on port or starboard tack.

POSITION LINE (US: LINE OF POSITION, LOP): line drawn on the chart as a result of taking a bearing, sight, sounding, etc., on which line a vessel is known to be. Two position lines give a fix.

PRAM: dinghy with a transom forward as well as aft.

PREVENTERS: (1) extra stays used to support a mast from astern; (2) (US & AUS) or to support spars; (3) US: line from boom end forwards which holds the boom in position in dipping seas.

PROHIBITED AREA: area where a vessel may not anchor.

PROPELLER: screw which is rotated by the engine to drive a vessel.

PULPIT: metal guardrail fitted at bows or stern to provide security for the crew working in the ends of a boat.

PURCHASE: tackle.

PUSHPIT: more correctly aft or stern pulpit, a pulpit at the stern of a vessel.

PUT ABOUT: cause another vessel to go about, for example when meeting on opposite tacks.

QUARANTINE FLAG: the yellow International Code flag Q, flown to indicate that a vessel has arrived from a foreign port and requests clearance by the health authorities and customs.

QUARTER KNEE: horizontal knee which ties the transom to the side of a vessel.

QUARTER, ON THE: about 45° abaft the beam, hence quartering sea, wind on the quarter, etc.

RACE: stretch of turbulent water owing to a strong current or tidal stream.

RACING FLAG (not US): flag worn at the truck when racing.

RADAR REFLECTOR: device, usually of sheet metal which, when assembled, offers three surfaces at right angles to each other. Hoisted in the rigging it produces a better image than a yacht on a radar screen.

RAFTING: when two or more vessels moor alongside each other.

RAIL: the top of a vessel's sides. Used frequently in the USA when 'gunwale' would be used in the UK.

RAKE: fore-and-aft angle with the perpendicular of a mast or other feature of a boat.

RANGE: (1) difference between the high- and low-water heights of a tide; (2) the distance which a light can be seen; (3) US: line of position formed by two fixed objects (UK: transit); (4) US: two objects in line which indicate the course a vessel should steer (UK: leading line) or which can be used to check whether the anchor is dragging.

RAP FULL (US): a little off the wind with sails drawing well.

RATE (US: DRIFT): see DRIFT (2).

RATING: a vessel is measured and given a rating which enables her to take part in handicap races.

RATLINES: small lines which run across between shrouds to provide steps for a man going aloft.

REACH: (1) sail with the wind roughly abeam (close- or fine-reach when the wind is slightly forward of the beam, beam-reach when the wind is dead abeam, broad-reach when the wind is abaft the beam); (2) long straight part of a channel or between two bends in a river; (3) US: long tack with the wind abeam or a little forward of the beam.

REACHING SPINNAKER: a spinnaker cut rather flat for use when reaching.

READY ABOUT: warning given preparatory to going about.

RECALL: at the start of a race a boat may be recalled if any part of her hull or equipment is seen to be over the starting line. If there is a general recall the entire fleet is recalled and the race restarted.

REEF: (1) line of rocks; (2) reduce canvas (see pp. 146–8).

REEF CRINGLES: thimbles in luff and leech which take the reef pennants or earings that pull down and secure the sail.

REEL WINCH: usually used for halyards; the wire halyard is permanently attached to the winch and is coiled round the reel when the sail is hoisted.

REEVE: pass rope through a block, ring, or hole.

RELATIVE BEARING: bearing of an object by comparison with the vessel's course.

RESTRICTED CLASS: class in which certain measurements are specified, but other aspects are left free for individual design and development.

RESTRICTED WATERS: waters in which there is little room for manoeuvre.

REVERSE SHEER: sheer line which rises between the bow and the stern producing a convex curve.

RIBS: timbers of a vessel to which the planking is fastened.

RIDE: vessels ride at anchor, ride out a gale, ride easily.

RIDING LIGHT: see ANCHOR LIGHT.

RIDING TURN (US: OVERRIDING TURN or OVERRIDE): when an earlier turn on a winch overrides a later turn and jams.

RIG: (1) general term covering the masting, yards and sails; (2) prepare a boat for sailing.

RIGGING: all the wires and ropes used to support masts and to control sails and yards, sub-divided into standing and running rigging.

RIGGING SCREW, BOTTLESCREW (US: TURNBUCKLE): device with a central frame or tubular central piece which turns on two opposite threads so that turning one way increases the length and turning the other way decreases the length of the screw. Used to adjust the tension of stays, shrouds, lifelines, etc.

RIGHT BANK: when looking downstream the right hand side of a river.

RING BOLT: bolt with a metal ring.

RISE: of a tide, the flood.

RISE OF FLOOR: see DEADRISE.

RISER: light fore-and-aft stringer on which the thwarts of a dinghy rest.

ROACH: curved area of leech in a fore-and-aft sail which extends beyond the direct line from head or peak to clew.

ROADS: sheltered anchorage for vessels.

ROCKER: upward curve of the line of the bottom of the hull towards the bows and stern.

RODE (US & AUS): anchor cable.

ROLLING: side to side motion of a vessel.

ROPE: cordage, correctly of 1in circumference and upwards. In the case of right-handed rope the fibres are twisted right-handed into yarns, the yarns are twisted left-handed into strands, and the strands right-handed into rope. US: any cordage until it has a specific purpose after which it becomes a 'line', i.e. sheet, dockline, guy, halyard, etc.

ROUND: sail round an object or headland.

ROUND BILGE: as opposed to hard chine, a vessel with a rounded bilge where topsides and bottom meet.

ROUNDLY: smartly, rapidly, as opposed to handsomely.

ROUND TURN: complete turn round a cleat, spar or another rope (AUS: two full turns).

ROUND UP: bring a vessel head to wind.

ROVE: past tense of reeve, q.v.

ROW: propel a vessel with oars.

ROWLOCK (US: also OARLOCK): crutch in which the oar is placed when rowing.

RUBBING STRAKE OR RUBBER (US & AUS: RUB RAIL): strip fitted outside the topstrake to protect the sides from damage.

RUDDER: flat vertical surface at the stern which is turned by the tiller or wheel to alter the course of a vessel.

RUDDER STOCK: upper part of the rudder between the blade and the tiller.

RUN: (1) sail with the wind aft; (2) distance covered; (3) after, lower part of the immersed hull of a vessel.

RUNNER LEVER: lever for tensioning running backstays.

RUNNERS: see RUNNING BACKSTAYS.

RUNNING: sailing with the wind aft.

RUNNING BACKSTAYS or RUNNERS: stays that can be set up or slacked off when the boat is sailing and which support the mast from aft.

RUNNING RIGGING: all moving rigging such as sheets and halyards, whether of wire rope or rope, as distinct from standing rigging. Running backstays, although movable, are classed as standing rigging because they support the mast.

SAG: fall off to leeward.

SAIL: canvas spread to catch the wind; square sails are bent to yards, fore-and-aft sails are bent to masts and/or gaffs, hanked to a stay or set flying.

SAIL TRACK: track on the mast and boom on which run the slides attached to a sail.

SAMPSON or SAMSON POST: strong post on a vessel to which mooring lines, etc., are secured.

SANDWICH CONSTRUCTION (US: CORED CONSTRUCTION): glassfibre is stiffened by sandwiching a layer of end-grain balsa wood or plastics foam between two layers of resin/glass laminate. End-grain balsa can also be laminated between layers of plywood.

SCANDALIZE: reduce the sail area by lowering the peak or topping the boom.

SCANTLINGS: dimensions of timbers used in the construction of a boat.

SCARF or SCARPH: joint used to join two pieces of wood end on whereby both pieces are tapered and overlapped, maintaining the same cross-section and avoiding a butt joint.

SCHOONER: fore-and-aft rigged vessel with two or more masts, the mainmast being as tall or taller than the foremast.

SCOPE: length of cable paid out when anchoring.

SCOW: boat with flat sections, often with transoms both fore and aft.

SCREW: propeller.

SCULL: propel a dinghy with one oar over the stern.

SCUPPERS: drain holes which allow water taken on board to escape from the deck.

SEA: (1) wave; (2) waves, when used with an adjective, as 'head sea', 'rough sea'.

SEA ANCHOR: drogue or combination of floating objects used to keep a vessel head or stern to wind in bad weather.

SEA BREEZE: blows from sea to land.

SEA-COCK: valve which shuts off an inlet or outlet passing through the hull.

SEAM: (1) space between planks; (2) join between the cloths of a sail.

SEA-ROOM: room to manoeuvre, especially clear of the land or dangers.

SECTION: shape of a boat when cut in any direction, longitudinally, horizontally or vertically, but usually taken as athwartships.

SECURE: make fast.

SEIZE: bind together with light lashing.

SELF-BAILERS: bailers which automatically suck water from a boat as she moves through the water.

SELF-DRAINING COCKPIT (US: also SELF-BAILING): cockpit with holes that allow the water to run out automatically.

SELF-STEERING GEAR: apparatus by which a vessel steers herself unattended.

SEPARATION SCHEME: in commercially congested waters, channels are defined for ships passing in opposite directions and are separated by a Separation Zone. Shipping is required to keep to the correct channel by maritime law and, if crossing, must do so at right angles.

SERVE: cover parcelling with marline.

SET: (1) to set sail is to hoist or spread sails; (2) the direction of a tidal stream or current.

SET FLYING: a sail not hanked to a stay, attached only at the three corners.

SEXTANT: instrument for measuring angles.

SHACKLE: metal link with a removable bolt, of various shapes such as D, U, bow, twisted.

SHAKE OUT A REEF: increase sail by untying a reef.

SHEATHING: covering protecting the bottom against marine borers such as teredo, usually copper or glassfibre.

SHEAVE: roller in a block or in a spar over which a rope is rove.

SHEER: fore-and-aft curve of the top of the sides or edge of the deck as seen from the side.

SHEER ABOUT: when at anchor, swing wildly from side to side.

SHEER PLAN or PROFILE DRAWING: fore-and-aft plan of a vessel viewed from the side.

SHEER STRAKE: topmost strake of a vessel.

SHEET: line which controls a sail.

SHEET HOME: haul the sheet hard in.

SHELF: fore-and-aft member which takes the deck beams.

SHIFT: alteration in wind direction.

SHIP: (1) take on board, whether gear or a sea; (2) put a thing in the proper place for working.

SHIP CHANDLER: supplier of marine equipment.

SHIP OARS: bring the oars inboard.

SHIP'S HEAD: direction in which the vessel is heading, indicated by the lubber's line on the steering compass.

SHORTEN SAIL: reduce sail.

SHROUDS: rigging which supports the mast athwartships.

SHY: a spinnaker is set shy when it is carried as close to the wind as possible.

SIGHTS: observations, angles, esp. of celestial bodies.

SINGLE-HANDER: (1) boat sailed by one person; (2) someone who sails alone.

SIT OUT: see HIKE OUT.

SKEG: (1) the extension of the keel which often supports the bottom of the rudder; (2) fin, separated from the keel, on which the rudder is hung.

SKIN: planking, plating, or shell of a hull.

SLACK: not taut.

SLACK AWAY or SLACK OFF: let out a line.

SLACK WATER: interval when the tidal stream (US: tidal current) is reversing and the water is hardly moving.

SLANT: favourable puff of wind.

SLAT: whip back and forth in the wind (sails, halyards, etc.).

SLICKERS: see OILSKINS.

SLIDING SEAT: see HIKING BOARD.

SLIP: (1) let go, e.g. the anchor by letting cable run out; (2) take a boat out of the water on a slipway; (3) quick release device for lifelines, anchor cables, etc.

SLOOP: fore-and-aft rigged vessel, usually with two sails, mainsail and headsail.

SLOT: gap between the headsail and the leeward side of the mainsail.

SNARLED: rope that does not run free, kinked or tangled.

SNUB: check a rope or line running out by taking a turn round a cleat or bitt.

SNUBBING WINCH: winch which does not have a handle.

SOLE: floor of the cabin or cockpit.

SOUND: (1) (opp. rotten); (2) determine the depth of water.

SOUND SIGNALS: signals made by vessels in sight of one another.

SOUNDING: depth of water.

SOU'WESTER: waterproof hat.

SPAR: general word covering masts, poles, yards, booms, gaffs, etc.

SPIDER BAND: a metal band which fits round a mast and takes the gooseneck. Has a number of lugs which carry belaying pins for securing the halyards.

SPIKE: see MARLINE-SPIKE.

SPILL THE WIND: allow some wind to escape from a sail to ease the pressure.

SPINNAKER: large, light sail set when the wind is free.

SPINNAKER CHUTE (UK); LAUNCHING TUBE (US): tube out of which a spinnaker is hoisted, fitted to small racing craft.

SPINNAKER POLE or BOOM: spar, attached to the mast at one end, which extends the spinnaker to windward.

SPITFIRE: small jib of heavy canvas for stormy weather.

SPLICE: method of joining two ropes or wires, or forming an eye in them, by interweaving their strands (see pp. 156–7).

SPLINED: a splined hull has wedge-section wooden splines glued between the seams in place of stopping.

SPLIT TACKS: when racing, to choose the opposite tack to an opponent, usually to obtain a clear wind.

SPOIL GROUND: area in which dredged material is dumped.

SPOON BOW: bow which, in profile, has a pronounced convex curve between the stemhead and the waterline.

SPREADERS or CROSSTREES: struts attached to the mast which extend to the shrouds to provide additional support.

SPRING: mooring line used to restrict fore-and-aft movement.

SPRING A LEAK: when a plank springs and allows water to enter.

SPRING TIDES: tides of greatest range (cf. neap tides).

SPRIT: spar which extends from the mast near the tack of a sail to the peak.

SPRITSAIL: fore-and-aft sail extended by a sprit in place of a boom.

SQUALL: brief but violent and sudden increase in wind.

SQUARE RIG: as opposed to fore-and-aft rig; square sails are extended by yards set across the vessel.

STALL: a sail stalls when the smooth flow of air over it breaks away.

STANCHION: metal post bolted to the deck to support lifelines or guardrails.

STAND: period when the tidal level of water does not alter.

STAND BY: (1) warning to be ready to act; (2) wait near a vessel that may need help.

STAND OFF: keep clear.

STANDING PART: the part of a rope that is made fast, as opposed to the running part.

STANDING RIGGING: the shrouds and stays of a vessel which are permanently set up, together with the running backstays (cf. running rigging).

STARBOARD: right-hand side of a vessel looking forward (opp. port).

STARBOARD TACK: the wind strikes the starboard side of the vessel first, and she sails with the boom to port. Starboard-tack vessels have right of way over port-tack vessels.

STARCUT: spinnaker made with the panels radiating from the centre, rather than running parallel to the edges. It resists distortion and therefore sets better on a reach.

START SHEETS: slacken or ease sheets.

STAYS: wires or ropes which support a mast in the fore-and-aft direction.

STAYSAIL: any sail set on a stay, but can be set flying.

STEER: keep a vessel on a selected course by using the tiller or wheel to control the rudder.

STEERAGE WAY: when a boat makes sufficient way through the water to answer the helm.

STEM: (1) timber at the bow from the keel upwards, to which the planking is fastened; (2) to stem the tide is to make way over the ground or hold one's own when sailing against the direction of the tidal stream or current.

STEP: (1) erect the mast; (2) mast step: the piece of wood or metal fabrication which locates the heel of the mast, or the recess in which the heel rests.

STERN: after part of a vessel.

STERNBOARD: making way astern.

STERN KNEE: knee on the centreline which connects the bottom of the transom to the hull structure.

STERNPOST: structural member to which rudder is usually attached; usually runs upward from aft end of hull.

STERN TO: when the stern is directed towards another vessel, seas, etc.

STERNWAY: when a vessel makes way stern first.

STICK: coll. mast.

STIFF: vessel which.can carry a lot of sail without heeling unduly (opp. tender).

STOCK-PRODUCTION BOATS: many sister ships built to the same plans, by one builder (cf. custom-built boats).

STOPPER: clamp which can be attached to a rope or wire to prevent it moving; length of rope used to achieve the same aim.

STOPPING: putty or pliable material used for filling seams and surface blemishes.

STOPS: (1) see IN STOPS; (2) US: line or canvas strips used to secure a furled sail (UK: gaskets, tyers, etc.).

STOPWATER: softwood plug fitted in a joint which swells when it gets wet and makes the joint watertight.

STORM JIB: small jib of heavy canvas for use in heavy weather.

STOVE IN: damage when any object breaks through the sides of a vessel.

STOW: put something away.

STRAKE: full length of hull planking.

STRAND: (1) yarns twisted together to make up into a rope; (2) the foreshore.

STREAM: run out a log line or rope aft.

STRIKE: lower something such as a flag or topmast.

STRINGERS: fore-and-aft members connected to the main structure.

STROP: ring, usually of rope, often with a thimble, used to attach rigging or a block to a spar.

STRUM BOX (not US): filter round the suction pipe of a pump.

SURGE: let out a rope or wire under control.

SWELL: continuous unbreaking rollers.

SWING: a moored or anchored vessel swings when the direction of the tidal stream (US: tidal current) changes.

SWING THE COMPASS or SWING SHIP: determine the amount of deviation on all headings in order to produce a deviation card.

SWINGING STRAPS (AUS): see HIKING STRAPS.

TABERNACLE: frame supporting the base of a mast in which the mast is pivoted when lowered or raised.

TABLING: reinforcing pieces on edges or corners of sails.

TACK: (1) lower, forward corner of a sail; (2) go about head to wind (opp. gybing); (3) see PORT TACK and STARBOARD TACK.

TACKING: work to windward close-hauled.

TACKING DOWNWIND: sail first on one broad reach and then on the other.

TACKLE: purchase composed of rope and blocks.

TAFFRAIL: rail at the counter or across the stern.

TAFFRAIL LOG (US): see PATENT LOG.

TAIL: (1) a rope tail is often attached to a wire halyard; (2) line attached to a block to connect it to an object; (3) pulling on a rope which is led round a winch.

TAKE IN: hand a sail.

TAKE UP THE SLACK: gather in the slack of a rope ready to haul.

TALLBOY: tall, narrow staysail set inside a spinnaker with its tack between the mast and the stemhead.

TANG: fitting on a mast to which a stay, shroud, or other object may be attached.

TAUT: tight, as opposed to slack.

TELL-TALE: light piece of material attached to the shrouds to indicate wind direction.

TENDER: (1) small dinghy used to ferry the crew of a larger vessel; (2) (opp. stiff), a vessel which heels easily.

THIMBLE: rigid eye around which a rope or wire is spliced.

THREE-QUARTER RIG: fore-and-aft rig with the forestay attached to the mast about three-quarters of the way from the deck to the masthead.

THROAT: upper, forward corner of four-sided fore-and-aft sail.

THWARTS: athwartship seats in a dinghy.

TIDAL CURRENT (US): horizontal movement of water owing to tidal causes.

TIDAL STREAM (UK): horizontal movement of water owing to tidal causes.

TIDAL-STREAM ATLAS (US: CURRENT CHART): publication showing the set and rate of tidal streams.

TIDE: vertical movement of water owing to the pull of the sun and moon (see SPRING TIDES and NEAP TIDES).

TIDE RIPS: patches of broken and disturbed water owing to strong tidal streams.

TILLER: bar connected to the rudder to steer the vessel.

TILLER EXTENSION (US: HIKING STICK): extension to the tiller for use when sitting or hiking out.

TIMBER: wood used for shipbuilding.

TIMBERS: the ribs of a wooden vessel which have been bent (cf. grown frames).

TOE RAIL: (1) any low rail which provides a foothold; (2) low bulwarks running around the outside of the deck.

TOE STRAPS (UK): see HIKING STRAPS.

TOP UP: raise an object such as a boom by means of a lift.

TOPMARKS (US: DAYMARKS): shapes placed on tops of buoys, beacons, etc., for distinguishing purposes.

TOPPING LIFT: a line which raises a spar, usually used in respect of the main boom.

TOPSIDES: from the waterline up, the part of the vessel's side that is out of the water.

TOW: pull another vessel through the water by means of a wire or rope.

TRACK: the course a vessel has made good over the ground.

TRANSIT (US: RANGE): two objects in line give a position line.

TRANSOM: flat or curved surface extending across the aft end of a vessel. Some craft, especially small dinghies, also have a transom forward.

TRANSOM FLAPS: flaps in the transom of a dinghy which hinge open so that water lying in the bottom may flow out.

TRAPEZE: wire support from the hounds enabling the crew to stand out to windward on a dinghy's gunwale to keep her level in fresher breezes. He wears a trapeze belt which is like a corset and fits round the buttocks. The belt is fitted with a hook which he attaches to the trapeze ring on the trapeze wire.

TRAVELLER: (1) ring or fitting which can be hauled out, along or up a spar; (2) fitting which slides on a track to which something is attached, thus allowing adjustment.

TRIATIC STAY: backstay which is led to another mast.

TRICE UP: lift something out of the way.

TRIM: (1) difference in draft between forward and aft; (2) the way a vessel sits in the water; (3) adjust the angle of the sails so that they are at their most efficient; (4) US: trim in, harden in the sheets.

TRIMARAN: boat with three hulls.

TRIP THE ANCHOR: break out the anchor.

TROT: mooring buoys laid out in a line.

TRUCK: the very top of the mast.

TRUE: course, bearings, etc., in relation to true north.

TRUNK (US); COACHROOF (UK): upper part of a cabin which extends above the deck.

TRYSAIL: small, heavy mainsail for stormy weather.

TUCK: sharp down-turn in a section where the hull fairs in to the keel or skeg.

TUMBLE HOME: the topsides curve inwards from the vertical (opp. flare).

TURN: take a turn is to catch a rope around a cleat, bollard, etc.

TURNBUCKLE (US): see RIGGING SCREW.

TURN OF THE BILGE: where the bottom and the topsides meet in a round-bilge boat, and the curvature is greatest.

TURN OF THE TIDE: slack water when the stream is turning from ebb to flood or vice versa.

TURTLE: bag from which a spinnaker may be hoisted.

TYERS or TIERS: see GASKETS and STOPS (2).

UNA RIG: only one sail.

UNBEND: undo a bend or lacing, or remove a sail from a boom or gaff.

UNDER SAIL: with sail hoisted and no engine working.

UNDER-STAND: when a sailing boat tacks for a mark or obstacle too soon and is forced to put in an extra tack in order to round it (cf. overstand).

UNDER THE LEE OF: sheltered from the wind.

UNDER WAY: when a vessel is neither anchored, made fast to the shore, nor aground (cf. making way).

UNFAIR: (opp. fair, q.v.).

UNREEVE: remove a line from blocks or sheaves.

UNSHIP: remove anything from the place where it is used.

UP HELM: pull the tiller to windward causing the boat to bear away.

UPSTREAM: towards the upper part of a stream whence the water flows.

UPWIND: to windward of (opp. downwind).

VANG or BOOM VANG; KICKING STRAP (UK): rope or tackle rigged to prevent the boom rising.

VARIATION: difference between true and magnetic north which varies both annually and according to the geographical location.

V-BOTTOM: the bottom meets the keel at distinct angle.

VEER: (1) (opp. back); the wind veers when it changes direction clockwise; (2) let out more cable.

WAKE: disturbed water astern of a vessel.

WARP: (1) heavy rope used for towing; (2) to warp a vessel is to move her from one place to another by means of warps.

WASH: disturbance caused by the movement of a vessel through the water.

WATCH: the part of the crew which is on duty is on watch.

WATERLINE: line at which a vessel floats.

WATERLINES: lines produced by cutting a vessel in the horizontal plane.

WATERWAY: (1) gap through which water may drain; (2) enclosed area of navigable water such as a canal.

WAY: movement of a vessel through the water.

WEAR: change tacks by gybing.

WEATHER: (1) side from which the wind is blowing (opp. leeward); (2) pass to windward of another boat, part of the coast, some danger, or a mark.

WEATHERBOUND: forced to stay in harbour due to foul winds.

WEATHER RAIL: rail on the weather side.

WEATHER SHORE: shore from which the wind is blowing (opp. lee shore).

WEIGH THE ANCHOR: raise the anchor.

WELL-FOUND: well-equipped vessel.

WETTED SURFACE: submerged area of the hull.

WHEEL: steering wheel by which a vessel is kept on course.

WHIP: bind the end of a rope or line with smaller yarn to prevent the ends unlaying.

WHISKER POLE: see JIB STICK.

WIDE BERTH: give a wide berth is to keep well clear of a vessel or object.

WINCH: mechanical device consisting of a revolving drum around which a line may be hauled taut.

WIND: moving current of air; heading wind, when a vessel has to haul in her sheets to maintain her course or has to bear away when close-hauled to keep her sails full; freeing wind, when she can ease sheets while maintaining the same course; a veering wind alters direction clockwise; a backing wind alters direction anti-clockwise.

WINDLASS: winch fitted with a warping drum and a gipsy which has sprockets to take the links of the chain. Usually used for the anchor.

WIND OVER TIDE: when the wind is blowing in the opposite direction to the set of the tidal stream or current. In strong tidal streams or currents and strong winds this leads to confused seas.

WIND SHADOW: area in which another boat's sails or some other obstruction interferes with the direction and strength of the wind.

WINDWARD: towards the wind (opp. leeward).

WING AND WING (US): when a headsail or mizzen is set on the opposite side to the mainsail with the wind dead aft.

WIRE ROPE: rope made of twisted iron or steel strands.

WORM: lay thin pieces of line in the grooves between strands of a rope, usually before parcelling.

WRECK: vessel that has been stranded or broken up.

WUNG OUT: sail held out to windward (see WING AND WING).

YACHT: (1) sailing or motor yacht used for pleasure; (2) vessel used for state occasions.

YANKEE: type of jib topsail.

YARD: spar used to extend a square sail and for other purposes.

YARN: (1) part of a strand of rope; (2) spun thread.

YAW: swing from side to side, not keeping on course.

YAWL: two-masted fore-and-aft rigged vessel, the mizzen mast being stepped aft of the rudder post (cf. ketch).

ABBREVIATIONS

AYF	Australian Yachting Federation
CCA	Cruising Club of America
CYA	Canadian Yaching Association
GRP	glassfibre reinforced plastics
FD	Flying Dutchman
FJ	Flying Junior
HW	high water
IOMR	International Offshore Multihull Rule
IOR	International Offshore Rule
IYRU	International Yacht Racing Union
JOG	Junior Offshore Group
LAT	Lowest astronomical tide
LOA	Length overall
LBP	Length between perpendiculars
LOP	Line of position
LPG	Liquid petroleum gas
LW	Low water
LWL	Load waterline
LWOST	Low water ordinary spring tides
MLWS	Mean low water springs
MORC	Midget Ocean Racing Club
NAYRU	North American Yacht Racing Union
ORC	Offshore Racing Council
PFD	Personal flotation device
RDF	Radio direction finder
RORC	Royal Ocean Racing Club
RYA	Royal Yachting Association
SORC	Southern Ocean Racing Circuit
USPS	United States Power Squadron
USYRU	United States Yacht Racing Union

Appendix II Notes on contributors

In the preparation of *The Complete Book of Sailing* the editors had the benefit of the co-operation of what is arguably the most experienced international team of authoritative yachting writers ever to have contributed to one book. Their names appear regularly in many of the world's leading yachting magazines; their sailing experience covers the widest range of boats and every type of sailing water from quiet inland rivers to the open oceans. Information provided by the contributors often found its way into more than one chapter, but the major contributors to each chapter are given below.

1 Centreboard dinghies *Wendy Fitzpatrick*
2 Keelboats *Malcolm McKeag*
3 Multihulls *Pat Boyd*
4 Sailing in Britain *Peter Cook*
5 Sailing in the United States of America *Theodore A. Jones*
6 Sailing in Australia *Bob Ross*
7 Sailing in Canada *Sandy McPherson*
8 Sailing in New Zealand *David Pardon*
9 Sailing in South Africa *Brian Lello*
10 The boat *Peter Cook*
11 Before going sailing *Barbara Webb*
12 Sailing and seamanship *Barbara Webb*
13 Safety, distress signals, flag etiquette and equipment *Barbara Webb*
14 Design considerations *Peter Cook*
15 Dinghy racing *Wendy Fitzpatrick*
16 Offshore racing *Jack Knights*
17 Cruising keelboats *Malcolm McKeag*
18 Weather *Ingrid Holford*
19 Navigation *Barbara Webb*
20 Rule of the road *Barbara Webb*
21 Racing rules *Eric Twiname*
22 Tactics *Eric Twiname*
23 Team racing *Eric Twiname*

NOTES ON CONTRIBUTORS
Patrick Boyd Sailed monohulls for twenty-five years before becoming interested in multihulls. Advertisement manager of *Yachting Monthly* in 1969. Left to open Camper & Nicholsons' London office. Runs a multihull brokerage and charter division.

Peter Cook Served his time as a boatbuilding apprentice and studied naval architecture. Various managerial positions in the boatbuilding industry in England and ran his own boat design and development business before taking up yachting journalism in 1966. Editor of *Yachts and Yachting* magazine. Has raced and cruised in all types of boat, former British Fireball champion. Active officer in the Royal Naval Reserve, member of the Royal Institute of Navigation, Associate of the Royal Institution of Naval Architects, sits on RYA Cruising Committee. Books on boatbuilding and co-author of *The Longest Race*.

Wendy Fitzpatrick Owner of many single-handed dinghies. British Open Laser champion 1972, Topper national champion 1976. Assistant editor of *Yachts and Yachting* before becoming secretary to the Topper class.

Ingrid Holford BSc (Econ) Trained as meteorologist and forecasted for the RAF for four years. Has written extensively about the weather, concentrating on aspects necessary to make yachtsmen self-reliant when afloat. Keen dinghy sailor, Rear Commodore of Thames Sailing Club. Books: *Interpreting the Weather*; *British Weather Disasters*.

Theodore A. Jones Internationally known authority and writer on sailing and sailboat racing. Contributing editor to *Yacht Racing Magazine*. Was Director of Offshore Activities for the USYRU, served on ORC committees and chaired USYRU Level Rating Classes Committee. Books include *The Offshore Racer* and *Racing for the America's Cup 1974*. Currently sails a 30ft Half Tonner which he designed.

Jack Knights An active competitor, races a Laser regularly, has competed in Solings, Tempests and Finns, winning British and American Finn championships, German Tempest championships and British Enterprise and Swordfish championships. World champion crew in a Dragon. Also races small offshore racers. Full-time yachting journalist, newspaper yachting correspondent for fifteen years and regular contributor to *Yachts and Yachting* for over twenty-five years. Publishes international yacht racing newsletter and contributes to US and many overseas magazines.

Brian O'Rafferty Lello, editor of *SA Yachting* for twenty years. Has sailed in all types of boat including trans-ocean racers. Designer of about eighty craft from dinghies to 140-tonners.

Malcolm McKeag, assistant editor of *Yachts and Yachting*, trained as a naval architect before gaining a BSc. Has sailed many boats from OKs to Eight Metres. Crewed in 1974 Edinburgh Cup-winning Dragon. Owns his own cruising boat. Lieutenant in the Royal Naval Reserve.

Sandy McPherson Has sailed from childhood in boats from dinghies upwards. Served in the Royal Canadian Navy. Owns an Alberg 30, *Tertius*. General Manager of the CYA 1965-9. Awarded Canadian Medal for services to sailing 1967. Has written six books on sailing in Canada and has contributed to magazines in Canada, UK, USA and Australia. Radio and TV commentator on sailing subjects.

David Francis Pardon British sports journalist, emigrated to New Zealand 1965. Editor of *Sea Spray* magazine since 1970. Regular contributor to overseas publications in USA, UK, South Africa and Australia.

Bob Ross Editor and publisher of *Sailing* magazine. Has reported Australian yachting for local and overseas magazines for fifteen years, including coverage of yachting's most important international events. A keen sailor, formerly active in Finns. Now races offshore in Half and Two Tonners.

Eric Twiname Former British Laser champion and member of team that won British Team Racing Championship. Primarily responsible for a number of revisions introduced to the IYRU rules in 1977. Rules adviser to the 1976 British Olympic squad. Contributes articles to most of the major sailing magazines worldwide. Television commentator on sailing. Books: *Start to Win, Dinghy Team Racing* and a rules book.

Barbara Webb Cruised and raced in dinghies, one-designs and five-tonners. Compiled *Yachtsman's Eight Language Dictionary*, author of *The Beginners Book of Navigation*, translator of *The Beginners Book of Sailing* and many books on marine subjects including racing tactics, glassfibre repairs, ancient ships and motor torpedo boats.

Acknowledgments

The publishers would like to thank the following for supplying and giving their permission to reproduce illustrations:

Black and white photographs
Ajax News and Feature Service, AMF Marine Products Group, F. J. Armes, Nick Armstrong, Australian Information Service.
Bahamas News Bureau, Bahama Islands Tourist Bureau, David Baker, Banks Yeldham, Beken of Cowes (pp. 27, 45 *top*, 52, 87, 197 and 222 *top*), Bermuda News Bureau, Jack Biscoe, Alastair Black, David E. Blundell, British Overseas Trade Board, Henry Browne and Son Ltd.
David Campbell-James, Carter Offshore, Howey Caufman, Comextra, Peter Cook, Peter Copley, Cox Marine, Cruising Yacht Club of Australia.
Trevor Davies, Anthony Dawson, Design Council, Dixon Accessories.
E. Emrys-Jones.
Financial Times, Bob Fisher, John Fitzpatrick, Daniel Forster, Pierre Fouquin.
F. E. Gibson, Malcolm Gray, Jenny Green.
Ingrid Holford, Jack Holt Ltd., John Hopwood, Rob Humphreys.
In-the-Water Boat Shows.
Tom Jarrett, Ted Jones.
Tom Lack, Lewmar Marine, Anthony J. Linton.
Sandy McPherson, Brian Manby, John Mellor, Miami-Metro Department of Publicity and Tourism.
National Photo Persbureau BV.
Ocean Youth Club.
David Pardon, Pearson Brothers Ltd., Hugh Perks.
Eileen Ramsay, RFD Inflatables Ltd., François Richard, Michael Roberts, Bob Ross, Rothmans Canada, RWO (Marine Equipment) Ltd.
Geoffrey Simpson, Helen Simpson, Small Craft (Blockley) Ltd., Roger M. Smith of Cowes, Swiss National Tourist Board.
Stephen Tester, Topix, Harry C. Turner.
Yachting News, Yachting World, Yachts and Yachting, Nick Yunge-Bateman.

Colour photographs and jacket
Alastair Black, Bob Fisher, Guy Gurney, Brian Lello, Eric North.

Line diagrams
Peter Cook, Harry Green, Peter Milne, Peter A. G. Milne, Barbara Webb.
For use of drawings in the preparation of figures:
Camper and Nicholsons Limited, Atlanta Marine Limited, Harris and Heacock, Scott Kaufman. The chart on pages 228 and 229 at the beginning of Part IV is produced from a portion of BA Chart 442 with the sanction of the Controller, HM Stationary Office and of the Hydrographer of the Navy.

Index